# Sea Dragons

Sea

UNIVERSITY PRESS OF KANSAS

RICHARD ELLIS

# Dragons

*PREDATORS OF THE PREHISTORIC OCEANS*

© 2003 by Richard Ellis

All rights reserved

Published by the University Press of Kansas
(Lawrence, Kansas 66049), which was organized
by the Kansas Board of Regents and is operated
and funded by Emporia State University,
Fort Hays State University, Kansas State
University, Pittsburg State University,
the University of Kansas, and Wichita
State University

Library of Congress Cataloging-in-Publication Data

Ellis, Richard.
    Sea dragons : predators of the prehistoric oceans / Richard Ellis.
       p. cm.
Includes bibliographical references and index.
    ISBN 0-7006-1269-6 (cloth : alk. paper)
    1. Marine reptiles, Fossil. 2. Paleontology—Mesozoic. I. Title.
    QE861.E45 2003
    567.9'37—dc21

                    2003006871

British Library Cataloguing-in-Publication Data is available.

Printed in the United States of America

10   9   8   7   6   5   4   3   2   1

The paper used in this publication meets
the minimum requirements of the American
National Standard for Permanence of Paper
for Printed Library Materials z39.48-1984.

# Contents

# Acknowledgments

When the world and I were somewhat younger, I started the research for a book that was going to be about the origin, evolution, and extinction of life in the sea. I wanted to write about the formation of the earth, the earliest and the later life-forms — invertebrates to vertebrates, trilobites to ammonites, lungfishes to whales. I was going to devote a certain amount of space to the fate of those creatures that are no longer with us and those that still are, as "living fossils." I thought I would also discuss the enigmatic disappearance of the dinosaurs and the ancient marine reptiles. It soon became obvious that those subjects were too many and too diverse to incorporate into a single book, so in a fashion that has come to define my modus operandi, I reduced the scope of the project, kept some of the material I had written, and filed the rest away for future use. In the original plan, one of the first subjects I tackled was the marine reptiles, because they seemed so close in spirit and habitat to other large vertebrates I had already dealt with — sharks and whales — and also because, as far as I knew, there hadn't been a proper book written about these neglected creatures since Samuel Williston's 1914 *Water Reptiles Past and Present*. (In 1997, Academic Press published *Ancient Marine Reptiles*, but this was a collection of disparate articles, and although they were all important, taken as a whole, it was not the book I had in mind.)

Not surprisingly, the material about ichthyosaurs, plesiosaurs, and mosasaurs was so extensive that it soon became evident that these marvelous creatures deserved more than a summary chapter in a book about everything, so they became the first casualties. (Also put aside was the question of whether there was water on Mars or on Jupiter's moon Europa; a discussion of the fascinating but ridiculously wrongheaded idea that all the fossils of *Archaeopteryx* were forgeries; and the whole section on extinction — past, present, and future — which will become another book.) In 2001, *Aquagenesis: The Origin and Evolution of Life in the Sea*, was published, and I still had a lot of neat stuff left over. In a manner of speaking, this book was rescued from the scrap heap.

In 1974, I was commissioned to do a series of whale paintings for *Audubon* magazine. Back then, before anyone had actually dived with whales and photographed them underwater, the only people who purportedly knew what they looked like were whalers and a small band of cetologists. I packed up my sketches and drove to Woods Hole, where I was planning to show them to Bill Schevill, probably America's foremost cetologist. I had never actually seen a living whale, so I needed someone to make sure that I wasn't too far off the mark. (He commented that my humpbacks were perhaps "too gaily spangled.") Bill's approval of the paintings essentially started me on the long journey through the subject matter of whales, dolphins, sharks, sea monsters, deep oceans, Atlantis, giant squid, and evolution. What a pleasant surprise, then, to see that Bill Schevill also played a role in the subject of this book, the extinct marine reptiles. In 1931, as a budding paleontologist, he led a Harvard University expedition to Queensland, Australia, where they unearthed an almost complete skeleton of the giant pliosaur *Kronosaurus,* now on display in the Museum of Comparative Zoology in Cambridge, Massachusetts.

Another person who played an inadvertent role in the preparation of this book was Bob Bakker. In 1975 (I was doing a lot of illustration work back then), the art director of *Scientific American* asked me to go to Harvard University to consult with a young paleontologist named Robert Bakker on an illustration of a distant dinosaur relative that was to appear on the cover of the April issue, featuring Bakker's groundbreaking article on warm-blooded dinosaurs. I met with Bakker, we "designed" a color scheme for *Longisquama,* and we talked a lot about dinosaurs. I was fascinated to learn that there had been all kinds of gigantic seagoing reptiles, all of which, like the terrestrial dinosaurs, were extinct. Over the years, Bakker and I talked about doing a book on the ichthyosaurs, mosasaurs, and plesiosaurs, and although he wrote many articles about them, we never managed to do the book together. That I have written this book is largely because of his introduction and inspiration, and I suspect that it would have been a better book—it certainly would have been more controversial—if we had collaborated.

Mark Norell's only connection with Harvard—as far as I know—is that he went to graduate school at Yale. As a friend (and also as the chair of the Department of Vertebrate Paleontology at the American Museum of Natural History), he has been steadfast in his support of my forays into the gullies and minefields of paleontology, even going so far as to make me a research associate in his department. This, of course, means that the extensive resources of this great museum are available to me, especially the library, where I work in wonderment at the richness of the published material, all under the creative stewardship of Tom Moritz, the head of Library Services (in other words, head librarian).

Chris McGowan of the Royal Ontario Museum has done more work on ichthyosaurs than anybody else, and some of that work was done in the venerable American Museum of Natural History in New York City. I first met Chris at the museum in 1997, and since then I have been corresponding with him on the fascinating lives of the ichthyosaurs. He read my chapter on the "fish lizards" and made many corrections, but any mistakes or errors of interpretation that managed to withstand his critical eye are mine alone. Another practicing ichthyosaurologist is Ryosuke Motani, who is now at the University of Oregon. I pestered him and McGowan with endless questions about the intricacies of ichthyosaur paleontology, phylogeny, and anatomy. Motani also maintains a marvelous website (www.ucmp.berkeley.edu/people/motani/ichthyo/index) that is devoted—as he is—to explaining the wonder and mysteries of ichthyosaurs.

In 1999, because I was working on *Aquagenesis,* a book about the origin and evolution of life in the sea, I attended a meeting in Copenhagen enticingly titled "Secondary Adaptation to Life in Water." I got a lot of material and references on the evolution of whales, seals, manatees, and penguins, but I also met Niels Bonde and Per Christiansen, participants in the meeting because they were working on a giant mosasaur skull from Israel that was at the Geological Museum in Copenhagen (described on page 225 of this book). Per read my description and corrected my misinterpretations. Also in Copenhagen was Betsy Nicholls of the Royal Tyrrell Museum in Alberta, one of the world's foremost authorities on marine reptiles. I bothered her in Copenhagen, and when she thought she had escaped safely to Canada, I found her there and continued to ask embarrassingly simple-minded questions. (At the Copenhagen meeting, Betsy presented an early discussion of the excavation of the giant ichthyosaur discussed on page 89.)

In 1997, I was invited to Edinburgh to repaint a giant squid model. (I was then working on a book called *The Search for the Giant Squid*, and I had developed a preternatural interest in the models found in museums around the world.) I painted the Scottish squid, but more important, I met Mike Taylor, who is the museum's curator of vertebrate paleontology. Mike was also at the 1999 Copenhagen symposium, and after listening to his presentation, I realized that I had found the perfect person to alleviate my confusion about almost everything. I shamelessly badgered him with inane and sophomoric questions, trying once again to master a subject (the marine reptiles) that I found utterly fascinating.

One of the first things I did when I commenced this study was the same thing any student does when beginning a term paper: I searched the Internet. To my surprise (and, I must admit, satisfaction), almost every quest for information on plesiosaurs, ichthyosaurs, and especially mosasaurs, produced the same website: "Oceans of Kansas," the brainchild and production of Mike Everhart, now adjunct curator of paleontology at the Sternberg Museum of Natural History in Hays, Kansas. Mike has collected and posted an incredible amount of information (and illustrations) on the fossils of Kansas, and although there is much to be found on his website, there was much that I wanted to know that *wasn't* there, so Mike became another victim of my unfulfillable curiosity. Thanks, Mike, for putting up with me, and congratulations on your forthcoming book called (of all things) *Oceans of Kansas*.

Ben Creisler of Seattle created the on-line "Translation and Pronunciation Guides" (dinosauria.com/dml/names/ples.html), but despite the comprehensiveness of this reference, the insatiable researcher always finds more questions to ask, and Ben was extraordinarily patient with me, providing answers that were probably right in front of me. A freelance researcher and linguist, Ben kindly gave me permission to use that information in these accounts and also provided valuable assistance in some problematic translations of scientific names from Greek or Latin, of which this book contains an inordinate number.

When I first encountered the name Theagarten Lingham-Soliar, he was affiliated with the Russian Academy of Sciences in Moscow, and he was difficult to contact. When he moved to the University of Durban-Westville in Kwazulu-Natal, South Africa, I finally got in touch with him. He has published extensively on marine reptiles—mostly mosasaurs, but also plesiosaurs and ichthyosaurs—and "Solly" was most generous with his time and expertise. He read my chapter on mosasaurs and made so many suggestions that he probably ought to be listed as a coauthor, and maybe even coillustrator. When I completed a mosasaur drawing, I would scan it and send it to him in Kwazulu-Natal. He would then comment on the drawing ("too fat; neck too short; stripes too prominent"), and with his suggestions before me, I would make the necessary changes. (For someone who is still drawing with pen and ink on illustration board, the idea of instantaneously sending drawings halfway around the world is breathtaking.) Others who read and commented on entire chapters were Ken Carpenter of the Denver Museum of Natural History; Leslie Noè of the Sedgwick Museum, University of Cambridge; Ryosuke Motani of the University of Oregon; and Mark Norell of the American Museum of Natural History. Even though they know far more about the various subjects than I do, there were times that I simply refused to change what I had written, and this stubbornness has undoubtedly resulted in mistakes. In other words, mea culpa.

A heartfelt note of gratitude goes to Darren Naish (University of Portsmouth, U.K.), who read the entire manuscript with such care that he made suggestions on every aspect of the work, ranging from spelling corrections to taxonomic interpretations. Without his meticulous attention to detail, this would have been a considerably less accurate study. The same gratitude is due to Colin McHenry of Queensland, whose specialty is plesiosaurs but whose knowledge of the literature, taxonomy, biomechanics, and a number of other marine reptile fields is encyclopedic. Darren and Colin both sent me elaborate notes and critiques of the manuscript, and I made many of the changes they suggested. To acknowledge every such correction in print would have been unwieldy, but when I quoted directly from their letters to me (which in Colin's case often took the form of ten-page essays), I credited them.

Among the others who answered my constant stream of questions (I am thankful for e-mail, but they may not be) with exquisite patience were Dave Martill of the University of Portsmouth (U.K.), Peter Doyle of the University of Greenwich (U.K.), Bill Sarjeant of the University of Saskatchewan, Dale Russell of North Carolina State University, Mike Caldwell of the University of Alberta in Edmonton, Judy Massare of the State University of New York at Brockport, Larry Witmer of the Ohio University College of Osteopathic Medicine, Robin O'Keefe of the New York College of Osteopathic Medicine, Michael Maisch of Tübingen, Nathalie Bardet of the Natural History Museum in Paris, Anne Schulp of the Natuurhistische Museum in Maastricht, Ben Kear of the South Australian Museum in Adelaide, Caitlin Kiernan, Kazuo Takahashi, Douglas Palmer, and Dan Varner.

At a symposium in Lawrence, Kansas, on Moby Dick in American art, I met the editor of the accompanying book, *Unpainted to the Last*. This was Mike Briggs, editor-in-chief of the University Press of Kansas, and when he agreed to publish *this* book, I dusted off the old files about mosasaurs, ichthyosaurs, and plesiosaurs and began to do the drawings that I thought would help reveal the long-hidden mysteries of the extinct marine reptiles. He edited this book too, and our chance meeting over a discussion of the white whale has produced a durable relationship of mutual respect and admiration. As he has done for the past 30 years, my agent Carl Brandt managed to place my ungainly and overstuffed manuscript in the capable hands of someone who could turn it into a proper book. Once again, Stephanie was along for the ride, and as always, I am grateful for her support and loyalty. She keeps me happy, and she also keeps me honest.

# Introduction
## Isn't That the Loch Ness Monster?

Come with me to the American Museum of Natural History on New York City's Central Park West. We walk up the broad stairs, dominated by the equestrian statue of Theodore Roosevelt, twenty-sixth president of the United States and a great benefactor of the museum. We enter the great Roosevelt Rotunda, where we are awed by one of the most dramatic dinosaur exhibits in the world—the mounted skeletons of a mother *Barosaurus* protecting her young one from an attacking carnivorous *Allosaurus*. The great sauropod rears up on her hind legs, her head 50 feet off the ground, towering high over the marauding *Allosaurus*, who appears to be trying to get at the baby. Although these dinosaurs are only bones, it is not difficult to flesh them out in our minds and see this tableau as a representation of what might have taken place when the world was about 150 million years younger than it is now, in the period known as the late Jurassic. (There is some controversy about whether *Barosaurus* could actually rear up on its hind legs—somebody suggested that it would have needed eight auxiliary hearts to pump the blood up that high—but a certain degree of "paleontological license" was exercised to make the dramatic fossil fill the spacious hall.)

We'll go up the stairs to the fourth floor and pass through the new Saurischian Dinosaur Hall on our way to the Hall of Vertebrate Origins. It's tempting to linger here, looking at the amazing *Tyrannosaurus rex* or the duckbilled hadrosaurs, larger than we remember them in the old halls (they're now standing on raised platforms), but we're on our way to something that I promise will amaze you. Now we're in the Hall of Early Mammals, where we can see the mammoths, the mastodons, and the lovely murals by Charles R. Knight. We pass through an orientation center that has a surprisingly realistic, fully realized little *Barosaurus* stationed here, a "photo op" if ever there was one. (The "little" *Barosaurus* is 32 feet long; the full-grown mother downstairs measures 90 feet from nose to tail tip.) But keep going around the corner, and here we are. Look up. The first thing you see hanging from the ceiling is *Dunkleosteus*, a weird-looking, 20-foot-long armored fish with jaws that resemble overgrown staple removers. Wasn't there a gigantic shark jaw around here somewhere? Oh yes, there it is, but when did it shrink? (It was rebuilt when the curators realized that it had been made half again as big as it actually was, because the original fabricators made all the palm-sized teeth the same size instead of making the ones at the corners much smaller.) To the left is the entrance to the library (probably the best natural history library in the country, if not in the world), but at the moment, we're going to continue to look up, as if bird-watching. And there, soaring high over the exhibit cases, is probably the single most astonishing fossil in a museum filled with astonishing fossils. It has a long neck and a tiny head; a broad rib cage with a second set of auxiliary ribs around the belly; a short tail (much shorter than its neck); and four broad fins, each with broadly flattened wrist bones and five long "fingers." What is the Loch Ness monster doing in the Museum of Natural History?

Better read the label to find out. It's kind of hard to find it, because the skeleton is way up in the air, but here it is:

### PLESIOSAURS

The greatly expanded shoulder and pelvic girdle in plesiosaurs provided attachment areas for the well-developed muscles that moved the limbs when the animal swam. Some of them like *Thalassomedon,* hanging from the ceiling, evolved a very long neck with as many as 70 vertebrae.

So even though there have been many claims that the Loch Ness monster is a plesiosaur left over from the past (and that a single animal somehow managed to remain alive for 100 million years), this is not the skeleton of "Nessie."* It is

* It now appears that the original "Nessie" is a fraud. On March 13, 1994, the London *Sunday Telegraph* published this headline: "Revealed: The Loch Ness Picture Hoax." The front-page story detailed a complicated plot involving a filmmaker and big-game hunter named Marmaduke Arundel Wetherell, his son and stepson, and Dr. R. Kenneth Wilson, the man who allegedly took the famous "surgeon's photograph" that has been the basis for all Nessie

the plesiosaur *Thalassomedon*, a representative of a group of marine reptiles that thrived for about 100 million years from the Triassic to the Cretaceous periods and then, for reasons not understood, became extinct. Some had long necks, some had short necks; some were petite, and some were gigantic. Some had sharp little teeth like a python, while others had 8-inch daggers that rivaled the fearsome dental equipment of *T. rex*. Like all reptiles, they breathed air, but some, unlike any living reptiles, probably gave birth to living young underwater. (Female sea turtles come ashore to lay their eggs.) Sea turtles are the only living reptiles that have four flippers, so we have to compare the four-finned plesiosaurs to them, but whereas the turtles are slow swimmers, some of the plesiosaurs were aggressive predators and had to chase down their prey. Turtles are encased in a pair of shells, known as the carapace (top) and the plastron (bottom), and although the plesiosaurs had no shells, they did have a set of belly ribs called *gastralia*. How they actually swam—whether they "flew," "rowed," or performed some combination of the two—has been a subject for much paleontological speculation. Plesiosaur fossils have been found all over the world, including England (the first one was found in 1811 by the famous fossilist Mary Anning), Kansas, Wyoming, Colorado, Germany, Russia, Japan, Africa, the Middle East, Madagascar, New Zealand, and Antarctica. A plesiosaur fossil found at Coober Pedy in Australia was completely opalized.

In this discussion and those that follow, it will become obvious that none of these creatures has a common name. We are used to referring to familiar animals by their vernacular names, such as lion, tiger, fox, whale, hummingbird, jellyfish, and so on. These animals also have scientific names, based on a system developed by Carl von Linné (Carolus Linnaeus) in the mid-eighteenth century. The lion is *Panthera leo*, the tiger is *Panthera tigris*, the red fox is *Vulpes vulpes*, the blue whale is *Balaenoptera musculus*, the ruby-throated hum-

hunting since 1933. Christian Spurling, Wetherell's stepson, revealed on his deathbed that he had participated in the manufacture and photographing of a foot-high model mounted on a toy submarine, and they had coerced Dr. Wilson—otherwise a man of impeccable credentials—to claim that he had taken the picture, when in fact it had been taken by Wetherell (Langton 1994).

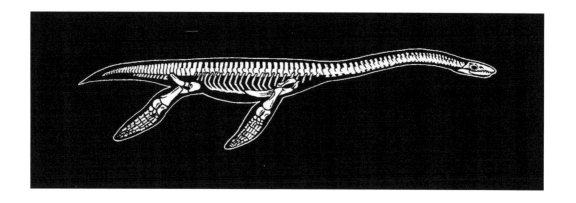

mingbird is *Archilochus colubris,* and the box jellyfish is *Chironex fleckeri.* The first
of these names identifies the genus (lions and tigers are in the genus *Panthera*),
and the second identifies the species. In all cases, the genus (generic) name is
capitalized, and the species (specific) name is not. Lion, tiger, blue whale, and
so forth are the names of these animals in English; in other languages, of
course, they are different. But whatever the language, the scientific name
remains the same. In a Polish, Chinese, Swedish, or Sanskrit discussion of the
lion, its scientific name still appears exactly as you see it here: *Panthera leo.*

There are no equivalents of lions or tigers among the marine reptiles. Just
as with the terrestrial dinosaurs, the scientific name is the only one used.
*Tyrannosaurus rex* is sometimes shortened to *T. rex,* but it is still known only by
its scientific name. The same is true for *Triceratops, Stegosaurus, Apatosaurus,
Velociraptor,* and even *Archaeopteryx.* The names of the major groups of marine
reptiles can be rendered into English, as in ichthyosaurs, plesiosaurs, and
mosasaurs, but each of these is also the generic name of a species within the
larger category, such as *Ichthyosaurus communis, Plesiosaurus dolichodeirus,* and *Mosasaurus hoffmanni.* Some of these names, like *dolichodeirus,* are more than a little
difficult to pronounce (it should be pronounced DOL-ik-o-DIE-rus), but
because nobody ever refers to this species as "longneck" (the meaning of
*dolichodeirus*), whenever this species appears in print it is *Plesiosaurus dolichodeirus.*
In this introduction to the marine reptiles, you will encounter jawbreakers like
*Ophthalmosaurus, Brachauchenius,* and *Pachycostasaurus,* but most of the names are
somewhat easier and more comfortable on the tongue. The lack of common

names might even help in recognizing the most significant characteristic of all the animals in this book: they are all extinct, and have been for millions of years. We would like to become more familiar with them, but time and nomenclature still remain formidable barriers.

As with many things paleontological, the evidence for the existence of long-extinct creatures consists of bones. Anatomists have given names to these bones, and they are the same for living animals as they are for extinct ones. The bones in your arm below the elbow are the radius and ulna, and they are the same—although sometimes of greatly differing size and proportion—for whales, zebras, chipmunks, and dinosaurs. Because there are very few instances in which anything but bones is preserved—and in those cases, rarely completely—those who describe extinct animals often limit themselves to detailed descriptions of the bones. If, for example, one finds a fossilized ichthyosaur with an upper jaw longer than that of another known fossil, the long-jawed ichthyosaur might be described as a new species. It might also be a juvenile as opposed to an adult, but other measurements can confirm its similarity to or difference from other known specimens.

Many of the descriptions of the creatures in this book—all of which are extinct, and all of which are known only from fossils—consist primarily of osteological terminology. (Osteology is the study of bones.) Even the size of the eye, so critical to the differentiation of various ichthyosaur genera, relies largely on the circle of bony plates in the eye socket known as the sclerotic ring. At least part of the behavior of a large-eyed animal can be postulated from the size of the sclerotic ring, and although we might suggest that such a creature hunted at night or in reduced light circumstances, we can only guess as to what it hunted. (Sometimes, remnants of its last meal are fossilized too; in some cases, squid beaks or sucker hooks have been found in the fossilized predator's stomach.) The ability to separate one species from another depends on these detailed descriptions, and when one fossil is compared with another and found to be different in its particulars, the result might be a new species. Comparative anatomy therefore is one of the cornerstones of paleontology, but it often results in complex technical descriptions not easily understood by the nonspecialist. Here, for example, is Edward Drinker Cope's

(1868a) description of a plesiosaur fossil that had been shipped to him from Kansas:

> The species represented a genus differing in important features from Plesiosaurus and its near allies. These were the absence of diapophyses on the caudal vertebrae, and the presence of inferiorly directed plate-like parapophyses which took the place of the usual chevron bones, in the same position; also in the presence of chevron-like bones on the inferior surfaces of the cervical vertebrae; further in some details of the scapular and pelvic arches. The diapophyses of the dorsal vertebrae originated from the centrum, and not from the neural arch.

Cope was reading the vertebrae backward, which resulted in his reconstructing the skeleton with the skull at the wrong end, but the point is the same: "the presence of inferiorly directed plate-like parapophyses" does not help the layperson understand what *Elasmosaurus platyurus* looked like. Most descriptions of fossils are like this, and only the most creative of paleontologists, or those attempting to make particular points about limb structure and movement or tooth structure and prey items, will extrapolate from the bones to the lifestyle. Because we are not all trained paleontologists, we would like to learn more about a given species than we can discover from the absence of diapophyses.

Although there are no "rules" governing the form of a scientific paper, most of them follow a recognized pattern, generally consisting of abstract, introduction, discussion, conclusion, and references. In a paleontological discussion, there is usually a section describing the location of the fossil find, its condition, and its eventual disposition; if possible, an attempt is made to place it in a recognizable phylogenetic category, such as ichthyosauridae or mosasauridae, so the reader will know the general nature of the fossil. (It is not always easy to place, say, a single tooth in a known category, and there have been instances when the description of the tooth was accurate but its designation was not.) Such organization is possible for scientific papers, but it is considerably more difficult with books. This book has certainly been organized into broad categories (ichthyosaurs, plesiosaurs, pliosaurs, mosasaurs), but the very nature of paleontology, with new specimens being unearthed or descriptions of old ones being revised in the literature, makes for an uneasy chronology. Does the writer talk about the sequence of discovery or the geological sequence of the specimens themselves? Is the "earliest" ichthyosaur the oldest, or the first one found by fossil hunters? The first discovery of a fossil mosasaur — in fact, the first discovery of a fossil marine reptile of any kind — occurred in a Belgian limestone mine in 1780. Later christened *Mosasaurus hoffmanni*, it was found to be one of the last of the mosasaurs; therefore, depending on who's doing the structuring, the story of the mosasaurs can either begin at the end or end at the beginning.

Many early paleontologists attempted to reconstruct the lifestyle of the marine reptiles or the dinosaurs, but because this exercise was speculative, often the safest thing to do was to describe the bones and leave the lifestyle to someone else. It is true that much can be learned from the size and shape of the bones and the muscle attachments, and from this evidence it can be ascertained how the animal might have moved, but what it did when it got there is often an enigma. Much can also be deduced from teeth. Just like today's animals, extinct large animals with big, sharp teeth were probably aggressive killers, and it is not difficult to imagine that a big marine lizard with teeth like a crocodile or a killer whale might have behaved in a similar fashion to these powerful predators. Animals with flattened teeth that look suitable for grinding were probably plant or shellfish eaters. Osteological descriptions are critical to understanding the relationships of extinct animals, but because we cannot observe them in action, we can only guess as to how the animals swam or hunted or gave birth. Whenever possible, therefore, I describe the animal's size, teeth, flippers, and tail (or where the fossil was found and by whom) and refrain from differentiating various species by the relative size and shape of the shoulder blade or pelvic girdle.

In many cases, there is enough fossil evidence to allow a fairly accurate reconstruction of the animal's size and shape, but except for the obvious — eyes are for seeing, teeth are for biting or tearing, backbones are for support — conclusions can rarely be drawn about how the animal actually used this equipment. As will be seen, the existence of four flippers in plesiosaurs has presented a virtually unsolvable question of how the flippers were used to propel the animals through the water, but we have a pretty good idea of the prey subdued by the enormous teeth of the giant pliosaurs. Most ichthyosaurs had a downward tailbend at the end of the vertebral column, which suggests that their swimming was powered by flexions of the lower lobe, so the comparison to the tail of a shark—where the vertebral column extends into the *upper* lobe—is obvious. We know what the tails of living sharks look like, but in only a few cases in which the outline of the entire animal was preserved do we know what the upper lobe of an ichthyosaur's tail looked like. The mosasaurs had scales, not unlike those of a snake, and at least some ichthyosaurs had smooth skin like that of whales and dolphins (Lingham-Soliar 2001); otherwise, with so few preserved fossilized impressions, we do not know whether the rest of them—particularly the plesiosaurs—were smooth-skinned or had scales, ridges, lumps, or bumps. And there is one thing that we know nothing about: we have no idea what color the marine reptiles were.

In order to re-create them, I could have made them monochromatic (I was, after all, working in pen and ink), but this seemed to detract from their vitality. We know that many living reptiles are brightly colored—think of snakes and lizards—so there is no reason to assume that the reptiles that lived 100 millions years ago were drab and colorless. Because these reptiles lived in the water, does that mean that they would be only countershaded, like many fishes—dark above and light below? Of course not. Fishes come in all the colors of the rainbow, and for good measure, some of them even light up. Well, then, aren't whales dull and monochromatic? Not on your tintype. Killer whales are spectacularly patterned in black and white; various dolphins sport elaborate haberdashery; and the fin whale, with its complicated asymmetrical pattern of swoops and swirls, may be the most intricately colored animal on Earth. In my drawings, I made some of the reptiles plain, and I patterned some of them with stripes, spots, and countershadings. All these color schemes are imaginary, designed (I hope) to breathe life into long-dead ichthyosaurs, plesiosaurs, and mosasaurs.

The fossil record is tantalizingly incomplete. There are any number of creatures that lived on Earth for which we have found no evidence whatsoever, so paleontologists have had to make do with the comparatively small number of fossils found and extrapolate from there. In *Atlas of the Prehistoric World,*

Douglas Palmer wrote, "there should be in the order of 500 million fossil species buried in the stratigraphic record. So far, paleontologists have described only a few hundred thousand fossil species. At less than 0.01 percent, this represents a very small sample of the estimated total." (Palmer says that real numbers are not available and his figure is a "guesstimate," but it is probably in the right range.) In 1994, David Raup summarized the fossil record for dinosaurs as follows:

> The dinosaur fossil record illustrates some of the more severe sampling problems. According to a review by Dodson, 336 of the named species of dinosaurs are taxonomically valid. Of these, 50% are known only from a single specimen, and about 80% are based on incomplete skeletons. The 336 species are grouped into 285 genera, and of these, 72% have been found in the rock formations where they were first discovered, and 78% have been found in only one country. These numbers are astonishing if viewed as if the data were complete.

In many instances, a single tooth, bone, or bone fragment has been found, and because there is no other possible explanation, the paleontologist identifies the animal that originally owned these bones and declares that it once lived (or died) here. How do they know? Comparison with specimens described in books and journals and those seen in museum collections, experience, and, of course, location. A great many species have been described from limited fragments of evidence, and the discovery of a complete or even partially complete specimen is a rare occurrence in paleontology. There are some notable exceptions where fossils are particularly plentiful, and they are occasionally even fairly complete. These special sites include the Burgess Shale in British Columbia, Holzmaden and Solnhofen in Germany, the seaside cliffs of Dorset in England, certain areas of the Gobi Desert, the Hell Creek Formation of Montana and the Dakotas, the Bear Gulch Formation in Montana, the Niobrara Chalk Formations of Kansas, and the Yixian Formation of the Liaoning province of China. Even when the fossils are relatively complete, an enormous amount of work is required to extract them and prepare them for study or exhibition.

Consider the fossils unearthed by New Zealand's "Dragon Lady," Joan

Wiffen. She and her colleagues (most of whom are amateurs) have been prospecting on North Island and have found "31 partial elasmosaur and 8 partial pliosaur specimens . . . collected over 10 years of summer fieldwork in the Mangahouanga Stream, inland Hawke's Bay." Wiffen and Moisley's 1986 paper, which occupies 47 pages in New Zealand's prestigious *Journal of Geology and Geophysics,* describes one skull (of *Tuarangisaurus keyesi,* "the only elasmosaurid skull . . . so far found in New Zealand"), and assorted teeth, vertebrae, pectoral girdle elements, and shoulder blades. From these fragments, Wiffen and Moisley have been able to postulate the existence of "young juveniles through to adult forms and provide a representative record of Late Cretaceous elasmosaurs and pliosaurs that lived in shallow estuarine or local offshore waters on the east coast of New Zealand during the Late Cretaceous." Not a single complete skeleton of any species was found, so the previously unsuspected presence of marine reptiles in New Zealand has been deduced from these fragments alone. In her 1991 book *Valley of the Dragons,* Wiffen wrote, "Those first fossil bones . . . were later identified as plesiosaur vertebrae, and plesiosaur remains proved to be the most common bone fossils found at Mangahouanga. Of these, the discovery of a complete skull in 1978 was by far the most exciting. It was the first found in New Zealand and one of less than a dozen complete elasmosaur skulls known anywhere." New Zealand is not unique; most of the world's fossiliferous locations have produced only scattered bits and pieces for paleontologists to work with. The history of the hominids—which includes us—is based largely on teeth and scraps of bone that have been found lying on the ground in Africa. Somewhere, perhaps buried deep in the earth or encased in impregnable rock, is the rest of the evidence, but it is reasonable to assume that it will never be found. Our understanding of ancient life-forms is often based on the skimpiest of evidence, but we are grateful that the earth has revealed as much as it has; much of our understanding of the processes of extinction and evolution has come from these shards of Earth's history.

None of this is meant to imply that paleontologists do not do proper science. They cannot directly observe the biology of their animals, but that does not mean that paleontology is any less rigorous a discipline than, say, ornithology. Despite the "data-poor" nature of their studies (missing parts, missing lineages, or even missing taxa), there are still many ways that good, testable hypotheses can be developed in studying the fossil record. Of necessity, the evidence collected is usually more indirect and circumstantial, but that does not make it less worthy than direct evidence, if used properly. Because paleontologists do not have the opportunity to observe the living subjects of their studies, their hypotheses must be tested by techniques of comparative biology, based on a thorough, detailed, and broad knowledge of living animals. There are no living ichthyosaurs, but they shared certain characteristics with sharks and dolphins, and comparisons with the living animals have given us great insights into the modus vivendi of the fish lizards. Mosasaurs resemble varanid lizards in some respects and crocodilians in others, and comparative studies have enabled paleontologists to make numerous assumptions about the lives and phylogeny of the great seagoing lizards. Unfortunately, there are few living creatures that resemble plesiosaurs (only today's sea turtles propel themselves with four flippers), and so much about their lives is still a mystery. The absence of living models, however, does not preclude creative analysis of the fossils. There is a substantial body of literature devoted to the locomotion of plesiosaurs, all based on the shape, structure, and relationship of the bony elements. Indeed, one does not have to compare fossil structures to analogous structures in living animals; the hydrodynamic capabilities of plesiosaur flippers have been compared to the wings of birds, bats, and even airplanes (O'Keefe 2002c).

Throughout this discussion of the marine reptiles, I cite the various chronological periods, which have been named by geologists and paleontologists so that they would have a consistent timetable with which to associate particular fossil faunas. The span under discussion here is generally known as the Mesozoic era, which lasted from 248 million to 65 million years ago. The Mesozoic is further broken down into three large periods, the Triassic (248 to 209 million years ago), the Jurassic (208 to 144 million years ago), and the Cretaceous (144 to 65 million years ago). These have been further compartmentalized into smaller, tighter groups; the late Cretaceous, for example, is subdivided into the Coniacian age (89.9 million years ago), the Santonian age (85.8 million years ago), the Campanian age (83.5 million years ago), and the

Maastrichtian age (71.3 to 65 million years ago). The dating of these periods is fairly firm—almost, but not quite, "written in stone." The dating of rocks by analyzing radioactive isotopes that decay at a known rate (the half-life) has provided geologists with an absolute scale of dating, and quite often, fossils themselves can be used to establish chronologies. Many invertebrates whose timeline is known can serve as "index fossils," and the particular period can be identified by the presence of these creatures. The coiled shells of ammonites, for example, are very common fossils, and because many species were incredibly numerous, we can identify a particular moment in time by the presence of certain ammonite fossils. Therefore, if we find fossilized animals (such as mosasaurs) alongside these cephalopod fossils, we can fairly safely assume that they lived (and died) at the same time. (But as we shall see, it is not so easy to figure out their interactions.)

Breaking down the chronology of the earth into convenient segments is enormously helpful in establishing an evolutionary sequence for groups of animals; if some are found, say, in Coniacian deposits, and similar forms are found in deposits that can be dated later as Maastrichtian, it can be assumed that the former are earlier and (perhaps) ancestral to the latter. This may not be accurate, for evolution does not necessarily consist of an unbroken chain of creatures that gradually morph into their modified descendants. Rather, evolution has been described as a bush, with branches that occasionally lead to other forms but more often end abruptly. As Darwin wrote in *On the Origin of Species*, "Though Nature grants long periods of time for the work of natural selection, she does not grant an indefinite period; for as all organic beings are striving to seize on each place in the economy of nature, if any one species does not become modified and improved in a corresponding degree with its competitors, it will be exterminated." That we have been able to identify the ancestors of any living (or extinct) creatures is the singular triumph of investigative paleontology, for it has been estimated that 99.9 percent of all the species that have ever lived are extinct.

When we see references to the Campanian (83.5 to 71.3 million years ago) and Maastrichtian (71.3 to 65 million years ago) ages, we might be able to understand the sequence, but this compression into comfortable categories erases the almost incomprehensible extent of time involved. Everybody is familiar with the comparison of the history of life on Earth to a 24-hour day, in which humans have been around for only the last few seconds, but such a construct *diminishes* the actual passage of time, probably in the ever-present interest of anthropocentrism—the belief that the world revolves around us and that we can understand things only in human terms. But human beings, as we know us, have been around for 100,000 years, a fleeting one-tenth of a million. The time of the mosasaurs, often described as "only" 25 million years, is 250 times greater than the total experience of *Homo sapiens,* from the moment he (or she) picked up the first rock and shaped it into an ax head to the moment you are reading these words. The ichthyosaurs lasted four times longer than the mosasaurs, so their time on earth was a thousand times longer than ours. To grasp the pace of evolution, we don't need to speed up the film, we need to slow it down. We must not be misled by the idea that a million years is a mere blink of the eye. That is the case only in geological terms; the planet is believed to be 4.5 *billion* years old, but a million years is a very long time indeed. If a human generation is 20 years, then 5,000 generations have passed in the entire history of *H. sapiens,* and if we were to last a million years— a highly unlikely scenario—50,000 generations would pass. If a generation of ichthyosaurs was also 20 years, then there were 7.5 million generations of fish lizards in their 150-million-year history. Evolution is a slow process, but during their "reign," the dinosaurs diversified into hundreds of different species, grew to enormous sizes, and even sprouted wings and feathers. Various ancestral reptiles took to the water, and through an inexorably slow and gradual process—comparatively speaking, glaciers move at the speed of bullets—became the aquatic reptiles that will be visited here.

The aquatic reptiles are all believed to have descended from terrestrial forebears, but those forebears were descended from animals that lived in the water. The first terrestrial tetrapods of the late Devonian period (circa 354 million years ago), such as *Acanthostega* and *Ichthyostega,* emerged from the water with their limbs modified to walk on land. Recent discoveries (Coates and Clack 1990) indicate that these early tetrapods had eight digits on the forelimbs and seven on the hind. This plan did not perdure, and the five-finger arrangement dominated the future of reptiles and mammals. (Stephen J. Gould wrote an essay on seven- and eight-fingered tetrapods, suggesting that polydactyly was a stepping-stone on the way to the normal five-finger plan that dominates vertebrate morphology. He was so taken with the idea that the 1993 book in which the essay appears is entitled *Eight Little Piggies*.) In their return to the sea, the ichthyosaurs, mosasaurs, and plesiosaurs exhibited what Michael Caldwell (2002) calls "an intriguing aspect of tetrapod limb evolution . . . the fin-to-limb-to-fin transition." He wrote:

> The recolonization of the water has occurred repeatedly in distantly re-
> lated tetrapod lineages, and in each case involves a major morphogenic
> reorganization of the limb to a paddle-like or fin-like structure. Among
> living groups of tetrapods this process of secondary radiation and mor-
> phogenetic evolution has produced the specialized limbs of cetaceans,
> seals, sea lions, manatees, walruses, and sea turtles. The fossil record also
> provides evidence of aquatic adaptation and extreme morphological spe-
> cialization in a number of extinct lineages of diapsid reptiles: mosasaurs,
> ichthyosaurs, plesiosaurs, pliosaurs, their basal sauropterygian cousins, and
> extinct crocodiles.

The marine reptiles all lived in the water. They all breathed air; some (the ichthyosaurs) are known unequivocally to have given birth to live young in the water, but the evidence is less convincing for the plesiosaurs and mosasaurs; and they were all descended from terrestrial reptilian ancestors. Some of them were contemporaries in time and place, but the ichthyosaurs finally went extinct at the Cenomanian-Turonian boundary, which was 93.5 million years ago, or 25 million years before the demise of the last of the plesiosaurs and mosasaurs. The final extinction of the plesiosaurs and mosasaurs is thought to be somehow connected to the event that took out the nonavian dinosaurs 65 million years ago, but how an asteroid impact and its consequences elimi-nated some of the seagoing reptiles while sparing the turtles and crocodiles is not clear.

Despite the apparent similarities in habitat and lifestyle, however, the three major groups of marine reptiles were quite different and were not closely related. The ichthyosaurs were more or less dolphin-shaped, but they had four flippers to the dolphins' two and a vertical tail fin where that of the dolphins is horizontal. The mosasaurs were also tail-powered swimmers, but their propulsion came from sinuous oscillations of the tail, quite different from the short power stroke of the ichthyosaurs. (Theagarten Lingham-Soliar believes that at least one mosasaur species — *Plioplatecarpus marshi* — "flew" through the water, using its fins as well as its tail, but not many agree with him.) And the plesiosaurs, with their short tails and four powerful flippers, moved through the water somehow, but the experts disagree as to how this might have been accomplished. However they propelled themselves, the short-necked plesiosaurs (known collectively as pliosaurs) met normal resistance from the water; the long-necked ones seemed to have problems that they were obviously able to solve (a long neck held out in front of a swimming animal would act as a rudder), but we still can't figure out how they did it.

Some 65 million years ago, at the geological boundary of the Cretaceous and Tertiary eras (known as the K-T boundary), a massive asteroid slammed into the earth at a place that would eventually be identified as Chicxulub, off the Yucatán peninsula in the Gulf of Mexico. Because this impact coincides with the last recorded terrestrial dinosaurs, there are those who draw a connection between the two events and claim that the environmental havoc caused by the impact led to the dinosaurs' extinction. Others hold that different variables, such as climate change, massive volcanic eruptions, and elimination of their food source, were at least partly responsible for the demise of the dinosaurs. Now it is believed that today's living birds are actually descended from terrestrial, feathered dinosaurs and that dinosaurs are not extinct after all.*

---

* In *The Evolution and Extinction of the Dinosaurs* (1996), Fastovsky and Weishampel answer the question, How can a bird be a reptile? "Clearly we have a decidedly different Reptilia from the traditional motley crew of crawling, scaly, nonmammal, nonbird, nonamphibian creatures that most of us think of when we think of reptiles. If it is true that crocodiles and birds are more closely related to each other than either is to snakes and lizards, then a monophyletic group that includes snakes, lizards, and crocodiles *must* also include birds. The implication of calling a bird a reptile is that birds share the derived characters of Reptilia, as well as having unique characters of their own."

In a 2002 paper entitled "Extinction of Ichthyosaurs: A Catastrophic or Evolutionary Paradigm?" Lingham-Soliar wrote:

> Lumping ichthyosaurs, plesiosaurs, mosasaurs, marine crocodiles and marine turtles into a marine reptile assemblage is fraught with problems, particularly when viewed over a range of functional attributes, e.g. reproduction, feeding and locomotion, irrespective of phylogeny. Jurassic and Cretaceous ichthyosaurs are the only marine reptiles thought to have used a thunniform mode of locomotion, with sustained speeds that were probably greater than that of the other marine reptiles. Some plesiosaurs are also thought to have achieved reasonably fast speeds although they employed a novel form of locomotion, viz. underwater flight. . . . The peculiar hydrodynamics of underwater flight in plesiosaurs had a number of definitive effects on the lifestyle of this unique group of marine reptiles. Ichthyosaurs gave birth to live young, a form of reproduction typical of mammals rather than reptiles. . . . Positions in the food pyramid would also presumably have differed in ichthyosaurs, plesiosaurs, mosasaurs, crocodiles and marine turtles. Thunniform ichthyosaurs were fast efficient predators that fed on fish and squid. They were secondary consumers in the food pyramid, comparable with e.g. present-day bottlenose and common dolphins. Mosasaurs in the late Cretaceous were ubiquitous archetypal ambush predators, feeding on a range of marine animals including sharks, other mosasaurs, birds, fish etc., and were probably at the top of the food pyramid. Their predecessors, pliosaurs (and certain fast swimming plesiosaurs such as *Cryptoclidus*) were probably adapted to both ambush and pursuit predation.

# The Marine Reptiles

## An Overview

*We have reviewed the various stages through which the ancestors of reptiles passed to be completely freed from the aquatic existence and become purely land-dwelling types. But, curiously, no sooner did the reptiles attain this terrestrial mode of life than many groups began to reverse the process and return to the water. We have noted that among the ruling reptiles the phytosaurs and crocodiles had returned to an amphibious type of existence, and also among the lizards several groups have become water dwellers.*
*— Alfred Sherwood Romer (1933)*

Until the mid-nineteenth century, almost everybody in the Western world — scientists included — accepted the traditional Christian view that the Bible was to be taken literally and that God had made all the mammals, birds, alligators, snakes, fishes, and insects, as well as all the trees, flowers, grasses, and ferns. His crowning achievement was "to make man in his own image, after our likeness; and let them have dominion over the fish of the sea, and over the fowl of the air, and over cattle, and over every creeping thing that creepeth upon the Earth." Aristotle believed that the animals had been divinely arranged in a ladder, with humans confidently perched on the top rung, the epitome of life. In the sixteenth century, there were only about 150 kinds of mammals known, approximately the same number of birds, and perhaps 30 snakes. For the first edition of his *Systema Naturae*, published in 1735, Carolus Linnaeus, a Swedish botanist, categorized all the known creatures (and plants) into an arrangement in which every living thing was given a binomial name, corresponding to its genus and species. Thus, in the Linnaean classification, the wolf is *Canis lupus*, the ibex is *Capra ibex*, and the blue whale is *Balaenoptera musculus*. Although the extinct marine reptiles also have proper binomials, none were mentioned by Linnaeus, because none of them had been recognized before he died in 1778.

Because Linnaeus was working in the middle of the eighteenth century, he was able to include some newly discovered beasts in his classification, but he firmly believed that all known species were unchanging creations of God, who had chosen to arrange things so that man resided at the top of the hierarchy. Whales and dolphins had been known since they demonstrated the unfortunate inclination to beach themselves. Two thousand years ago, Aristotle wrote, "It is not known for what reason they run themselves aground on dry land; at all events, it is said that they do so at times, and for no obvious reason." Until whalers and other seafarers took to the sea, the only cetaceans that could be known were those that washed ashore. The discovery of fossils, known since ancient Greece, suggested that there were some life-forms that were no longer with us, but for European and American minds, this meant only that the Great Flood, identified in the Bible, had drowned those that Noah hadn't loaded onto the ark. (How the fishes, whales, and dolphins managed to board the ark was never explained; maybe they swam along in its wake.) As humankind's horizons widened, animals that Linnaeus never knew of began to appear. In North America, there were raccoons, pronghorns, and mountain lions; South America had weird and wonderful monkeys with prehensile tails, sloths, anteaters, llamas, and armadillos; and there was an entire continent in the southern sea that was populated by the strangest fauna of all: kangaroos, wallabies, koalas, and wombats—mammals that raised their young in a pouch. The "dark continent" of Africa had giraffes, water buffaloes, zebras, baboons, chimpanzees, and gorillas, not one of which was mentioned in the story of the biblical flood.

None of these animals, no matter how bizarre, would astonish the scientist and the layperson the way the great fossil reptiles did. After all, deer and antelopes are relatively familiar; llamas sort of look like camels, and even the fantastic fauna of Australia fit—albeit roughly—into a range of sizes and shapes that would hardly cause people to question their fundamental beliefs about life on Earth. But here we had evidence of 40-foot-long lizards with huge teeth; dolphin-like creatures with long snouts and four legs; and, most wondrous of all, a long-necked something with a tiny head and what looked like flippers! Everything people thought they knew about the living world was being stood on its head. There was nothing remotely resembling a comprehensible framework that could enclose these fabulous creatures. A whole new way of looking at life would have to be developed—and quickly. Fortunately, there were men like Baron Cuvier, Geoffroy Saint-Hilaire, and the Chevalier de Lamarck; Dean William Daniel Conybeare and Professor William Buckland; Richard Owen and Henry De la Beche; Carolus Linnaeus and Charles Lyell; and, ultimately, the men who would furnish the system that could incorporate the lizards, the llamas, the lions, and the kangaroos—Charles Darwin and Alfred Russel Wallace.

Like the first of the dinosaurs, the first of the great sea reptiles was found in England. Although the British were the first to find and publish descriptions of the extinct marine and terrestrial reptiles, fossils would soon be appearing in other European countries, in North America, and eventually on every continent. In 1719, Dr. William Stukely was apprised by Robert Darwin (Charles's grandfather) of a "human Sceleton (as it was then thought)" that had been found in the bluestone quarries of Nottinghamshire. Stukely examined the specimen and realized that "it cannot be reckoned Human, but seems to be a Crocodile or Porpoise." (That there were "no less than Eleven Joints of the Tail" probably helped in his diagnosis.) In his discussion of the "sceleton," he wrote: "What Creature this has been, for want of a Natural History of Sceletons, well worthy of the Endeavors of this society, we cannot possible determine; but generally find the like to be amphibious or marine Animals." Stukely's was the earliest authenticated reference to a plesiosaur, but the name hadn't been invented yet. More than a century would pass before Conybeare and De la Beche would coin the term in their 1824 discussion of *Plesiosaurus dolichodeirus*, the long-necked near-lizard. (Stukely's "sceleton," now properly identified as a plesiosaur, is on exhibit in the Natural History Museum, London.)

In 1818, William Buckland, a professor of geology at Oxford, was shown the bones of a huge carnivorous beast, and when he couldn't identify the original owner, he sent them to Baron Cuvier, the world's foremost authority on fossils and anatomy, who helped Buckland see that they had indeed come from a giant reptile. Six years later, Buckland published "Notice on the *Megalosaurus*, or the great fossil lizard of Stonesfield." He did not call it a dinosaur, because the term would not appear until Richard Owen introduced it in 1842. He had the fossil lower jaw (with teeth in place), several vertebrae, some fragments of the pelvis, and the shoulder bones of large, unknown animals that he had been collecting for about a decade from the Stonesfield quarries near Oxford. In his 1824 paper, Buckland identified it as a species of giant extinct lizard (*Megalosaurus* means "great lizard") that exceeded 40 feet in length and had a bulk equal to that of a large elephant.

In 1821, while walking through Tilgate Forest in Sussex, Mary Ann Mantell found a toothlike fossil that she gave to her husband, Dr. Gideon Mantell, who went on to become a compulsive collector of fossils (Mary Ann left him because there was no more room in their house, among other reasons). Mantell felt that the tooth did not belong to a crocodile or an ichthyosaur,* so he sent it to Cuvier, who identified it as belonging to an extinct form of rhinoceros. But when Mantell compared the tooth with that of an iguana, he realized that the tooth his wife had found was almost a replica of the tooth of the living lizard, but 20 times larger. He named it *Iguanodon* ("iguana-tooth"), and although it was in fact the first dinosaur ever described, it entered the literature only as the "Newly discovered Fossil Reptile from the sandstone of the Tilgate Forest in Sussex." Cuvier rescinded his misidentification in a letter to Mantell in in 1824. Buckland and Mantell both believed that their creatures were (or had been) giant lizards, and the parade of the dinosaurs had begun.

The seagoing reptiles were actually discovered a couple of years before the land-dwelling dinosaurs and were therefore the first prehistoric animals to

---

* According to Chris McGowan (2001), "This is a wonderful story of the discovery of one of the most important fossils of the time. Unfortunately, it is without foundation, and Mantell himself was largely to blame for this. Not only did he fail to record at the time how the unique tooth was discovered, but he also gave somewhat different accounts of the find after the fact. . . . Dennis Dean, an authority on Mantell, is of the opinion that the first tooth was probably supplied to Mantell by Mr. Leney, the quarryman at Cuckfield. . . . Regardless of the provenance of the first tooth, it must have astonished and baffled Mantell because it was so entirely different from anything he had ever seen before."

come to light (as it were). In 1839, De la Beche made a drawing for Mary Anning that he titled *Duria Antiquior* ("Ancient Dorset"), copies of which Mary offered for sale – probably along with fossils – to her customers. The drawing depicted ichthyosaurs, plesiosaurs, sharks, squid, ammonites, and pterodactyls, all "realistically" portrayed in or around the water. (A plesiosaur plucks a pterodactyl out of the air, but two others fly freely overhead.) Of De la Beche's *Duria Antiquior*, Rudwick (1992) wrote that it "was the first true scene from deep time to have received even limited publication" and was thus the first such illustration to place these long-extinct animals into something approximating natural surroundings. In 1840, Thomas Hawkins wrote *The Book of Great Sea-Dragons*, which was illustrated by John Martin, whose animals, with their bulging eyes and forked tongues, looked more like mythological dragons than real animals. But drawings showing the fossil skeletons fleshed out, whether in "natural surroundings" or not, encouraged the public to believe that these long-extinct creatures had once been as real as the cats, dogs, and horses they could see every day.

It wasn't long before these great dragons made an appearance in literature. In his 1864 *Journey to the Center of the Earth*, Jules Verne postulated that the earth was hollow, and his heroes, who had descended into the throat of a dormant volcano in Iceland, found a huge "central sea" that was "horribly wild – rigid, cold and savage." With some convenient trees (!) they build a raft, which they sail across the sea, hoping to find "some of those Saurians which science has succeeded in reconstructing from bits of bone or cartilage." Always willing to oblige, Verne produces the chapter called "Terrific Saurian Combat," in which the subterranean adventurers are surrounded by a whale of supernatural dimensions, a turtle 40 feet wide, and "a serpent quite as long, with an enormous head peering from out the waters." Then they witness a battle between "two hideous and ravenous monsters," the first of which has "the snout of a porpoise, the head of a lizard, the teeth of a crocodile; and in this it has deceived us. It is the most fearsome of all antediluvian reptiles, the world-renowned Ichthyosaurus or great fish lizard." The other is "a monstrous serpent concealed under the hard vaulted shell of the turtle, the terrible enemy of its fearful rival, the Plesiosaurus or sea crocodile." Verne describes the battle:

These animals attacked one another with inconceivable fury. Such a combat was never *seen* before by mortal eyes, and to us who did see it, it appeared more like the phantasmagoric creation of a dream than anything else. They raised mountains of water, which dashed in spray over the raft, already tossed to and fro by the waves. Twenty times we seemed on the point of being upset and hurled headlong into the waves. Hideous hisses appeared to shake the gloomy granite roof of that mighty cavern—hisses which carried terror to our hearts. The awful combatants held each other in a tight embrace. I could not make out one from the other. Still the combat could not last forever; and woe unto us, whichsoever became the victor. One hour, two hours, three hours passed away, without any decisive result.

In the end, the Ichthyosaurus triumphs and "returns to his mighty cavern under the sea to rest." It is obvious that Verne had read some of the contemporaneous descriptions of plesiosaurs and ichthyosaurs and had seen some of the more spectacular illustrations, perhaps those in Louis Figuier's 1863 *La Terre avant le Déluge* (Earth before the Deluge).* Figuier's book includes illustrations by Edouard Riou, one of which depicts an ichthyosaur confronting a plesiosaur, which Martin Rudwick calls "a visual cliché." The discovery of fossils of gigantic marine reptiles clearly captured the imagination of the public. The ichthyosaurs and plesiosaurs were bigger, fiercer, and more terrifying than any puny crocodiles, and now it was up to the scientists to explain where they had come from and, Jules Verne notwithstanding, what had happened to them.

* As a novelist, it was Verne's prerogative to exaggerate the size and ferocity of the saurians, but what Figuier actually wrote (in Rudwick's 1992 translation) was: "we bring together these two great marine reptiles of the Lias, the Ichthyosaur and the Plesiosaur. Cuvier says of the Plesiosaurus 'that it presents the most monstrous assemblage of characteristics that has been met with among the races of the ancient world.' It is not necessary to take this expression literally; there are no monsters in nature; the laws of organization are never positively infringed; and it is more accordant with the general perfection of creation to see in an organization so special, in a structure which differs so notably from that of animals of our days, the simple augmentation of a type, and sometimes also the beginning and successive perfecting of these beings."

In early-nineteenth-century Europe, most educated people believed that all the creatures God had made had been around since the Creation, so the idea that there were some that had mysteriously disappeared or died out was anathema to the prevailing religious doctrines. Georges Léopold Chrétien Frédéric Dagobert, Baron Cuvier (1769–1832), was the founder of comparative anatomy and probably the first paleontologist; as the "Magician of the Charnel House," he demonstrated that he could reconstruct an entire animal from a single fossilized bone. He believed that fossil sequences were the result of periodic catastrophes, with groups of animals being replaced by new forms in successive creations, and that each new form was a step in the progressive sequence that would eventually lead to man, the most sublime of God's creations. In addition to the biblical flood, he believed that the earth had been subjected to a succession of natural catastrophes throughout its history. Cuvier died 30 years before Darwin published his theory of evolution, and throughout his life, he believed that the extinct types were the ones that had been swept away by successive disasters, and fossils were the irrefutable evidence of those disasters. In reference to a series of (imagined) floods, he wrote:

> These repeated [advances] and retreats of the sea have neither been slow nor gradual; most of the catastrophes which have occasioned them have been sudden; and this is easily proved, especially with regard to the last of them, the traces of which are most conspicuous. . . . Life in those times was often disturbed by these frightful events. Numberless living things were victims of such catastrophes; some, inhabitants of dry land, were engulfed in deluges; others, living in the heart of the seas, were left stranded when the ocean floor was suddenly raised up again; and whole races were destroyed forever, leaving only a few relics which the naturalist can scarcely recognize.

No matter how it happened, however, Cuvier was among the first to recognize that certain species were no longer among the extant. Of course, there was always the possibility that new animals might turn up in some remote corner of Africa or South America, but exploration in those regions was making it more and more unlikely.* After comparing the skulls of the Indian and African elephants, Cuvier announced ("with remarkable self-assurance — some might term it arrogance," wrote Rudwick) that they were different species and, furthermore, that the mastodon, recently unearthed in Ohio, was distinct from either of the two living elephants. He believed that the mastodon was extinct, as were the previous owners of many fossil animal parts, but he was unable to determine why so many living species had survived the catastrophes while the extinct species *(espèces perdus)* had not. Cuvier wrote (translated in Rudwick 1972), "the most important question being to discover if the species that then existed have been entirely destroyed, or if they have merely been modified in their form, or simply transported from one climate into another."

In 1808, Cuvier was shown the fossilized jaws of an enormous reptile that had been found in a limestone mine in Maastricht in what is now the Netherlands. The jaws looked something like those of a modern monitor lizard, but they were more than 3 feet long. The jaws would later be described by Conybeare as belonging to the first mosasaur (named for the Meuse River near which they were found), a gigantic marine lizard that was also, mercifully, extinct. Cuvier's ability to reconstruct entire animals from a single bone meant that any unexplainable fossils would be brought to him for identification. From a small scrap, he was able not only to identify the animal it came from but also to postulate its way of life. It was not long before he was shown the bones of a reptile that appeared to have wings, which he named *Ptero-dactyle*, meaning "winged fingers." Cuvier realized that some animal species had

---

* But not impossible. During the twentieth century, when most people would assume that all the large animals had already been discovered, the okapi was found in central Africa in 1901, the coelacanth off South Africa in 1938, and the megamouth shark in Hawaii in 1975. In 1993, the saola or Vu Quang ox *(Pseudoryx nghetinensis)*, a previously unknown deer-sized animal with horns like an antelope, was discovered in a mostly unexplored rain forest on the Vietnam-Laos border. In 1997, scientists in Myanmar (formerly Burma) found the world's smallest deer, *Muntiacus putaoensis*, about the size of a large beagle and half the size of the smallest deer previously known. And in 1999, Pitman et al. identified *Indopacetus pacificus*, a new species of bottlenose whale from the tropical Indopacific — a 25-foot-long cetacean whose existence was suspected but unconfirmed.

disappeared—at least from some parts of the world—which meant that they had been destroyed, had somehow turned into something else, or had wandered far from the spot where the fossils had been found and were still alive somewhere. It would be another 40 years before Charles Darwin would suggest that extinction was somehow related to evolution, but Cuvier proposed periodic mass extinctions caused by catastrophes like the biblical deluge. He believed that the unrecognizable forms appeared after each flood and that fossils were remnants of the most recent previous creation. (He would go to his death, however, proclaiming that there would never be a human fossil; he declaimed emphatically, *L'homme fossile n'existe pas!*) For hundreds of years, educated humankind had believed in the "Great Chain of Being" *(Scala Naturae)*, a hierarchical arrangement of every living thing in the universe. There were "base" metals like lead, and "noble" ones like gold and silver. Given the authors of the list, it is not surprising to find man at the top, just below God and the angels. The chain progressed ineluctably upward, from the "lower" animals such as insects and worms to the "higher" animals, the birds and mammals.

Those who would reconstruct or study the terrestrial dinosaurs tried to imagine how they might have oriented their bodies and how they moved. At first, it was no problem, because Sir Richard Owen was utterly certain about what he was doing, even when he was wrong. His first reconstructions, sculpted in concrete by Waterhouse Hawkins for exhibition at Sydenham in 1854, were more or less patterned after known mammals and were low-slung, with sturdy, columnar legs. Because of their size, Owen found it impossible to combine them with the known lizards, so he coined the term *Dinosauria,* to include the huge "terrible reptiles" *Megalosaurus, Hylaeosaurus,* and *Iguanodon.**

* When Owen coined the term *dinosaur* in 1842, he intended it to apply to fossils of giant reptiles that had been unearthed in England and were different from any known reptiles. His definition reads as follows: "The combination of such characters, some, as the sacral bones altogether peculiar among Reptiles, others borrowed, as it were, from groups now distinct from each other, and all manifested by creatures far surpassing in size the largest of existing reptiles, will, it is presumed, be deemed sufficient ground for establishing a distinct tribe or suborder of the Saurian Reptiles, for which I would propose the name *Dinosauria.*"

Incomplete fossils of Gideon Mantell's *Iguanodon* were used by Hawkins as a basis for the "life-sized" model, in which Owen hosted a dinner party to celebrate the opening of the Crystal Palace. (Before the model was completed, it had no back so that people could sit in it, like a giant bathtub on columnar legs.) The nose of Hawkins's *Iguanodon* was decorated with a horn like that of a rhinoceros, but this bone is now believed to be a defensive "thumbspike." Indeed, Owen's *Iguanodon*, as seen in contemporaneous drawings, looks like an enormous scaly rhino, which is nothing at all like the most recent reconstructions. Modern paleontologists now think that *Iguanodon* was a somewhat graceful, long-legged animal with a long neck and peculiar "hands," each of which was equipped with a forward-pointing spike. Its tail was stretched out behind and probably never touched the ground unless the animal lay down.

Large reptiles were believed to be sluggish and slow-moving, and the dinosaurs, larger than anything previously imagined, were believed to be even slower and more ponderous. (As reconstructed by Waterhouse Hawkins, *Iguanodon* was close to 40 feet long.) Some of the larger sauropods, such as *Apatosaurus,* were thought by some to have been too large and heavy to walk on land, so it was suggested that they must have spent their lives neck-deep in ponds or lakes, with their great weight supported by the water, like whales. Or they were believed to feed from the tallest treetops and drag their tails behind them. The first *Tyrannosaurus* was found in Montana in 1902 by Barnum Brown of the American Museum of Natural History. Because the fossils included large, powerful hind leg bones, tiny forelimbs, and huge tails, the first reconstructions of *T. rex* were made to look like gigantic, big-headed kangaroos, resting upright on their tails with their little forelimbs tucked in. The huge jaws armed with 8-inch-long, serrated teeth were decidedly unkangaroo-like, however, and whereas kangaroos can pick up and manipulate objects in their forepaws, the function—if there was one—of *T. rex*'s tiny, two-clawed forelimbs is still a mystery. The latest interpretations have *Tyrannosaurus* standing with its back held horizontally and its powerful tail, stiffened by strong tendons, held out behind it. Some paleontologists have even suggested that *T. rex* was not an active predator at all but a scavenger that fed on carrion.

Nowadays, the answer to the question "What is a reptile?" is an easy one: it is the vernacular term for scaly, cold-blooded vertebrates and includes lizards, snakes, alligators, crocodiles, gharials, tortoises, and turtles. (The tuataras, which look like lizards, are classified as sphenodonts, separated by certain skull characteristics from the lizards.) The Reptile House at the zoo usually contains snakes, lizards, and crocodiles. The term *reptile* is generally used to mean a nonmammalian, nonavian amniote, but biologists are now shying away from such inclusive and undefined terms. (Current phylogenies put birds in the class Reptilia, because of their common origins.) All reptiles are air-breathers, and although most are terrestrial, some have adapted to an aquatic existence. None have gills, and nearly all lay eggs. (Many snakes and lizards are viviparous.) Reptiles invest more in their eggs than amphibians do, and therefore lay fewer of them. Mammals, for the most part, do not lay eggs (the exceptions are the egg-laying monotremes, the platypus and the echidna) but are classified as amniotes because the fertilized egg inside the body of the mother has an amnion. Birds, which all lay eggs, are also amniotes.

The reptilian egg is porous, and the shell contains the chorion, which surrounds the embryo and yolk sac; the allantois, which is involved in respiration (oxygen in, carbon dioxide out) and stores waste materials; and the amnion, which lies within the chorion and surrounds the embryo. The amnion creates a fluid-filled cavity in which the embryo develops, and the chorion forms a protective membrane around the amnion. The allantois is closely applied against the chorion, where it performs gas exchange and stores metabolic wastes. The presence of these membranes permits respiratory exchange between the egg and its environment without desiccation. The moist nature of the membranes is perfect for the developing embryo: too dry, and the embryo dies; too moist, and it drowns. The porous nature of the outer shell means that it cannot be laid in the water, and even snakes and turtles that are almost wholly aquatic have to come ashore to lay their eggs. (Amphibians and egg-laying fishes lay their eggs in the water.) Reptiles differ from the other major classes of terrestrial vertebrates — birds and mammals — in that they lack an internal system for controlling their body temperature and are largely dependent on the temperature of the environment. Amniotes include most of the land-dwelling vertebrates alive today, namely, mammals, turtles, tuataras, lizards, crocodilians, and birds. Although fundamentally terrestrial, several types of amniotes, such as ichthyosaurs, plesiosaurs, pinnipeds, sirenians, and cetaceans, have returned to the sea.

Until recently, the earliest known amniote was the 8-inch long *Hylonomus,* dating from the early Pennsylvanian period (310 million years ago) of Joggins, Nova Scotia, described by J. William Dawson in the mid-nineteenth century. It is characterized by a lack of openings in the skull behind the eye and was therefore classified as an *anapsid,* which simply means "no opening." The primitive nature of *Hylonomus* made it a candidate for the common ancestor of later reptiles, but a "supposed amniote" known as *Westlothiana* was discovered in Scotland and has been dated from the early Carboniferous period, 350 million years ago. Although its affinities are in dispute, Benton (1997a) wrote, "It could perhaps be a reptile, as suggested by some characters at the back of the skull, but other evidence suggests it might be a microsaur, a group of superficially reptile-like amphibians." Believed to be even earlier is *Casineria kiddi,* found by an amateur collector in Cheese Bay, Scotland, in 1992 (*Caseus* is Latin for "cheese"). Twenty million years later than the primitive tetrapods *Acanthostega* and *Ichthyostega,* it bore certain similarities to them but was considerably smaller and had five digits on each of its limbs instead of seven or eight. Whereas *Acanthostega* and *Ichthyostega* would have been awkward and ungainly on land—if indeed they ever came ashore—*Casineria* was clearly designed to spend more time out of the water. For one thing, it was only about 6 inches long—not nearly as big or heavy as the others—and its fingers were designed to flex separately, an adaptation for walking on irregular terrain. Its vertebrae locked together in such a way as to provide strong support for its body when it was lifted off the ground, unlike that of the earlier tetrapods, whose looser backbones were more like those of fishes (Paton et al. 1999). It is not clear if *Casineria* was a reptile, but if it was, it would certainly be listed among the first of its kind.

Reptiles are divided into two groups, anapsids (turtles and their extinct relatives) and diapsids. The diapsids—reptiles with two holes in the skull behind the orbit—have been further separated into two principal groups—the lepidosaurs ("scaly reptiles"), which includes the living snakes and the lizards (including the extinct mosasaurs), and the archosaurs ("ruling reptiles"), which includes crocodiles, dinosaurs, and flying reptiles. Although the nothosaurs, placodonts, plesiosaurs, and ichthyosaurs had only a single skull opening, they are classified as diapsids, but of unknown relationships.

The first reptiles lived on land, as did the ancestors of the living crocodiles, lizards, snakes, and tuataras. These proto-reptiles were small and light-boned, not unlike most lizards today, probably because smaller bodies were easier to maintain on the small grubs, insects, and worms that could be found on the floor of the Carboniferous forests, and also because small bodies are easier to heat up in whatever sunlight managed to break through the canopy. Richard Cowen (2000) believes that the first reptiles evolved "either on the riverbanks or in the canopy ecosystem of the Early Carboniferous, not on the forest floor," and may have even lived in the hollowed-out stumps of tree ferns. However they accomplished it, Carboniferous reptilomorphs like *Westlothiana* or *Hylonomus* were among the first animals on Earth to lay amniotic eggs, in which the embryo develops in a leathery shell, instead of the jelly-covered eggs of amphibians and fishes. Unlike typical amphibian and fish eggs, which have to be laid in water, reptile eggs must be fertilized before they are laid, and they must be laid on land. The shell prevents the embryo from drying out, and the developing reptile emerges as a miniature adult only when it is competent to survive on its own. (Most amphibians pass through an aquatic larval phase, like the tadpole stage in frogs, before they come onto land.) All the future amniotes (later reptiles, birds, and mammals) developed because of this innovation. But the reptiles, which are characterized by a scaly integument, never developed the ability to heat themselves metabolically and were, for the most part, dependent on ambient temperatures. (We don't really know about the terrestrial dinosaurs, which were reptiles. But modern birds, which are their descendants, are certainly warm-blooded.) It is likely, however, that some of the marine reptiles, particularly the ichthyosaurs, were warm-blooded, as were some of the dinosaurs. Some of the marine reptiles even "advanced" beyond the limitations of the amniotic egg, to the point where they became viviparous, giving birth to live young underwater, the way whales and dolphins do today.*

Reptiles evolved on land, but after their dispersal to various terrestrial habitats, some returned to the sea. In geological time, this turnaround occurred soon after the conquest of the land, because there are records of anapsids known as mesosaurs ("middle lizard") that evidently achieved an aquatic existence as soon as the early Permian, almost 300 million years ago. *Mesosaurus*, the first known marine reptile, was a 3-foot-long, fully aquatic lizard-like animal that propelled itself underwater with its elongated tail and webbed hind feet. Some thought that its elongated jaws, equipped with fine, sharp teeth that were too delicate for snagging fish, might have formed a sieve to strain plankton from the water, but modern analyses render this an unlikely explanation. The mesosaurs died out about 250 million years ago and evidently left no direct descendants. Because mesosaur fossils have been found in southern Africa and eastern South America, a good case can be made for continental drift. Since *Mesosaurus* could not have swum across the ocean from one continent to the other, its presence on both sides of what is now the South Atlantic supports the notion that the two land masses were once joined.

As Samuel Williston wrote in 1914, "Were there no turtles living we should look upon the fossil forms as the strangest of all vertebrate animals—animals which had developed the strange habit of concealing themselves inside their ribs, for that is literally what the turtles do." If it wasn't for the 250 species of turtles living today, trundling around on land and swimming in the sea or in lakes and ponds, these animals encased in mobile homes could easily be

* Giving birth to live young (viviparity) may not be the "advance" that us live-bearers think it is. In a letter to me, Mike Caldwell wrote, "Many groups of living squamates are viviparous/ovoviviparous while closely related forms (sister taxa) are egg-layers (e.g., pythons lay eggs, boas give live birth). Which is more advanced? I don't know and couldn't begin to guess. The problem intensifies as you go up the tree—many vipers lay eggs while crotalids (rattlesnakes) are live bearers. Between boas and rattlesnakes there are thousands of species and millions of years. Which is the advanced condition? Again I don't know. I do not think the amniotic egg and shell is a limitation. Ichthyosaurs and mosasauroids simply bypass the egg shell and retain the embryo in the body—as do boas and rattlesnakes."

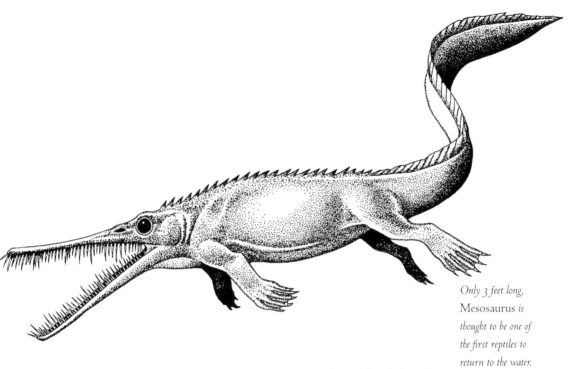

*Only 3 feet long, Mesosaurus is thought to be one of the first reptiles to return to the water. The flattened tail fin would have helped propel it through the water, but exactly how it fed with those long, delicate teeth is a mystery. It lived almost 300 million years ago.*

viewed as bizarre evolutionary experiments that were ordained for failure. Sea turtles were much more varied and diverse than they are today, but some of the earliest turtles, known from the late Triassic (200 million years ago), had a shell and an anapsid skull — a solid block of bone, with no openings for jaw muscles. The first known turtle was *Proganochelys quenstedi*, which had a fully developed shell and a turtle-like skull and beak, but it also had several primitive features not found in turtles today, including tiny teeth on its palate, a clavicle, and a simple ear. The early turtles were unable to withdraw their heads or legs into their shells, but by the middle of the Jurassic, turtles had split into the two main groups of turtles found today, the side-necked turtles (pleurodires) and the arch-necked turtles (cryptodires). They probably had terrestrial ancestors, but the sequence of descent is not evident.*

* Although this is the traditional view, Rieppel and Reisz presented a paper in 1999 in which they argued that the opposite conclusion was possible: "Within Amniota, the turtle body-plan is highly derived (autapomorphic) which results in functional constraints that are indicative of an aquatic origin for turtles. The most important of these traits is the

The steps required to get from a Permian scaly reptile to a fully armored creature with flippers for feet are also unclear. The turtles are probably descended from reptiles that inhabited swampy areas, where their bodies widened while their feet became webbed and they lost the articulation of their digits altogether. (Terrestrial tortoises have clawed toes, not unlike those of crocodilians.) The shell, which consists of an upper element (the carapace) and a lower one (the plastron), is unique to turtles and tortoises—indeed, unique in the animal kingdom. The path from Permian proto-turtle to recent turtle or tortoise was not without detours, and there were numerous variations on the armored reptile theme that did not perdure. *Proganochelys* is no longer with us, nor are the horned turtles *Niolamia* from Argentina and *Meiolania* from Lord Howe Island, an isolated speck of land 300 miles east of Sydney, Australia. In addition to "horns"—actually, flanges of bone behind the eyes—*Meiolania* had a spiked tail that was also fully armored. Then there was *Stupendemys geographicus,* a side-necked turtle that lived only 10,000 years ago in South America, whose shell reached a length of 8 feet. In 1976, Roger Wood described a specimen from the late Tertiary Urumaco Formation of northern Venezuela that he labeled "the world's largest turtle," but he also wrote that "*Dermochelys* [the leatherback] is reputedly the largest of all turtles, living or fossil." It also is not clear if *Stupendemys geographicus* was fully aquatic. Wood wrote, "Whether it was a fresh water or marine turtle, however, cannot be determined with certainty from the present evidence. One or perhaps both pairs of limbs may have been modified into flippers, and the head may not have been fully retractable."

Today, there are several species of large marine turtles, found mostly in the tropical and subtropical oceans of the world but occasionally wandering into

---

development of a carapax and plastron, which results in the reorganization of the paraxial mesoderm in the trunk region. The consequences of this ontogenetic repatterning affects locomotion and respiration in profound ways, necessitating structural and functional changes that are more easily achieved in an aquatic rather than a terrestrial environment. An aquatic origin of turtles is also suggested by the earliest appearance of the clade in the Middle Triassic Muschelkalk of Germany, an appearance that matches quite closely the time of the origin of the turtle clade suggested by the molecular data."

*Although "tortoise-shell" can easily be replaced by plastic, the 30-inch-long hawksbill turtle (Eretmochelys imbricata) is still hunted throughout its worldwide tropical habitat for its beautifully mottled shell.*

colder waters, such as those of Alaska (Hodge and Wing 2000). They all have flippers for forelimbs, lightweight shells, and heads that cannot be drawn into their shells. They spend most of their lives in the water, but the females come ashore to dig a nest in the sand and lay their eggs. All species are declining in numbers because the eggs are frequently "harvested" for human consumption, and the meat is also eaten. The shell of the hawksbill turtle *(Eretmochelys imbricata)* is the source of tortoiseshell, still popularly used for decorative objects, even though plastic has replaced most uses. The green turtle *(Chelonia mydas)*, highly valued for soup, has been known to weigh 800 pounds, but most specimens today are not half that size. The loggerhead *(Caretta caretta)* is a large-headed, chiefly carnivorous species that occasionally comes ashore to bask in the sun. The Pacific leatherback *(Dermochelys coriacea)* is the largest of the living sea turtles; an 8½-foot-long specimen weighed 1,908 pounds. The Atlantic leatherback (same species), which ranges from the Gulf of Mexico and the Caribbean to the British Isles in the north and to Argentina and South Africa in the south, is smaller. Leatherbacks have no visible shell; instead, they have a series of longitudinal ridges on the back and underside.

*A loggerhead is a ball of iron on the end of a long handle used in the melting of tar or pitch. The loggerhead turtle (Caretta caretta) has a proportionally large head and weighs between 200 and 400 pounds.*

The smallest of the sea turtles are the ridleys; the 2-foot-long Kemp's ridley (*Lepidochelys kempii*) breeds only in the Gulf of Mexico, and the slightly larger Pacific ridley (*L. olivacea*) is found in the Indian and Pacific Oceans. Kemp's ridley is seriously endangered, and there may be no more than 1,500 left in the world. The nonmigratory flatback turtle (*Natator depressus*), found only in northern Australia, is the only species of sea turtle that is not considered threatened or endangered.

After the mesosaurs, the earliest known marine reptiles are the nothosaurs, which had slender bodies, long necks and tails, and webbed feet. The nominal genus (*Nothosaurus*) had a long, narrow skull with splayed teeth that intermeshed when the mouth was shut, or, as Rieppel (2001b) put it, "As in all species of *Nothosaurus*, the anteriormost two fangs erupt from their respective premaxilla immediately lateral to the middle of the rostrum, and as in *Nothosaurus tchernovi*, the two anteriormost fangs fit between the two anteriormost symphyseal fangs when the jaws are closed." Nothosaurs flourished in Europe during the middle Triassic, about 225 million years ago, and were probably able to come out of the water, rather like modern pinnipeds do. The nostrils, which would normally be at the tip of the snout, were actually set further back, an adaptation that supports the suggestion that *Nothosaurus* was at least semiaquatic. They are classified as sauropterygians, a diversified group that includes the placodonts and pachypleurosaurs and the later plesiosaurs.

*With its webbed feet, Nothosaurus was a swimmer, but it was capable of moving on land too, perhaps like some of today's water monitors. Nothosaurs preceded plesiosaurs and may be ancestral to them.*

The sauropterygians (the name means "winged lizards" and refers to their paddle-like flippers) were related to one another but are of unknown ancestry. Rieppel (1997) wrote: "A number of basic subgroups of the Sauropterygia were readily recognized, such as the plesiosaurs and pliosaurs, with their streamlined skulls, needle-shaped teeth, elongated necks, and limbs transformed to hydrofoils. Nothosaurs and their allies were perceived as a distinct group, but the distinction between the relatively large nothosaurs and the generally smaller pachypleurosaurs of similar habitus was less easily drawn."

Some of the sauropterygians were semiaquatic, but most seem to have been aquatic. As Carroll (1988) wrote, "The sauropterygians provide the most complete evidence of the sequence of events that leads to a specialized aquatic way of life." The long-necked, long-tailed *Claudiosaurus,* from the Upper Permian of Madagascar, resembles a primitive sauropterygian but actually belongs to a different group. The primitive cervical vertebrae and unossified sternum place it close to the ancestry of all lizards, snakes, and crocodilians. The proportions of this 3-foot-long early reptile suggest that it swam like today's crocodilians, powered by undulations of the rear portion of the trunk and the tail, with its forelegs tucked in alongside the body, but it could probably walk on land as well. A similar species, also from Madagascar, was *Hovasaurus,* with a tail more than twice as long as its body and vertically compressed into a broad paddle, obviously useful for propulsion.

Closely related to the nothosaurs was *Pachypleurosaurus* ("thick-ribbed liz-

*Using a tail that was twice as long as its head and body,* Hovasaurus *plied the late Permian seas, about 250 million years ago. Adults were less than 2 feet long.*

ard"), found in deposits from the European middle Triassic and displaying a remarkable size range, from 8 inches to 13 feet (Benton 1990a). The skeleton shows poor ossification of the limb girdles, suggesting that it could not walk very well, but because its limbs were also not specialized into paddles, it probably moved by undulations of the long tail. As O'Keefe (2002a) wrote, "Plesiosaurs were advanced over their 'nothosaur-grade' forebearers in the evolution of wing-shaped fore and hind flippers that generated thrust via lift as well as drag." Like other sauropterygians, the pachypleurosaurs had an array of gastralia, the belly ribs that formed a ventral support system under the animal's underside and, along with the ribs, completely enclosed it in a shield of internal bony armor. Carroll and Gaskill (1985) described *Pachypleurosaurus* as having a moderately long neck and a particularly small skull, with widely spaced, peglike teeth that suggested that it chased and caught fish. A tiny nothosaur, possibly *Pachypleurosaurus*, was reported from Switzerland, with large eyes and unossified limbs that indicate that it was certainly an embryo (Sander 1988). Because it was not found in conjunction with an adult, this suggests that the nothosaurs laid eggs—perhaps on land.

The monotypical *Pistosaurus* is believed to be morphologically intermediate between the nothosaurs and the plesiosaurs proper. It is known only from the

*With skeletal characteristics of both nothosaurs and plesiosaurs, Pistosaurus may have been ancestral to the plesiosaurs. This 10-foot-long creature lived in the middle Triassic, about 230 million years ago.*

middle Triassic of Germany, so it seems to have had a limited distribution. *Pistosaurus* had a nothosaur-like body with a plesiosaur-like head, and it has been variously classified as a nothosaur or a plesiosaur, depending on what characteristics are used to define each group. Even if it is a nothosaur, it is acknowledged to be closely related to the ancestors of plesiosaurs. These may have been oceangoing creatures, but there has been no morphological analysis of the way these animals moved, so we do not know whether it swam like a crocodile (as nothosaurs did) or paddled (or rowed) like a turtle or sea lion.

Placodonts were sturdy-bodied reptiles that fed on shellfish, harvesting them with their shovel-like front teeth and crushing them between the heavy, platelike teeth on the roofs of their mouths and their lower jaws. (*Placodont* means "plate-teeth.") Their feet were webbed and less flipper-like than those of other marine reptiles, so they might have paddled in shallow water in search of food, but like today's marine iguanas, they also might have spent time out of the water. However, like the nothosaurs, their limb girdles were too weak to support these large, heavy animals on land, so they may have rested in the shallows when not feeding. Like that of the iguana, the tail of *Placodus* was long and laterally compressed and probably helped in aquatic propulsion. *Placodus*, which appeared and disappeared in the Triassic, was characterized by a massive skull and the presence of massive gastralia. There was a single row of dermal ossifications above the neural spines of the vertebrae, which was probably expressed as a row of spines running down the middle of the back. Placodonts looked something like overgrown, buck-toothed iguanas, and they came in armored and unarmored varieties. *Placodus* may have reached a length of 6 feet, including the tail.

*Henodus* was a sort of armored placodont, with a body as wide as it was long. At a length of about 3¼ feet, it had a boxlike head and a flexible tail, which was probably used in locomotion, along with its feet. It looked something like a toothless *Placodus* peeking out from under a heavy, horny blanket. *Henodus* was well armored, with protective shells top and bottom composed of bony plates covered in horn. This unusual marine reptile also had short fore- and hind limbs, and its relatively small feet might have been webbed. *Henodus* — which means "one tooth" — lacked the large, crushing teeth typical of the placodonts, and it was originally assumed that its hard, horny beak was used to get and crush shellfish, but recent studies have revealed numerous small teeth that formed a comblike structure that probably served as a sieving apparatus for small crustaceans. Even though Benton (1990a) described it as "startlingly similar in body form to the turtles," *Henodus* was not a turtle. Whereas the shell of a turtle develops largely from its skeletal bones — most of the carapace (upper shell) from the neural spines of the vertebrae and the ribs, and the front end of the plastron (lower shell) from elements of the shoulder girdle — the armor of *Henodus* developed exclusively from bony plates in the skin. Furthermore, the rhomboidal horny scutes of *Henodus* were quite different from — and much more numerous than — the plates of a turtle's shell.

*The placodonts ("plate-teeth") probably used their*
*projecting teeth to gather mollusks from the sea bottom.*
*Shown here is* Placodus, *which was 6 feet long.*

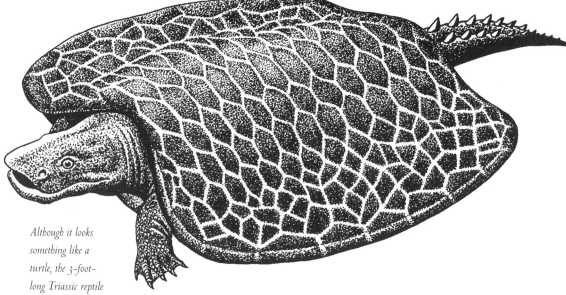

*Although it looks something like a turtle, the 3-foot-long Triassic reptile* Henodus *was actually an armored placodont. Grooves in the jaws may have held a baleen-like sieve, but how* Henodus *fed — or what it fed on, for that matter — is still a mystery.*

The term *convergent evolution* is used to describe unrelated creatures, such as the seagoing turtles and *Henodus*, that developed similar modifications because they lived the same kind of life in the same sort of habitat. *Henodus* lived during the late Triassic period, and the single species *(Henodus chelyops)* is known only from the Gipskeuper deposit of Tübingen-Lüstnau in southern Germany.

In 1999, Michael Caldwell described a new species of a primitive marine lizard known as *Coniasaurus*, from the chalk deposits at Brighton in southeastern England. (An earlier species, *Coniasaurus crassidens,* from the same location had been described by Richard Owen in 1850.) The coniasaurs were smallish lizards, probably no more than 3 feet long, with small heads and elongated necks, bodies, and tails. Although they do not figure in the ancestry of snakes (or mosasaurs), the small size, elongated body, and small head suggest a feeding strategy not unlike that of some extant sea snakes, that is, probing in crevices in coral reefs and rocky shores.

Whether or not birds are dinosaurs, the ancient marine reptiles certainly were not. They were not descended from dinosaur ancestors and represent a completely different vertebrate lineage. In any case, the nonavian dinosaurs were terrestrial and the marine reptiles were, well, marine. For an aquatic existence, the marine reptiles had fins, while the terrestrial dinosaurs had legs. Based on the structure of their pelvic girdles, dinosaurs have been divided into two groups, the bird-hipped (ornithischian) and the lizard-hipped (saurischian). The hips and hind limbs of dinosaurs are designed for weight bearing and bipedal or quadrupedal upright walking, whereas those of the ichthyosaurs and plesiosaurs could not possibly have borne any weight on land. In fact, the hip bones of the ichthyosaurs are not connected with the vertebral column at all; they are only reduced vestiges, buried in the abdominal wall. (Many living whales, which have no pelvic bones at all—and no hind legs, either—have tiny, vestigial hind limbs buried in the muscle where the hips would be.) The limbs of a plesiosaur demonstrate that it was a swimmer, not a walker. Plesiosaurs had four limbs of approximately the same size and propelled themselves through the water with some combination of flapping and rowing motions. Ichthyosaurs were built not unlike dolphins, except that the seagoing reptiles had hind limbs, and the dolphins have lost their hind limbs altogether. Like dolphins, ichthyosaurs steered with their fins and propelled themselves with their tail fins, but whereas the tails of dolphins and whales are horizontal, those of the ichthyosaurs were vertical. To the best of our knowledge, the dinosaurs were terrestrial—except, of course, those that returned to the water as birds (e.g., the hesperornithiformes). Some of the nonavian dinosaurs may have ventured into the water, as do many present-day terrestrial animals such as hippos, elephants, and penguins, but all the plesiosaurs and ichthyosaurs were aquatic and had flippers and other appropriate skeletal modifications for the marine environment. Regardless of how well adapted they seemed for a marine lifestyle, however, they all had to come to the surface to breathe.

The nothosaurs, placodonts, ichthyosaurs, plesiosaurs, and mosasaurs were oriented horizontally, like whales, dolphins, and most fishes, because that is the best way to swim through the water. (A few species of living fishes—sea horses, for example—orient themselves vertically, but they move slowly and inefficiently, which is surely not what the great marine predators did.) The long-necked plesiosaurs almost certainly oriented their bodies horizontally, with their long, flexible necks stretched out in front, swinging their heads and toothy jaws in pursuit of fish. (The long-necked dinosaurs, such as the sauropods *Diplodocus* and *Apatosaurus,* were herbivores whose prey rarely tried to escape.) But whether they sank to the bottom and struck at passing fish like a snake or floated at the surface with their heads dangling below is not known. In 1903, J. William Dawson (the discoverer, with Charles Lyell, of the Carboniferous reptile fossils of Joggins, Nova Scotia), wrote:

> The Ichthyosaur was fitted to struggle with the waves of the stormy sea, to roll therein like modern whales and grampuses, to seize and devour great fishes, and to dive for them into the depths; and its great, armor-plated eyes must have been well adapted for vision in the deeper waters. The Plesiosaur, on the contrary, was fitted for comparatively still and shallow waters; swimming near the surface with its graceful neck curving aloft, it could dart at the smaller fishes at the surface, or stretch its long neck downward in search of those near the bottom.

When Richard Harlan obtained a fossil fragment from a trader around 1830, he was told that it came from "the skeleton of an alligator-animal about seventy feet in length," with a head that appeared to be about 3 or 4 feet long. The end of the snout — the only part that Harlan had — reminded him of an ichthyosaur, so he described it as such, only to have his identification overturned by later examiners, who realized that it was actually part of a mosasaur. In the paper in which he misidentified the fossil, Harlan (1834a) expressed a sense of wonderment at the discovery of such strange creatures in the American West:

> Future discoverers will no doubt demonstrate that our country, already rich in fossil reliquiae, possesses numerous species of fossil Sauriens, those extraordinary inhabitants of a former state of our planet, which sported on the bosom of the ocean, or enlivened the shores of primordial worlds, ere yet the "lord of the eagle eye" had scanned the creation, or waved his magic sceptre over the beats of the earth. Strange indeed are the forms, structures and habits of these beings with which geological researches are making us acquainted: in the beautiful and sublime at least, the pre-adamitic *Fauna* and *Flora* are as yet unsurpassed by those of the present day.

The marine reptiles had also developed skull modifications that would serve them well for moving through the water and capturing their prey. For the most part, the ichthyosaurs had long, narrow, tooth-lined beaks, ideal for catching and holding fast, slippery prey such as fishes and squid. The prey-capturing equipment of the plesiosaurs was more varied. Some had small heads with mouths full of needle-sharp teeth; others, such as the 50-foot pliosaur *Liopleurodon*, had a 10-foot-long head and massive jaws armed with foot-long spikes. (The plesiosaurs are sometimes divided into two groups: the long-necked plesiosaurs and the short-necked, big-headed pliosaurs.) The skulls of most of the marine reptiles were flattened or tapered to reduce water resistance. As Robert Carroll (1997) wrote:

> Approximately 20 lineages [of Mesozoic marine reptiles] have independently adapted to an aquatic way of life. The major groups are represented by many superbly preserved fossils, frequently showing every bone in the body in nearly perfect articulation. Even where specific ancestry cannot be established, the polarity of character changes and their functional association with the physical properties of water can be readily determined. Several exhibit modifications associated with hearing and respiration. The ichthyosaurs provide the most extreme example of aquatic adaptation, with a body comparable to that of the fastest swimming modern fish, and were apparently unique in giving birth to living young in the water.*

The ichthyosaurs swam in the Mesozoic oceans when dinosaurs walked on the land. They appeared slightly earlier than the nonavian dinosaurs (240 million versus 230 million years ago) and disappeared earlier (90 million versus 65 million years ago). While the ancestral dinosaurs were heading toward their destiny as rulers of the land, the "fish lizards" and plesiosaurs were beginning their domination of the ocean. Several groups of marine reptiles didn't make it through the Permian extinction, but the first ichthyosaur skeletons appear in early Triassic formations, and although their

* The presence of embryos within the fossils of mature animals has shown that mosasaurs were also viviparous, and the case for live birth in plesiosaurs is also strong, if not yet conclusive.

ancestors remain unidentified, they were beginning to fill the same apex predator positions in the water that the carnivorous dinosaurs did on land. The ichthyosaurs lived from the early Triassic (about 240 million years ago) until about 93 million years ago – 32 million years before the mass extinctions at the end of the Cretaceous period. During their tenure, they developed a basic body plan that consisted of a dolphin-like shape; a tooth-filled beak; a vertically oriented, lunate tail fin like that of a shark; and, in most of the later species, a dorsal fin. The earliest ichthyosaurs were about a yard long, but they later grew to impressive lengths, such as the 45-foot-long *Shonisaurus,* which got as big as a humpback whale, and the so-far unnamed ichthyosaur from British Columbia, which was even larger. The ichthyosaurs of the Jurassic period are the most numerous, suggesting a flowering of these animals some 140 million years ago. The best-known genus was *Ichthyosaurus,* preserved mostly in England, but also from southern Germany and western Canada.

Jurassic seas were also occupied by plesiosaurs, marine reptiles with long necks, and their relatives the pliosaurs, short-necked animals with powerful jaws and teeth. Giant marine crocodiles with long, eel-like tails competed for prey in Jurassic seas, but unlike ichthyosaurs, which were pelagic and never left the water (although they had to surface to breathe, like the dolphins they resembled), the crocs occupied a nearshore environment and probably came ashore to rest and lay their eggs. The ichthyosaurs were gone for 25 million years when the asteroid (or comet) hit in the area that would become the Gulf of Mexico. The plesiosaurs were extinct by the end of the Cretaceous, the same time that the last of the nonavian dinosaurs disappeared.

The dinosaurs, crocodiles, pterosaurs (flying reptiles), and marine reptiles (ichthyosaurs, plesiosaurs, and mosasaurs) are all broadly classified as ruling reptiles, but not all of them were dinosaurs. And although the dominance of the sea by the great marine reptiles coincided with the dominance of the land by the dinosaurs (and, to a lesser extent, the dominance of the air by pterosaurs), the reptiles were as popular in the Victorian era as dinosaurs are today. The fashionableness of ichthyosaurs and mosasaurs was due almost entirely to the fact that their discovery predated that of the first dinosaurs. Their remains were far more complete – and therefore far more dramatic – than the first discoveries of fragmented dinosaur fossils. Because the marine reptiles were the first "prehistoric" animals uncovered in English fossil beds, they led to a great upsurge in the study of extinct animals. Public interest in the ichthyosaurs, plesiosaurs, and mosasaurs declined after the nineteenth century, but recently there has been a revival of interest, probably sparked by the discovery of various spectacular new species, such as gigantic mosasaurs from Israel and New Zealand and ichthyosaurs that were larger than full-grown sperm whales.

Just as there is an ongoing discussion about whether dinosaurs were warm-blooded, there is a comparable question about the marine reptiles: how could these "cold-blooded" reptiles possibly have lived and hunted in the heat-sapping oceans if all their living relatives become slow and sluggish when the ambient temperature drops? Because the ichthyosaurs, plesiosaurs, and mosasaurs were reptiles, it has been assumed that, like their living relatives, they were cold-blooded. (The blood of reptiles is not actually "cold"; some desert-dwelling lizards have higher body temperatures than mammals of comparable size.) Mammals and birds are *endothermic*, which means that they produce their own heat metabolically and maintain a high, constant body temperature, regardless of the surrounding conditions. If the temperature of most birds and mammals falls a few degrees below normal, they die. Modern lizards, snakes, and crocodiles rely on the heat of the sun to warm up their bodies so that they can perform their everyday activities. When the temperature drops too low—at night in the desert, for example—lizards become sluggish and inactive. As might be expected, the larger the reptile, the longer it takes to warm up the body, but the longer it can store heat within. When paleontologist Robert Bakker applied this formula to some of the fast-moving dinosaurs, he realized that, as reptiles, they could not rely on the sun to heat them up because it would take too long, and besides, they would not function very well on cool or cloudy days.*

* The original studies of the time it took large reptiles to warm up were performed in the late 1940s by Charles Bogert and Edwin Colbert of the American Museum of Natural History and by Raymond Cowles of the University of California. Working with alligators, they saw that the smallest specimens could warm up quickly: a 7-inch-long specimen took only 90 seconds to raise its body temperature 1°C, while it took a 30-pounder five times as long. They wrote in 1946, "Continuing this line of reasoning, it would seem probable that in

In 1964, John Ostrom of Yale University discovered the fossil of a bipedal dinosaur in the mountains of southern Montana. From its structure, it was obvious that *Deinonychus* had been an agile, swift predator, but because it was a reptile, and because reptiles were believed to be (and to have been) slow-moving, sluggish creatures, the only way that this animal could have run the way it was designed to run was if it had been warm-blooded. Ostrom compared dinosaurs to high-energy mammals and said, "The correlation of high body temperature, high metabolism, and erect body posture is not accidental. The evidence indicates that erect posture and locomotion are not possible without high metabolism and high uniform temperature." One of Ostrom's students on that Montana dig was Robert Bakker, who was beginning to develop the idea of warm-blooded dinosaurs. In a 1968 article in Yale University's *Discovery* magazine, he wrote, "although much work remains to be done on dinosaur functional anatomy, the mammal-like posture has convinced me that these rulers of the Mesozoic were fast, agile, energetic creatures that lived at a high physiological level reached elsewhere among land vertebrates only by the later, advanced mammals." The cause was taken up by Adrian Desmond in 1976 in *The Hot-Blooded Dinosaurs* and summarized in John Noble Wilford's *The Riddle of the Dinosaur* in 1986.

Bakker published *The Dinosaur Heresies* in 1986, in which he presented his theories about dinosaurs and many other creatures, extinct and extant. In his analysis of the lifestyle of living reptiles, Bakker wrote that, unlike mammals and birds, they grow slowly and eat infrequently, unless they are kept in an artificially heated environment and force-fed protein-rich foods. In a 1972 paper, he cited the 1950s work of Enlow and Brown, which showed that the presence of haversian canals in the bones of dinosaurs pointed to a rapid rate

---

an adult ten-ton dinosaur . . . the rate of temperature change would be very much slower than a large alligator. Indeed, if the same difference in temperature rise were applied to the dinosaur (an animal 700 times greater in body mass than the large alligator) then one might suppose that it would have taken more than 86 hours to raise the body temperature by 1°C in the adult extinct giant." Later, Colbert, Cowles, and Bogert would reduce their estimates of the amount of time it would have taken a dinosaur to warm up, but they continued to believe that large reptiles had to modulate their body temperature by moving in and out of the sun.

of growth comparable to that of modern mammals. (The role of haversian canals in bones is not clearly understood, but Bakker wrote, "Whatever their role, densely packed Haversian canals are clearly marked 'for warm bloods only.'") Dinosaurs, according to Bakker, "grew mammal fashion; they grew fast and bred early. And their dynamic approach to quick maturity must have been one of the most powerful weapons in their adaptive arsenal." (Chris McGowan disagrees with Bakker's conclusions, saying that Bakker might have confused haversian bone with fibrolamellar bone, which indicates high body temperature rather than rapid growth.) And in a study of dinosaur growth patterns published in 2001, Erickson et al. concluded that "dinosaurs exhibited . . . growth curves similar to those of other vertebrates, but had unique growth rates with respect to body mass. All dinosaurs grew at accelerated rates relative to the primitive conditions seen in extant reptiles."

As far as we can tell, the extinct marine reptiles differed from living reptiles in one way: they lived all their lives in water, a circumstance achieved only by sea snakes today. (Female sea turtles come out of the water to lay their eggs; males hardly ever leave the water.) Of stamina, McGowan (1991a) asks, "why have reptiles got so little?" and answers by saying, "They have a very limited capacity for aerobic exercise and are therefore unable to sustain any fast activities." He does recognize, however, that reptiles can be very fast during periods of intense activity; "just consider how quickly lizards dart from place to place, or the speed with which a venomous snake can strike its victim." He concludes his discussion of stamina with:

> Reptiles, then, in contrast to mammals and birds, have a limited capacity for aerobic activity and this severely limits their sustainable activity levels. They lack the stamina for anything more than a slow jog, and when they need to run fast, or participate in other intense activities, they rely on glycosis. We have attributed this lack of stamina to a metabolic rate that is an order of magnitude below that of birds or mammals, but there are other contributing factors. They include the way they ventilate their lungs, their posture, and the anatomy of their heart.

Some sharks, particularly the lamnids such as the great white, mako, and porbeagle, have a heat-exchange circulatory system that warms up the muscles, making it possible for them to swim faster and more efficiently than their colder-bodied relatives. Some fast-swimming fishes, such as tuna and billfish, have similar arrangements, and they are among the fastest fishes in the ocean. The lamnid sharks and these fast-swimming fishes have tails of a similar design—crescent shaped, with the upper lobe equal in size to the lower. These similarities do not indicate a phylogenetic relationship between these sharks and fishes, but they do suggest that in their history, the same systems evolved convergently. What do these fishes and sharks with efficient radiators and homocercal (equal-lobed) tails have in common? They are powerful predators and unusually fast swimmers. (The mako shark and the sailfish are believed to be the fastest swimmers of their respective groups.) If we look at the body plan of many of the later ichthyosaurs, we find the same deep-bodied shape, tapering to a narrow tail stock and, in many cases, a homocercal tail fin.

Bony fishes, for the most part, are not warm-blooded. As McGowan (1991a) wrote, "Fishes, being surrounded by water, quickly lose the heat generated by their actively contracting muscles. This is because the heat that leaves the muscles is lost when the blood passes through the gills. Some fishes, like the tuna, are able to maintain some of their swimming muscles at a relatively high and constant temperature, through modifications in their blood vascular system." But most fishes do not have heat exchangers, so how do they function? "First," says McGowan, "the costs of aquatic locomotion are about one-tenth those of locomotion on land, one important factor being that fishes do not have to spend energy in supporting their body weight. Another consideration is that as swimming speed increases, the flow of water over the gills increases, facilitating the uptake of oxygen. A third factor that needs consideration is the metabolic rate of high-performance fishes like the tuna. . . . Given their elevated body rate, high body temperature, and high activity level, the tuna should probably be regarded as being as endothermic as a bird or mammal."

The ability to deliver live young underwater is another hint that many of the marine reptiles were endothermic. No living reptiles lay eggs in the water (reptile embryos must respire through the egg's permeable shell), and although there are major differences between the living and extinct groups, this is probably not one of them. The evidence that ichthyosaurs delivered live young is massive and incontrovertible, and although there is less evidence to support viviparity in plesiosaurs and mosasaurs, there seems to be little question that they too delivered live babies. In an article about the reproductive biology of ichthyosaurs, Deeming et al. (1993) wrote, "Viviparity has both advantages (production of small numbers of precocial young) and disadvantages (such as a need for the adult to feed herself and the embryos, and a higher level of predation)." As Bakker (1986) wrote:

> Fast rates of reproduction are powerful evolutionary weapons; they provide an enormous advantage in coping with predators or surviving climatic catastrophes. The surest method of speeding up rates of breeding is to become warm-blooded. . . . But reptiles cannot exploit their full capacity for growth, because their cold-blooded physiology makes them less effective in gathering food than a warm-blooded creature. Their fluctuating body temperature forces them to operate their food procurement and growing processes at levels far below maximum for much of their lives. Warm-blooded birds and mammals, on the other hand, may be absorbing nourishment in their digestive systems at rates very close to the biochemical maximum.

There are many lizards and snakes, some amphibians, and numerous fish species that are viviparous, but the endothermic mammals are the predominant vertebrate group that gives birth to living young. (The monotremes, an ancient and anomalous group of mammals that includes the platypus and echidna, lay eggs.) Birds, the other endothermic vertebrates, are all egg-layers, descended from reptilian ancestors. Since reptiles cannot lay eggs in the water, and it is clear that most of the ancient marine reptiles were viviparous, the plesiosaurs, ichthyosaurs, and mosasaurs might have been at least partially endothermic.

In the 2000 edition of his book *History of Life*, Richard Cowen addresses many of the mysteries of marine reptile metabolism. Quoting Carrier (1987), he points out that "many fishes have no problem maintaining high levels of locomotory performance and exercise metabolism. Many sharks swim all their lives without rest, for example. Gill respiration gives all the oxygen exchange necessary for such exercise levels." But because the early tetrapods inherited the fishlike flexion of the body, walking compresses first one side of the thorax and then the other, meaning that both lungs cannot be simultaneously inflated when the animal is walking, and should the animal break into a run, breathing becomes impossible. Living amphibians cannot breathe and run at the same time, a situation Cowen refers to as "Carrier's Constraint."* But this constraint is not applicable to air-breathing marine reptiles; they obviously do not have to breathe and "run" at the same time, because their high-performance locomotion takes place underwater, and their breathing occurs at the surface.

Cowen also addresses what he calls "the ichthyosaur problem," pointing out that even though they were reptiles, their major propulsion came from the tail, "anatomically rather decoupled from the main body by a narrow caudal peduncle." Because ichthyosaurs are shaped remarkably like dolphins, it is easy to suggest that they were fast, flexible swimmers like their mammalian counterparts. "If the body was flexible," says Cowen, "ichthyosaurs really hadn't solved Carrier's Constraint," because flexion of the thorax—even if generated from the "decoupled" tail—would alternately close the lungs down and make it difficult if not impossible for the animal to breathe. If they had no stamina, but only ambushed their prey from short distances while holding their breath, the streamlined shape would make ecological sense. However, Cowen prefers a somewhat unexpected interpretation, based on observations of penguins and dolphins, the closest analogues to the streamlined shape of some ichthyo-

---

* Mammals can breathe and run at the same time because their four legs support the body equally and the thorax is not twisted, says Cowen. "In fact, quadrupedal locomotion encourages breathing on the run. The backbone flexes and straightens up and down with each stride, alternately expanding and compressing the rib cage evenly. So horses, dogs, and jackrabbits running at full speed take one breath per stride." Marine mammals also avoid the lateral thoracic compression because their undulations are dorsoventral, as might be expected in animals that are descended from terrestrial mammals. Contra Cowan's hypothesis, however, there are several species of monitor lizards that are, according to a letter from Colin McHenry, "lizards who think they are mammals. . . . The perentie (*Varanus giganteus*) acts like it's on speed. Check out the perentie pens in any reptile park [McHenry lives in Australia] and they'll be racing around their pens non-stop, more like a dog than a lizard."

saurs. (The marine reptiles were quite diverse, and not all of them would behave in the same way.) He wrote:

Ichthyosaurs are not penguins or dolphins, but it is possible that leaping could provide yet another way to avoid Carrier's Constraint. An ichthyosaur could swim at high speed in an undulating path, with the pectoral fins providing upward or downward forces as needed. With appropriate control, the ichthyosaur could "porpoise," lifting clear of the water, pointing straight ahead, and in that position, could breathe at high speed, exactly as [penguins do]. Propulsion by the laterally flexing body would be resumed during the underwater phase, with the body traversing the high-drag surface zone at a reasonably high angle. In this situation, the performance of an ichthyosaur could certainly approach that of a dolphin of the same body size.

Cowen, a senior lecturer in geology at the University of California at Davis, added limericks in the margins of *History of Life,* perhaps as memory aids for his students. Here's the one about Carrier's Constraint:

> Fast-swimming air-breathers are rare
> But ichthyosaurs did it with flair
> They swam up in a leap
> (It's energetically cheap)
> And they took a deep breath in mid-air

Although "Carrier's Constraint" is applicable to terrestrial reptiles, it probably had nothing to do with the ability of marine reptiles to swim efficiently at high speed and still be able to breathe. Dolphins, penguins, and sea lions, and probably ichthyosaurs and some plesiosaurs, are all subject to "drag" (loss of momentum) as they move through the water. As McHenry wrote (personal communication 2002):

As soon as a swimming animal approaches the surface, the drag it incurs increases significantly. If dolphins, for example, came up only to get their blowholes out of the water (as they do when swimming at a more leisurely pace), then they'd end up spending a great deal of their time in the high drag zone near the surface. To approach the surface in a controlled manner, exhale and then inhale without drowning, and then dive again, would all take time. By porpoising, the animal bursts through the high-drag zone at high speed, and then enters a zone of zero drag — the atmosphere. Its momentum gives it plenty of time to breathe before it re-enters the water at high speed, allowing it to quickly get down below the high-drag zone and keep its speed up.

Some recently evolved marine reptiles had little trouble making the transition from land to water. Terrestrial snakes are ectotherms, of course, and because surface area relative to weight is higher in long, thin animals than in shorter, rounded ones, their serpentine bodies give them a great deal of control of their heating and cooling rates. Because ectotherms rely on external sources of heat, they do not have to expend energy in keeping their bodies warm and therefore require much less food than comparably sized mammals or birds do. (Some living reptiles, such as large crocodiles or very large snakes, may eat only three or four times a year.) Sea snakes, therefore, simply moved into the water with their metabolic heritage intact, and because water holds heat much better than air does, they were able to benefit from the relatively stable temperatures of warm tropical seas. And like their terrestrial relatives, sea snakes don't have to eat very often.

Most fossils consist of bones, shells, or teeth and rarely reveal the soft parts. Our knowledge of the muscles, ligaments, skin, viscera, eyes, and circulatory systems of long-extinct animals usually consists of educated guesses based on osteological analysis. We can tell how big an animal was, and whether it was a tree-climber or a cursorial predator, but we cannot tell how its circulatory system worked or what kind of noises it made. Available spaces can tell us a lot, such as the size of the brain that could be contained in a particular skull, or what sort of bone structure would support what sort of muscles, but beyond that, we enter the realm of speculation. One subject rarely discussed in relation to marine reptiles is fat (which, of course, would not fossilize), yet it is extremely important in the lives of some marine mammals. Indeed, it is

*The heaviest living reptile, the leatherback turtle (*Dermochelys coriacea*) can reach a length of 8 ½ feet and weigh more than a ton. It is also the deepest diving of all modern sea turtles, going as far as 3,000 feet.*

not the metabolism of whales and dolphins that enables some of them to live in cold water but rather the thick envelope of blubber that encases them and keeps the body heat in and the ambient cold out. Sperm whales, among the deepest divers of all whales and therefore subjected to the most intense cold, have a thick blubber layer that enables them to hunt at depths up to a mile. Other cetaceans such as bowheads, narwhals, and belugas live their entire lives in arctic ice-filled waters with no ill effects. Some pinnipeds, such as walruses and elephant seals and even some of the larger penguins, have evolved an insulating layer of fat that enables them to live in cold water, and even though the Cretaceous seas may have been a lot warmer than the waters of modern Greenland, it is possible that some of the larger ichthyosaurs, plesiosaurs, and mosasaurs had a layer of blubber. Besides insulating them, it would have provided additional buoyancy as they floated at the surface to breathe.

The leatherback, the largest and most widely distributed of all living sea turtles, is well known for its frequent appearance in cold water. The FAO species guide *Sea Turtles of the World* (Márquez 1990) lists as its high-latitude appearances "the North Sea, Barents Sea, Newfoundland and Labrador in the North Atlantic, and Mar del Plata, Argentina, and South Africa in the South Atlantic; it also occurs throughout the Indian Ocean, in the Northern Pacific, to the Gulf of Alaska and south of the Bering Sea, in the southwestern Pacific to Tasmania and New Zealand, and in the southeastern Pacific to Chiloé (Chile)." The leatherback can also dive to depths of 3,000 feet, where the water is icy cold. How can turtles function under such conditions? They might be able to thermoregulate like mammals. Even though their metabolic rate is low, they can maintain a large temperature differential between their body core and the surrounding water. As James Spotila wrote (1995): "Deep dives by leatherbacks appear to be supported by an increased $O_2$ carrying capacity of blood and tissue because the lungs undoubtedly collapse owing to increased hydrostatic pressure. Hematocrits and hemoglobin and myoglobin concentration are among the highest recorded in reptiles, and approach levels found in diving mammals." Indeed, the increased oxygen carrying capacity, lung collapse, and hemoglobin and myoglobin concentrations are the same modifications that enable the deepest-diving mammals (sperm whales, bottlenose whales, and elephant seals) to dive to such prodigious depths. For protection from the cold, the cetaceans and seals have a thick blubber layer, and so does the leatherback. With a large adipose tissue layer and large body size, leatherbacks "can use changes in blood flow to the skin and periphery to regulate body temperature such that they maintain warm temperatures in the North Atlantic and avoid overheating in warm tropical waters" (Spotila et al. 1997). Although we cannot know how (or if) the extinct marine reptiles were able to control their body temperature, in the leatherback we can observe a living marine reptile and perhaps make some educated guesses about the ichthyosaurs, plesiosaurs, and mosasaurs.

In a 1992 article, Kenneth Carpenter of the Denver Museum of Natural History offered an explanation as to why several different reptile lineages took to the sea:

One clue comes from studies of the energy needs of modern reptiles. These show that a swimming reptile needs only one-fourth the energy it would need for walking on land. This difference is due to buoyancy in the water; the only energy that is needed is that required to propel the animal through the water. On land, the reptile needs energy to overcome the pull of gravity and to hold the body off the ground, and energy to move the limbs during locomotion. Another possible clue as to why reptiles adapted to life in the sea is the abundance of fish, squid, and belemnites (a squid-like cephalopod) parts found in the stomachs of many marine reptile fossils. This suggests that the Mesozoic seas were an enormous larder of animal protein waiting to be tapped. Ocean production is greatest in shallow coastal water, so it is not surprising that marine reptiles evolved in the shallow seas of the Mesozoic.

Writing of the Western Interior Seaway, Nicholls and Russell (1990) said, "Studies of oxygen isotope ratios in belemnites suggests a temperature range . . . of 17–27°C [62–80°F] in the seaway between latitudes of 73°N and 40°N. While a thermal gradient was present in the seaway, it was not as pronounced as today and there is no evidence of cold, arctic conditions." If the ancient seas were much warmer than they are today, the reptiles would have had no real problem maintaining their metabolic levels. Sea snakes, which live only in the tropics, obviously do not have a problem with cold water. In answer to a question I asked him about the metabolism of marine reptiles, Carpenter wrote:

Throughout most of the Mesozoic, global temperatures were much higher and nowhere is there evidence of continental glaciation. Early Triassic: Coal found in Antarctica, situated pretty much where it is now, implying warm, wet conditions. Evaporites (salt, gypsum, etc.) deposits formed under arid conditions common in western US, Europe and Middle East. Late Triassic: Initial rifting of Pangea. Development of warm, shallow seas between Europe and N.A. Giant amphibians in Antarctica. Early Jurassic: Continued rifting. Abundant coal in Antarctica, Australia, Asia. Evaporites along North Africa. Late Jurassic: Continuation of above, large Sahara-like deserts in Western US. Oceanic anoxic events in deep sea indicate high sea surface productivity, hence high sea surface temperatures. Ferns occur as far as 60° north, farther than their present range. Cretaceous: Oxygen isotope data indicates sea surface temperatures of 80–95°F.

"The gist of the data," said Carpenter, "is that marine reptiles had no problems as you raise." Even if the surface temperature of the water was as high as 95°F, the depths would be considerably cooler, so the marine reptiles could have dived in pursuit of prey, then returned to the surface to digest it and reenergize their systems. Many of these animals were the size of whales, which means that their body mass would have held a lot of internally generated heat. Heat exchangers would have enhanced their performance—as in the case of today's tunas and mackerel sharks—which would mean that the ichthyosaurs, plesiosaurs, and mosasaurs had been even *more* effective as predators. It is unlikely that the explanation for the activity level of the marine reptiles will be found in a single factor; rather, it was likely a combination of internal metabolism, large size, warmer water, and increased activity.

When I asked Michael Caldwell why he thought the marine reptiles could adapt to the unwelcoming conditions of cold water, he answered: *enzymes.* He went on to write:

> Most morphologists, paleontologists, etc. forget about biochemistry. Enzyme activation levels (concentrations and temperatures) are the key to successful metabolism in varied environments.
>
> Enzymes are proteins. They are produced directly by nucleotide sequences and can therefore rapidly evolve (unlike morphology, which is the product of major genetic and epigenetic evolution). Therefore, organisms which evolve new enzymes can readily adapt to specific problems, e.g., temperature or other metabolic needs like increased swimming speed.
>
> Thermoregulation per se, is not the issue. An arctic cod can swim in 4°C water. In water that would inactivate your enzymes, the fish muscle contracts and moves and works extremely well. The question is not the success or failure of endo- versus ectothermy, but rather the variety of enzyme systems and whether they work in cold temperatures or hot.
>
> Ectotherms with such competent enzyme systems are actually much better adapted to thermally stable (homeothermic) environments than are endotherms. Heat is not an issue the way it is for mammals. To function successfully, aquatic endotherms must insulate and eat tremendous amounts of food. In short, it is rather surprising that endotherms returned

to the water at all. In contrast, in a number of terrestrial environments that are not thermally stable, endothermy is a good solution. Enzymes actually have a fairly precise activation range insofar as temperature is concerned. Where external temperatures vary widely, endothermy is a much better solution, as the *internal* environment is homeothermic, and biochemical activation levels are always optimal for physiological needs.

So either keep the essence of the (salty and thermally stable) sea inside the body as endotherms do, or, live in it, as most aquatic ectotherms do. Otherwise, it's a continual fight if the environment is thermally unstable.

For the Mesozoic and Tertiary history of marine reptiles, we see numerous groups that independently evolve successful enzyme chemistries that allow aquatic adaptations in activity levels that seem endothermic-like in quality and quantity, but really only represent very advanced enzymes that work at cold temperatures. Mammals, on the other hand only re-invade the water when they can insulate themselves properly against the cold. Enzymes may have evolved as well, but it is really unnecessary if you can keep them warm and working.

Throughout the history of marine life, certain "solutions" to problems have appeared when unrelated groups—many of which became extinct, no matter how well adapted they appeared to be—developed similar morphological adaptations. We can never know what "caused" the first reptiles to forsake the land and return to the depths from which they had so recently emerged, but they began a trend that would continue, albeit sporadically, up to the present. The "sieve feeding" of the mesosaurs (if indeed that is what they did) would reappear 200 million years later in the baleen whales; the return to the sea (with the attendant transformation of legs into flippers; migration of nostrils; development of a fusiform, hydrodynamically advantageous shape; and so on), would occur several times, in completely unrelated animals. First the ichthyosaurs, then the plesiosaurs and the mosasaurs, then 15 million years after they had disappeared from the world's oceans, terrestrial mammals accomplished the same thing—if it can be called an accomplishment—by returning to the sea and becoming whales, dolphins, and porpoises.

The cetaceans and pinnipeds that evolved long after the great marine reptiles had left the scene forever were descended from terrestrial forebears, and all took the remarkable step of returning to the sea from whence they came. In the process, they acquired (or reacquired) profound adaptive modifications that enabled them to engage in a fully or partially aquatic lifestyle. Where there had been legs there were now flippers. In most marine reptiles, scales were lost in favor of a slick skin that would pass smoothly through the water. Some developed long, narrow, tooth-studded jaws, the better to gobble up slippery fish and squid, while others followed a different path and developed huge heads and powerful jaws that were suited for killing and crushing prey as large as or larger than themselves. Still others grew impossibly long necks that somehow enabled them to snatch fish that were 30 feet away. Vision and hearing were modified for life in a viscous medium that transmits light poorly but sound wonderfully well. (We do not know if any of the marine reptiles echolocated, but we do know that dolphins, the modern-day analogues of ichthyosaurs, have perfected a system of sound transmission and reception that far surpasses anything that *Homo technologicus* has managed to come up with.) At least some of them renounced egg-laying—a plan that most modern reptiles adhere to—and, like the whales and dolphins, learned to give birth to living young underwater.

The largest living marine reptiles are the saltwater crocodile and the leatherback turtle, descendants of ancient lines whose origins predated that of the ichthyosaurs, plesiosaurs, and mosasaurs. Living birds are now considered the lineal descendants of dinosaurs, so we can see "dinosaurs" just by looking at our bird feeders. Like so many large, dominant groups of animals in the history of life on Earth, the large marine reptiles are gone, and they left no descendants. (The imaginary Loch Ness monster is not descended from a plesiosaur—or anything else, for that matter.) There are no saucer-eyed, four-flippered ichthyosaurs; there are no 50-foot liopleurodons or kronosaurs (for which we can probably be grateful); and there are no huge mosasaurs, crushing ammonite shells in their double-hinged jaws. There are living monitor lizards, of course, and although the Komodo dragon *(Varanus komodoensis)* is a formidable beast, it is a pussycat compared with the lion that was *Tylosaurus.* (In Pleistocene Australia there lived an enormous monitor lizard that was twice the length and weight of the Komodo dragon; *Megalania prisca* reached 22 feet long and weighed about 1,300 pounds. It became extinct 10,000 years ago.) If snakes are closely related to the group including mosasaurs, they may be heirs to a great tradition of aquatic reptiles that once dominated the seas, but even the largest pythons and boas are but legless shadows of the mighty mosasaurs.

The apex predators of today's oceans are considerably less fearsome than those that swam in Mesozoic seas. The *ne plus ultra* of today's marine predators is the great white shark, usually an eater of fish and marine mammals but whose reputation for anthropophagy has been greatly enhanced by the author of *Jaws*. The killer whale, which hunts in packs and grows much larger and heavier than the white shark, is a more efficient and dangerous hunter, but only of selected victims, ranging from salmon and squid to seals, sea lions, porpoises, and even the great whales. Sperm whales, at 60 feet and 60 tons, are the largest predators alive today, but they feed mostly on squid. There were no humans around to see the great marine reptiles, and we know of their existence only from the fossil evidence. In our mind's eye, we can conjure up images of the swift ichthyosaurs coursing after fishes and squid; plesiosaurs stretching their necks out to grab at passing prey; monstrous pliosaurs with their bone-crushing jaws, grabbing at anything and everything that came within range; and 40-foot-long mosasaurs, lizards that menaced the life of the inland seaways. Just as the terrestrial dinosaurs ruled the land and the flying reptiles dominated the skies, the marine reptiles were the lords of the sub-aqueous realm. The sea dragons have been gone for 65 million years, but from the fossils, some of them beautifully preserved, we can make them live again. Enter their ancient underwater world and see how they lived, how they hunted, how they gave birth, how they died.

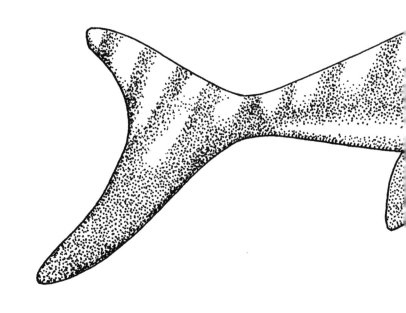

# The Ichthyosaurs

If a casual observer looked at a drawing of an ichthyosaur and identified it as a dolphin, the mistake could be easily forgiven. A closer examination would reveal small hind flippers and, more critical, that the tail fin, instead of being horizontal as it is in cetaceans, is vertical, as it is in sharks. Those differences notwithstanding, the ichthyosaurs of the middle Triassic through the Cretaceous demonstrate an incredible example of convergent evolution, with similar traits developing in totally unrelated groups of animals. In this case, the ichthyosaurs would adapt to a life in the ocean, flourish, and die out 40 million years before the earliest cetaceans. In shape, they were streamlined like

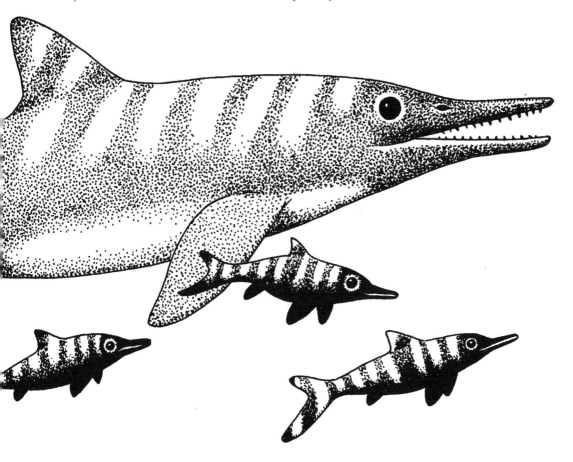

*From top: An ichthyosaur, a porbeagle shark, a bottlenose dolphin, and a bluefin tuna demonstrate similar evolutionary solutions to the problem of moving swiftly through the water. The ichthyosaur, the shark, and the tuna use a vertical tail fin for propulsion, although the vertebral column in the ichthyosaur is in the lower lobe of the tail, and that of the shark is in the upper (the vertebrae of the tuna do not extend into the tail). The tuna is probably the best designed of them all and is generally considered one of the fastest fish in the sea.*

the fastest fishes, and they breathed through nostrils located close to the eyes, not on the tip of the snout. Unlike the plesiosaurs, the ichthyosaurs did not use their forelimbs for propulsion but used their lunate caudal fins, much the way sharks do today. They were reptiles and therefore had well-developed ribs from their necks to their tails — some of the post-Triassic ichthyosaurs had more than 80 pairs of ribs — which suggests a rigid trunk, with propulsion deriving from undulations of the vertical tail fin.* (Early ichthyosaurs, such as *Chaohusaurus,* had shorter ribs and probably swam by undulating the entire body.)

The origin of ichthyosaurs is unknown, but their shaftlike limbs indicate that they were certainly descended from terrestrial reptiles. Colbert (1965) wrote that "the ichthyosaurs comprise an isolated order of reptiles ultimately derived from the cotylosaurs," which group Carroll (1988) describes as "a wide range of primitive tetrapods . . . including a host of primitive amniotes," which is not particularly helpful. "The typical ichthyosaurs of the Jurassic are so highly modified for marine life" wrote Romer (1948), "that they show no clear indications of relationship to any other reptilian group." The sudden appearance of the ichthyosaurs in the fossil record, with nothing even remotely resembling a transitional form, has provided much support for the creationists' dismissal of evolutionary theory. In *Dinosaurs by Design,* Duane T. Gish quotes Edwin Colbert, Alfred Romer, and assorted other scientists, all of whom say that there are no clues to the ancestors of the ichthyosaurs. This, says Gish,

> shows that . . . explanations of the evolutionary process are really fairy tales. . . . If ordinary land reptiles changed into marine reptiles, then one of these land reptiles must have ventured into the water, and after eons of time and a long series of genetic mistakes, it gradually changed into a fish-

* The presence of multiple pairs of ribs is one of the defining characteristics of reptiles, which have many more ribs than mammals do. Mammals have separate ribs only on the vertebrae connected to the sternum — the so-called thoracic vertebrae. Reptiles have ribs on the neck and tail vertebrae as well. In reptiles that have distinct necks, such as plesiosaurs and dinosaurs, the neck ribs are often but not always short and reduced. In reptiles with little or no distinct neck region, there are long ribs on almost all vertebrae. This arrangement can be found in ichthyosaurs, mosasaurs, pliosaurs, and snakes.

like reptile or *Ichthyosaurus.* If this were true, we ought to find at least some in-between kinds. Perhaps an animal with feet and legs gradually changing into paddle like fins would give evidence of this evolution. But not one such transitional form has ever been found! Every one of the marine reptiles just popped into the fossil record fully-formed at the very start. . . . This is exactly what we would expect to find if God is the Creator of these creatures. These fossils give powerful evidence against evolution.

Here, however, we will assume quite the opposite: these fossils constitute powerful evidence *for* evolution. As with the mammals that evolved into whales and dolphins, some of the reptiles returned to the sea and, in time, acquired those characteristics that made life in the water possible: a fishlike shape, flippers instead of feet, a mouthful of sharp teeth for capturing slippery prey, and the ability to deliver their young alive in the water. Although the evidence exists only for *Stenopterygius,* many of the ichthyosaurs are believed to have had a dorsal fin to provide stability while swimming, since it has developed independently in cetaceans, sharks, and bony fishes. Like the cetaceans that were to follow them—and to which they are in no way related—ichthyosaurs retained their air-breathing requirements and were therefore restricted in the amount of time they could spend underwater.

The ichthyosaurs lived from the early Triassic (about 250 million years ago) and went extinct about 93 million years ago. During their 150 million–year history, they developed many varied forms, all of them conforming to the same basic body plan, with thematic variations. Some were small and snub-nosed; others had long, pincer-like jaws; still others had an overhanging upper jaw like that of a swordfish. The earliest ichthyosaurs were smallish, no more than 3 feet long, but there were some monsters that reached a length of 50 feet, and some were even larger. We know that they were all aquatic because, as Michael Taylor (1987c) wrote, "Paleontologists find ichthyosaur fossils only in coastal or marine rocks." Besides, unless it was a snake, an animal without functional legs would have had a rather difficult time on land.

In the March 6, 1999, issue of *New Scientist,* Kate Douglas wrote about ichthyosaurs in an article called "Dinodolphin," which included this discussion of the adaptive process:

More than 245 million years ago the ichthyosaur's terrestrial ancestor made the plunge back into the watery world. With a body designed for walking on land, getting around underwater would have been a major challenge. By shortening and flattening the long bones of its limbs and extending and covering the existing fingers and toes, evolution carved out a set of paddles front and rear. Fossils of the earliest ichthyosaurs have five distinct rows of bones in each. Later, the number varied from three to seven, with up to 100 individual bones in each paddle. But ichthyosaurs needed more than oars and a streamlined shape if they were to take their place as top predators. The solution was obvious: ditch the reptilian tail and replace it with a model with a good track record for speed. Why go back to the drawing board when sharks had solved that problem millions of years earlier? With a little tinkering, the ichthyosaur's existing tail could be bent downward near the end to support the lower fluke of its new tail fin. Constructing a scaffold for the mirror image lobe on top would have been more tricky, but a blade of cartilaginous material did the job. With another lump of cartilage on the back to use as a stabilizing dorsal fin — also similar to a shark's — the transformation was complete.

Douglas makes it appear as if evolution was a sort of mail-order design firm where otherwise unsuited animals could look through a catalog and select the adaptations that would enable them to acquire new and better lifestyles. Would that the process was that simple.

In 1699, a Welshman named Edward Lhwyd published a book of drawings of the British fossils that were housed in the Ashmolean Museum at Oxford. Underwritten by ten subscribers, including Hans Sloane, Samuel Pepys, and Isaac Newton, *Lithophylacii Britannici Ichonographia* was limited to 120 copies and, according to its author, "contains the Grounds of a new Science in Natural History," namely, palaeontology, the study of the lithified remains of long-extinct animals. According to Howe et al.'s 1981 *Ichthyosaurs: A History of Fossil Sea-Dragons,* the collection included "a number of ichthyosaur vertebrae and limb bones collected from the Jurassic of Purton Passage, Gloucestershire. However, as large marine reptiles such as ichthyosaurs were unthought of at that time, and as the true nature of many fossils was not generally understood, Lhwyd believed that the bones belonged to fish and called them *Ichthyospondyli.*"

While walking on a Yorkshire beach in 1758, Captain Chapman and Mr. Wooler came upon some fossil bones embedded in a cliff. They identified the bones as belonging to an "allegator" and sent their written descriptions to the Royal Society of London, where they were read into the *Philosophical Transactions.* (The fossil, classified as the primitive crocodilian *Steneosaurus bollensis,* is now in the Natural History Museum in London.) In 1821, Britain's first vertebrate paleontologist, the Reverend William Daniel Conybeare (1787–1857), an Anglican from Bristol, examined some fossils found at Lyme Regis in southwestern England. His account, cowritten with Henry De la Beche (1796–1855), contained the first descriptions of long-extinct reptiles that they called *plesiosaurs* ("near lizards"). They identified the ichthyosaur thus: "A marine quadruped, nearly resembling the crocodile, in the osteology of its head, and its mode of dentition. Vertebrae having both faces of their body deeply concave as in fishes. Extremities having no distinct radius and ulna, but the humerus immediately supporting a very numerous series of small polygonal bones, forming a very flexible paddle. Anterior extremities much larger than the posterior."*

* The Reverend Conybeare certainly helped in identifying some of the recently unearthed fossil animals, but his ideas of where they came from were — not surprisingly — firmly rooted in church doctrine. In a footnote to their 1821 description of "a new fossil animal forming a link between the Ichthyosaurus and the crocodile," De la Beche and Conybeare strongly objected to the idea of evolution and wrote, "When alluding to the regular gradation, and, as it were, the linked and concatenated series of animal forms, we would wish carefully to guard against the absurd and extravagant application which has been made of this notion. In the original formation of animated beings, the plan evidently to be traced throughout is this. That every place capable of supporting animal life should so be filled and that every possible mode of sustenance should be taken advantage of; hence every possible variety of structure became necessary, many of them such as to involve a total change of parts, slight indeed in external appearance, yet important in subserving the peculiar habits and economy of the different animals; in these cases the unity of general design was preserved while the requisite peculiarity of organization was superinduced; nor can there anywhere be found a more striking proof of the infinite riches of creative design, or of the infinite wisdom which guided their application. Some physiologists however . . . have most ridiculously imagined

In 1975, Justin Delair and William Sarjeant published an essay on Joseph Pentland (1797–1873), an amateur geologist and paleontologist who was a friend and adviser to Conybeare and Buckland and seems to have played a part in the early identification of the ichthyosaurs. Delair and Sarjeant wrote (of Pentland), "he was generally far in advance of most of his contemporaries, especially those in Britain, with regard to understanding reptilian osteology; . . . even with comparatively meager material at his disposal, he was able to correctly diagnose the true affinities and probable mode of life of the *Ichthyosaurus;* and still more significantly, . . . he recognized that it represented an entirely distinct reptilian group." Conybeare described the first ichthyosaur from a skull found in Somerset, but when Mary Anning or members of her family found a complete skeleton at Lyme Regis (Dorset) in 1823, the discovery sparked a nationwide interest in the extinct marine reptiles.

Mary Anning was born in 1799 in Lyme Regis, the daughter of Richard Anning, a cabinetmaker and amateur fossil collector who died when she was eleven. His death left the family £120 in debt and without a source of income, so Mary walked the cliffsides looking for fossils that she might sell. (The tongue-twister "she sells seashells by the seashore" was written about her.) In 1817, Thomas Birch, a well-to-do collector, befriended the family and agreed to sell his collection at auction for the Annings' benefit. Joseph Anning, Mary's brother, actually found the first ichthyosaur in 1811, and Mary found the remainder of the skeleton nearly twelve months later. The ichthyosaur was described in 1814 by Sir Everard Home, an anatomist with the Royal College of Surgeons. Home first affiliated the fossil with fishes, opined that it was some sort of a link between fishes and crocodiles, and finally decided that it fell between lizards and salamanders.* In 1819, he named it *Proteosaurus,* based

---

that the links hence arising represent real transitions from one branch to another of the animal kingdom; that through a series of such links . . . that which was once a polypus becomes successively a mollusca, a fish, a quadruped; an idea so monstrous, and so completely at variance with the structure of the peculiar organs considered in the detail . . . and no less so with the evident permanency of all animal forms, that nothing less than the credulity of a material philosophy could have been brought for a single moment to entertain it – nothing less than its bigotry to defend it."

* The almost impossible duckbilled platypus had only recently been discovered in Australia

on the salamander *Proteus,* but the name *Ichthyosaurus* ("fish lizard") had precedence and was subsequently applied to all the fossils. Five years later, in 1824, the Reverend George Young found a fossil "fish lizard" at Whitby in Yorkshire. Called by Roger Osborne "a great figure in the beginnings of geology in Yorkshire," Young described it as having the features of a crocodile, a fish, and a dolphin, but "to what class of animals this skeleton and others found at Whitby should be assigned, it is difficult to determine." From the drawing in his 1820 description (the actual fossil cannot be found), the animal has been identified as *Leptonectes acutirostris,* the ichthyosaur now known as *Temnodontosaurus.* Young believed that ichthyosaurs might still be found swimming in uncharted waters and wrote, "It is not unlikely, however, that as the science of Natural History enlarges its bounds, some animal of the same genus may be discovered in some parts of the world . . . and when the seas and large rivers of our globe shall have been more fully explored, many animals may be brought to the knowledge of the naturalist, which at present are known only in the state of fossils."

Because they have been extinct for 93 million years, no living ichthyosaurs were ever found in the "seas and large rivers of our globe," but in the fossilized skeleton of the ichthyosaur, Young did catch a glimmer of the idea that Darwin would publish 40 years later: that animal species were designed for their particular function. Predictably, however, he assigned this determination to God: "Some have alleged, in proof of the pre-Adamite theory, that in tracing the beds upwards, we discern among the inclosed bodies a gradual progress from the more rude and simple creatures, to the more perfect and completely organized; as if the Creator's skill had improved by practice. But for this strange idea there is no foundation: creatures of the most perfect organization occur in the lower beds as well as the higher." As Simon Winchester wrote, "The Reverend Young could not, however, go any further than

---

and a specimen sent to England. Home wrote, "I by no means consider it wholly a fish, but rather view it in a similar light to those animals met with in New South Wales, which appear to be so many deviations from ordinary structure, for the purpose of making intermediate connecting links, to unite in the closest manner the classes of which the great chain of animated beings is composed."

this. The forces ranged against him — of custom, history, doctrine and common acceptance — were just too formidable." The concept of extinction was completely alien to people of Young's time and disposition.

Mary Anning also discovered the first complete skeleton of the reptile Conybeare and De la Beche named *Plesiosaurus dolichodeirus*. Thomas Birch bought it from Mary and made it available to Conybeare, but it ultimately ended up in the collection of the Duke of Buckingham. Mary and Joseph Anning made many important fossil finds, but it was Mary who was famous throughout Europe for her knowledge of the various fossilized animals she was uncovering. As quoted in Hugh Torrens's 1995 biographical sketch of Mary Anning, Lady Harriet Silvester wrote in her diary in 1824:

> The extraordinary thing about this young woman is that she has made herself so thoroughly acquainted with the science that the moment she finds any bones she knows to what tribe they belong. She fixes the bones on a frame with cement and then makes drawings and has them engraved. . . . It is certainly a wonderful instance of divine favour — that this poor, ignorant girl should be so blessed, for by reading an application she has arrived at a degree of knowledge as to be in the habit of writing and talking to professors and other clever men on the subject, and they all acknowledge that she understands more of the science than anyone else in this kingdom.

In addition to the ichthyosaurs and plesiosaurs, Mary found Britain's first pterodactyl. In 1838, for services rendered, Mary Anning was given an annual stipend from the British Association for the Advancement of Science, and she was made the first honorary member of the Dorset County Museum in 1846, a year before she died of breast cancer.

Mary Anning is the reigning heroine of British paleontological history, but her life story is somewhat more complicated than the one usually told to schoolchildren. She was indeed the most famous fossil collector of her time, but her story has been oversimplified and romanticized because it was an uplifting Victorian tale of a young girl who discovered a "crocodile" in the cliffs of Lyme Regis and sold it to an understanding gentleman just in time to save her family from the poorhouse. According to Chris McGowan (2001), "Fossils were Mary Anning's salvation, and not simply because they kept her fed and clothed. Fossil hunting provided intellectual sustenance as well as a sense of self worth." Although, as McGowan wrote, "everything was set against her; her sex, her parents' low social rank, their poverty," she was lucky to have been in the right place at the right time. According to Benton and Spencer (1995), "Lyme Regis is the most famous British Early Jurassic reptile site, and one of the best in the world."

Thomas W. Hawkins (1810–1889) lived comfortably in Somerset on an inherited fortune and, as a fossil enthusiast, often accompanied Mary Anning on her collecting expeditions. He spent a vast amount of money accumulating a superb collection of ichthyosaurs and plesiosaurs from Lyme Regis and the quarries around Street in Somerset, which he described in an 1834 book called *Memoirs of Ichthyosauri and Plesiosauri.* The book was sold on subscription for the price of £2.10s, and because a workingman's wage in 1834 was 9 shillings a week, this was an extremely expensive book.* One of the most bizarre characters in the history of paleontology, Hawkins was referred to by Gideon Mantell as "Mad Hawkins," and Conybeare wrote to William Buckland, "What capital fun Hawkins' book is. I only wish it had been published before Walter Scot [*sic*] died. It might have furnished him a character, a Geological bore far more absurd than all his other ones put together."

Hawkins's enormous collection, which weighed 20 tons, cost him more than £4,000 to accumulate, but he sold it for £1,300. His memoir, described by Martin Rudwick (1992) as "a peculiar mixture of the straightforwardly scientific and bizarrely idiosyncratic," included depictions of the fossils in

---

* The book includes poems and dialogue between the workmen who were helping Hawkins dig, reproduced in dialect. Here is a colloquy between two quarrymen over a plesiosaur fossil:

"I wonder what tes."

"O a viery dragern a-maa-be."

"One that stinged Moses a-maa-be."

"Here's at'un." A tremendous blow with the mallet.

"How he do zound: I wonder of the stwoone be holler."

"Tes vire stwoone, vire stwoone is terrible hard — hit un agean Jack."

"There's hes baak-bwoone."

"An ther's hes ribs."

situ, as well as drawings made under Hawkins's direction by landscape painter John Samuelson Templeton, which purported to show the various reptiles in their natural habitat. The reconstructions depicted the crocodiliform ichthyosaurs swimming or hauling themselves out of the water to bask on rocks, with long, poorly defined flippers and straight tails.

Neither Conybeare nor De la Beche thought that ichthyosaurs came out of the water—in a drawing caption, De la Beche wrote, "*I. communis* . . . is represented on dry land, where it probably never reposed, for the purpose of exhibiting its form"—but when Sir Richard Owen included ichthyosaurs in the outdoor display at Sydenham in 1854, he opted for a straight-tailed, rock-basking reptile. Owen, the most celebrated anatomist of his time, originally believed that the downward-pointing tail of the fossil was a postmortem artifact and that it should have been straight, so early-nineteenth-century illustrations of ichthyosaurs showed them out of the water with straight tails. He later concluded that the tailbend existed in living ichthyosaurs and wrote, "The appearance on the tail of the *Ichthyosaurus* . . . is too uniform and common to be due entirely to an accidental and extrinsic cause. I am therefore disposed to attribute it to an influence connected with some structure of the recent animal; and most probably to the presence of a terminal caudal fin." It was obvious that the downward tailbend was characteristic of the later ichthyosaurians and that it supported the lower lobe of the tail, unlike the caudal vertebrae in sharks, which extend into the *upper* lobe of the tail.*

In 1846, Chaning Pearce was examining a newly excavated fossil of *Ichthyosaurus communis* from Somersetshire when he found "a series of small vertebrae lying on three or four posterior ribs; on removing another portion

---

* In an article devoted specifically to the tailbend in ichthyosaurs, Stephen J. Gould (1990) documents the history of the discovery and recognizes the role that Owen played, but he chooses to see the shape of the ichthyosaur as a convergence with fishes, as in "ichthyosaurs are most celebrated for their convergence upon the external form of superior swimmers among fishes." But if there is any convergence, it is surely with dolphins—which developed 100 million years later. As Simon Conway Morris (2002) wrote (of the similarity between ichthyosaurs and dolphins), "the streamlined bodies of the mammal and the reptile cleave the ocean in much the same way, even though the ichthyosaur evolved from something like a lizard and the dolphin from something like a dog. It's a textbook example of convergence."

of the clay the rami of the jaws, and other parts of the head were visible." He described how the tiny skeleton lay in the body cavity of the larger one and observed, "while the posterior two thirds of the little animal is within the pelvis, the head appears to protrude beyond it, and apparently being expelled at the time of death." After consulting with Richard Owen, Pearce concluded that he was indeed looking at the frozen moment when an ichthyosaur mother had died in the process of giving birth. In his 1880 "Report on the Mode of Reproduction of Certain Species of *Ichthyosaurus* from the Lias of England and Wurtemburg," Harry Govier Seeley, professor of geology at King's College, London (and author of the first definitive work on flying reptiles), examined the various fossils that appeared to contain miniature ichthyosaurs. Some of these tiny skeletons associated with mature ones had been interpreted as stomach contents, as if the larger ones had eaten the smaller ones, but when skeletons were found in the pelvic region – that is, beyond the stomach in the digestive process – it became clear that these were fetuses and that ichthyosaurs gave birth to living young underwater, much the way whales and dolphins do today. In England and Germany, Seeley examined as many of the fossils-with-embryos as he could and wrote:

> I therefore submit that the evidence indicates that these Ichthyosaurs were viviparous, and were probably produced of different relative bulk in different species; and it may be from feeble health of the parent or from some accident of position in the young that they were not produced alive, and thus have left a record of their mode of reproduction to which no allied extinct group of animals has shown a parallel. There is some evidence that in certain cases many young were produced at a birth, and although the specimens are not in the best state of preservation, analogy strongly suggests that this is a distinctive character of certain species.

*Ichthyosaurus communis* (the "common ichthyosaur," if you will) is the species most often found in the limestone of Lyme Regis and Street. It was a medium-sized ichthyosaur with a sharply pointed snout; a tuna-like, lunate tail fin; and probably a prominent dorsal fin. In a specimen found at Kilve (Somerset) in 1985, a tiny embryo was found in the immediate vicinity of a fossilized adult; the proportionally large skull, head, and orbit of the little one made it clear that it was an embryo. (In a 1993 discussion, Charles Deeming, Beverly Halstead, Mankato Manabe, and David Unwin described "the reproductive biology of ichthyosaurs"—quite an extraordinary accomplishment with regard to animals that have been extinct for 85 million years.) Because cetaceans usually deliver their young tail first, so that the neonate remains attached to the female as long as possible and will not drown if there is a hitch in the birthing process, the same assumption was applied to ichthyosaurs. But because many of the "small associated" individuals are preserved in the headfirst position, Deeming et al. assumed that in these cases, "complications during the birth process (perhaps the embryo was too large for the pelvic opening and lodged in the birth canal) led to the death of the embryo by drowning. Moreover, the retention of such a large embryonic corpse would almost certainly have caused the death of the mother." This explanation accounts for those fossil ichthyosaurs that appeared to show a mother in the process of giving birth; a normal birth would not have killed the mother, and there would have been no reason for the fossilization of the pair, but if a difficult birth resulted in the death of the mother, the fossils

*The stripes on this mother Ichthyosaurus and her babies are conjectural, but it is certain that these reptiles gave birth to live young underwater. Adults of this species reached a length of about 7 feet.*

make sense. There is a fossil of the ichthyosaur *Stenopterygius* from Holzmaden, Germany, with seven preserved embryos inside the body cavity.*

Many ichthyosaurs have been discovered in and around Lyme Regis in Dorset and Whitby in Yorkshire, but the premier site for these fossils is Holzmaden in Germany. As McGowan (1979a) wrote, "More ichthyosaur skeletons have been collected from the Lower Jurassic of southern Germany than any other locality." It was here that the best-preserved fossils were found, many of them so detailed that the complete outline of the animal was revealed, including the dorsal fin and the lunate tail. The first identification of ichthyosaur embryos was also made from Holzmaden specimens. When German zoologist Willy Ley (1951) described Holzmaden, he wrote, "There were numerous small open quarries and a few of them (those that happened to cut into the epsilon stratum) yielded ichthyosaurs. Two hundred of them per year! . . . Old Professor Oskar Fraas of the Museum of Natural History in Stuttgart, knew all the details of the 'ichthyosaur business' and wrote a report about it in 1866," in which he said:

> There they lie in their stone coffins of many millennia, wrapped in slate, and one can just discern a rough outline like in a wrapped-up mummy. One may see the head stick out, the spine, the position of the extremities, the over-all length of the animal, and even the workman needs only a glance to see whether it is an animal with paddles or one with "paws." One with "paws" is worth three times as much. But this is not the only criterion for the price . . . a complete animal may bring as much as a hundred guilders. The workman does nothing about selling, he quietly puts his find aside in the secure knowledge that prospective buyers, representatives of scientific institutions, will call every week. No horse trading was ever performed with more zeal, with such an expenditure of eloquence and tricks, and nothing requires as much knowledge and cleverness.

* McGowan (1991a) points out that a baby protruding from the cloaca does not always mean that the mother died that way. When a school of false killer whales stranded and died on a beach in Tasmania, they were buried, but not deeply enough. When the site was revisited several months later, fetuses were seen partly protruding from the genital slits, "presumably because of the mounting gas pressure in the carcass."

But for all the "knowledge and cleverness," ichthyosaurology in Holzmaden was in a chaotic state. As Axel Hungerbühler wrote in a 1994 study, "when the Lower Jurassic ichthyosaurs of Germany were reviewed by McGowan, he found it impossible to identify most of the specimens described by [German geologist Friedrich] Quenstedt. . . . Labels on most of the type specimens* were missing and the type material is scattered throughout the collection. But above all, it is Quenstedt's idiosyncratic approach to taxonomy that has caused the most taxonomic confusion for later authors." Quenstedt's descriptions, often resorting to trinomials and even quadrinomials, were published in the mid to late nineteenth century, and when McGowan examined the material in the museum at Tübingen, he wrote that of the 28 names erected, only ten were valid, and to these ten he added two new ones, *Stenopterygius cuniceps* and *S. macrophasma.* The osteological and taxonomic reasons for McGowan's revisions are too technical for this discussion, but when Hungerbühler examined the specimens whose names and identifications Quenstedt had mangled, he wrote that "the taxonomy of Toarcian ichthyosaurs is far from certain and further investigations are needed to establish the validity of a number of species from Germany."

Christopher McGowan of the Royal Ontario Museum in Toronto has devoted his professional life to the study of ichthyosaurs. Born and educated in England, he wrote his doctoral dissertation at the University of London on "The Cranial Morphology and Interrelationships of Lower Liassic Ichthyosaurs." Since then, he has published more than 40 papers on these marine reptiles. In *Dinosaurs, Spitfires, and Sea Dragons,* which includes a comprehensive, eminently readable study of the ichthyosaurs, McGowan defined them chronologically, that is, ichthyosaurs of the Triassic (the earliest known, from 250 to

---

* Under the formal rules for naming species in the International Code of Zoological Nomenclature, each species of animal or plant must be represented by a type specimen, or holotype, which is the single specimen selected by the original describer of a species to be the standard-bearer for the new name. In simple terms, it is the original specimen of a species. The holotype specimen may or may not be the first ever collected, and it may or may not be a good example of its kind, but it has the official designation. Thus, the first time Conybeare decided to call a particular fossil *Ichthyosaurus communis,* that fossil became the type specimen. These rules apply to recent as well as fossil species.

205 million years ago), ichthyosaurs of the Jurassic (205 to 140 million years ago), and those of the Cretaceous (140 to 85 million years ago). In the first group is the yard-long *Mixosaurus cornalianus,** found mostly in Switzerland and northern Italy but also in other locations. Other mixosaurs have been found in Alaska, British Columbia, Nevada, China, Germany, Turkey, and the Indonesian island of Timor, suggesting that this was one of the most widespread of all ichthyosaur genera. In this early form, the vertebral column was not turned down, so it did not have the crescent-shaped caudal fin of the later species; more likely it had a long, trailing tail fin. Its limbs were modified into fins, but they had the five-fingered inner structure that showed that they were descended from land animals, but there is no indication what the ancestors of ichthyosaurs might have been. In his 2000 discussion of ichthyosaurs, Martin Sander wrote, "One of the most striking things about the evolution of the ichthyosaurs is that they appear fully formed in the late Early Triassic without any known intermediates to terrestrial animals. The strong aquatic adaptation of the group would suggest that it had a long evolutionary history with ample opportunity for proto-ichthyosaurs to fossilize. However, the Early Triassic was marked by rapid evolution rates and the origin of many new groups as the result of the mass extinctions at the end of the Permian."

The most common of the middle Triassic ichthyosaurs was *Mixosaurus* ("mixed lizard"), whose fossils have been found in many different regions, notably France, Norway, China, and New Zealand; several hundred specimens have come from Ticino, in the Monte San Giorgio region of the southern Alps at the Swiss-Italian border. (One of these specimens, described by Massare and Callaway in 1988, is a pregnant female and shows the earliest evidence of live-bearing in ichthyosaurs.) Triassic ichthyosaurs had not yet

* The rules of binomial nomenclature are applied as rigorously to fossil species as they are to recent ones, and all ichthyosaurs have been given a two-part name, with the generic name preceding the specific. For convenience, the specific name is omitted in discussions of those animals when there is only one species. Also, although there are several described species within a genus such as *Ophthalmosaurus* (*O. icenicus, O. natans, O. cantabrigensis*), except in publications identifying a new species or commenting on the differences within a particular genus, only the generic name is used. Unless otherwise specified, in this general discussion, use of a generic term such as *Ophthalmosaurus* refers to all known species.

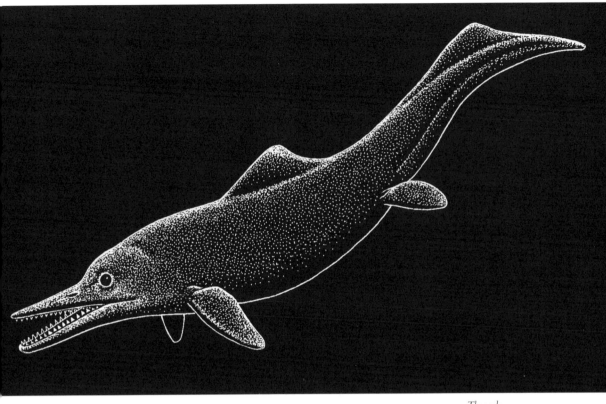

developed the vertical, sharklike tail fin and had a trailing tail, perhaps with an incipient upper lobe. Like many of the ichthyosaurs that followed, *Mixosaurus* had enormous eyes, set in a circular framework of bony plates known as the sclerotic ring. Primitive crocodilians had sclerotic rings, but modern crocs and alligators do not. Living fishes, birds, and some lizards have sclerotic rings, and their function is to support the eyeballs. Birds and most reptiles do not have muscles attached to their lenses and therefore cannot change the focus of their eyes. Instead, they compress the eyeball using the sclerotic ring, thus pushing the lens farther from the back of the eyeball. The principle is the same as using the focus knob on a pair of binoculars to shorten or lengthen the focal length. The term *accommodation* in this context refers to any mechanism that allows an eye to bring closer objects into focus on the retina. Animals generally

*The early ichthyosaurs, such as the 3-foot-long* Mixosaurus, *did not have the pronounced upper tail lobe of the later ones. Fossils of this species have been found in China, Indonesia, Europe, North America, and Spitsbergen.*

*The 5-foot-long Triassic ichthyosaur* Utatsusaurus *did not have the vertical tail fin that characterized later species; it moved by flexing its entire body. It was discovered in Japan.*

accommodate by changing the shape or position of the lens within the eye, but some animals such as snakes accommodate by squeezing the eye, thus causing it to change shape as well as moving the lens within it. (Even humans sometimes squint in an attempt to correct poor focus, which also changes the shape of the eyeball.) Conversely, some birds—cormorants, for example— drastically change the shape of their lenses when they go underwater so that they can compensate for the fact that their corneas no longer provide much focusing power.* Because we cannot do this, we can't see well underwater without trapping a layer of air around our eyes in a diving mask.

Like Chris McGowan, Ryosuke Motani, formerly of the Royal Ontario Museum but now at the University of Oregon, is a paleontologist who has devoted himself to the study of ichthyosaurs. (His 1997 doctoral dissertation at the University of Toronto was "Phylogeny of the Ichthyosauria with Special Reference to Triassic Forms.") In their 1998 discussion of *Utatsusaurus*, Motani, Minoura, and Ando wrote that the 5-foot-long ichthyosaur (which they called "phylogenetically basal among ichthyosaurs") had about 40 vertebrae in the front part of its body—the same number as living catsharks (Sciliorhinidae),

* M. P. Rowe (2000) wrote that the conventional interpretation of sclerotic rings was that they altered the focus of the eye by changing the shape of the eyeball. In some fishes and early tetrapods, sclerotic rings occur along with double cones on the retina, indicating enhanced color vision. We see such adaptations in birds, for example, and other animals that are active during daylight hours. This suggests that ichthyosaurs and other marine reptiles with sclerotic rings were active during the day and had some color vision. The large eyes of ichthyosaurs suggest low-light visual acuity, especially helpful in the fast pursuit of prey (Motani 2002).

which lack a high, vertical tail fin and move by flexing their entire bodies. The eel-like swimming style of the earliest ichthyosaurs suggests that they lived and hunted in shallow water, where maneuverability would be more advantageous than in the open ocean, where greater speed is required. Later ichthyosaurs would develop a lunate, vertical tail fin like that of the speedy mackerel sharks (great white, mako, porbeagle) and the tunas, which provides propulsion with little or no body flexion. Lingham-Soliar (1991a) identified this type of locomotion as "axial oscillation" and wrote, "in this mode the entire body, which is spindle or torpedo shaped, remains stiff or nearly so. . . . The force is transmitted from the massive musculature to the stiff caudal fin, via a strong series of tendons."* The vertebrae of the early ichthyosaurs were long and narrow, conducive to flexible, oscillatory swimming, but they became shorter and flatter in later forms, modifications that were required for the swimming style of heavier-bodied, tail-propelled swimmers.

The ichthyosaurs for which fossils have been found were a large and varied group, but they all conformed to a basic body plan (known to paleontologists as a *bauplan,* from the German for "work plan"): streamlined body, long snout, four flippers, and, in the later species, vertical tail fin and dorsal fin. There was enough variation, however, to create many genera, which differed in such particulars as length of rostrum, size of eyes, number of bones in the flippers, and overall size. The first ichthyosaurs were long and skinny, almost eel-like in form, but later species were deeper-bodied like the mackerel sharks, particularly the porbeagle (*Lamna nasus*) and the great white (*Carcharodon carcharias*). "Sharks evolved several body forms," wrote Motani et al. (1996), "some of which are also found in ichthyosaurs. Because of these similarities, sharks provide the best analogue for ichthyosaurs in overall body shape and locomotion, although differing in details."

The earliest ichthyosaurs—in contrast to the earliest discovered ichthyo-

---

* This description is equally applicable to some of the small, swift cetaceans, such as the spinner, spotter, common, and bottlenose dolphins, all of which are as streamlined as anything that swims and as fast as any fish in the ocean—except perhaps the bluefin tuna. The difference between cetaceans and ichthyosaurs, of course, is that the cetaceans move their horizontal tails up and down, while the ichthyosaurs (and the sharks and fishes) move their vertical tail fins from side to side.

saur fossils—were small, with a five-fingered forefin, a relatively short snout, and no sign of the downturned vertebral column that would characterize later forms. Among these early Triassic forms are *Grippia* from Spitsbergen, *Utatsusaurus* from Japan, and *Chaohusaurus* from China. According to Massare and Callaway (1990), "Triassic ichthyosaurs had less compact, more elongated bodies than the Jurassic species, a factor that must have affected their swimming capabilities." Indeed, the long, unbent vertebral column probably meant that they had not developed the bilobed caudal fin, probably swam with an undulating motion like crocodilians or mosasaurs, and were probably ambush predators. (The alternative form of predation is "pursuit," whereby powerful swimmers—like the later ichthyosaurs and the pliosaurs—actively chase their prey over greater distances.) Massare and Callaway conclude their article by noting, "the Triassic probably represents a period of experimentation and fine-tuning for the ichthyosaurs."

"Primitive Early Triassic ichthyosaurs are rare," wrote Mazin et al. in 1991; "up to now only seven species, referred to six genera have been described." They are *Grippia* (Spitsbergen), *Chaohusaurus* (China), *Utatsusaurus* (Japan), *Svalbardosaurus* (Spitsbergen), *Omphalosaurus* (Nevada), and two species of *Chensaurus* (China). (*Chensaurus* is now considered a junior synonym for *Chaohusaurus*.) In 1988, three specimens of a new Triassic ichthyosaur were found in Thailand, significantly expanding the database for the study of early ichthyosaurs. It had a long, pointed snout and high, conical teeth. The skull, which was incomplete, was approximately 6 inches long, suggesting an overall body length of 2 feet. The new species was named *Thaisaurus chonglakmanii*, for Thailand and Chongpan Chonglakmani, the man who found the specimens in a limestone quarry near the city of Phattalung. But in his 1999 "Phylogeny of the Ichthyopterygia," Motani downgraded *Thaisaurus* to the ignominious classification of *incertae sedis* ("affinities uncertain"), because it appears to be very similar to *Chaohusaurus geishanensis*, and also because the material analyzed by Mazin et al. is "too poorly known to be included in the cladistic analysis."

Describing the discovery of a new specimen of *Utatsusaurus* in Japan in a *Scientific American* article, Motani (2000b) wrote: "When I saw the skeleton for the first time, I knew that *Utatsusaurus* was exactly what paleontologists had been expecting to find for years: an ichthyosaur that looked like a lizard with flippers. . . . *Chaohusaurus* occurs in rocks the same age as those harboring *Utatsusaurus,* and it, too, had been found before only in bits and pieces. The new specimen clearly revealed the outline of a slender, lizardlike body."

A great number of marine reptiles have been recovered from the black bituminous marine shales of Holzmaden in Germany.* Because of the fine-grained nature of the stone, it was (and still is) used in the manufacture of lithographic plates. The quarries of Holzmaden are still active, and according to McGowan (1991a), "about thirty-five ichthyosaurs are found each year and the total number of specimens that have ever been found in that area is in the order of three thousand." Whereas *Ichthyosaurus communis* is the most common fossil of the English shales, three genera are represented at Holzmaden: *Stenopterygius, Eurhinosaurus,* and *Temnodontosaurus.* Similar in size to *Ichthyosaurus communis,* adults of the species *Stenopterygius quadriscissus* (the most common German species) are characterized by an almost total absence of teeth. Perhaps the most interesting aspect of the Holzmaden ichthyosaurs is how many of them are females with embryos. Why is this? Judy Massare (1992) offered this suggestion:

> I believe that Holzmaden was a breeding and birthing ground similar to some of the shallow, nearshore areas frequented by whales today. Like such whales as grays and humpbacks, ichthyosaurs were wide-ranging. Such animals could well have developed a behavioral adaptation for congregating at a certain time of year in a spot particularly favorable for giving birth. The nurseries may have been calm waters, and the sheer numbers of mothers and young may have afforded them some protection from such predators, such as the ferocious ichthyosaur *Leptopterygius.*

*Leptopterygius* is now known as *Leptonectes* (McGowan 1995c), and in January 1995, another specimen was found in England from the Belemnite Marls at Seatown, Dorset. Except for a somewhat shorter snout — which suggests that

---

* There are two regions of Germany where the close-grained stone preserves incredible detail in fossils: Holzmaden, located about 20 miles southeast of Stuttgart, and the more famous Solnhofen, the home of *Archaeopteryx* and *Compsognathus,* which is in Bavaria, about 60 miles northwest of Munich.

this was an immature individual—this specimen bears a striking resemblance to *L. tenuirostris* (Conybeare) and was named *L. moorei*, for its discoverer Chris Moore. The incomplete skeleton comprised the skull, forefins, and anterior trunk, and its size was estimated at about 8 feet. As with most ichthyosaurs of this type, the eye sockets were enormous, and in this specimen, they formed an almost perfect circle (McGowan and Milner 1999). In 1998, M. W. Maisch showed that *Leptonectes, Excalibosaurus,* and *Eurhinosaurus* form a clade for which the name Leptonectidae was erected, characterized by their long, slender snouts; elongate, slender fins with three or four primary digits; enormous orbits; and a tendency to develop an overbite.

Prospecting in southeastern France, Hugo Bucher came across an ichthyosaur fossil in the bottom of a ravine near the village of Le Clapier. The disarticulated skull and some teeth were brought to the Musée Géologique at Lausanne, but Bucher (and Martin Sander) felt that there was not enough material for a positive identification. The authors finally decided that because of its size—the skull suggests an animal about 16 feet long—it was probably *Stenopterygius,* regarded as the most common of the Liassic* ichthyosaurs, having been found in the United Kingdom, Germany, France, Switzerland, and Portugal (there is a possible record from Argentina, but it is not certain). We cannot tell whether the fossil record shows that the animals themselves were widely distributed or whether the fossils have been found because conditions in particular areas are conducive to their appearance. As McGowan (1979a) wrote, "Attempts to construct geographical ranges for extinct taxa are always circumscribed by the vagaries of the fossil record, and possibly only reflect the distribution of good fossiliferous exposures. . . . Ichthyosaurs were probably highly mobile animals, comparable to present day cetaceans, and I suspect the complete fossil record would reveal that most taxa were widely distributed geographically."

* The terms *Lias* or *Liassic* are used in England and Germany for the earliest part of the Jurassic, from about 205 to 180 million years ago. The name probably derives from the Gaelic word *leac,* for a flat rock. In terms of standard geology, it extends from the Hettangian to the Toarcian and is divisible into the Lower Lias (Hettangian–Lower Pleinsbachian), Middle Lias (Upper Pleinsbachian), and Upper Lias (Toarcian). The famous Holzmaden material is all Toarcian; the Lyme Regis material is Lower Lias.

The identification, classification, and naming of ichthyosaurs is an ongoing enterprise; as various paleontologists examine and reexamine the material—which is often fragmentary and sometimes goes missing—the phylogeny of these marine reptiles is stretched, compressed, modified, altered, and corrected to such a degree that the subject can only be described as a work in progress, as far from completion as the ichthyosaurs themselves are from modern reptiles. McGowan (1979a) wrote:

> Any attempt to produce a stable taxonomy is circumscribed by the uncertainty of recognizing natural groupings of individuals. It is impossible to estimate the range of individual variations, and the effects of allometric

growth (which are compounded by the large size ranges encountered) make taxonomic conclusions conjectural. Von Huene sought a solution to these problems by extreme taxonomic splitting, but the differences between his groups were often small, and often within the range which might be expected for extant species. In contrast to von Huene, I have tended to lump specimens together, rather than referring them to different species.

Many workers have had a go at resolving the confusion, most recently Ryosuke Motani. In 1999, he published "Phylogeny of the Ichthyopterygia," in which he wrote, "The Ichthyopterygia is a group of aquatic reptiles with fish shaped bodies. Ichthyopterygians have been known to the scientific community for over 180 years, yet their phylogeny is very poorly understood. . . . Recent cladistic studies all agree that they are all modified diapsids, as suggested by some earlier works, but their position among the diapsids is still controversial." In this paper, Motani proposed two new genera, *Macgowania* and *Isfjordosaurus* — the former for Chris McGowan,* and the latter for Isfjord in Spitsbergen, where the specimen was found. (He lists many other genera that, because of limited space and technical differentiation, will not be discussed here, including *Parvinatator, Besanosaurus, Toretocnemus, Hudsonelpidia,* and *Caypullisaurus.*)

Georg Baur, a Ph.D. from Germany, worked for O. C. Marsh in New Haven, Connecticut, for many years and provided a much-needed background in biology to Marsh's expertise in geology and mineralogy. Like all Marsh's assistants, Baur was underpaid, underappreciated, and restricted in what he was allowed to publish under his own name. Still, in 1887, he wrote "On the Morphology and Origin of the Ichthyopterygia" in which he opined that "the Ichthyopterygia were developed from land-living reptiles which very much approached the Sphenodontidae. . . . Their fins are not original but secondary formations, like the paddles of cetaceans." The family Sphenodontidae is a mostly extinct group of land reptiles represented today by the tuataras *(Sphenodon)*, the only surviving members of the order Sphenodontia. All other members of the order (and family) are known only from the

* The International Code of Zoological Nomenclature recommends the use of "Mac" rather than "Mc" in scientific names, hence the apparent misspelling.

Mesozoic. *Sphenodon* and the crocodilians resemble each other and differ from all other living reptiles in that they have diapsid skulls, as did the ichthyosaurs. It was on the basis of the skull that Baur affiliated the ichthyosaurs with the Sphenodontidae ("turning now to the upper part of the skull," he wrote, "we find the parietal bones of exactly the same structure as in *Sphenodon*, and in front of those very small frontals.") But Maisch believes that Baur (and others who suggest that ichthyosaurs are descended from diapsids) was dead wrong and that "the ichthyosaurian ancestor was an anapsid amniote or proto-amniote."* Diapsid, anapsid, amniote, or proto-amniote, the ancestors of the ichthyosaurs remain well hidden in the rocks.

The family Mixosauridae was erected in 1887 by Baur, and he included the species that had previously been classified as *Ichthyosaurus cornalianus* and *I. atavus*. The animal now known as *Mixosaurus cornalianus* was described from specimens found in Basano, Italy, but they were destroyed when the Milan Museum of Natural History was bombed during World War II. The best material now available is from Ticino, Switzerland, and is housed in the museum in Zurich, but as Callaway (1997b) points out, "this material remains undescribed to the present date . . . because access to researchers has been denied or severely limited." Nevertheless, Callaway managed to examine some of the Zurich material and wrote "an interim update on various aspects of *Mixosaurus*." He synonymized *Mixosaurus maotaiensis*, *M. natans*, *M. nordeskioeldii*, and the various *Phalarodon* species into two recognized species, *Mixosaurus*

---

* Anapsids are tetrapods characterized by the lack of temporal fenestrae, large holes in the side of the skull. Whereas anapsids have no holes behind the eye socket, diapsids have two on each side of the skull. The function of these holes has long been debated, but no consensus has been reached. Many believe that they allow muscles to expand and lengthen, which would result in a stronger jaw musculature, and the longer muscle fibers would allow an increase in the gape. The taxon Anapsida includes turtles and their extinct relatives. Amniotes are vertebrates that possess an extraembryonic layer called an amnion within the egg or womb, which replaces the aquatic environment required for developing vertebrate embryos. Amniotes may reproduce on land and may respire without the assistance of a body of water. Their development was a monumental event in vertebrate evolution, allowing for domination of the land and exploitation of the food resources growing there. All birds, reptiles, and mammals are amniotes.

*cornalianus* and *M. atavus.* The mixosaurs have well-developed belly ribs (gastralia), but what function they performed is uncertain. Some plesiosaurs also had these tightly knit structures that formed a sort of plastron or bony shield on the underbelly, but, Callaway writes, "they may simply represent a feature retained from terrestrial ancestors, although they seem very well developed for mere vestigial structures." He concludes, "*Mixosaurus* became the quintessential Triassic ichthyosaur used to illustrate both scientific and popular literature. . . . Mixosaurs are not the most primitive of ichthyosaurs, as often depicted in much of the older literature, but are in some respects as derived as or more derived than Late Triassic and post-Triassic forms."

In 1998, Michael Maisch, a German ichthyosaurologist working in Tübingen, wrote that there might be another species of mixosaur from Monte San Giorgio. With Andreas Matzke, he created the new genus *Wimanius,* "for Prof. Dr. Carl Wiman of the University of Uppsala (Sweden) for his excellent contributions to paleoherpetology, particularly on the Triassic ichthyosaurs."* Maisch also reexamined the specimen from Holzmaden originally designated *Leptopterygius disinteger* by von Huene in 1926 and renamed it *Suevoleviathan* — from *Suevo,* Latin for Swabia in Germany, and *leviathan,* the Hebrew name for "a sea dragon of the antediluvian earth." Known from only a single specimen, the Swabian leviathan was a largish ichthyosaur, about 13 feet long, with medium-sized eyes. In their 2001 study, Maisch and Matzke recognized *Phalarodon* (Nicholls et al. 1999) and wrote, "Here we focus on a third valid ichthyosaur taxon, hitherto known as *Mixosaurus major* and usually dismissed as a nomen dubium (e.g. Callaway and Massare 1989). It is demonstrated that

---

* But when Motani (1999a) reexamined the bone that was described as having teeth, he noted that "this bone is possibly a broken pterygoid. Maisch and Matzke noted that the only other ichthyopterygian with teeth on the palate was *Grippia,* and that the teeth were on the palatine in that genus, citing Wiman (1933). They accordingly identified the bone in their new genus as the palatine, however what was described as the palatal teeth by Wiman have been shown to be the second row of maxillary teeth. The only ichthyopterygian with teeth on the palate is *Utatsusaurus,* and these teeth are on the pterygoid. It is therefore possible that the bone is actually a pterygoid rather than palatine." Although Maisch and Matzke point out the differences between *Wimanius* and *Mikadocephalus,* they share many characteristics in common and may in fact be the same species.

the type material of this species, despite its fragmentary nature, is diagnostic on the generic and specific level and can be referred to the genus *Phalarodon* Merriam 1910, which was up to now unknown from the Germanic Muschelkalk."

In 1998, Maisch and Matzke published the first description of "a crested predatory mixosaurid from the Middle Triassic of the Germanic Basin," which they identified as a new genus and called *Contectopalatus* ("closed palate"). It reached a length of 16 feet, more than twice that of other mixosaurids, but it differed from all others in the shape of its skull, which Maisch and Matzke (2000) called "the most bizarre of any known ichthyosaur." It had a high sagittal crest, which the authors interpreted as "correlated with a unique arrangement of the jaw adductor muscles . . . with the internal jaw adductors extending over most of the skull roof up to the external narial opening." They believed that this arrangement greatly increased the biting force of the jaws and made *Contectopalatus* a particularly effective marine predator. It was long thought that the mixosaurs were primitive versions of what was to follow, but *Contectopalatus* was extremely specialized, capable of crunching the hard shells of ammonites and perhaps even preying on smaller ichthyosaurs.

A (possible) later development in ichthyosaurs was durophagy, which means the eating of hard objects, such as bivalves and ammonites. The teeth of *Omphalosaurus* (*omphalos* is "navel" in Greek) consisted of an irregular pavement of button-like teeth set in short, massive jawbones. The original specimen was discovered in Nevada by J. C. Merriam (1906), who believed that it represented a distinct group of reptiles related to placodonts or rhynchosaurs. In 1910, fossils were found in Spitsbergen that Carl Wiman believed were the limb bones of ichthyosaurs, and he assigned them to the species *Omphalosaurus nevadanus.* McGowan (1991a) wrote that it was a "problematic and poorly-known Triassic ichthyosaur," and according to Sander (2000), there is a question of whether *Omphalosaurus* is really an ichthyosaur and whether the limb bones of the Spitsbergen specimen actually came from the same animal as the jaws. Motani (2000a) argues that "there is insufficient reason to consider *Omphalosaurus* as ichthyopterygian . . . [because] the characters used to unite the two groups are all inconclusive because none are unique to the two and most are lacking in basal ichthyopterygians." (In 1860, Richard Owen

*Whatever its proper name,* Shasta-saurus *(named for Shasta County, California) probably looked something like this — except for the color pattern, which is imaginary. It is shown chasing squid.*

arbitrarily changed Blainville's Ichthyosauria to Ichthyopterygia ["fish flip-pers"], "a name which is often, though incorrectly, used to designate this order of reptiles" [Callaway 1997a].)

At the turn of the nineteenth century, paleontologist John C. Merriam of the University of California at Berkeley was working in northern California and Nevada, ably assisted by Annie Alexander, a wealthy amateur collector. Alexander sponsored many of Merriam's expeditions, and in recognition of her considerable contributions to paleontology — and to her founding of the Museum of Paleontology at Berkeley — he named the species *Shastasaurus alexandrae* for her in 1902 (*Shastasaurus* was named for Shasta County, California). But even now, wrote McGowan (1994b), with new material being uncovered, *Shastasaurus* is not a well-understood genus. "Many of the species," he noted, "were erected on inadequate material — especially vertebrae and rib frag-ments — and should be considered nomina dubia ('doubtful names'). Al-though there is information for the skull, fins, and girdles, most of the material is incomplete. Thus there is no complete skull, forefin or hindfin, nor is the vertebral column known much beyond the pelvic girdle." Beginning in 1986, McGowan led expeditions to Williston Lake, British Columbia, and found "the most complete skeleton to date," which he named *Shastasaurus* neoscapularis (*neo*, "new"; *scapula*, "shoulder blade"). In his 1994 discussion, McGowan wrote that Merriam's five species (plus another added by von Huene in 1925), "aside from cluttering the literature with dubious names, . . . have given a false sense of security in our knowledge of *Shastasaurus.*" Summing up, McGowan found that *Shastasaurus pacificus* (the type species), *S. alexandrae*, and *S. neoscapularis* were valid species, but *S. careyi, S. carinthiacus, S. osmonti,* and *S. altispinus* were all nomina dubia. So what was left of the shastasaur grab bag was three species, all of which were medium-sized ichthyosaurs with characteristically large eyes. But as might be expected, that situation didn't last long.

Since 1992, paleontologists from the Royal Tyrrell Museum in Drumheller, Alberta, have been working the late Triassic Pardonet Formation in the Pink Mountain region of British Columbia. To date, 65 ichthyosaur specimens have been collected (Nicholls and Manabe 2001) from this region, which is about 60 miles north of the area where McGowan worked before them. From reports received from helicopter pilots, collectors excavated the remains of a medium-sized ichthyosaur and brought the fossils to the Royal Tyrrell Museum. Elizabeth Nicholls and Makoto Manabe reexamined the material that McGowan had named *Shastasaurus neoscapularis* and concluded "that the [new] species does not belong in the genus *Shastasaurus,*" so on the basis of skull characters and the osteology of the front flippers, they placed it in a new genus altogether, which they named *Metashastasaurus* (*meta* means "changed," referring to differences from the *Shastasaurus* skull). But just before Nicholls and Manabe's paper appeared, Maisch and Matzke named the species *Callawayia*, which, because it appeared in print first, became the senior synonym; therefore, the International Code of Zoological Nomenclature recognizes *Callawayia* as the official name of the species. (Nicholls and Manabe were not particularly happy about this sequence of events.)

In 1991, archeologist Keary Walde was wandering deep in the forests of British Columbia when he happened upon the fossilized remains of a giant animal beside the isolated Sikanni Chief River. Walde reported his discovery to the Royal Tyrrell Museum, where it was brought to the attention of curator Elizabeth Nicholls, one of the world's leading authorities on prehistoric marine reptiles. Nicholls visited the site and saw that the 75-foot-long fossil skeleton was 50 percent longer than the largest previously known ichthyosaur,

*Shonisaurus* from the Nevada desert, and was by far the largest marine reptile ever found. Through the combined efforts of the Royal Tyrrell Museum, the National Science Museum of Tokyo, and the Discovery Channel, a team led by Nicholls managed to excavate the skull in pieces in 1999. The skull alone was 18 feet long, and the largest piece (the braincase and orbit) weighed 8,860 pounds. It was airlifted from the site by a cargo helicopter usually used to carry trucks and other heavy equipment. Nicholls has spent the last six years painstakingly excavating and studying the ichthyosaur, overcoming countless obstacles to extract the fossil from its limestone bed on a remote riverbank flooded for part of the year. For her efforts, Nicholls was named a Rolex laureate in 2000, which includes a stipend of $100,000, meaning that the Swiss watch company is financing a substantial portion of her very expensive excavations.*

When Nicholls publishes the results of her excavations, the specimen will be recognized as the largest ichthyosaur, and probably the largest marine reptile, that ever lived. But for now, the largest of the ichthyosaurs is *Shonisaurus.* Named for the Shoshone Mountain Range, where the fossilized remains of 40 ichthyosaurs were discovered in 1928 by Simeon Muller in a naturally eroded area of what is now Berlin-Ichthyosaur State Park, *Shonisaurus* is the state fossil of Nevada. Excavations began in 1954 under the direction of Charles Camp and Samuel Welles of the University of California at Berkeley. At a length of 50 feet, this gigantic reptile was approximately equal in size to an adult humpback whale. Its long backbone bent downward at the posterior end, supporting the lower lobe of a sharklike tail. Its jaws were greatly elongated, with teeth only at the front, and its flippers were 5 feet long and of equal size in the front and back. When Camp was excavating the specimens,

---

* In December 2001, in response to my question about how the excavation was going, Nicholls wrote to me: "Work on our giant ichthyosaur is coming along well. . . . The skull is almost finished. It is not as complete as we had hoped, as the front of it was so badly crushed. But we have a good part of the back of the skull, and the palate is in good shape. Sounds funny doesn't it, to be enthused about a 'good palate'? The tail is prepared, and we are working on front limbs and ribs. Hope to have a preliminary publication on it submitted next year, and will tell you more about it when that is out. . . . I am not one to release my data to the popular press before it is published."

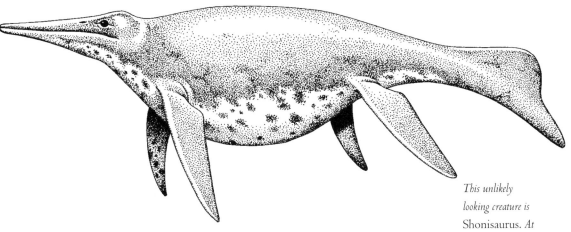

he noticed that they were all aligned in more or less the same direction, leading him to suggest that they might have been mass stranded, much the way certain whales do today.

More recently, paleontologists have come up with alternative explanations for the sudden mass mortality of the shonisaurs of Nevada. Stranding requires a shallow, coastal location, but examination of the site led Orndorff et al. (2001) to conclude that "the ichthyosaur bones were deposited on a deep ocean shelf environment." If they didn't strand, then how to explain the bodies of so many giant ichthyosaurs in the same place? "One intriguing possibility," say the authors, "is that the ichthyosaurs ate fish or shellfish tainted with a neurotoxin that paralyzed them." They refer to "mass kills of modern whales along the coast of New England" as a paradigm, but unfortunately for the neurotoxin explanation, these "kills" occurred on the very shallow beaches that the authors say are absent in the ichthyosaur deaths, and besides, there is no evidence that these whale kills are in any way related to shellfish poisoning. (Ichthyosaurs probably ate ammonites, but modern whales do not eat shellfish, and although many whales and dolphins eat squid, these cephalopods have not been shown to carry poisons toxic to cetaceans.)

Camp collected the Nevada specimens from 1954 to 1957, with additional field seasons between 1963 and 1965. He excavated the partial remains of 35 to 40 animals, but not one was complete. He typed up a monograph on

*Shonisaurus,* but ill health prevented him from seeing it through to publication. Just before his death in 1975, Camp entrusted his manuscript and accompanying illustrations to his friend Joseph Gregory, which resulted in two publications in 1976 and 1980 (both appear under Camp's name). In the 1980 publication, there was a reconstruction of the skeleton of *Shonisaurus popularis,* depicted as a deep-bodied creature with huge fins and a skull that was nearly as long as its downturned tail. This image of the gigantic ichthyosaur appeared in numerous popular and scientific publications, and it was generally acknowledged that *Shonisaurus,* with its narrow, pointed head and unnaturally deep rib cage, was one weird-looking animal. In 1990, Bradley Kosch of the Berlin-Ichthyosaur State Park in Nevada revised the interpretation of Camp's skeleton, noting that "Camp's often reproduced skeletal reconstruction contains significant discrepancies from both his published description and his unpublished field notes." Kosch realized that "as much as eight feet of the dorsal region might not have been represented," and the ribs were too long, which gave his restoration its exaggerated potbellied appearance. Then McGowan and Motani (1999) remeasured the actual specimens housed at the Natural History Museum of the University of Nevada at Las Vegas and also at the Berlin-Ichthyosaur State Park. Camp had identified three species: *Shonisaurus popularis* (the most common, represented by 37 of the 40 individuals), *S. silberlingi,* and *S. mulleri.* But after a careful examination of the fossils, McGowan and Motani declared that "the likelihood of their having been three species of *Shonisaurus,* the largest of the ichthyosaurs, seems unlikely," and there was probably only a single species, *S. popularis.*

When Martin Sander of the Institute for Paleontology in Bonn examined a fossil that had been exposed in the Muschelkalk beds of Karlstadt, he found that it was a small shastasaurid, to date the most complete ichthyosaur skeleton from that region of Germany. In 1997, he named it *Shastasaurus neubigi,* for Bernd Neubig, who had discovered the fossil during railroad construction work in 1985. In the early Triassic period, the Tethys Sea covered much of what is now central northern Europe, and because large ichthyosaurs are otherwise rare in the Muschelkalk Sea, Sander opined that the individual might have accidentally entered the shallow basin. Sander erected the species *Shastasaurus neubigi,* "based on the structure of the vertebrae, in particular the nature of the rib articulations, and of the pubis." Again, this illustrates the ever-changing nature of paleontology, with some of the older specimens relegated to the scrap heap of nomina dubia, some combined with others (the correct term is *synonymized*), and others rejected completely because the original material was too fragmentary for an accurate diagnosis or simply because a later worker decided that the earlier description was inaccurate. Have we arrived at a point where we can say that we really understand ichthyosaur phylogeny? As long as paleontologists keep digging, reexamining material in existing collections, or arguing about which name ought to have priority, the book on the fish lizards will remain open.

The shastasaurs — some of which grew to enormous sizes — represent an example of convergent or parallel evolution with the toothed whales of the Cenozoic era, although in terms of the rapid evolutionary tendency to hugeness, there is a similarity with the baleen whales, which likewise grew from medium-sized to enormous creatures in the space of some 5 or 10 million years. Reaching lengths of 30 to 50 feet, and with bodies that were quite deep and sturdy, the shastasaurs were the largest ichthyosaurs and among the largest of the marine animals of the Mesozoic. The still-unnamed giant ichthyosaur being excavated by Nicholls might turn out to be a shastasaur. The first of the really large ichthyosaurs was the 33-foot-long *Cymbospondylus.* It was originally believed that the tail portions of this species and of the giant shastasaurids lacked the tailbend that characterized the later ichthyosaurs, but Jennifer Hogler (1993) reexamined the tail portion of *Cymbospondylus* and *Shonisaurus* and found the wedge-shaped caudal vertebrae that are the hallmark of the tailbend, suggesting that these early ichthyosaurs had a tail structure similar to that of the later forms.

Found in the middle Triassic deposits of Nevada, *Cymbospondylus* was about the size of an adult male killer whale, with a short (or perhaps no) dorsal fin. The first evidence of the existence of this giant ichthyosaur was a 3-foot-long skull found by Annie Alexander in Nevada in the early years of the twentieth century, but afterward, more specimens were found, including an almost complete skeleton. *Cymbospondylus* fossils have been found in North America, Spitsbergen, and Europe, and recently, two skulls were found in the Upper Triassic Falang Formation in Guizhou province, China, extending its range to

*The 30-foot-long ichthyosaur* Cymbospondylus *with a juvenile. Ichthyosaurs delivered their young alive, but it is not known whether they cared for them. The pattern on the tail is conjectural, as is the flap at the tip.*

another continent (Li and You 2002). The lower jaw contained teeth only on the forward part, and it has the smallest orbit (and therefore the smallest eyes) of any known ichthyosaur. *Cymbospondylus asiaticus* is a new species, younger than the middle Triassic specimens found earlier.

Paleontologists do much of their work in the field, but there are occasions when digging through museum collections also produces some interesting results. In the collection of the Academy of Natural Sciences of Philadelphia, Chris McGowan may have found *another* ichthyosaur that was as big as *Shonisaurus,* or maybe even bigger. In 1996, he described a "giant ichthyosaur of the Early Jurassic," identified from a mislabeled bone in the academy's collection. Because of its size, it had originally been identified as a coracoid, which is part of the shoulder girdle and one of the larger parts of any ichthyosaur skeleton. As he recounts in *The Dragon Seekers* (2001), McGowan saw that "the robust element was not part of the shoulder at all but part of the skull, namely a quadrate bone." And what a quadrate bone! "The entire animal must have been colossal — larger than any ichthyosaur ever found in England." McGowan then revisited the collection in the Natural History Museum in London, where he found a massive scapula and teeth that were much larger than those of any known ichthyosaurs. He wrote, "I suspect the massive isolated teeth belong to the unknown giant . . . as large as *Shonisaurus* . . . all we know so far about this enigmatic giant is that it reached lengths upwards of about fifty feet (15 meters) and that it had massive teeth with sharp edges and short crowns."

Most ichthyosaur fossils have been found in Europe and North America, with England and Germany as the prime locations. Some fragmentary material was found in Argentina, but recently, more complete fossils of various marine reptiles, including pliosaurs, turtles, and ichthyosaurs, have been found in Neuquén province of the Argentine Andes. As Marta Fernández (2000) of the Museo de La Plata wrote, "a rich fauna of marine reptiles has been discovered from Tithonian levels of the Vaca Muerta Formation, exposed as several localities in the Neuquén Basin." The first Argentine ichthyosaurs were referred to *Ophthalmosaurus* (Gasparini 1985), but one of the recent specimens has been reassigned to a new genus, *Caypullisaurus,* which differs from *Ophthalmosaurus* in the osteology of the forefin. There is also a long-snouted species named *Chacaisaurus* (Fernández 1994) and another new species from the Los Molles Formation that was named *Mollesaurus* (Fernández 1999). The Argentine *Ophthalmosaurus* from the Tithonian levels of Vaca Muerta ("dead cow") was about 148 million years old, but *Mollesaurus* was from the Bajocian, perhaps 25 million years older.

Investigators continue to uncover more ichthyosaur fossils, often in unexpected locations. For example, when Dino Frey, Marie-Céline Buchy, and Wolfgang Stinnesbeck examined the material in the collection of the Faculty of Geosciences in Linares, Mexico, they found (but have not yet described) "a large number of vertebrae and segments of columnae vertebrates of ichthyosaurs . . . but no cranial material." In their 2001 abstract (in which they also discussed the giant pliosaur known as the "Monster of Aramberri"), Frey et al. wrote that they were planning to return to Mexico because they "expect to discover more material in order to determine the taxonomical and paleobiogeographical importance of these assemblages."

In recent years, China has become one of the world's most important sources for fossils, particularly of the specimens that have led paleontologists to recognize that many early dinosaurs had feathers, demonstrating a direct connection between creatures such as *Archaeopteryx* and today's birds. China is also offering up fossil ichthyosaurs. In 1999, Chun Li reported on an ichthyosaur fossil from Guizhou province in southwestern China that he named *Qianichthyosaurus*, for Qian, which is another name for Guizhou. Then Betsy Nicholls, Chen Wei, and Makato Manabe published a lengthy description of a complete specimen of *Qianichthyosaurus*, also from Guizhou, that had a short snout; small, closely spaced teeth; and huge eyes. It is believed to be closely related to *Toretocnemus*, found in late Triassic deposits in Shasta County, California, and originally described by Merriam in 1903. "The close relationship between *Qianichthyosaurus* and *Toretocnemus* indicates a trans-Pacific distribution of [ichthyosaur] faunas in the late Triassic," wrote Nicholls and her colleagues in 2003.

In May 2000, Nathalie Bardet and Marta Fernández published a description of a new ichthyosaur from the Upper Jurassic lithographic shales of Solnhofen, one of the first new specimens described from the area in almost 50 years. "Indeed," they wrote in their historical review, "with the exception of Meyer's [1863] skull, kept at London, the ichthyosaur collections from the lithographic limestones of Bavaria (then housed in the Munich State Museum) were completely destroyed during World War II." The new species is based on two specimens, one unearthed in 1954 (originally referred to as *Macropterygius posthumus*), and another found in 1990 and called *Macropterygius trigonus*. The type specimen is one that had previously been identified as *Ichthyosaurus leptospondylus* (Wagner 1853), but it was destroyed in the bombing of Munich. Because the two specimens of *Macropterygius* were found to differ significantly from known *Ichthyosaurus* specimens, Bardet and Fernández proposed that the species be renamed *Aegirosaurus leptospondylus*, from Aegir, god of the oceans and seashores in German and Scandinavian mythology. It was a medium-sized ichthyosaur, about 6 feet long, with a long, slender snout packed with small teeth strongly anchored in the jaws. Its eyes were large, and the sclerotic rings were composed of fourteen overlapping thin plates (*Ophthalmosaurus*'s eyes had fifteen plates). Impressions of the soft tissue were preserved all around the body, except on the skull, and showed the typically lunate tail and four limbs. The gracefully curved forelimbs were long and narrow, and the hind limbs were shorter and broader.

The Solnhofen limestone occasionally preserves impressions of the skin,

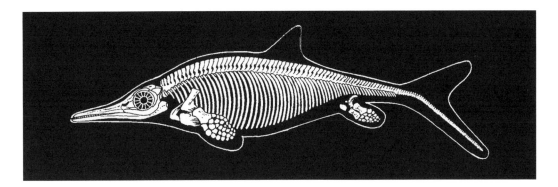

and in the case of *Aegirosaurus*, Bardet and Fernández observed what they tentatively interpreted as "minute scales covering the ichthyosaurian skin, an opposite opinion to Martill (1995)." In his paper, Martill had written, "A surprising aspect of all ichthyosaur soft tissue specimens is the lack of preservation of typical reptilian scales," and for the most part, negative evidence — that is, the absence of scales in any known specimens — has led most researchers to conclude that the skin of ichthyosaurs was smooth, like that of dolphins. In an 1853 study, Henry Coles described scales for ichthyosaurs ("when grouped together on the surface, they appear like hairs or spines; but when detached, by their short and generally flattened shapes, they approximate more nearly to scales"), but it is obvious, just by looking at the plate in Coles's paper, that the "scales" were actually cephalopod hooklets. What was supposed to indicate what the skin of the ichthyosaur looked like actually showed what it ate.

In his 1973 discussion of the cranial morphology of *Ichthyosaurus*, McGowan discussed the size of the brain: "By reptilian standards the brain was extensive. . . . The cerebellum was very large, a condition which is indicative of a high level of locomotor integration. . . . The corpus striatum is the seat of innate behavioral activity and it seems reasonable to conclude that the ichthyosaur possessed a wide spectrum of instinctive behavioral patterns." Then he wrote:

From observations of specimens in which the unborn offspring are preserved it is clear that few were born at any one time and these were delivered from the cloaca tail first. The birth would certainly have been

*Skeletal reconstruction of the ichthyosaur* Ophthalmosaurus. *Note the particularly large eye ring, the downturn in the vertebral column, and the profusion of ribs.*

attended by a considerable degree of parental care, and may also have been accompanied by displays of social co-operation by other individuals. It is very probable that ichthyosaurs were gregarious and some evidence for this is available from Germany where aggregations of specimens have been found in some quarries. The gregarious habit is associated with co-operative behavior which is further evidence of cerebral activity at a high center.*

Based on size, tooth structure, comparison with living animals, and many other variables, paleontologists can make educated guesses about the diet of a particular kind of animal. It is rare that fossils yield evidence of the actual prey items (the fossils of some predatory fishes have been found with the fossils of undigested smaller species in their stomachs), but some ichthyosaurs have been found with the fossilized hooks of cephalopods in their gut, giving a clear indication of what they ate. How the ichthyosaurs actually caught their prey has also been a subject of speculation, and for those with dolphin-like jaws and teeth, the answer appears obvious: they swam through a school of fishes or squid and snapped up the smaller animals, much the way many dolphin species do today. We know that dolphins have an additional weapon in their arsenal in the form of echolocation; they can emit sounds and listen to the returning echoes to get a fix on the location, speed, and even type of prey. Could the ichthyosaurs echolocate? Probably not. Unlike the ears of dolphins, which are surrounded by a layer of spongy tissue, the middle and inner ear bones of ichthyosaurs were uninsulated and part of the skull, which precludes the directional hearing necessary for the analysis of returning echoes. In his discussion of the cranium of *Ichthyosaurus,* McGowan (1973a) also wrote that "the last piece of evidence to support the absence of direction location is the nature of the sensory receptor. It has already been noted that the lagena [an extension of the saccule of the ear] was probably a small structure, and this evidence, slender as it is, is not suggestive of an acute sense

* Several specimens found in the same place does not necessarily show gregarious behavior, because a number of specimens might have died in the same place but not necessarily at the same time.

of hearing. . . . It is therefore concluded that the possession of directional hearing capabilities in the ichthyosaurs is extremely doubtful."

In 2001, with radiographer George Kourlis, paleontologist Ben Kear of the South Australian Museum performed a computed tomography scan on the skull of a specimen of the ichthyosaur *Platypterygius* and found that the tiny inner ear bones were too thick to detect sound vibrations; therefore, ichthyosaurs — or at least the one he examined — might have been stone deaf. The scan also revealed delicate structures deep in the animal's palate (the pterygoid bones) that may have been related to the sense of smell, and channels and grooves that suggest that this ichthyosaur might have had an electroreceptor system like that of some fishes and sharks (Perkins 2002). The *Platypterygius* ichthyosaurs unearthed at Hughenden in Queensland also revealed a fetus in a fossilized female, incontrovertible evidence of live birth in ichthyosaurs, as well as the mother's last meal, which consisted of belemnites, fish, and hatchling turtles.

Although many toothed whales (odontocetes) have a device for generating and focusing sound (the melon), no such apparatus has been found in ichthyosaurs. Odors disperse too quickly in moving water to be of much value in locating prey, so without echolocation, the ichthyosaurs probably relied heavily on vision, and many species had enormous eyes that enabled them to find their prey in the reduced light of the ocean depths. Their streamlined shape and powerful caudal fins probably made the ichthyosaurs fast and agile swimmers, capable of capturing darting prey species in their toothy, snapping jaws. In a 1993 article about marine reptile extinction, Bakker wrote that the ichthyosaurs "grabbed quick breaths of air at the rear corner of their jaws," but we don't really know if ichthyosaurs breathed through their mouths. They certainly breathed through their nostrils, which were located in front of their eyes but not at the tip of the snout, and certainly not on top of the head, where the blowhole of dolphins is found. We also have no way of knowing what color ichthyosaurs were, but it would be safe to assume that some were countershaded, darker above and lighter below, which helped camouflage them as they hunted. It's also safe to assume that they were not bright orange or Day-glo chartreuse. Examining the fossilized dermis of an ichthyosaur from Dorset, Whitear (1956) believed that she had identified some brown pigments.

Evidence has recently been uncovered from a clay quarry in Peterborough, England that might demonstrate that Jurassic ichthyosaurs ate belemnites, and what's more, after they ate them, they vomited up the indigestible guards. According to paleontologist Peter Doyle of Greenwich University in London, the find consisted of fossilized shells, whereas previous discoveries had contained only the arm hooklets. In an interview in *New Scientist* (Pearce 2002), Doyle said, "It showed that ichthyosaurs behaved much as sperm whales do today"; that is, they ate the belemnites and then vomited up the bullet-shaped shells. How did Doyle know they were vomited up? Because the shells showed distinctive signs of being etched by the ichthyosaur's digestive juices. How did he know they came from ichthyosaurs? Because 160 million years ago, as shown by other fossils, ichthyosaurs lived there. In an earlier paper, Doyle and Macdonald (1993) wrote that "[belemnite] hooks would effectively interlock in the stomachs of predators making the normal process of excretion difficult and regurgitation a more likely disposal process." Other paleontologists are not so sure that these shells were regurgitated, let alone regurgitated by ichthyosaurs. Also, it has not been shown unequivocally that it was stomach acids that etched the guards; the marks might have been made by acidic sediments in the waters in which the fossils were found.

Dolphins do it, but did ichthyosaurs do it? Richard Cowen suggested that ichthyosaurs leaped out of the water, but the question is unanswerable from the fossil record—which is all we have to go on with ichthyosaurs. Their sleek shapes imitate those of dolphins and argue for leaping ability, as does their need to remain near the surface in order to breathe.* Also, it has been shown

---

* Michael Caldwell of the University of Alberta at Edmonton does not believe that ichthyosaurs should be compared with dolphins. In a November 1999 letter to me, he wrote, "There is nothing dolphin-like about an ichthyosaur. However, there is something ichthyosaur-like about a dolphin. . . . Ichthyosaurs did metabolic things that some extant reptiles do—some more or less closely related (crocodiles and marine iguanas) and unrelated (sea turtles)—all of which, like sharks and tunas, accomplish their active marine habits in ways that are metabolically unfamiliar to metabolic solutions of mammals. There are

that "porpoising"—leaping out of the water when traveling at speed—is an energy-saving proposition, utilized today by dolphins and penguins. In his 1983 study of the energetics of leaping in dolphins and other aquatic animals, R. W. Blake wrote, "Leaping is energetically less efficient than swimming close to the surface up to a certain speed . . . after which it is more efficient." (For a 1999 article in the *Journal of Experimental Biology,* Yoda et al. attached accelerometers to Adélie penguins in the Southern Ocean and calculated that the birds expended as much energy leaping from the water as they did while swimming underwater, concluding "that porpoising may be a better strategy for breathing without reducing swimming speed.") Like their swimming, dolphin leaps are powered by their tail flukes, but penguins use only their wings for propelling themselves in and out of the water. The downstroke of a dolphin's tail is obviously capable of propelling a 500-pound animal completely out of the water, and even killer whales, which can weigh 10 tons, are capable of prodigious aerial gyrations. The side-to-side oscillation of an ichthyosaur's tail is not an ideal engine for an upward leap out of the water, but many game fishes such as marlin, swordfish, and even mako sharks can launch themselves into the air, and they too use a vertical tail fin that moves from side to side. L. B. Halstead (1982) wrote: "In most popular books, ichthyosaurs are shown leaping out of the water rather like dolphins. The main skeleton was in the lower part of the tail, so the side to side movement of the tail not only drove the body forward in undulating movements, but also pulled the tail downwards, which raised the forepart of the body. This meant that the main propulsive force from the tail would have driven the body upward towards the surface and might have lifted it out of the water."

―――――

similarities, but each similarity represents either ancient common ancestry (they are all vertebrates) or convergence (fins in tuna, ichthyosaurs, and dolphins). I see no imperative to explain some unique mechanism that was mammalian-like. Rather, to simply indicate that mammals have neither a superior nor inferior metabolism and physiology. That many animals work with non-mammal systems to accomplish what mammals accomplish. The marvel is not in the mammal-like condition, but rather in the diverse physiologies that achieve similar results. Kind of a 'there's more than one way to skin a cat' sort of thing."

We will probably never know if ichthyosaurs leaped out of the water for greater swimming efficiency, for more effective fish capture, or just for fun, but the image of a fish lizard flying through the air is an intriguing one.

Swimming with fins and tail seems a simple enough business: flexing the tail against water resistance provides forward movement, and the fins act as planes to adjust the angle. But it is not nearly that simple, and opinions differ on the properties of the ichthyosaur tail, with the vertebral column in the lower rather than the upper lobe as it is in sharks. When Keith Thompson and David Simanek (1977) studied locomotion in sharks, they concluded that the heterocercal (one lobe longer than the other) caudal fin is also instrumental in changing the pitch of the shark's body in the water, and subtle adjustments enable the shark to turn and accelerate quickly. Because the ichthyosaurs had to come to the surface regularly to breathe, they had another set of problems to solve in addition to swimming through the water: they had to compensate for the downward thrust generated by the tail fin. Michael Taylor (1987b) wrote that "the caudal fin of ichthyosaurs is usually assumed to have the primary function of propelling the animal, but this does not explain why many ichthyosaurs had a caudal fin of the reversed heterocercal type." He suggested that the tail fin alone could compensate for residual buoyancy, and "there would be no need for the pectoral and pelvic fins to produce any lift." In 1992, McGowan wrote a paper in which he contended that simply reversing the tail structure did not mean that the tails of sharks and ichthyosaurs functioned in the same way, just because the bones were in one lobe rather than the other. "The two structures," he wrote, "are not strictly analogous, and there are functional grounds why the ichthyosaurian tail should not generate vertical forces." He then suggested that even though they operate in a horizontal plane, the symmetrical tail flukes of cetaceans might make a better analogue for the tail fin of ichthyosaurs. Because no human has ever seen an ichthyosaur, our discussions about the dynamics of its swimming only point up the problems inherent in interpreting fossil animals.*

* In 1986, German paleontologist Jurgen Riess published an article in which he argued that ichthyosaurs did not use their tails for locomotion but rather "flew" underwater like penguins, using their foreflippers for propulsion. In his third-year dissertation at the University of Southampton (UK), Darren Naish refuted this peculiar notion, and in a

In a chapter of the 1994 book *Mechanics and Physiology of Animal Swimming,* Judy Massare summarized the literature on ichthyosaur swimming:

De Buffrénil & Mazin (1990) examined the microstructure of limb bones of *Ichthyosaurus* (Late Jurassic) and *Stenopterygius* (Early Jurassic) and *Omphalosaurus* (Early Triassic). They found that the bones displayed woven fiber bone tissue, which is considered indicative of a high absolute rate of bone growth; it is absent among living, slow-growing ectotherms. . . . Buffrénil & Mazin concluded that ichthyosaurs may have had a high metabolic rate, thus an endothermic or incipiently endothermic physiology.

In 2002, in an article in *Nature,* Ryosuke Motani presented a mathematical model of swimming kinematics and fluid mechanics and compared the typical "thunniform" swimmers: eponymous tunas, lamnid sharks, dolphins, and the ichthyosaur *Stenopterygius quadriscissus.* Based on his calculations, he rejected the "popular yet rather teleological view that thunniform tails were selected for their high aspect ratios that increased propulsive efficiency" and substituted the prediction that "wide caudal fin spans, typical of thunniform swimmers, are necessary for large cruisers." He concluded that *Stenopterygius* had raised metabolic rates, and the Jurassic ichthyosaurs "probably had optimal cruising speeds and basal metabolic rates similar to living tunas" – quite an accomplishment, since tunas are usually considered among the fastest fishes in the ocean.

McGowan (1991a) also thinks that ichthyosaurs may have been endothermic, because their body form was like that of the tuna and its relatives, which "suggests that some ichthyosaurs, at least, were capable of maintaining high swimming speeds. It must be emphasized that this did not necessarily apply to all fast swimming ichthyosaurs, no more than it applies to all scombroid fishes. The swordfish, for example, is a large scombroid fish that appears to be every bit as active as a tuna, but it is not endothermic as the tuna appears to be." He also suggests that the larger ichthyosaurs, "just by virtue of their size,

---

popular article in 1998, he wrote, "One clear correlation that does appear to be true for swimming vertebrates concerns the tail. Essentially, if an animal has a propulsive surface on the end of its tail, it uses it."

could probably not have escaped being inertial homeotherms and they probably maintained body temperatures greater than that of the surrounding sea." Size or similarity of body plans does not automatically confer endothermy on ichthyosaurs, but such comparisons are steps in the direction of understanding how these marine reptiles functioned. Unfortunately, other extinct large marine reptiles did not resemble tunas or sharks; some looked like crocodiles, others like swimming sauropod dinosaurs, and some like no other creatures before or since. How did marine crocodiles, plesiosaurs, and mosasaurs manage to retain enough body heat to chase and capture their prey in the ocean? In a 1993 article about predatory marine reptiles, Bakker described the ichthyosaur *Baptanodon* (a synonym for *Ophthalmosaurus*) as "having the deadly advantage of slashing speed. Their bodies have the 40-knot shape preferred by evolution for all its fastest swimming creations." Nowhere in this article does he address the thorny question of how an ichthyosaur might have achieved this "slashing speed." This is a curious omission for Bakker, who is a champion of the idea that ancient predators (theropod dinosaurs) had to have been warm-blooded.

In a 1996 discussion of *Chensaurus* (with *Grippia* and *Utatsusaurus*, the earliest known ichthyosaur), Motani, You, and McGowan described this genus as long and slender (the fossil is about 30 inches long), with a very high vertebral count that suggests an anguilliform (eel-like) swimming motion, probably similar to that of some scyliorhinid sharks. Later ichthyosaurs developed a body plan that was carangiform (shaped like a jacklike fish) and finally thunniform (shaped like a tuna). By the time of the Triassic *Shonisaurus*, swimming efficiency had been sacrificed for sheer size.

Early paleontologists recognized two forms of ichthyosaurs: a broad-finned type they called latipinnate, from the Latin *latus*, meaning "broad," and *pinna*, for "fin"; and longipinnate, from *longus*, which means "long." As earlier defined, latipinnate ichthyosaurs tended to be moderate in size, not exceeding 12 to 13 feet in length, but some of the longipinnates were gigantic; *Cymbospondylus* reached a length of 33 feet, and *Shonisaurus* was 50 feet long, bigger than an adult gray whale. Although the two types of ichthyosaurs occupied the same waters, the latipinnates became extinct by the late Jurassic, while the longipinnates lasted another 40 million years, into the late Cretaceous. Although it might be an artifact of the fossil record, the longipinnate *Platypterygius* appears to have been the last of the ichthyosaurs. The system of separating ichthyosaurs on the basis of fin shape, though useful in the past, is no longer used. In 1972, McGowan published "The Distinction between Longipinnate and Latipinnate Ichthyosaurs," in which the fin structure was correlated with certain cranial features that made it possible "to distinguish between latipinnate and longipinnate ichthyosaurs on the basis of the skull alone." But seven years later, McGowan (1979a) wrote, "I have recently had reason to question the validity of dividing the ichthyosaurs into latipinnates and longipinnates . . . it appears that there are no unequivocal distinctions between latipinnate and longipinnate ichthyosaurs, and that a systematic dichotomy of the group is probably unjustified."

Latipinnate, longipinnate, or intermediate, the forefins of ichthyosaurs are unusual appendages indeed. We are used to seeing the five-fingered manus in animals we know to be descended from early tetrapods, and of course the evolutionary history of cetaceans is partially predicated on the existence of five fingers in the forelimbs, demonstrating that these marine mammals are descended from terrestrial ancestors. What a surprise, then, to see that the fossilized forelimbs of ichthyosaurs exhibit a completely different way of solving the osteological problem of flipper design. As with the cetaceans, there is a compressed humerus (bone of the upper arm) and radius and ulna (bones of the lower arm), but instead of separate fingers, there is an ensemble of tile-shaped bones arranged on the long axis as digits, but squashed together so that they form a solid, flipper-shaped mosaic. There are ichthyosaurs with three digits per flipper; a couple with four; many with five; and some with six, seven, or eight. The foreflippers of *Ichthyosaurus breviceps*, from the Lower Liassic of England, have 27 elements in the longest digit, and Wade (1984) counted 30 in the flipper of *Platypterygius*.

Now considered by some to be the same genus as the British *Temnodontosaurus* (McGowan 1995c), *Leptopterygius* ("narrow fin") was a fast-swimming predator of the Jurassic seas. (*Leptopterygius* has been renamed *Leptonectes*.) *Temnodontosaurus* reached a length of 29 feet and did not share the toothlessness of *Stenopterygius*. It was as large as a modern killer whale, but its teeth were smaller. Its eyes were as large as or larger than those of *Ophthalmosaurus*, and like many

*Bones of the left foreflipper of Ichthyosaurus. Instead of the familiar five fingers, the ichthyosaurs developed tile-shaped bones arranged on the long axis as digits, but squashed together so that they formed a solid, flipper-shaped appendage.*

*The 30-foot-long early Jurassic ichthyosaur* Temnodonto-saurus *had eyes that were 9 inches across, the largest eyes of any animal that has ever lived. It seems reasonable to assume that it hunted in reduced light conditions. The dramatic black and white pattern is purely conjectural.*

ichthyosaurs, it was a teuthophage—a squid eater (Pollard 1968). There are several species of *Temnodontosaurus*, the largest of which is *T. burgundiae*, but it was only about two-thirds as large as the gigantic *Shonisaurus* and had teeth in proportion to its size, suggesting that it fed on large prey items, probably including smaller ichthyosaurs.

One of the most common ichthyosaurs of the English Lower Lias (Lower Jurassic) is *Leptonectes tenuirostris*, found mostly in Somerset. As suggested by its name (*tenuirostris* means "narrow rostrum"), this is a long-snouted species, but not as long-snouted as those that would follow. Its jaws were long and narrow but of equal length, rather like today's franciscana dolphin. The southwestern coast of England has been intensively scoured for fossils since little Mary Anning found the first ichthyosaur in 1811, but in Somerset in 1984, an ichthyosaur was found whose upper jaw extended a considerable distance beyond the lower, or, as McGowan (1986) described it: "mandible shorter than skull but exceeding 60% of skull length. Snout extends well beyond anterior tip of mandible but length of snout . . . not greatly exceeding length of mandible." McGowan named it *Excalibosaurus*, both for its swordlike jaw and for the fact that it was found in the west country, the place of the emergence of King Arthur's sword. There seemed to be a tendency for the upper jaw of *Leptonectes* to extend beyond the lower (McGowan 1989c), so one can postulate a direct evolvement from the geologically older *Leptonectes* to *Excalibosaurus* and finally to *Eurhinosaurus,* the ichthyosaur that looked much like a swordfish, only with teeth.

The first of the swordfish ichthyosaurs was described by Dr. Gideon Mantell in 1851, from the Upper Liassic of Whitby, Yorkshire. He named it *Ichthyosaurus longirostris,* but it was later determined that it differed enough from the other known *Ichthyosaurus* species to warrant its own genus, so it became *Eurhinosaurus longirostris,* the "broad-nosed lizard with a long beak." *Eurhinosaurus* has long, slender pectoral fins and a tail that was probably lunate like that of the broadbill swordfish *Xiphias gladius.* Today's swordfish has a single, fleshy pelvic fin, but like all ichthyosaurs, *Eurhinosaurus* had a pair of hind flippers. Other significant differences included the absence of gills in the ichthyosaurs (they were air-breathing reptiles and had to surface to breathe, whereas fishes breathe water) and the presence of teeth in the jaws (the swordfish is toothless). The *bauplan* of the two is so similar that a layperson shown silhouettes of *Eurhinosaurus* and *Xiphias* would be hard-pressed to differentiate one from the other. The ichthyosaur was considerably larger than

*The 100-million-year-old ichthyosaur* Eurhinosaurus *(top) bears a remarkable resemblance to the modern swordfish* Xiphias gladius. *Unlike the swordfish, the ichthyosaur had teeth.*

the fish, however; swordfish can reach a length of 15 feet (including sword), but some fossils of *Eurhinosaurus longirostris* are more than twice that length.

Those ichthyosaurs that resembled swordfish are a problem for paleontologists, because even today, we are not sure how a swordfish actually uses its sword. It is horizontally flattened and sharp on the edges, so it has been assumed that the swordfish enters a school of fishes and slashes wildly, cutting and otherwise incapacitating the prey items, which it then eats at its leisure. But since nobody has ever witnessed this activity, the actual use of the sword is conjectural.* And if the function of an elongated rostrum has to be conjectured in a living fish, imagine the problems involved in trying to figure out how an animal that has been extinct for 180 million years might have used its elongated upper jaw.

McGowan recognized the usefulness of swordfish studies in relation to the long-snouted ichthyosaurs and studied swordfish in an attempt to learn how *Eurhinosaurus* might have earned a living. (In a 1988 paper, he wrote, "There has been much speculation on the function of the sword, and while it may serve an important hydrodynamic role, much attention has focused on its possible use during feeding. Anecdotal accounts are given of swordfishes slashing their

* In their 1968 study, "Food and Feeding Habits of the Swordfish," Scott and Tibbo wrote, "There is a special appeal in studies of food and food-getting among the swordfish and spearfishes because of the unique spear-like rostral development and its use as a slashing instrument to maim or injure smaller fishes upon which they feed. The swordfish differs from the spearfishes (marlins and sailfishes) in that the sword is long and it is dorsoventrally compressed (hence the name broadbill) whereas the spearfishes have a shorter spear and it is slightly compressed laterally. Thus, the swordfish appears to be more highly specialized for lateral slashing. Such a specialization would seem to be pointless unless directed to a vertically oriented prey, or unless the swordfish slashes while vertically oriented, as when ascending or descending." In contrast to almost every other suggestion about swordfish feeding techniques, Charles O. Mather (1976) wrote, "Essentially a bottom feeder, a broadbill is believed to use his bill as a tool to obtain crustaceans from their cracks or attachments and to enjoy crabs and crayfish." In *Living Fishes of the World* (1961), ichthyologist Earl Herald (who ought to have known better) wrote, "the sword may be used to impale fishes during feeding," which seems highly unlikely, because the prey fish would offer no resistance to the impaler, and even if such a process could work, the swordfish would be unable to get at the dead fishes stuck on the end of its nose.

way through schools of fishes and gathering up the incapacitated victims, but inherent problems make direct observations virtually impossible.") Most ichthyosaurs had teeth, and they undoubtedly used them to catch their prey. It is not clear, however, what purpose was served by the teeth in that part of the upper jaw of *Eurhinosaurus*. Because of the severe overbite, the upper teeth could not make contact with the teeth in the lower jaw or, for that matter, with anything at all.

While excavating a drainage channel near Stowbridge in Norfolk, England, in 1958, workmen came upon a large, long-snouted ichthyosaur skull, along with some vertebrae, ribs, and other fragments. It was provisionally identified as a species of the Jurassic ichthyosaur *Ophthalmosaurus*, but the eye sockets were not nearly as large, so it was reclassified in 1976 by McGowan. Because it had powerful jaws and teeth, he named this killer whale–sized ichthyosaur *Grendelius mordax*—the generic name from Grendel, a legendary monster in *Beowulf*, and the specific name from *mordax*, Latin for "biting." Along with *Excalibosaurus*, *Grendelius* was one of McGowan's more inspired names, but alas, it didn't endure. In 1989, another specimen was found in the Kimeridge Clay of Dorset, and when McGowan examined the new material (particularly the newly excavated forefin), he realized that it should actually be placed in an existing genus *(Brachypterygius)* that had been erected in 1922 by German paleontologist Frederich von Huene. Too bad; *Grendelius* was a wonderful name.

Many of the ichthyosaurs had large eyes, but the largest relative to body size belonged to the appropriately named *Ophthalmosaurus;* its eyes were 8 inches across in a 15-foot-long animal. (The eyes of a 15-foot pilot whale are about an inch across, and the eyes of a 100-foot blue whale, probably the largest animal that has ever lived, are about 8 inches across.) In a 1999 study, Motani, Rothschild, and Wahl measured the sclerotic rings of *Temnodontosaurus* and found that a 30-foot-long individual had an eye that measured nearly 10 inches in diameter, making it the "largest eye in the history of life." But *Ophthalmosaurus* had the largest eyes relative to body length of any vertebrate that has ever lived.* The authors found that the f-number (the measure

---

* The giant squid *(Architeuthis)* is usually said to have the largest eyes in the animal kingdom, often described as being "as big as dinner plates" (a standard dinner plate is 10 inches in

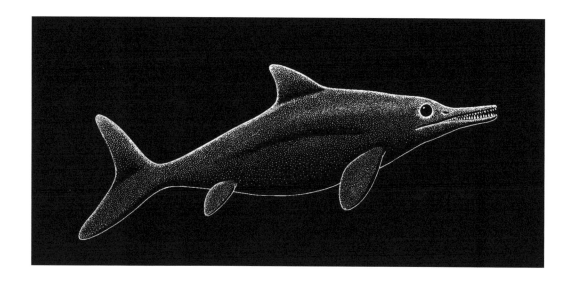

of relative aperture used in camera lenses) for *Ophthalmosaurus* was the lowest of any of the ichthyosaurs (the lower the f-number, the more light the eye picks up). They believe that this ichthyosaur had the ability to see where light barely penetrated and that it "probably had higher visual sensitivity than a cat," an animal justly renowned for its vision in low light. We know that these big-eyed reptiles were habitual deep divers, because their fossilized skeletons showed evidence of the bends. We have no way of knowing if the squid that *Ophthalmosaurus* fed on were bioluminescent, but because so many living squid species are, it seems a reasonable assumption, and big eyes with a very low f-number would be especially useful in picking up flickering flashes of light from squid in the otherwise pitch-blackness of the depths.

"Why did some ichthyosaurs have such large eyes?" asked Stuart Humphries and Graeme Ruxton in a 2002 article in the *Journal of Experimental Biology.* They answered, "sensitivity to low light at great depth has recently been

---

diameter) or even "automobile hubcaps," but the scientific literature contains no such dimensions (Ellis 1999). Motani et al. (1999) cited Roper and Boss's 1982 *Scientific American* article, which states that the eyes of the giant squid are "enormous, larger than the headlights of an automobile . . . with a diameter approaching 25 centimeters (10 inches) they are the largest eyes in the animal kingdom."

suggested, [but] previous estimates may be even more interesting than they first appear." Humphries and Ruxton found that harp seals (*Phoca groenlandica*) can see at light levels found at approximately 2,000 feet, but because the eyes of the ichthyosaurs were so much larger than those of harp seals, the ichthyosaurs may have been able to see at substantially greater depths. Using the data of Motani et al. (1999), the investigators found that *Ophthalmosaurus* had a sensitivity two and a half to four times that of an elephant seal, so it could probably see in light that was approximately 25 percent of the minimum requirements of the elephant seal. These large seals are known to forage at depths of more than 3,280 feet, and Humphries and Ruxton realized that "visual sensitivity is insufficient to explain why these ichthyosaurs had such large eyes." But in addition to being able to see at very low light levels, the large-eyed ichthyosaurs were able to resolve fine detail into an image, indicating an extraordinarily high level of visual acuity. They concluded: "A further possible consequence of selection for high visual acuity is the use of visual signaling or individual recognition between ichthyosaurs, perhaps related to mating or coordinated foraging. . . . In summary, we suggest that the large eyes of *Ophthalmosaurus* are the result of simultaneous pressure for sensitivity, allowing prey detection at considerable depths, combined with pressure for high acuity, allowing these animals to hunt small, fast-moving prey."

Of all the ichthyosaurs, *Ophthalmosaurus* was also the most streamlined, with a teardrop-shaped body tapering to a narrow, pointed snout at one end and a lunate tail at the other. "Repeated Diving Was Not for All Ichthyosaurs" was the title of an abstract by Rothschild, Motani, and Wahl presented at the September 1999 Society for Vertebrate Paleontology meeting in Denver. By examining the bones of post-Triassic fossil ichthyosaurs, they suggested that those species with a pronounced downward tailbend (and therefore an efficient heterocercal caudal fin) were probably capable of continuous swimming, which meant repeated dives. Unfortunately, the researchers found that the ichthyosaurs that dived the deepest and most frequently, such as *Ophthalmosaurus*, were susceptible to the bends. When animals dive deeply, nitrogen in the blood is forced into solution by the increased pressure, and as they ascend, it becomes a gas again, but often as bubbles that remain in the joints. Nitrogen bubbles in the brain can be lethal, but they usually form in other places where they are painful but not life-threatening. That ichthyosaurs got the bends suggests that they had not perfected their diving physiology the way today's marine mammals have. (Rothschild and Martin have also found evidence of the bends in deep-diving mosasaurs.)

The eyes of *Ophthalmosaurus* may have been among the largest relative to body size (those of *Temnodontosaurus* were larger in absolute size), but how these big-eyed ichthyosaurs captured their food is not immediately evident. One might assume that a creature built like a dolphin would have a similar diet, but most of the known fossil skulls of *Ophthalmosaurus* are toothless, a condition called *edentulousness.* This has led to an assumption (Andrews 1910) that *Ophthalmosaurus* must have fed on soft-bodied animals like squid and may have used some sort of suction method to capture them. But when Angela Kirton (1983) examined the skulls of various Jurassic ichthyosaurs from England, she found that many of the large skulls did indeed have teeth. There are two ways of explaining edentulousness in adult *Ophthalmosaurus:* either they lost their teeth as they matured, or they had perfectly serviceable teeth that were loosely attached (like the teeth of some sharks) and were lost during the hundreds of millions of years between the time the animal died and the time the fossils were discovered. Some believe the former explanation, and others subscribe to the second theory. Ryosuke Motani, who provided this infor-

*The 22-foot-long ichthyosaur* Platypterygius *shown chasing an ammonite, an extinct cephalopod.*

mation (personal communication 2000), said, "After seeing the specimens [Kirton] mentioned, I decided that she was probably right. I have been using Kirton's reconstruction of the *Ophthalmosaurus* skull with robust teeth, but I think I belong to the minority at this point."

Teeth or no teeth, these ichthyosaurs were squid eaters, like many dolphins and beaked whales today, and they probably sucked them up. Suction feeding has long been postulated in various living cetaceans, particularly sperm whales and beaked whales (Heyning and Mead 1996). In a study published in April 2000, Alexander Werth noted that "several authors . . . have postulated the use of suction feeding by odontocetes, particularly large teuthophagous (squid-eating) species with blunt rostra and reduced dentition." Werth filmed captive pilot whales that had been stranded and rehabilitated and observed that "food was often ingested without grasping with teeth." *Ophthalmosaurus* is anything but short-snouted, but the beaked whales — whose common name comes from their elongated rostra, which have been likened to birds' beaks — are largely edentulous, and they are known squid eaters. In most species of beaked whales, the females and juveniles are toothless, and the males have teeth that are believed to be used in intraspecific fighting.

By the mid-Cretaceous (105 to 85 million years ago), the day of the ichthyosaurs was passing, and only one clearly defined genus remained. As the sole surviving genus of a long and rich heritage, *Platypterygius* was one of the most widely distributed of all ichthyosaurs, appearing in fossil formations in North and South America, England, Europe, Russia, India, and Australia. The first Australian ichthyosaur remains were discovered in Australia in 1865 near the Flinders River in Queensland. Since then, several other fossils have been found in Queensland, all of which were described as *Ichthyosaurus australis*, but they have since been reassigned to *Platypterygius australis* and then renamed again as *Platypterygius longmani*. These ichthyosaurs are characterized by their broad front flippers, and because they have multiple accessory digits, they are popularly (but incorrectly) known as longipinnate ichthyosaurs. The most complete specimen was found in Queensland in 1934. An 18-foot-long sub-adult, it lacks all but one tail fin vertebra, the pelvic girdle and hind limbs, parts of the pectoral girdle, and some ribs. A larger specimen was 23 feet in total length, probably an adult.

The "youngest" ichthyosaur fossils (so far) are about 93.5 million years old and were found in the Upper Cenomanian of Bavaria (Bardet et al. 1994). *Platypterygius* was a large animal, reaching a length of 23 feet. Its jaws were long and slender, its eyes were relatively small (but only when compared with its huge-eyed relatives such as *Ophthalmosaurus*), and its foreflippers were the widest of any ichthyosaur's (*Platypterygius* means "broad fin"). This species was also polydactylic, with as many as ten rows of squarish bones in the flipper. Sander (2000) wrote, "this is the only instance of polydactyly in amniotes that is not pathologic." Like all later ichthyosaurs, this genus had a symmetrical tail fin, with the vertebral support in the lower lobe. The tail was certainly used for propulsion, but the narrow-based fins were probably used for sculling, adding another element to the propulsive powers of this reptile. (The reduced hind fins were probably not particularly useful and are comparable to the paired pelvic fins of sharks, which probably function as secondary stabilizers in swimming.)

Several attempts have been made to place ichthyosaurs in deposits later than the Cenomanian (93.5 million years ago), but these have proved unsuccessful; in her 1992 review of the stratigraphic evidence, Nathalie Bardet wrote, "A review of these post-Cenomanian ichthyosaur remains reveals that all are doubtful either from a stratigraphic or systematic point of view." After listing the various "systematically doubtful specimens" and the "stratigraphically doubtful specimens," Bardet speculated on the extinction of the ichthyosaurs:

> The group, being pelagic since the Jurassic, was potentially insensitive to the great anoxic event characterizing this period. Biological factors such as replacement by mosasaurs are debatable, as these two groups probably did not occupy the same ecological niche. The great extinction suffered by marine invertebrates, especially cephalopods, at the Cenomanian-Turonian boundary, may have preferentially affected specialized predators such as ichthyosaurs more than generalist ones such as plesiosaurs, in terms of a break in their food chain. If the extinction of ichthyosaurs is linked to the Cenomanian-Turonian extinction events, such a break in the food chain may be proposed as an extinction scenario.

But Theagarten Lingham-Soliar disagrees with Bardet on the reasons for the disappearance of the ichthyosaurs. In the introduction to his 2002 paper "Extinction of Ichthyosaurs: A Catastrophic or Evolutionary Paradigm?" he wrote,

> The present study proposes a biological explanation, consistent with the evolutionary paradigm, viz., that by the end of the Jurassic/early Cretaceous, ichthyosaur monopoly of a thunniform body shape and commensurate mechanical design ended and that this heralded their demise. The emergence of fast-swimming fishes with streamlined bodies placed new energetic costs on ichthyosaur predation from the perspectives of both more evasive prey and more effective predators. Furthermore, ichthyosaurs were K-strategists, producing a small number of large young. Predator avoidance in ichthyosaur juveniles, by high-speed flight, was placed under greater stress from the newly emerging, streamlined, fast-swimming bony fishes and sharks. . . . By the closing stages of the Late Cretaceous pursuit predation in marine reptiles was almost completely replaced by lie-in-wait or ambush predatory tactics. The hydrodynamic body shape of ichthyosaurs gave way to the long-bodied design, exemplified in the mosasaurs, a group of marine reptiles that arose in the latest stages of the Cretaceous. The latter design is more effective for rapid starts and burst speeds, useful in ambush predation. Among plesiosaurs, only the less hydrodynamic long-necked elasmosaurs survived to the last stages of the Upper Cretaceous. Their extremely long necks, rather than long bodies, may have been an alternative adaptation for ambush strikes.

In a 1999 article devoted to the aberrant African mosasaur *Goronyosaurus*, Lingham-Soliar speculated on the extinction of the ichthyosaurs:

> An understanding of mosasaur evolutionary success is critical to our understanding of the extinction and reduction of other marine vertebrates during the Cretaceous. Jurassic and Cretaceous ichthyosaurs had torpedo-shaped bodies and a deep, hydrodynamically-shaped tail, resulting in high-speed swimming. It is almost paradoxical that they should have given way to the hydrodynamically inferior mosasaurs. It points, however, to a chang-

ing environment that was clearly conducive to long-bodied animals. Jurassic ichthyosaurs had become "boxed in" by too much specialization. High-speed, highly evasive fishes were becoming dominant in Cretaceous waters and pursuit predatory tactics of ichthyosaurs, for instance, are energetically very expensive. . . . The sit-and-wait or ambush strategies favored . . . mosasaurs and it is no coincidence that Cretaceous ichthyosaurs were reverting to longer forms such as first seen in their early history in the Triassic. But it was too little and too late for them. It is even less of a coincidence that at precisely this time the ichthyosaurs became extinct and the supreme long-bodied mosasaurs arose.

The ichthyosaurs are among the most highly developed reptiles that ever lived. They were superbly designed for earning a living, with their tooth-studded beaks, large eyes, powerful tails, and two sets of steering fins. They came in all shapes and sizes, from small to extra large. Some of them might have been endothermic. They bypassed the limitations imposed by having to lay eggs on land by giving birth to live young. They were to the oceans what the (nonavian) carnivorous dinosaurs were to the land, and for the same amount of time. What happened to them? We can only speculate. "Well before the close of the Jurassic," wrote McGowan (1973a), "their numbers began to dwindle, and relatively few [species] survived into the Cretaceous. While the last chapters of the Age of Reptiles were being written on the land, the last of the ichthyosaurs slipped quietly and unpretentiously into oblivion."

# The Plesiosaurs

*There were no real Sea Serpents in the Mesozoic Era, but the Plesiosaurs were the next thing to it. The Plesiosaurs were reptiles who had gone back to the water because it seemed like a good idea at the time. As they knew little or nothing about swimming, they rowed themselves around in the water with their four paddles, instead of using their tails for propulsion like the brighter marine animals. This made them too slow to catch fish, so they kept adding vertebrae to their necks until their necks were longer than all the rest of their body. Then they would dart their heads at the fish from a distance of twenty-five or thirty feet. Thus the Plesiosaurs resembled the modern Sea Serpent above the water-line, though they were almost a total loss farther down. They might have had a useful career as Sea Serpents, but they were before their time. There was nobody to scare except fish, and that was hardly worth while. Their heart was not in the work. As they were made so poorly, Plesiosaurs had very little fun. They had to go ashore to lay their eggs and that sort of thing. They also tried to get along with gizzards instead of stomachs, swallowing pebbles after each meal to grind their food. At least, pebbles have been found near fossil Plesiosaurs, and to a scientist that means that the Plesiosaur had a gizzard. During the Cretaceous Period many of the inland seas dried up, leaving the Plesiosaurs stranded without any fish. Just about that time Mother Nature scrapped the whole Age of Reptiles and called for a new deal. And you see what she got.*

*— Will Cuppy (1941)*

Less enjoyable—but probably more useful—than Cuppy's definition is Glenn Storrs's 1997 classification of the genus *Plesiosaurus,* one of the many genera that make up this fascinating group:

> Plesiosaurs (Diapsida: Sauropterygia: Plesiosauria) are extinct Mesozoic marine reptiles comprising one of the most successful and widely distributed groups of marine reptiles. They developed a wide range early in their history and some representatives of the clade survived into the Maastrichtian, becoming extinct perhaps only at the terminal Cretaceous. The evolutionary and systematic relationships of the Plesiosauria, however, are almost completely unknown. The group appears as isolated bones and associated partial skeletons in the Middle Triassic (Anisian) of Germany, but the first unambiguous, fully articulated specimens occur in the uppermost Triassic and Lower Jurassic (Liassic) of England. By Liassic times, the plesiosaurs were particularly diverse, already fully marine, and highly modified from the presumed terrestrial condition of their forebears.

The name *plesiosaur* means "near reptile," and it was bestowed on the earliest fossils by Conybeare because he believed that they represented animals that were on their way out of the sea to become the terrestrial reptiles.* We now know that it was actually the reverse—they are descended from land reptiles that returned to the sea. These great oceangoing creatures dominated Mesozoic seas and were powerful predators, armed with a mouthful of sharp teeth. Unlike the ichthyosaurs, which looked rather like dolphins, plesiosaurs came in all shapes and sizes, many of them unique. Some had short necks and huge heads, while others had long necks and tiny heads. All four limbs were modified into flippers, and the shoulders and pelvic girdle were formed of broad sheets of bone to which the powerful swimming muscles were attached.

* On the subject of the name, Robin O'Keefe (2002a) wrote: "The term 'plesiosaur,' meaning 'near lizard' is not an informative name from a modern perspective. However, when Conybeare (1822) coined the term to describe fossils from the English Lias, little was known concerning any extinct marine reptile. The realization that plesiosaurs were a completely extinct group was significant at a time when the occurrence of extinction itself was uncertain. These 'near-reptiles' were named at a time when there was no need, and no context, for a more specific term."

The flippers were long and narrow, but there is no consensus among paleontologists as to how these great reptiles actually moved through the water. Did they pull through the water in a "breaststroke," or "fly" like turtles or penguins? There are no fossil plesiosaurs that contain unborn fetuses, so we do not know if these reptiles gave birth to live young in the water or came ashore to lay their eggs. The dense rib cage, especially in the belly region, has suggested to some that they might have come ashore, but with flippers instead of feet and, in some cases, an extremely long neck, they would have been very awkward out of the water and susceptible to predation by land animals such as crocodiles or carnivorous dinosaurs. It now seems unlikely that the plesiosaurs ever left the water.

The description of a plesiosaur as "a snake threaded through the body of a turtle" has variously been attributed to Conybeare, De la Beche, Mantell, Owen, and both William Buckland and his son Frank, but its actual origin remains a mystery. In his 1824 description of the first plesiosaur fossil, Conybeare wrote, "In its motion, the animal resembled the turtle more than any other, and the turtle also, as it was better remarked, could we divest it of its shelly case, would present some slight approach in its general appearance to the plesiosaurus." In 1837, Mantell wrote, "The reptile combines in its structure the head of a lizard with teeth like those of a crocodile, a neck resembling the body of serpent, a trunk and tail resembling of the proportions of a quadruped, with paddles like those of turtles." In his 1914 *Water Reptiles of the Past and Present*, Samuel Williston wrote, "It was Dean Buckland who facetiously likened the plesiosaurs to a snake threaded through the shell of a turtle, but what Buckland actually wrote (in the 1836 *Bridgewater Treatise*), was: 'To the head of a lizard, it united the teeth of a crocodile; a neck of enormous length, resembling the body of a serpent; a trunk and tail having the proportions of any ordinary quadruped, the ribs of a chameleon and the paddles of a whale.' "

The enigmatic *Pistosaurus*, which gets its name from the Greek *pistos*, for "liquid," the medium in which it lived, was found in the Muschelkalk (middle Triassic) of Germany. It is known only from a skull and a postcranial skeleton that was found in the same location, but not in direct articulation (Sues 1987b). "If this association is correct," wrote Carroll (1988), "this genus combines a postcranial skeleton like that of the typical nothosaurs with a skull similar to that of plesiosaurs." This 10-foot-long reptile bears some skeletal similarities to both nothosaurs and plesiosaurs, but, as is nearly always the case, the skeletal material that would show a transition between the two groups has not been found. So even though the "transition" cannot be documented, it seems likely that the pistosaurids are somehow connected with the evolution of true plesiosaurs and are, according to McHenry (personal communication), "highly tempting candidates for the role of plesiosaur ancestor."

One of the earliest plesiosaurs (as opposed to one of the earliest found plesiosaur fossils) was *Archaeonectrus*, whose name means "ancient swimmer." Previously known as *Plesiosaurus rostratus* (Owen 1865), this 12-foot-long species was found in the early Jurassic formations of Charmouth, England, and later in Siberia. Both regions were semitropical 200 million years ago. *Archaeonectrus* had a large, elongated head with a narrow snout, only 20 vertebrae in its neck, and hind flippers that were larger than its forelimbs. When Richard Owen described *Plesiosaurus rostratus* in 1865, he noted that some of the centra of the tail vertebrae were compressed, suggesting the presence of a vertical tail fin.

Plesiosaurs seem to have evolved during the Triassic, some 250 million years ago, but only began to flourish and proliferate in the Jurassic, 200 to 140 million years ago. The earliest forms were probably small, no longer than about 10 feet from nose to tail, and had comparatively short necks, with about 32 vertebrae. In time, they became larger and their necks became longer, and the latest forms, from the Cretaceous (140 to 65 million years ago), had incredible snakelike necks and reached lengths of 47 feet. They had four paddle-like limbs that look smaller in the Cretaceous forms, indicating a reduced dependence on maneuverability and an increased emphasis on ambush predation. These marine reptiles have been divided into two major groups, differentiated by the length of their necks. Traditionally, the plesiosaurs were long-necked, small-headed creatures, whereas the pliosaurs had short necks and large heads. A succinct differentiation is given by Thulborn and Turner (1993):

The adaptive radiation of aquatic reptiles in the order Sauropterygia culminated in two extremes of body form. At one extreme were the Cretaceous elasmosaurs (plesiosaurs of the family Elasmosauridae, superfamily Plesiosauridae), readily identified on account of the remarkably long neck and a relatively small and delicate skull. At the other extreme were the Jurassic and Cretaceous pliosaurs (superfamily Pliosauroidea) distinguished by a relatively short neck and a massive skull that some times attained a length of more than 3 meters. Elasmosaurs were probably slow-cruising feeders on fishes and cephalopods, whereas the biggest pliosaurs have been regarded as savage predators, with habits broadly similar to those of the Late Cretaceous mosasaurs and the existing killer whales.

The plesiosaurs and the pliosaurs shared the oceans with the ichthyosaurs for about 150 million years, but the last of these giant marine reptiles died out around 65 million years ago (around the time of the departure of the dinosaurs), leaving no descendants.

There are, however, some who believe that there is still at least one plesiosaur swimming around in a lake in Scotland. Although it has been identified as a dinosaur, a fish, a snake, a sea serpent, a giant eel, an otter, or an elephant, the Loch Ness monster is most often described as some sort of plesiosaur. The idea of a long-necked, plesiosaur-like creature has caught the fancy of "Nessie" watchers, and many of the "sightings" describe such a creature, largely based on the famous "surgeon's photograph" of 1934 (now revealed as a hoax involving a sculpted model and a toy submarine), which shows an animal with a long, sinuous neck and a small head. Nessie seems to have vanished into the mists of hoax and folklore, although there are many who travel to Inverness hoping for a sighting. The ancient plesiosaurs are all gone, as are the dinosaurs — unless you believe that birds are their lineal descendants, in which case there are feathered dinosaurs perched in the trees outside your windows.

Stranger than the other plesiosaurs were the incredible elasmosaurs. It is difficult enough to visualize a creature like *Muraenosaurus,* from the Jurassic, with a neck so long that it was likened to an eel, but some of the elasmosaurs had necks longer than their bodies and tails combined. At the end of the neck was a tiny head that looked altogether too small. The earliest plesiosaurs had only moderately long necks, but they got longer and longer until we get to

*Elasmosaurus*, which, at a known length of 47 feet (more than half of which was neck, ending in a tiny head), was among the longest of the plesiosaurs. (*Elasmosaurus* means "thin-plated lizard," for the platelike nature of its pelvic bones.) Whereas some of the earlier plesiosaurs had 28 neck vertebrae, *Elasmosaurus* had more than 70.* "An active piscivore with a long, flexible neck," *Hydrotherosaurus* ("fishing lizard") *alexandrae* (for Annie Alexander) was one of the longest of the elasmosaurs according to S. P. Welles (1943), who unearthed it in Fresno County, California. With 63 cervical (neck) vertebrae, 17 dorsals (back), and 30 caudals (tail), *Hydrotherosaurus* was one of the longest-necked (and longest) of all the elasmosaurs, reaching an estimated overall length of 42 feet. In his restoration, Welles raked the ribs sharply backward, claiming that some of the earlier reconstructions were misinterpretations, based on postmortem crushing of the skeletons.

* The 70-vertebrae neck makes *Elasmosaurus* the longest of the plesiosaurs, but it is not the longest-necked animal on record. That distinction goes to the terrestrial sauropod dinosaur *Mamenchisaurus*, which had a *neck* that was 46 feet long — equal to the total length of *Elasmosaurus* — but *Mamenchisaurus* had only 19 cervical vertebrae.

*One of the longer-necked elasmosaurs,* Muraenosaurus *gets its name from* muraena, *the Latin name for the moray* eel, *and* saurus, *for reptile.* Muraenosaurus *was 20 feet long.*

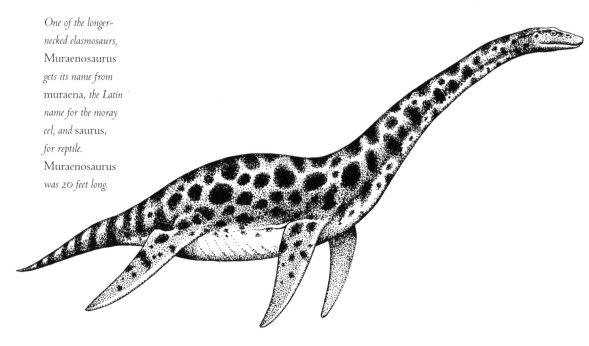

In an 1824 letter to De la Beche (quoted in Rudwick 1992) about the newly discovered plesiosaur, Conybeare wrote, "He probably swam at the surface and fished with his long neck, or lurked in shoal water hid among the weeds, poking his nose to the surface to breathe and catching all the small fry that came within reach of his long sweep, but he must have kept as much as possible out of reach of *ichthyosauri*, a very junior member of whom with his long powerful jaws could have bit his neck in two without ceremony."

In 1821, De la Beche and Conybeare published "Notice of the Discovery of a New Fossil Animal, Forming a Link between the *Ichthyosaurus* and the Crocodile, Together with General Remarks on the Osteology of *Ichthyosaurus*," based on material found by Mary Anning of Lyme Regis. They named the creature *Plesiosaurus dolichodeirus*, which means "near lizard with a long neck." The skeleton, now in the Natural History Museum in London, was 7½ feet long from the tip of its skull to the tip of its tail. Its little head and long neck were approximately the same length as its torso and tail, and it had needle-like teeth in both the upper and lower jaws. Some recent books indicate incorrectly that *Plesiosaurus* means "ribbon lizard," supposedly for the ribbon-like

*This is Plesiosaurus dolichodeirus, described in 1821 by Henry De la Beche and William Conybeare from the skeleton of a "fossil animal" found by Mary Anning at Lyme Regis. The skeleton, now in the Natural History Museum in London, is 7½ feet long.*

appearance of the neck spines along its backbone, but there is no basis in Greek or Latin for such a reading. Conybeare wrote, "The name I have originally given to this animal, *Plesiosaurus* (approximate to the Saurians), may appear rather vague in this stage of our knowledge, and an appellation derived from its peculiar length of neck might be preferred; but for the present I shall retain the old generic name, adding for specific distinction the well-known Homeric epithet *Dolichodeirus* ("long-necked"), as characterizing the most striking peculiarity of its osteology." The archetypal genus *Plesiosaurus* (De la Beche and Conybeare 1821) became a sort of grab bag for subsequently discovered plesiosaurs, even though many of them were dramatically different (Storrs 1997).

Joseph Pentland, who was so helpful to Conybeare and Buckland in the proper identification of the ichthyosaur, also contributed to their understanding of the plesiosaurs. In a letter to Buckland dated June 20, 1820 (reproduced in Delair and Sarjeant 1975), Pentland wrote, "As to Mr. Conybeare's new Animals, I will not pretend to judge, but the disposition of the bones of the arm seem to put beyond a doubt that it is very different from the *Ictyosaurus* [*sic*]. . . . From the sketch, I clearly see that the bone can only be the Coracoid . . . so if you have any influence with Mr. Conybeare you would do well to suggest to him to correct the fault he is about to commit by calling it the Clavicle. . . . The name of Plesiosaurus is a very good name I think, perhaps a little too relative; would it not be better to give some other name which would express either some peculiar structure in the animal, or one relative to its high antiquity, while retaining the termination *Saurus,* which I think has been very happily chosen." Conybeare seems to have been impressed with Pentland's suggestions about nomenclature; although he stuck to the name *Plesiosaurus,* he added *dolichodeirus* ("long neck") to the more complete specimen found by Mary Anning in 1824.

In 1832, Dr. Richard Harlan was presented with several enormous vertebrae by a gentleman named Bry, who had found them on the Ouchita River in Louisiana. Harlan submitted a description of the bones to the American Philosophical Society in Philadelphia, and his description ("Notice of the Fossil Bones Found in the Tertiary Formation of the State of Louisiana") was published in the society's *Transactions* in 1834. Evidently, Harlan had read (or read of) Conybeare's 1824 paper "On the Discovery of an Almost Perfect Skeleton of the Plesiosaurus," for he wrote that his fossils possessed "characters which enable us to refer it to an extinct genus of the order 'Enalio-Sauri,' of Conybeare, which includes numerous extinct genera of marine lizards or crocodiles, generally possessing gigantic proportions, which have hitherto been found only in the sub-cretaceous series . . . from England, France, and Germany, and in the supposed equivalent formations in North America." Harlan compared the bones to those of the various gigantic reptiles that had been identified by 1834 (*Mosasaurus, Geosaurus, Megalosaurus, Iguanodon, Ichthyosaurus,* and *Plesiosaurus*) and concluded that his bones belonged to a plesiosaur, 80 to 100 feet in length. Accordingly, he named it *Basilosaurus,* "king of the lizards."

It wasn't actually a plesiosaur — in fact, it wasn't a reptile at all — and it wasn't 100 feet long. Eight years later, Harlan brought the bones to England and showed them to Richard Owen, who compared the double teeth of *Basilosaurus* with those of other reptiles and mammals and concluded that the teeth were actually those of a primitive whale. Because it wasn't a lizard, the name *Basilosaurus* was completely inappropriate, so Owen proposed the name *Zeuglodon,* which means "yoked teeth." In the 1842 Geological Society report on Owen's observations, we read: "Mr. Owen, in compliance with the suggestion of Dr. Harlan, who, having compared with Mr. Owen the microscopic structure of the teeth of the Basilosaurus with those of the Dugong and other animals, admits the correctness of the inferences of its mammiferous nature, proposes to substitute for the name of the *Basilosaurus* that of *Zeuglodon,* suggested by the form of the posterior molars which resembled two teeth tied or yoked together." Unfortunately, the rules of zoological nomenclature dictate that the first name has priority, no matter how misguided, so because Harlan named it first, the early whale is still known technically as "king of the lizards."

Genuine plesiosaur fossils, among the first of the marine reptiles to be discovered in England, were highly prized by museums and collectors and often commanded high prices. When a fossilized skeleton of *Plesiosaurus dolichodeirus* was found in 1841 at Saltwick (Yorkshire), it was first displayed in a room over the Whitby shop of one Matthew Green, where this notice was posted:

NOW EXHIBITING DAILY,
In a Room over the Shop owned by Mr. Matthew Green, Haggersgate,
A SPLENDID AND VERY VALUABLE FOSSIL
"PLESIOSAURUS DOLOCHODEIRUS"

Recently Found in Whitby Cliffs.

This unparalleled Organic Specimen of so extraordinary an Animal measures 15 feet in length, and 8 feet 5 inches across the fore Paddles. The Neck is 6 feet 6 inches long, exclusive of the Head.

Among the multiplicity of Fossil Petrifactions discovered in the neighbourhood of Whitby, this by far surpasses all, even the famed Crocodile in the Whitby Museum; indeed it is questioned whether any fossil remains were ever discovered equal to that of this wonderful species of the Plesiosaurus tribe. The specimen is entire, without, we believe, a single joint wanting, and very cleverly excavated from the strata in which it was found. Among the notes appended to Goldsmith's Animated Nature, by Alexander Whitelaw, we find the following remarks in reference to this singular species: "Perhaps there has been no animal created of a more extraordinary form than the *Plesiosaurus Dolochodeirus.* In the length of the neck it far exceeds even the longest necked birds. It is in this species five times the length of its head; the trunk of the body four times the length of the head; and the tail three times; while the head itself is only a thirtieth part of the whole body. From the whole physiology of the Animal, Mr. Conybeare says, that it was aquatic is evident from the form of its paddles; that it was marine is equally so, from the remains with which it is universally associated; that it may have occasionally visited the shore, the resemblance of its extremities to those of the turtle, may lead us to conjecture; its motion, however, must have been very awkward on land; its long neck must have impeded its progress through the water, presenting a striking contrast to the organization which so admirably fits the Ichthyosaurus to cut through the waves. May it not therefore, be concluded, that it swam upon or near the surface, arching back its long neck like the swan, and occasionally darting it down at the fish, which happened to float within its reach."

The "splendid and very valuable fossil" soon became the subject of a bitter dispute between the museums at Whitby and Cambridge, and after many acrimonious letters between the two institutions, it was finally bought by the Fitzwilliam Museum of Cambridge for £230 (Osborne 1998). It is an almost complete skeleton, 15 feet from the tip of the snout to the end of the tail, and its "paddles" were so large that Owen originally named it *Plesiosaurus grandipinnins*. It can be seen today in the Sedgwick Museum of Geology, Cambridge.

In America, nothing did more to publicize the budding science of vertebrate paleontology than the feud between Edward Drinker Cope and Othniel Charles Marsh. In 1868, they were collecting fossils in western Kansas, digging on their own, but also employing various "collectors" to find material and ship it back east to them. (Cope was affiliated with the Academy of Natural Sciences of Philadelphia, Marsh with Yale University.) In 1867, Theophilus Turner, a physician at Fort Wallace, Kansas, collected three vertebrae and sent them to Cope, who asked Turner to collect the rest of the fossil and ship it to Philadelphia. When Cope examined the bones, he realized that the original owner was obviously related to the plesiosaurs, but in addition to its short neck and unusually long tail, there was something strange about the vertebrae. In the 1869 *Proceedings of the Boston Society of Natural History*, Cope published descriptions of various reptiles, including one that he named *Elasmosaurus platyurus* ("flat-tailed, thin-plate reptile"). Because most plesiosaurs had long necks and short tails, he erected a new order to accommodate it, which he called Streptosauria, from the Greek *streptos*, which means "turned" or "reversed," referring to the "articular processes of the vertebrae [which are] reversed in their direction, viz., the anterior looking downwards, the posterior upwards." Unfortunately, Cope had completely misunderstood the vertebrae, assembled the skeleton backward, and put the head at the wrong end. He was embarrassed into correcting his blunder when Marsh gleefully pointed it out, exacerbating the bitter rivalry between the two paleontologists that would last until Cope died in 1897.

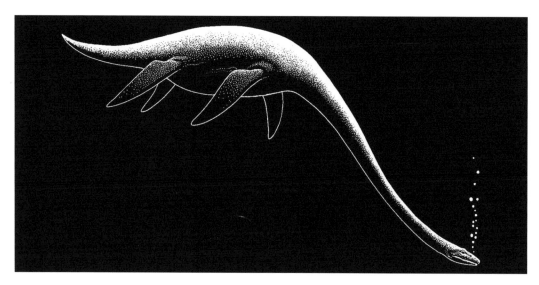

*Did the long-necked plesiosaurs, such as* Elasmosaurus platyurus, *lie on the bottom, weighted down with stones they had swallowed, and reach upward? Or did they hang head-down to snatch their food from the surface?*

In a letter to the *New York Herald* in 1890, Marsh described the moment that he pointed out Cope's mistake:

> The skeleton itself was arranged in the Museum of the Philadelphia Academy of Sciences, according to this restoration, and when Professor Cope showed it to me and explained its peculiarities I noticed that the articulations of the vertebrae were reversed and suggested to him gently that he had the whole thing wrong end foremost. His indignation was great, and he asserted in strong language that he had studied the animal for many months and ought at least to know one end from the other. It seems he did not, for Professor Leidy in his quiet way took the last vertebra from the end of the tail, as Cope had placed it, and found it to be the atlas and axis, with the occipital condyle of the skull in position.

Cope corrected the mistake when Marsh identified it, but he first claimed that he had never made it and then said that Leidy was responsible. He tried to buy up all the copies of the original publication, but a few have survived that show the head and tail reversed and the limbs on backwards.*

With the head on the right end, *Elasmosaurus platyurus* now hangs from the ceiling of the Inland Sea Exhibit at the Academy of Natural Sciences of Phila-

* At a meeting of the Academy of Natural Sciences on March 8, 1870, Leidy discussed

delphia, and visitors marvel at its impossibly long neck, short tail, and massive flippers, which look much too big, even for an animal that was 40 feet long. It looks for all the world as if another museum managed to find a fossil of the Loch Ness monster. A pair of comparable skeletons swim high above the entrance hall of the Denver Museum of Natural History, but these are of the elasmosaur *Thalassomedon hanningtoni,* from the late Cretaceous of Baca County, Colorado. In 1970, S. P. Welles published a brief note entitled "The Longest Neck in the Ocean" in the Museum Notes of the University of Nebraska State Museum, in which he discussed the discovery of an elasmosaur in the Graneros Shale of eastern Nebraska in 1964. It was another 40-foot-long *Thalassomedon hanningtoni,* nearly as long as Cope's *Elasmosaurus platyurus.*

In their haste to outcollect and outpublish each other, Cope and Marsh made a muddle of the identification and classification of plesiosaurs.* As Glenn Storrs (1999) wrote, "At the most general level, however, the taxonomic status of many plesiosaurian taxa remains chaotic, and this particularly applies to the several species that have been described from the Niobrara Chalk. Niobrara specimens are uncommon and are often incomplete and the historical holotypes of such early workers as Cope and Marsh are notoriously so."

———

Cope's mistakes ("Professor Cope has described the skeleton in a reversed position to the true one"), but at the same time, he reflected on the modus vivendi of *Elasmosaurus platyurus:* "We may imagine this extraordinary creature, with its turtle-like body, paddling about, at one moment darting its head a distance of upwards of twenty feet into the depths of the sea after its fish prey, at another into the air after some feathered or other winged reptile, or perhaps when near shore, even reaching so far as to seize by the throat some biped dinosaur."
* Cope and Marsh were not only rivals for collecting and naming fossils but also—albeit inadvertently—were competitors for the title of greatest blunderer in paleontological history. Cope had put the head of *Elasmosaurus* on the wrong end, but Marsh took the prize, for he put the *wrong head* on a dinosaur, a mistake that was not corrected for a century. When Marsh collected the bones of the huge sauropod *Apatosaurus* in the Como Bluffs region of Wyoming in 1880, the head was lacking, so he simply used the head of another gigantic sauropod named *Camarasaurus,* which he had found 4 miles away from the body. Although some people recognized the mistake as early as 1915, it was not corrected until 1979, when the Carnegie Museum in Pittsburgh replaced the head on its *Apatosaurus;* shortly thereafter, the American Museum of Natural History followed suit.

Setting out to rectify this situation, Storrs (1999) and Carpenter (1999) independently examined the holotypes of all the plesiosaurs described from the Niobrara Chalk and attempted to clean up the mess. Of the nine named species, they found that only three were valid: *Polycotylus latipinnis* (named by Cope in 1869), *Styxosaurus snowii* (named by Williston in 1890), and *Dolichorhynchops osborni* (named by Williston in 1902). The remainder of the Niobrara plesiosaurs were synonymized with species from other localities or relegated to the category of nomina dubia (doubtful names). This is all very complicated, but it points up the state of plesiosaur taxonomy in the nineteenth century. These gigantic sea creatures (identifiable by paddles instead of feet) had only recently been discovered, and the understanding of their taxonomic differences was vague. It was little wonder that Cope and Marsh identified too many animals or confused one specimen with another. They were working with a fossil fauna the likes of which had never before been seen on Earth.

Since Cope and Marsh so muddled their identifications, other plesiosaurs have been found in the American West. Welles and Bump (1949) excavated the fossil remains of a long-necked elasmosaur that they named *Alzadasaurus pembertoni,* for Ralph Pemberton, M.D., who found the fossil in South Dakota. (The name *Alzadasaurus* comes from the town of Alzada in southeastern Montana, where the holotype had been found.) In Carpenter's 1999 revision of the North American elasmosaurs, he concluded that there were "only five valid genera and species: *Elasmosaurus platyurus, Hydralmosaurus serpentinus, Libonectes morgani, Styxosaurus snowii,* and *Thalassomedon hanningtoni. Alzadasaurus kansasensis, A. pembertoni,* and *Thalassonomosaurus marshi* form an ontogenetic series of *Styxosaurus snowii* from the Smoky Hill Chalk, and Sharon Springs Member of the Pierre Shale. The holotype of the genus of *Alzadasaurus* is synonymized with *Thalassomedon,* leaving '*Alzadasaurus*' *columbiensis* without a generic name, and therefore a new name is proposed." (That name is *Callawaysaurus,* for Jack Callaway, a vertebrate paleontologist who died in 1997.)

After Carpenter's 1999 revision, we lost all the alzadasaurs to *Styxosaurus* and *Thalassomedon,* the new genus set up by Carpenter to include the alzadasaurs and assorted *Elasmosaurus* species (but not *E. platyurus*), as well as *Thalassiosaurus* and *Thalassonomosaurus,* species with names almost as long as their necks. Now *Thalassomedon hanningtoni* (*thalassa* means "sea" in Greek) can be

It is almost
impossible to picture
Thalassomedon
moving through the
water. The
incredibly long neck
must have acted like
a rudder on the
front of the animal
as it paddled through
the water, requiring
constant course
corrections.

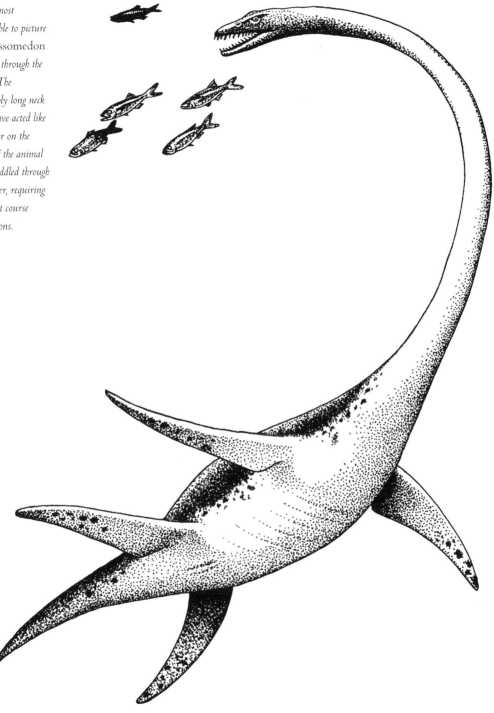

seen in the Denver Museum of Natural History, and because the Denver specimen has been licensed to Valley Anatomical Preparations of Chatsworth, California, casts of the Colorado elasmosaur have been sold to the Royal Tyrrell Museum in Drumheller, Alberta; the Milwaukee Public Museum; and, in Japan, the Iwaki Municipal Museum, the Toyohashi Municipal Museum, the Mie Prefecture Natural History Museum, and the Nagoya City Aquarium. The cast in the Hall of Vertebrate Origins in the American Museum of Natural History, discussed in the introduction, was also made by Valley Anatomical Preparations.

Another spectacular elasmosaur is the Australian *Woolungasaurus glendowerensis,* named for Woolunga, a reptile in Aboriginal mythology, and the Glendower Station in Queensland, where the fossil was found in 1982. At an estimated length of 30 feet, it was smaller than *Elasmosaurus* but similarly proportioned, with a neck as long as the body and tail combined. One specimen was found with its skull showing signs of having been bitten by *Kronosaurus,* the giant pliosaur that was the scourge of Australian Cretaceous seas (Thulborn and Turner 1993). In 1997, *Woolungasaurus* appeared on an Australian postage stamp, splendidly tricked out in a suit of black and yellow, a product of the artist's imagination. No matter what else we have learned about the extinct marine reptiles, their coloration remains largely a mystery.

Although the plesiosaurs have been known to science and the public for almost two centuries (De la Beche and Conybeare published the first *Plesiosaurus* paper in 1821), their taxonomy is still poorly organized. There are dozens of named species from all over the world, many of which are known from partial or fragmentary material, and some of which undoubtedly belong in different genera. In a 1981 review of the late Jurassic Plesiosauridae, D. S. Brown recognized four genera and six species: *Cryptoclidus eurymerus, C. richardsoni, Muraenosaurus leedsii, M. beloclis, Tricleidus seeleyi,* and *Colymbosaurus trochanterius.* In 1892, Harry Seeley first described *Cryptoclidus* ("hidden clavicle"), named for the small clavicle bones that rest in shallow depressions on the inner surface of the front limb girdle and are thus hidden from view. Seeley's actual specimen, found in the Oxford Clay* of Bedford, England, has been lost; it

---

* England's Oxford Clay is one of the most famous and productive fossiliferous regions in

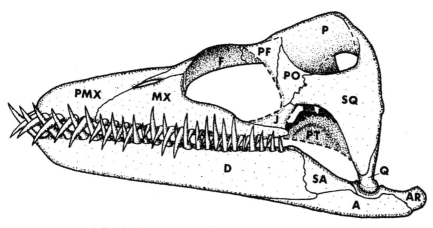

*Reconstruction of the skull of the plesiosaur* Cryptoclidus eurymerus
*(from Brown and Cruickshank 1994).*
A = *angular;* AR = *articular;* D = *dentary;* F = *frontal;* MX = *maxilla;* P = *parietal;*
PF = *prefontal;* PMX = *premaxilla;* PO = *postorbital;* PT = *pterygoid;* Q = *quadrate;*
SA = *surangular;* SQ = *squamosal.*

consisted of a forelimb that was originally mistaken for a hind limb, leading
to the name *Plesiosaurus eurymerus* ("wide femur"). Brown therefore designated
a British Museum specimen as the neotype and established the corrected
name as *Cryptoclidus eurymerus.* Found in a brick pit near Peterborough and
described by C. W. Andrews in 1910, it is one of the most complete skeletons
of an adult plesiosaur ever found. (Brown also declared *Cryptoclidus oxoniensis* a
nomen dubium.) Although *Cryptoclidus* is known mostly from the Oxford
Clay, fragments have been found in Russia, Greenland, Cuba, and Argentina.

The body of the long-necked plesiosaurs was broad, flat, and inflexible,
because it was well plated with bones both dorsally and ventrally (some,
however, were rather barrel shaped). The bones served as anchors for the

---

the world. It runs in an irregular, snaky line from Yorkshire south to Dorset, and across the
English Channel into the sea cliffs of Normandy. The uppermost layers date from the
Lower Oxfordian, 150 million years ago, and the oldest fossils are from the Lower Callovian,
161 million years ago. The Oxford Clay "mud rocks" contain innumerable ammonites,
belemnites, and brachiopods, as well as vertebrates such as plesiosaurs, ichthyosaurs, marine
crocodiles, fishes, and sharks.

powerful muscles of the paddles, which sometimes contained as many as 18 joints per digit. (Only some ichthyosaurs had more phalanges; *Platypterygius* had as many as 30.) As reconstructed in Brown's paper, *Cryptoclidus eurymerus* was a heavy-bodied, long-necked plesiosaur with a shortish tail and a broad, lightly built skull, with as many as 100 small sharp teeth that interlocked outside the jaws. This uncommon arrangement is believed to have functioned as a sort of trap for fishes and soft-bodied cephalopods. Brown showed it "flying" underwater, with the forelimbs raised on the upstroke and the hind flippers trailing behind: "the flattened body shape provides additional dorso-ventral stabilization during subaqueous flight locomotion as in marine turtles."

In 2002, Arthur Cruickshank and R. Ewan Fordyce published a detailed description of a New Zealand cryptoclidid plesiosaur that they named *Kai-whekea kaitiki*. The name, taken from the Maori language, means "squid eater of Katiki." The fossilized skeleton was largely complete and included the skull; all cervical, pectoral, thoracic, and sacral vertebrae; much of the right and left rib cage; some gastralia; and an almost complete right hind limb and part of the left. The entire specimen was more than 21 feet long, and because the tail was missing, the animal in life would have been even longer. The authors wrote that "there is not currently a consensus on plesiosauroid classification; the diagnoses and content are still debated for the Plesiosauridae, Elasmosauridae, and Cryptoclididae," but based on their cladistic analyses, they assigned *Kaiwhekea* to the Cryptoclididae. With its long neck and powerful, tooth-studded jaws, *Kaiwhekea* probably fed on fast-moving, medium-sized to large prey, probably fishes and cephalopods. The structure of the neck vertebrae "provide no evidence of a serpentine mobility, although the craniocervical joint allowed significant movement horizontally and vertically . . . the degree of ventral movement is hard to assess." (As we shall see, the flexibility of plesiosaur necks is a popular subject for paleontological controversy.) Like other cryptoclidids (but unlike the elasmosaurs), *Kaiwhekea* had large eye sockets, suggesting the ability to hunt deeper in the water column where the light levels were lower.

When Harry Seeley examined a plesiosaur specimen collected from the Oxford Clay by Charles Leeds of Exeter College, he noted the similarities to *Cryptoclidus* but observed that its neck was nearly twice as long. Named for an eel *(Muraena)* on account of its long, eel-like neck and for Leeds, *Muraenosaurus leedsii* was first described by Seeley in 1874. The skull was about 16 inches long, and the entire animal was estimated at between 15 and 21 feet. Benton (1990a) wrote that "*Muraenosaurus* . . . took the long-necked adaptations to an extreme. Some had as many as 70 cervical vertebrae, and the neck could bend around itself two or three times." Whereas the numerous teeth of *Cryptoclidus* were smooth, those of *Muraenosaurus* were fewer, larger, and vertically ridged. "The hindermost teeth look directly upward," Benton wrote, "but as they approach the front of the jaw they are necessarily directed more and more outward and forward." Like *Cryptoclidus*, its tail was short and its paddles proportionally small, suggesting that it was a slow-swimming ambush predator. There is another *Muraenosaurus* species, surnamed *beloclis*, referring to the shape of its clavicle *(belemnon* is "arrow" or "spear" in Greek; it is also the root of the name of the cephalopods known as belemnites).

The Leeds collection also contained disarticulated elements of a plesiosaur that C. W. Andrews (1909) named *Tricleidus seeleyi*. Also from the Oxford

Clay, this species is monotypical, meaning that it is the only species in the genus. It differs from *Cryptoclidus* and *Muraenosaurus* in the number of teeth, which also were more strongly ridged. It too was probably a trap feeder, dining on soft-bodied cephalopods and crustaceans. *Colymbosaurus* ("diving lizard") *trochanterius,* identified and named by Owen in 1840, was the largest and most massive of the English long-necked plesiosaurs, reaching an overall length of 22 feet, about a third of which was neck. Because *Colymbosaurus* is known only from skeletons without skulls, the skull of *Kimmerosaurus* (a new genus erected by Brown in 1981 and named for the Kimmeridge Clay of Dorset) might belong to the same animal, which would make *Colymbosaurus* a junior synonym of *Kimmerosaurus.* With Milner and Taylor in 1986, Brown wrote, "The possibility that *Kimmerosaurus* might be synonymous with *Colymbosaurus* is discussed, in which case *Colymbosaurus* would have to be reassigned at family level as a long-necked cryptoclidid." Whatever its name, this was another of the Upper Jurassic long-necked plesiosaurs that trapped their prey in a mesh of sharp teeth.

There are many ways of moving through the water. Most marine vertebrates (fishes, sharks, sea snakes, and crocodilians) use an oscillating, vertical tail fin to provide propulsive power. Cetaceans and sirenians use an analogous arrangement, but the movement of their flukes is up and down rather than side to side. Ichthyosaurs had four flippers, but their caudal fins had developed into vertical, flattened crescents that moved from side to side and served, like the tail of a shark, as the propulsive engine. For the four-flippered, short-tailed plesiosaurs, there were essentially three alternatives. One is "paddling," where the feet of the animal are pulled through the water in the vertical plane; this is the way ducks swim or the way humans use their arms doing the crawl stroke. (A nonanimal example is a canoe or, in a form that moves the water without moving the paddler, a waterwheel.) In the paddling recovery stroke, the duck closes its webbed foot and brings it forward; the human swimmer raises his arm out of the water. In paddling, the limbs usually alternate the propulsive strokes, but in principle, they can be used together. "Rowing" uses the same technique of pulling a flattened blade through the water, except that it is in the horizontal plane and the "oar" has to be "feathered," which means that in the recovery stroke, it is turned to present its least-resistant face to the water. Few living animals actually row through the water, but the human breaststroke can be used as a paradigm. Finally, there is underwater "flying," where the limbs move at a right angle relative to the direction of motion as the animal moves forward; this results in a "figure-eight" pattern made by the fin. Examples of subaqueous "fliers" are sea turtles, penguins, and sea lions. Penguins (like their terrestrial avian ancestors) use their forelimbs for flying; otariids also use their forelimbs; and the four-flippered sea turtles use the forelimbs for propulsion and the hind ones for steering.

The locomotion of plesiosaurs has always puzzled and fascinated those who have studied these extinct marine reptiles. In 1824, Conybeare speculated that "in its motion, this animal must have resembled the turtles more than any other," and in 1851, Owen corroborated Conybeare's opinion. Then in 1924, working with the fossil remains of *Plesiosaurus dolichodeirus,* D. M. S. Watson reconstructed the limb muscles (it was the first time anyone had ever done that with a plesiosaur and decided that they didn't "fly" like turtles but "rowed." Storrs (1993a) summarized the myriad discussions of plesiosaur locomotion and wrote:

> The model for underwater "flight" for plesiosaur paraxial locomotion is not a perfect one. Rather, it is probable that the plesiosaurian power stroke combined elements of "flight" and subaqueous "rowing" with both vertical (lift-based) and fore-and-aft (drag-based) components. Robinson (1975) was correct in highlighting the hydrofoil-shaped limbs of plesiosaurs. Their distally tapering configuration created a relatively high aspect ratio for each limb and this minimized trailing vorticity and lift-induced drag. Nonetheless sea lions, with limbs constructed in a functionally similar pattern, do not rely exclusively on lift-induced thrust. . . . An inertial gliding phase may have existed between periodic power strokes, again as in sea lions. At least in pliosaurs, this gliding phase would have been relatively unencumbered by drag because of their comparatively small surface to mass ratio (less likely in elasmosaurs whose long necks increased surface area relative to mass).

When the remains of a large reptile were unearthed by workers at the London Brick Company in Bedfordshire in 1958, work was stopped and paleontologists from the British Museum were called in. The remains consisted of the back part of an animal and the front of the head, the total length estimated at 36 feet. It was *Liopleurodon,* and according to Barney Newman and Beverly Tarlo, the reconstruction enabled them to arrive "at a result different from other restorations in suggesting a much more streamlined animal." Although they "discovered evidence that the plesiosaurs had a tail fin on the upper part of the tail," they did not reveal in their 1967 paper what that evidence was. They did explain, however, why the bones in the "paddles" of plesiosaurs are rarely disturbed while the other bones are often scattered: "they were fixed in cartilage or gristle and were not capable of any movement on each other, as, for example, our fingers are." They further concluded that the forelimbs and hind limbs of pliosaurs functioned differently; the forelimbs could be raised above the horizontal, but the hind limbs could not, which indicated to them that the animal could dive in pursuit of food.

In 1975, Jane Ann Robinson wrote an article entitled "The Locomotion of Plesiosaurs," which was filled with sentences such as, "The action of this muscle parallels that of supracoracoid-coracobranchial complex in the pectrum, providing most of the power for adduction." She concluded:

> Plesiosaurs, long considered to be rowing animals, are shown to have employed subaqueous flight, modifying both fore- and hindlimbs into virtually identical wings. These can be compared functionally point for point with the wings of subaqueous flyers (sea turtles, penguins, and otariids), but not with the limbs of rowing or paddling animals. . . . Differences in limb and head/neck proportions in plesiosaurs are related to relative maneuverability; the short-necked forms were agile and pursued their prey as sea lions do, while the *long-necked* forms were endurance swimmers and not particularly agile.*

* Robinson's paper, published in the *Neues Jahrbuch für Geologie und Paläeontologie* in Stuttgart, is so replete with typographical errors that it is sometimes difficult to understand. Some of the harmless errors are "1924" for the date of Conybeare's paper or "1941" for Owen's, but the last sentence of her paper actually reads, "the short-necked forms were agile and pursued their prey as sea lions do, while the short-necked forms were endurance swimmers and not particularly agile." Based on a careful reading of the paper, I have taken the liberty of changing it as italicized above.

Instead of solving the problem, Robinson's paper only opened the flood-gates for a barrage of criticisms and revised interpretations. In a paper published in the same journal in 1982, Tarsitano and Riess looked at Robinson's "elaborate study" and found that her errors had to do with "either incorrect interpretations of the morphological data and/or the lack of understanding of basic biomechanical concepts and morphology." In addition, her paper was "hampered by faulty comparisons with the non-analogous underwater flight of penguins, sea turtles and sea lions." They wrote that the comparison to the wings of penguins was flawed because "most tetrapod underwater flyers have a functional elbow joint, the exception being plesiosaurs and humpback whales."* Tarsitano and Riess didn't exactly offer an answer and only succeeded in pointing out where Robinson was wrong. "As yet," they wrote, "it is unknown how the two sets of wings functioned together in plesiosaurs."

In the same issue—in fact, on the next page—Frey and Riess added a footnote to the article and wrote, "Muscles inserting at the internal area of the coracoids or pubices and ischia respectively (Robinson 1975) have to be rejected for anatomical reasons. . . . More likely it seems to us that muscles of the proximal basis of the limbs migrated dorsally to insert at the long neural spines. Here they could function as levitators. However, this cannot serve as the answer to the question, why was it necessary for plesiosaurs to develop 4 large 'wings.' All recent tetrapods which fly underwater (i.e., penguins, marine turtles, sea lions, etc.) are perfectly well-equipped with just 2 wings."

The follow-up to Robinson's 1975 article appeared two years later. In the same Stuttgart journal she published "Intracorporal Force Transmission in Plesiosaurs," the "second part of a doctoral dissertation prepared at the University of California at Los Angeles," which might explain the length and detail of this paper and its predecessor. "Intracorporal force" is the energy, set up by the motion of the limbs, that (according to Robinson) is stored in the pectrum (pectoral region), pelvis, and gastralia (belly ribs) and helps provide the propulsive force for the next stroke of the limbs. Robinson compared

---

* Humpback whales have long flippers, but they use them for steering, not propulsion. Like all other cetaceans, humpbacks propel themselves with their tail flukes. In a 1995 paper, Fish and Battle discussed the hydrodynamic design of the humpback whale flipper.

other subaqueous fliers (otariid pinnipeds, penguins, and sea turtles) to plesiosaurs and then, after much structural, osteological, and muscular analysis, concluded that all four limbs of plesiosaurs functioned as propulsive hydrofoils; that plesiosaurs were probably unable to emerge on land; and that forces distributed through the body include those that arise from the restraining actions of major limb muscles arising from the inner and outer surfaces of the girdles, and are absorbed directly by the ventrally located platelike girdle elements. She concluded that other propulsive forces result from the hydrodynamic thrust that tends to drive the limbs forward and are transmitted by the "bowstring" construction of the ventral basket. "The archer's bow construction of the dorsal and ventral elements of plesiosaurs is able to accommodate asymmetry of force direction and magnitude in anterior and posterior, as well as bilateral, wing pairs without intermobility of bony elements or distortion of the body as a whole."*

Gastralia, also called gastric or belly ribs, have been defined as ossifications in the belly wall. They lie just posterior to the sternum and provide sites for muscle attachment as well as support for the abdomen. In living animals, they are found in some lizards, crocodiles, and the tuataras, but whereas the theropod dinosaurs had them, the ornithischians and most of the sauropods did not. (Modern birds lack gastralia, but *Archaeopteryx* and other primitive birds had a full set.) It is likely that muscles linked to the gastralia were used to expand the volume of the body cavity in breathing. Gastralia were present in many of the earlier marine reptiles, such as placodonts and nothosaurs, and although they were retained by later forms, particularly the ichthyosaurs and plesiosaurs, they were absent in mosasaurs. In most Jurassic ichthyosaurs, the gastralia were fairly small, but they were larger in some of the Triassic forms and much larger in the plesiosaurs. When it was thought that plesiosaurs might have occasionally emerged from the water—perhaps to lay eggs—it was suggested that the gastralia provided support for the body on land, but now

* With the exception of obvious typographical errors, I have quoted and paraphrased Robinson's arguments to the best of my ability. Her elaborate arguments for a "force transmission system" are completely theoretical and almost completely incomprehensible to me. I have included them under the assumption that others might be able to understand what she is talking about.

that most paleontologists believe that plesiosaurs never left the water (and, despite the lack of evidence, that they probably gave birth to live young there), the function of gastralia in the marine reptiles is still unknown. In her discussion of the locomotion of plesiosaurs, Robinson (1977) suggested that the gastralia functioned as a component of a dorsoventral stabilizing system (the "archer's bow construction") that absorbed the up-and-down motion of the fore and hind limb girdles while transmitting the propulsive force to the body. However, this complex explanation has been questioned, most recently by Lingham-Soliar (2000c), because of the ineffectiveness of an inflexible backbone in storing strain energy in something like an archer's bow. Instead, he suggests that the ribs (and gastralia) aided force transmission more like the cables in a suspension or bowstring bridge from fixed supports analogous to the plesiosaur backbone.

In a letter written to me in January 2002, Lingham-Soliar articulated his ideas about the function of gastralia:

> In early ichthyosaurs, especially massive-bodied forms, robust gastralia probably provided support, whereas in the later streamlined or thunniform ichthyosaurs, lighter more delicate gastralia may have played a very important part in maintaining an advanced hydrodynamic body shape. In plesiosaurs, where large ventral body mass (gut) was concentrated over a relatively short body length the gastralia may have played a vital role in support. . . . Furthermore, a more rigid thorax is essential in a paraxial flyer. Gastralia are probably made redundant in birds by the enormous sternum and in marine turtles by the plastron. In the latter group a rigid plastron (the lungs are dorsally placed anyway) almost certainly meant that breathing was facilitated by the enormous pectoral musculature during contraction and expansion (possibly a good analogue for plesiosaurs). Mosasaurs, in contrast, lacked gastralia. Being more slender and elongated the ribs were probably adequate to assist in breathing and in maintaining body shape. Furthermore the ventral mass was probably better spread over the length of the animal. In enormous mosasaurs such as *Mosasaurus hoffmanni* the thoracic and anterior abdominal ribs are extremely deep, offering a good deal of support. The disadvantages of gastralia in an advanced

undulatory swimmer, e.g. compromising flexibility, may have outweighed the advantages. In crocodiles a weak diaphragm may indicate breathing as an important function of gastralia. But support too may have been highly important, particularly in high-walking and twist feeding.

In a 1981 article, Michael Taylor reproduced Robinson's 1975 drawing of *Liopleurodon,* which has no body outline and thus no tail fin, although he did say that "plesiosaurs did have small vertical tailfins, presumably for stabilising the animal directionally and for controlling direction of motion." He wrote that the forelimbs and hind limbs of the pliosaur were "self-contained power units," and "the ability to vary independently the action of each limb would be most useful, as it made possible rapid changes of direction in pursuit of prey, or when diving from a position at the surface. One can also conclude that the plesiosaurs could move and breed on land, *pace* Robinson, as the arched vertebral column prevented the collapse of the lungs. Ichthyosaurs and modern whales cannot move on land and perforce give birth in the water to live young; certainly there are specimens of ichthyosaurs—but not plesiosaurs—with unborn young still in the body cavity. Plesiosaurs may have given birth to live young or laid eggs in pits scraped out with their tails, like modern turtles."

Robin O'Keefe (2001, 2002c) analyzed the "flipper geometry" of plesiosaurs with regard to the aspect ratio* and presented "new data on the aspect ratios (ARs) of plesiosaur flippers, and interpreted these data via comparison with AR in birds, bats, and aircraft." Thus, bombers and transport planes have higher ARs than attack planes, which have to be more maneuverable. Long, thin wings, such as those of long-distance cruisers like albatrosses, have a high AR, while birds with short, wide wings, such as the extremely maneu-

---

* McGowan (1991a) wrote that "the relative narrowness of an inclined plane is expressed as the *aspect ratio* which is the ratio of the length to the width. A plane 10 units long and 10 units wide has an aspect ratio of one, whereas one that is 20 units long and 5 wide has an aspect ratio of four. One of the reasons inclined planes (and wings) with high aspect ratios have a higher lift-to-drag ratio is that they generate less of a vortex at the tips. The lift-to-drag ratio of a plane is also increased by its having a streamlined profile . . . a streamlined body experiences lower drag forces than one with a rectangular profile."

verable goshawk, have a comparatively low AR. The plesiosaurs, with their high-AR flippers, "are inferred to have hunted by cruising long distances searching for small, dispersed food items, [while] pliosauromorphs are inferred to have actively hunted single, large food items on the wing" (O'Keefe 2002c). But whereas the aspect ratios of fighter planes and long-range bombers are specifically *designed* to achieve their particular purposes, no such "design" was responsible in the various plesiosaurs, which developed along different lines and achieved different results. These creatures did not develop their particular aspect ratios so that they could specialize in a certain type of prey capture; rather, the flipper types evolved over time, and the animals developed attack strategies commensurate with their capabilities.

In 1989, Beverly Halstead published an article simply titled "Plesiosaur Locomotion" in which he proposed that the plesiosaurs used all four fins for propulsion, and because theirs was an undulatory trajectory through the water, their motion was not affected by the turbulence created by the vortices of the front flippers' power stroke. He wrote: "Once an undulating or porpoising mode is acknowledged then plesiosaurs can be allowed to swim like sea lions." This is "Newman's porpoising solution," which was in fact proposed by Newman and Halstead himself in a popular article published in 1967.* In this article (which is nominally about the discovery of a *Liopleurodon* skeleton in Bedfordshire), the word *porpoising* does not appear, but the authors wrote:

> Both the fore and hind-limbs could only move in a horizontal plane. The fore-limbs were incapable of being raised, and we are thus forced to

---

* To the eternal confusion of biographers and bibliographers, the man born Lambert Beverly Halstead (1933–1991) was at one point given the name of his stepfather and became Lambert Beverly Tarlo. In paleontological publications from 1954 to about 1968, he used the name Tarlo. Then for a brief period he used both names and became Halstead Tarlo, but from 1969 onward, he used only Halstead (Sarjeant 1993). This change led to some rather peculiar constructions, such as this one from "Plesiosaur Locomotion" (whose author is L. B. Halstead): "On the basis of an unusual bone identified as a scapula, Tarlo (1958) reconstructed the musculature of a giant plesiosaur." This was obviously intended to identify the reference, but it presupposes that the reader will know that Tarlo and Halstead are the same person, which might not be evident to those unfamiliar with Halstead's convoluted nomenclatural history.

conclude that these creatures were unable to dive after their prey. Furthermore, we can see from the structure of the shoulder girdle that the associated muscles that drew the limb forward were just as strong as those which drew it back. This means that these long-necked plesiosaurs could twist and turn extremely well by combining a normal swimming stroke of one limb with a backing stroke of the other. This sort of action was simply not possible for a pliosaur—it did not have sufficient muscle power for an effective backing stroke.

In a 1994 study of the swimming capabilities of the marine reptiles, Massare wrote that "the two lineages of plesiosaurs, the plesiosauroids (Superfamily Plesiosauroidea) and the pliosauroids (Superfamily Pliosauroidea) shared a similar mode of locomotion, that of subaqueous flying, using their two pairs of winglike appendages as hydrofoils," but the swimming of plesiosaurs is not that simple. In 1975, Robinson argued that the animals "flew" like overgrown penguins—but where penguins have only two flippers, the marine reptiles had four, which presented a more complicated problem in hydrodynamics. According to Massare's 1994 summary:

> The old idea of subaqueous rowing assumed that the two pairs of wings would move simultaneously. Would underwater flyers with an asymmetric power stroke necessarily beat their four limbs in unison? Riess and Frey argued that the two pairs of wings were out of phase by half a stroke, such that the forelimbs were in the power phase (backward, downward movement) while the hindlimbs were in the recovery phase (forward, upward), and vice versa. Thus the plesiosaur was always generating thrust. Alexander pointed out, however, that swimming would be very inefficient with the fore and hind limbs out of phase because the hindlimbs would be accelerating water that was already in motion. It would be more efficient for the fore and hind limbs to work together and simultaneously accelerate a larger mass of water.

Bakker (1993a) wrote that "the plesiosaur body was short, compact, oval in cross-section, and strongly-braced below by thick central ribs that resisted the compressional forces generated by the pulsating cycles of the swimming strokes. Modern penguins are equipped with only one set of propellers—those of the forelimbs (wings)—and yet penguins are exceptionally fast, quick in turns, and capable of dramatic bursts of acceleration. Plesiosaurs, endowed with two sets of propellers, fore and aft, must have exceeded the penguins in the top speed possible for a given body size in the capacity for maneuvers in three dimensions." Of course, not every activity required high-speed swimming, and the animals might have been able to change their "gaits," similar to the way a horse varies its leg movements when walking, trotting, or galloping. Also, the requirements of the long-necked plesiosaurs were probably quite different from those of the pliosaurs; the former were mostly fish eaters that plucked their prey from schools, whereas the latter were large-prey predators that had to chase their prey down and thus needed more maneuverability as well as more speed—especially if the prey was as maneuverable and fast as they were. As Newman and Tarlo (1967) wrote, "From studying the muscle actions in the two kinds of plesiosaur we get a picture of two different ways of swimming that we never would have suspected from the general appearance of the skeletons alone. The long-necked forms were adept at twisting and turning with great speed, but all their time was spent at the surface of the sea. The pliosaurs were powerful swimmers that hunted down their prey; although they did not have the agility of their cousins, they were adapted to diving down after their food."

Lingham-Soliar then wrote a lengthy piece in 2000 called "Plesiosaur Locomotion: Is the Four-Wing Problem Real or Merely an Atheoretical Exercise?"* It was introduced with these words:

* In response to my question about the word *atheoretical* in his title, Lingham-Soliar answered as follows: "I use *atheoretical* essentially to mean lacking sound biological or functional theory. It was not, however to impugn or undermine previous discussions on four-wing flight but simply to state that despite many of the ideas proposed being good, they frequently lacked theoretical basis (i.e. they were more empirical, often without due regard for system and theory). By this I mean anatomical and morphological theory (musculature and joint construction) was often ignored when they didn't coincide with four-wing flight hypothesis, body weight and lifting surface areas, despite all the postulations, were never investigated, anterior and posterior wing shape and design were taken for granted, flight theory in living animals and machines was poorly addressed, the bowstring hypothesis was

Recent workers have regarded the four wings of plesiosaurs as four organs performing essentially the same function, i.e., an integration of the components of thrust, lift, stability, and steering in one and the same system. In extant vertebrates on the other hand (e.g., sharks, whales, dolphins, ichthyosaurs, flying fish, etc.) and in machines (airplanes, powered gliders) the efficiency of lift and thrust components is maximized by largely independent generation. . . . In birds the same organ performing distinctly different functions accounts for the complexities of their wing structure. In a number of large marine vertebrates e.g., lamnid sharks, whales, dolphins, and large ichthyosaurs, efficient locomotion is dependant upon a separate pair of hydrodynamic organs to achieve stability, passive lift, and steering.

Lingham-Soliar dismisses Robinson's elaborate "archer's bow theory," whereby an inflexible bow composed of the dorsal and ventral elements of the skeleton serve as the basis for propulsive forces on the four hydrofoils during underwater flight, and also Riess and Frey's (1982) theory of passive upstroke of the limbs. He replaces them with his own synthesis, published in great detail in *Neues Jahrbuch* and then as a popular article in the British newspaper *The Guardian* on November 16, 2000:

Traditionally all four plesiosaur limbs have been treated as identical structures. This is far from so. The anterior limbs are swept back as in swallow's wings—the posterior ones are relatively straighter. Research has shown that the swept-back or crescent shape is dynamically more efficient than the straight wing for flight. There is no elbow or wrist-joint in plesiosaur limbs, so the ability to make delicate changes in pitch, direction etc., was limited. Of further significance is the way in which marine animals such as sharks and ichthyosaurs rise or descend in the water by elevating or lowering the leading edge of the paddles. However, lift in a hydrofoil works best

theoretically weak, so was Riess and Frey's 'passive supination' hypothesis, the gastrolith and ballasting hypothesis is highly dubious . . . etc. Most later theories were simply taking earlier statements of four-wing flight as read (undoubtedly an alluring proposition), despite the fact that it was never really soundly investigated or tested in the light of alternative theories—in truth they depended on a wing and a prayer (pun intended)."

when it is inclined at a precise angle to the water flow — known as the angle of attack. Hence, the wing's capacity to act simultaneously as a rudder and flight organ is impractical. For a pursuit predator chasing elusive prey, this would be disastrous. The solution? Sharing flight functions between the anterior and posterior limbs. Think of plesiosaurs as using a front-wheeled drive engine (thrust and lift) with the steering and a number of other functions at the back (ideal for rotating and maneuvering because of their greater distance from the centre of balance). . . . At other times the hind limbs could also be used in rowing — the predominantly ventral musculature would allow this. While the glamorous notion of plesiosaurs as four rather than two-winged fliers is appealing, reality suggests a very effective division of functions between the anterior and posterior limbs, necessitated by mechanical and anatomical limitations, but every bit as unique.

In a book revealingly called *In the Presence of Dinosaurs,* John Colagrande resurrects the lifestyle of various long-extinct reptiles, with only a brief nod to the idea that he might be making it all up. In the introduction, he says, "The behaviors we ascribe to the animals are by nature speculative, but no more 'radical' than some of the forms of behavior exhibited by modern animals." In other words, because some living animals exhibit enigmatic behavior, there is no problem in fabricating equally strange behavior for creatures that have been extinct for 100 million years and are known only from fossils, some of them mere fragments. Here is Colagrande's account of the egg-laying procedure of elasmosaurs:

They normally start approaching just before sunrise, while the moon is still above the horizon. Like an invading armada, scores of the giant reptiles head for the beach, enter the surf zone, thrust themselves out of the foam, and laboriously pull themselves onto the sand with a loud grating hiss. Every once in a while one of the leviathans will stop momentarily and with a shake of its head, snort a great spray of salty water from its nostrils. Some marine reptiles absorb great amounts of salt, which can kill them if allowed to build up. Special glands in their heads remove the excess salt from their blood and dump it into their nasal passages, where it is unceremoniously expelled.

This may be Colagrande's idea of "weird" behavior, but it is remarkably close to a description of the egg-laying behavior of modern sea turtles. Elasmosaurs may have hauled themselves en masse onto the sand (with or without a "grating hiss"), or they might have come ashore individually, but it is most likely that they didn't come ashore at all. And as for the "special glands in their heads," they may have had them, but we really have no idea at all about the soft tissue of plesiosaur skulls. Colagrande, a high school science teacher and self-described "dinosaurologist," has none of the problems faced by paleontologists when it comes to describing the way plesiosaurs fed:

> Superbly suited for life at or near the surface, elasmosaurs feed in one of two ways. Rising quickly from the depths, snaking their heads through the water, they can shoot their heads up to twenty feet out into a school of small fish or squid. Or, by lifting their heads high above the surface, they can drop down onto their unsuspecting prey. Long, needle-sharp teeth pierce their victims and seldom allow an escape. With a quick jerk of the head, the reptile flips its slippery prey up to dislodge it from the sharp teeth, then catches it in mid-air. A few adjustments, and the fish is poised to go down the long neck headfirst, so the fins and scales can't injure the lining of the elasmosaur's throat.

Because no living creature is built along the same lines as a plesiosaur, we can only speculate about the mode of propulsion of these long-extinct water reptiles. The subject has captured the imagination of many paleontologists, and because it is so complex, it seems to encourage long-winded explanations. Halstead managed to cover the subject in 4 pages, but Robinson produced two mammoth articles (each one evidently half of her doctoral dissertation), the first 46 pages long and the second 42, filled with graphs, charts, tables, diagrams, and illustrations of plesiosaurs. There were some brief responses to Robinson's two-part thesis, and then Lingham-Soliar chimed in with another 42-pager. The locomotion of the long-necked plesiosaurs is somewhat less problematical than that of the pliosaurs, because the former probably moved fairly slowly, depending on their long necks and sharp teeth for the capture of fishes, ammonites, or other prey; in contrast, the latter, with their powerful jaws and teeth, were probably fast-moving predators that had to chase down their prey, which consisted of other swift marine reptiles such as ichthyosaurs, as well as large fishes and perhaps even cephalopods. Did pliosaurs row or fly through the water? Was their swimming similar to that of turtles? Sea lions? Penguins? Did they pull with their forelimbs and let their hind limbs trail behind, or did they flap hind and forelimbs in some sort of synchrony? Did the long-necked plesiosaurs locomote differently from the short-necked pliosaurs? Did any of them ever come out of the water?

Harry Seeley, who in 1880 was one of the first to recognize fossilized unborn ichthyosaurs, later claimed to have discovered the same for plesiosaurs. In 1888, he published a short note in which he described "four more or less complete specimens regarded as foetal plesiosaurs, together with fragments of at least three others. They are remarkable for having the flesh mineralized with phosphate of lime, and still show many of the characters of the external form of the body, but slightly distorted by decomposition. Only one individual has the head preserved; its extreme length is about 14 mm [½ inch]. . . . Hence, the author regarded this specimen as showing that Plesiosaurus was viviparous, and that in one species from the Lias many were produced at one birth." It is likely that plesiosaurs were viviparous, but Seeley's "evidence" cannot be used to demonstrate it. When R. A. Thulborn (1982) decided to reexamine the material in London's Natural History Museum that Seeley had described, he found that it consisted of "an irregular nodule of pyritic mudstone and shale; a small fragment, broken from the main nodule; five slides each with a thin section; a slide with twenty-three stained sections of a modern lizard embryo." Examining the material that Seeley had so carefully identified as heads, necks, bodies, tails, and limbs, Thulborn found "no evidence of organic structure in any of the supposed embryos . . . and some of the anatomical features identified by Seeley are no more than surface irregularities, scratches, pits, and similar weathering effects."

What, then, were Seeley's "embryos"? Thulborn reinterpreted the original fossils as a crustacean burrow system, with "only one structural feature (the 'dorsal ridge' noted by Seeley) that I have been unable to match in any other thalassinoid burrows." In his 1994 discussion, Storrs wrote, "The so-called 'embryos' had been acquired by Seeley after passing through the hands of a local fossil dealer. They had been, furthermore, highlighted or 'enhanced' by rather crude preparation, possibly by the dealer. . . . As yet there is no answer to the question of 'live' vs. oviparous birth in plesiosaurs or other sauropterygians and discussions of their mode of reproduction remain speculative." The smallest known plesiosaur was found in 1990 on the coast of Dorset, near Charmouth. It was described in 1994 by Storrs, who estimated its total length at between 4 and 5 feet, making it "one of the smallest reported plesiosaur skeletons from Dorset, perhaps the smallest Liassic individual known, and certainly one of the smallest individual plesiosaurs yet discovered." It was too large to be a neonate, so the record of no newborn plesiosaurs is still intact.

"The discovery of a pregnant female plesiosaur," wrote Taylor (1986), "would settle the question, but none has yet been found. Perhaps we have not looked inside the bodies of enough plesiosaurs, or perhaps the embryos decomposed before they could become fossilized." There are numerous fossils of immature plesiosaurs, but nothing has been found that might be a neonate or a hatchling—unless the mother was *very* large. But negative evidence does not prove that plesiosaurs were not viviparous. As Taylor wrote to me: "nobody disputes the live birth of whales—but as far as I know or can remember, nobody has reported a gravid fossil whale, or for that matter, a pinniped." Reconstructing the plesiosaurs from the fossils strongly suggests that they could not come out of the water; their flippers appear utterly ill suited for walking (or even crawling, as turtles do), and the enormous weight of some species controverts the idea of the plesiosaur as an even partially terrestrial creature. Picturing one of the long-necked elasmosaurs crawling around on the beach is even more difficult than imagining these impossible animals in the water. We have evidence of viviparity in ichthyosaurs and mosasaurs, so it is likely that at least some of the plesiosaurs were live-bearers. In 1994, James Martin of the South Dakota School of Mines collected a partial skeleton of an "extremely young pliosaur . . . near [what was] the middle of the North American epicontinental seaway." In his description, Martin wrote:

> The occurrence of an articulated skeleton of a very small juvenile plesiosaur may suggest live birth and/or parental care; the chances of survival of

such a small pliosaur swimming from distant shores to the middle of the epeiric sea seem remote. If accompanied by parents, or in a pod, survival chances would be greater. Another obvious alternative is that the baby was born well developed far from the shores of the seaway. This circumstance of course does not preclude subsequent parental care. Overall, this occurrence suggests possible live birth and parental care by a group of highly derived pliosaurid reptiles.

Next to the little pliosaur fossil was a gaping hole that Martin described as "extensive evidence of vandalism," suggesting that the site had already been vandalized and that perhaps some indications of an adult had been removed. Poaching of fossiliferous sites is bad enough, but in this case, the only conclusive evidence for live birth in plesiosaurs might have been removed before a scientist ever got to see it.

Rumors abound within the paleontological community about undescribed plesiosaur embryos in unopened crates, but so far, none of these mysterious crates has been opened, and the contents – if they exist – remain hidden from sight and from science.*

Plesiosaurs have raised the art of paleontological guesswork to new heights. We do not know how these great reptiles hunted, how they swam, or how they gave birth. Even with sufficient fossil material, we are unable to tell how the plesiosaurs actually used their four flippers for propulsion. (The ichthyosaurs also had four flippers, but their swimming was powered by their

---

* The following tantalizing paragraph appears on the South Australian Museum's website, without elaboration or explanation. The author is paleontologist Ben Kear: "One of the more surprising discoveries is that most of the South Australian plesiosaurs found are in fact juveniles. About 95 per cent of the fossils we find are juveniles or babies. That's a staggering amount considering that baby plesiosaur fossils are basically unknown. What this means is South Australia was possibly a birthing ground. Plesiosaurs could have come to SA seasonally to breed, give birth to their young then maybe move north again. It would have been a whale-like migration up-and-down the coast. Plesiosaurs would have been attracted to the colder waters because they would have been teeming with plankton, small fish and squid. If you've got a glut of food it's a good place to have a child because they'll be fed."

vertical tail fins.) And if we can't tell how an aquatic reptile moved in the water, we are utterly in the dark about how—or even if—these great reptiles moved on land. For example, Michael Taylor wrote, "Plesiosaurs may have given birth to live young or laid eggs in pits scraped out with their tails." Note the use of the words "may have," which indicates that Taylor is only guessing about what the plesiosaurs might have done—a far cry from Colagrande's descriptive phrasing, which makes it sound like he has actually observed plesiosaurs laying eggs or hunting fish. Some paleontologists delight in spec-ulation about the way their subjects walked or swam or flew; it gives life to the otherwise mute fossils. But to describe in unequivocal terms how a long-extinct animal like a plesiosaur caught its prey does a disservice to the science of paleontology by removing the element of mystery and replacing it with an ill-conceived and unwarranted certainty. Without a time machine, we can only *wish* that we knew how they hunted.

The long-necked plesiosaurs were probably among the slowest of the ancient marine reptiles, with their barrel-shaped bodies creating substantial drag. Judy Massare, in her 1988 analysis of the swimming capabilities of Mesozoic marine reptiles, wrote that "the plesiosauroids . . . do not fall within the range of optimum fineness ratios. This would have resulted in greater drag for a given size than for ichthyosaurs and pliosaurids, and suggests that the more elongate forms probably had slower continuous swimming speeds." Lateral movements of the long neck would also affect the plesiosaurs' ability to steer, creating considerable yaw (deviation from a straight course) as the animals plowed through the water. Movement of the head and neck as the animal paddled must have been the functional equivalent of having a rudder on the front end, requiring constant course corrections. It is possible that the animals compensated for these deviations by developing a swimming style that was constantly veering from one heading to another, because it seems certain that they could not have moved in a straight line if the head was in motion from side to side or up and down. With a long, snaky neck and a mouthful of sharp teeth, the "swan lizards" (Bakker's 1993 name for them) were almost certainly fish eaters, but how they captured their prey is not immediately evident. Did they take a breath and dive after fishes (the way some toothed whales do today), or did they float at the surface with head and neck hanging down underwater, like a snake hanging from a branch? Did they float at the surface with the head raised, and then plunge it downward to capture a fish in the manner of herons and egrets?*

Some have assumed that plesiosaurs, because of their incredibly long necks, could coil their heads back and strike at passing prey like a snake. In 1897, Charles R. Knight illustrated *Elasmosaurus platyurus* with its neck curved into a figure eight, looking like a python grasping its prey.† "But," argued Samuel Williston (1914), "the plesiosaurs could not and did not use their neck in such ways. They swam with the necks and head, however long, directed in front, and freedom of movement was restricted almost wholly to the anterior part. The posterior part of the neck was thick and heavy, and could not have been moved upward or downward to any considerable extent and not very much laterally." (In a letter to me in 2002, Ken Carpenter wrote, "When the *Elasmosaurus* mounts were done at Denver, I played with the neck to determine the true range of motion, not with sketches on paper. I concluded that Williston was right.") Michael Benton, author of *The Reign of the Reptiles* (1990) and *Vertebrate Paleontology* (1997), the latter a respected textbook, disagrees—as do many other paleontologists. In *Reign of the Reptiles,* he wrote (of elasmosaurs of the Jurassic, such as *Muraenosaurus*), "Some had as many as 70 cervical

---

* The study of fishing birds actually offers little help in determining how plesiosaurs might have fed. Swans, with comparably long necks, are not fish eaters; they churn up aquatic plants from the bottom. Flamingos, with even longer necks, stand on their stiltlike legs and, with their heads upside down, filter tiny organisms from the water with a sievelike arrangement in their beaks. Cormorants and anhingas (the latter sometimes known as "snakebirds") provide perhaps the best analogue; they dive beneath the surface and swim after fish, capturing them with their beaks. The cormorant grabs its prey, but the anhinga spears it and then, rising to the surface, flips it up and catches it headfirst. The long-necked herons and egrets are not swimmers at all but stand in the shallows, poised to snatch swimming fish or frogs.

† Knight's illustration was made under the direction of E. D. Cope for the American Museum of Natural History. In their 1982 book about Knight (*Dinosaurs, Mammoths and Cavemen*), Sylvia Czerkas and Donald Glut wrote, "The depiction of the extremely serpentine neck, although now known to be an error, was based on the evidence available to Cope at the time. Despite this inaccuracy, the painting is a stunning work of art conveying the drama of Mesozoic marine life."

vertebrae, and the neck could bend around upon itself two or three times. The elasmosaurs no doubt jabbed their snake-like necks rapidly among the scattering clouds of teleost fishes. They could have darted the head in and out and seized several fish without moving the body at all." It is known that they swallowed stones for ballast (or to help grind their food), so they might have sunk to the bottom to wait for unwary fish to come into striking range. This scenario is supported by the position of the eyes in the skull, facing slightly upward.

In contrast, Newman and Tarlo (1967) wrote, "in the long-necked plesiosaurs, both sets of limbs could only move in a horizontal plane, and since they could not raise their forelimbs, they could not dive." They concluded that "the long-necked forms were adept at twisting and turning with great speed, but all their time was spent at the surface of the sea." In his 1968 book *The Pattern of Vertebrate Evolution*, Halstead (a.k.a. Tarlo) wrote, "The inevitable conclusion is that the head and greater part of the neck were lifted out of the water during rapid manoeuvring, swinging over the surface and dropping in again on the sighting of fish. This high degree of manoeuvrability not only enabled the long-necked plesiosaurs to fish efficiently but must also have been equally advantageous in helping them to escape the attention of predators." As with their method of locomotion, the plesiosaurs have managed to turn the simple business of feeding into another paleontological conundrum.

A subject not often mentioned with regard to the elasmosaurs is the great degree of vulnerability represented by the long, exposed neck. Very long necks are rarely evolved because they are costly in terms of growth and maintenance, as well as the extra respiratory work needed to breathe through elongated trachea. Because all the energy spent on a longer neck means less energy that could go elsewhere—tail, limbs, growth, parturition, tougher hide, and so on—there must have been a significant metabolic advantage to a long neck. It might have enabled the animal to catch enough food to support this anomalous structure, but this seems like circular reasoning: an animal would not have developed a long neck so it could harvest the energy necessary to support such a structure. Moreover, the neck is one of the most vulnerable spots in an animal, since the nervous, circulatory, and respiratory systems all run through it in close proximity. With such dangerous predators as giant mosaurs lurking around, the long-necked elasmosaurs must have lived in constant danger of decapitation.* Could they, as Halstead suggests, "escape the attention of predators" by swimming with the head and neck lifted high out of the water?

Many scientists do not believe that a long-necked plesiosaur could actually lift its head and neck out of the water. In his popular article on plesiosaurs, Mike Everhart (2000b) wrote:

Unless the laws of physics were suspended on the behalf of these extinct creatures, it would have been impossible for them to lift much more than their head above water to breathe. If you would like to prove this for yourself, try lifting something long and heavy from one end while floating in water and not touching the bottom. As you try to raise the object, your feet and the lower part of your body will also begin to surface to counter-balance any weight above the water. In elasmosaurs, the weight of the long neck (as much as a ton or more in an adult animal) dictated that the center of gravity was just behind the front flippers. Holding the head and neck above the surface was something that could never happen unless the rest of the body was setting on a firm bottom in shallow water (a possibly fatal situation for the elasmosaur!). Even then, the limited movement between the vertebrae, limited musculature, and the sheer weight of the neck would severely limit the height to which the head could have been raised.

When a partial skeleton of a Cretaceous short-necked plesiosaur was discovered in Japan in conjunction with a large number of isolated ammonoid jaws, it provided clear evidence of the diet of these marine reptiles. (Cicimurri and Everhart [2001] listed no fewer than fifteen occurrences of the stomach contents of plesiosaurs being recorded; most of the contents consisted of cephalopods, but there is also plentiful evidence of plesiosaurs feeding on fishes.) The skeleton, which was found in an outcrop along the Obirashibe

* The long-necked terrestrial dinosaurs faced the same problems. We do not know how (or even if) creatures such as *Apatosaurus, Brachiosaurus,* and *Diplodocus* raised their heads to such astounding heights, because studies of the biomechanics of their skeletons have so far proved inconclusive. With the carnivorous theropods such as *Tyrannosaurus rex* and *Allosaurus* on the prowl, they too would have been extraordinarily susceptible to attack.

River in Hokkaido, consisted of the right half of the pectoral girdle, a nearly complete right forelimb, disarticulated vertebrae, several gastralia, and fragments of the pelvic girdle. The skull was nowhere to be found, making a specific identification impossible, but the skeleton indicated an animal approximately 10 feet long (Sato and Tanabe 1998). Like living squid and nautiluses, ammonites had beaklike jaws, and in the region that corresponded to the plesiosaur's gut, researchers found about 30 ammonite jaws, suggesting that the tiny jaws (none larger than ½ inch) were the contents of the plesiosaur's stomach. With their slender teeth, unsuitable for crushing the sturdy shells of ammonites, plesiosaurs had to have swallowed the cephalopods whole, but curiously, there was no sign of the outer shells.

In Samuel Williston's 1903 discussion of North American plesiosaurs, he mentioned that "pebbles" were often associated with plesiosaur remains. "What the use of these pebbles was I will not venture to say," he wrote, "they may have served as a sort of weight to regulate the specific gravity of the animals or they may have been swallowed accidentally." Upon reading Williston's report, dinosaur collector Barnum Brown (1904) wrote a note for *Science* in which he said, "The conclusion seems evident that invertebrate animals formed a large part of the food of plesiosaurs and that, in default of crushing teeth, the breaking up of the food was effected by the aid of these stomach stones, the presence of which further implies a thick-walled, gizzard-like arrangement in the alimentary canal." Harvard University paleontologist Charles Eastman (1904) was so offended by Brown's remarks that he submitted a rebuttal to *Science*, writing that "the history of the gizzard shows that it was developed first amongst cold-blooded vertebrates, then lost by them and afterwards acquired independently by birds." He concluded: "For our part, we are willing to consign to birds the exclusive enjoyment of gizzards and feathers. . . . Before asking us to believe that all plesiosaurs had 'gizzard-like arrangements' let it be shown that all plesiosaurs and related reptiles had the habit of gorging themselves with foreign matter to the extent asserted of the American species, and let no doubt remain that these pebbles are not of adventitious origin." The last word in this 1904 donnybrook went to the man who had started the whole thing, Samuel Williston (1904b). He too wrote a letter to *Science* in which he said, "Apropos of Dr. Eastman's letter . . . permit me to state that there is not a shadow of a doubt that the plesiosaurs, both Cretaceous and Jurassic, had the habit of swallowing such stones. At least thirty instances are now known of the occurrence of the very peculiarly worn pebbles between the ribs or with the remains of plesiosaurs in Europe and America. The fact was first published by Professor Seeley in England, in 1877."

Around 1884, Seeley found the fossil of a medium-sized plesiosaur in the English Lias that was associated with many smoothly polished stones ranging in size from grape to potato. According to Williston (1914), Seeley "believed that their occurrence with the skeleton was not accidental, but that they had been intentionally swallowed by the animal when alive, and formed at its death a part of its stomach contents." At about the same time, Williston "found several species of plesiosaurs in the chalk of Western Kansas in which similar pebbles were associated. . . . Since then, numerous discoveries have made it certain that the plesiosaurs usually, if not always, swallowed such pebbles in considerable quantities." Williston could only guess at the purpose of these "gastroliths," but because chickens swallow grit as an aid in grinding food in the gizzard, he and many other paleontologists believed that the stones served the same purpose in the marine reptiles. Williston wrote, "That the plesiosaurs picked up these siliceous pebbles, sometimes weighing half a pound, accidentally with their food is highly improbable; they surely had something to do with their food habits." But in 1981, Michael Taylor (referring to a 1980 study by Darby and Ojakangas) wrote that "plesiosaurs neutralized their upward buoyancy by swallowing masses of pebbles and retaining them in their stomachs much in the same way as modern crocodiles do." Thus ballasted, crocodiles can lie on the bottom, waiting for a prey animal to happen by. Although the plesiosaurs didn't have the powerful jaws and teeth of crocs and alligators, they might very well have been able to rest on or near the bottom with their long necks outstretched, waiting for their prey—usually fish—to swim by. (Some herbivorous dinosaurs also swallowed stones, but they probably did it as an aid to digestion, as chickens do. Neither dinosaurs nor chickens worry very much about buoyancy.)

When Samuel P. Welles and James D. Bump (1949) examined fossils of the elasmosaur *Alzadasaurus pembertoni* from Iona, South Dakota, they found 253 rounded stones "immediately in front of the pelvic girdle in a concentrated area about thirty inches square and seven inches deep. . . . As these gastroliths are composed of materials [mostly quartzite] of a common sedimentary variety, it is obvious that their original source could never be traced. In all probability the animal was many scores of miles from a shoreline at the time of its death." The function of the stones seemed perfectly obvious to Welles and Bump: "The 'gizzard stones' relieved the head of all masticatory responsibilities, leaving it free to dart after the prey, snap it up, and start it down the long neck. The creature could thus devote his full time to fishing and wasted none on ingestion."*

Mike Everhart likes the term *lithophagic,* which he uses to mean "stone-eating." Chris Whittle (then of the University of New Mexico) and Everhart wrote a paper in 2000 entitled "Apparent and Implied Evolutionary Trends in Lithophagic Vertebrates from New Mexico and Elsewhere" in which they listed the various lithophagic vertebrates, including fishes (a basking shark was found with "several pails full of pebbles in its stomach"); various reptiles, including alligators, crocodiles, lizards, snakes, and turtles; birds; and mammals, mostly pinnipeds, such as sea lions and fur seals, and, of course, dinosaurs and marine reptiles. "There is," they wrote, "enough conflicting evidence on extant lithophagic animals to prevent an accurate statement on the extinct animals' uses of the stones, but conservative comparison of animals in similar niches would be a good place to start, that is, once we decide what the contemporary vertebrates are doing with the stones."

In 1991, a rancher found plesiosaur bones in conjunction with 38 smooth, rounded pebbles piled close together at an exposure of the Pierre Shale in Logan County, Kansas. He contacted Larry Martin (of the Natural History

---

* These authors also had no doubt about the way plesiosaurs locomoted: "His paddles are highly specialized oars. The great development of the head of the prepodials indicates a considerable use of these powerful propelling mechanisms. They were undoubtedly 'feathered' on the return stroke, and then turned with the leading edge down for the propulsive stroke. It has been shown that the animals had a flexible streamlined body and that normal locomotion was probably undulatory, the paddles used probably as starters and for sudden accelerations. The relatively short, stout tail undoubtedly was a powerful organ of propulsion." This seems rather unlikely.

Museum at the University of Kansas) and Mike Everhart, and arrangements were made to perform an exploratory dig at the site. The plesiosaur, cataloged as KUVP 129774, was not identifiable from the bones, but it was clear that the stones were gastroliths. They were among the largest ever found, and, according to Cicimurri and Everhart (2001), they were "even larger than those reported from the giant sauropod *Seismosaurus.*" (The largest of the stones was more than 6 inches long and weighed 3 ¼ pounds.) Michael Taylor's idea that the "gastroliths can be eaten or vomited to change buoyancy quickly" did not convince Cicimurri and Everhart, because "it is doubtful . . . that this would have been a useful strategy for an elasmosaur with a 5–6 m (16–20 ft.) neck, especially one that was living and feeding hundreds of kilometers from the nearest sources of such stones." As to the function of the gizzard stones, Cicimurri and Everhart concluded: "The location of the gastroliths within the abdominal region . . . and their intimate association with the remains of small fish supports the hypothesis that these stones aided the plesiosaurs in the breakdown of food."

Ellis W. Shuler, dean of the Geology Department of Southern Methodist University in Dallas, invited paleontologist Samuel Welles of Berkeley to describe a new plesiosaur fossil found in the Eagle Ford Shale of Texas. Welles (1949) named the new species *Elasmosaurus morgani*, after Charles G. Morgan, the preparator of the skeleton. A year after Welles's technical description was published, the more rhetorical Shuler wrote a lengthy article about this species (now known as *Libonectes morgani*) and reflected on plesiosaurs in general: "The Cretaceous elasmosaurs had a worldwide distribution, and they developed into gigantic 'sea-serpents.' Their extinction at the close of the Cretaceous Period is even more mysterious than their origin." About a large number of gastroliths that had been found near the fossil, he wrote: "There is a feeling of silkiness to the smaller pebbles and a smooth lustrous polish that distinguishes them from other polished pebbles. Perhaps the secret of this lustre is the uniformity of the flint. Definitely the pebbles are not rounded like marbles. The spherical shapes given in the rotating grind of the ball mill are not seen in these gastroliths. An alternating rhythmic squeeze of the great gizzard muscles give the flints their beautiful polish." But Shuler also wondered about the cause of death of *Elasmosaurus morgani:* "Was its death due to a new bacterial disease sweeping over the ocean, a typhoid-pneumonia type of bacteria which was attacking even the most resistant denizens of the deep; or was it 'stomach trouble'? Or perhaps in its eagerness to pick up a supply of fine new flints for its stomach mill, our elasmosaur took in an overload. Then when it pursued downwards a school of fish it was not able to rise again because of the pressure on its lungs from the water above."

Plesiosaur fossils from England often wander from one institution to another or get reclassified with some degree of regularity. Some of the earliest fossils found at Street, in Somerset, were collected by Thomas Hawkins, who eventually assembled a huge collection, most of which he donated to the British Museum (Natural History);* he also gave some to the museums at Oxford and Cambridge. One of the Cambridge donations was a small plesiosaur fossil that had originally been named *Plesiosaurus hawkinsii* by Owen in 1838, "in honour of the gentleman to whose remarkable skill and indefatigable labour, the beautiful skeletons of it are exclusively due." Owen (1838) noticed that the neck of *P. hawkinsii* contained 27 vertebrae, while that of *P. dolichodeirus* had 35, and that the proportions were different as well, but nearly 160 years later, Storrs and Taylor (1996) revealed that it was so different from *Plesiosaurus* that it didn't even belong in the same genus. They erected the new genus *Thalassiodracon,* which means simply (and elegantly) "sea dragon." Despite its name, however, *Thalassiodracon* was hardly a dragon in the manner of *Rhomalaeosaurus* or the giant pliosaurs; it was only about 7 feet long, and its dentition suggested that it fed on small prey items such as fishes. Its eyes were large and equipped with sclerotic rings, "perhaps indicating an adaptation to low light intensities. Dark conditions occur at night, or at great water depth (unlikely in this case) or in water that is darkened by suspended solids." They concluded that the "eye was primarily adapted, as one might expect, for underwater vision." Although this seems obvious at first—plesiosaurs were aquatic, after all—it really means that vision in water was more important

* The British Museum was created by an act of Parliament in 1753, and its Natural History Department was formed from collections bequeathed by Sir Hans Sloane. In 1881, when Sir Richard Owen superintended the building of the new structure in South Kensington, it was known as the British Museum (Natural History). In 1963 it officially became the Natural History Museum, London, or, more popularly, the NHM.

than vision in air because they had to capture their prey underwater and had to see above the surface only when they breathed or rested. *Thalassiodracon* is known only from the late Triassic to early Jurassic shales of England.

Some plesiosaur fossils, after lasting for 100 million years, did not survive the blitzkrieg bombing of England during World War II. *Plesiosaurus conybeari* was first described in 1881 from Charmouth, England, and kept in the collection of the Bristol City Museum. It was an almost complete skeleton, lacking only the tip of the tail, and remarkably, what appeared to be an impression of the skin was preserved in a thin film over the body. There were no scales or scutes, so this species—and perhaps the other plesiosaurs—may have had smooth skin, in contrast to most living reptiles, which have scales of one sort or another. The fossil was destroyed in 1940, but the British Museum (Natural History) in London had made a cast, and it survived the raids. Bakker (1993a) examined it and reclassified *Plesiosaurus conybeari* as *Attenborosaurus* (after filmmaker David Attenborough), because "it is the only plesiosaurian of any age that combines a very long neck with a long, massive, evenly tapered snout, and very large, conical tooth crowns."

In their 1999 description of *Plesiosaurus tournemirensis* (named for the southern French village of Tournemire), Bardet, Godefroit, and Sciau wrote:

> During the Mid and Late Jurassic, elasmosaurs apparently began to spread all over the world, as they have been reported from Argentina, Wyoming, and India. . . . During the Late Cretaceous, elasmosaurs achieved a worldwide distribution as they have been found in both the northern and southern hemisphere. They are especially abundant in North America, where most of the genera have been described, but they also occur in western Europe, Russia, Japan, Africa and the Middle East, Madagascar, South America, New Zealand, and Antarctica. The Elasmosauridae disappeared at the end of the Maastrichtian, during the K/T biological crisis.

In a 1994 study of the extinction of the marine reptiles, Nathalie Bardet noted that by the mid to late Triassic (234.3 to 227.4 million years ago), the placodonts and the mixosaurid ichthyosaurs were gone; by the late Jurassic (150.7 to 144.2 million years ago), the cryptoclidid plesiosaurs and the family Ichthyosauridae were gone; and in what is known as the early late Cretaceous

One nineteenth-century description of a plesiosaur was "a snake threaded through the body of a turtle." This is Plesiosaurus conybeari, whose name Bakker changed to Attenborosaurus, after British nature filmmaker David Attenborough.

(98.9 to 93.5 million years ago), the last of the ichthyosaurs (the Platy-pterygidae) were gone. Sixty-five million years ago (the end of the Creta-ceous), when the Chicxulub asteroid hit, the pliosaurs, elasmosaurs, and mosasaurs, along with the terrestrial dinosaurs, disappeared forever. A high incidence of extinction among marine invertebrates (ammonites, bivalves, corals) has been detected at the end of the Jurassic (144.2 million years ago), but it is not known whether these extinctions contributed to the downfall of the placodonts and mixosaurs or whether the same thing that eliminated the invertebrates also wiped out the reptiles. When the Cenomanian stage of the Cretaceous period ended 93.5 million years ago, there was another mass extinction of marine invertebrates (Raup and Sepkoski 1986), but again, the cause-and-effect relationship cannot be established. Bardet said, "The fact that plesiosaurs may have been more opportunistic predators than ichthyosaurs could explain why they have not been directly affected," but whatever the reason, the ichthyosaurs died out long before the plesiosaurs did. The asteroid that struck the earth 65 million years ago was somehow responsible for a precipitous drop in the phytoplankton of the oceans' surface, and this may have caused a massive break in the food chain, the effect of which was felt all the way up to the top predators, the plesiosaurs and mosasaurs.

In a 1993 article called "Plesiosaur Extinction Cycles," Robert Bakker wrote, "It is well known that the terminal Cretaceous event exterminated all plesiosaurs and all mosasaurs in the Western Interior [Seaway], as well as elsewhere. However, most traditional plesiosaur classifications give the impression that this mass extinction was a most unusual event and that, for most of the Jurassic and the Cretaceous, the major plesiosaurian clades had been evolving continuously and without serious disruption." This, Bakker believes, was not at all the case; instead, "plesiosaur history was punctuated by a series of sudden mass extinctions that define natural units of marine history." He lists successive radiations and extinctions, beginning with the "Terminal Triassic Extinction and Early Liassic Re-Radiation" and concluding with the "Mid-Cretaceous Extinction and Re-Radiation," which eliminated the ichthyosaurs and opened new opportunities for plesiosaurs. Extinctions of some dinosaur species on land occurred at the same time—the Jurassic-Cretaceous boundary—and Bakker points out that roughly in the middle of the period, there was "a marked turnover among herbivorous dinosaurs—the Iguanodontidae are replaced nearly entirely by the Hadrosauridae. . . . All the available evidence favors the view that the replacement at the family level among dinosaurs occurs at the same general interval as do the extinction events among large, specialized marine reptiles." As to the identification of the extinction agent, he wrote, "Draining of the cratonic interior and continental margins would remove much of the productive area of the shallow sea." In other words, when the Western Interior Seaway dried up, the animals that lived in it died off.

In their discussion of plesiosaur remains found in the Mons Basin of southern Belgium, Mulder et al. (2000) also summarize the (limited) material on Maastrichtian elasmosaurs worldwide. Rare in the Mons Basin region, they are much more common in Californian and Moroccan deposits of the same age and type, that is, late Cretaceous marginal seas such as the coast of California, the Western Interior Seaway, the Mississippi Embayment, and the North Atlantic Basin. The authors note that Bakker (1993b) suggested that "the absence of fast-swimming plesiosaurs could be explained by the presence of an exceptionally dense algal forest. Only the California coast had an abrupt continental slope, with a narrower zone of shallow water where an algal forest could grow." Mulder and his colleagues, however, believe "that the presence of an abrupt continental slope also coincided with an upwelling of nutrient-enriched water, which favored the presence of a high biomass, being an ideal condition for open-water predators such as elasmosaurids." The worldwide distribution of elasmosaurs indicates that, like the mosasaurs, they were widespread and diversified during the late Maastrichtian, the end of which (65 million years ago) was marked by an explosion of an extraterrestrial object that hit in what is now the Yucatán. They conclude, therefore, that "the extinction of the elasmosaurids at the K/T boundary thus appears to be sudden rather than gradual."

# The Pliosaurs

*One of the relatives of the Plesiosaurs, the Pliosaur, of which genus several species of great size are known, perhaps realized in the highest degree possible the idea of a huge marine predacious reptile. The head in some of the species was eight feet in length, armed with conical teeth a foot long. The neck was not only long, but massive and powerful, the paddles, four in number, were six or seven feet in length and must have urged the vast bulk of the animal, perhaps forty feet in extent, through the water with prodigious speed. The capacious chest and great ribs show a powerful heart and lungs. Imagine such a creature raising its huge head twelve feet or more out of the water, and rushing after its prey, impelled with perhaps the most powerful oars possessed by any animal. We may be thankful that such monsters, more terrible than even the fabled sea-serpent, are unknown in our days. — J. W. Dawson (1903)*

There are those who would—with good reason—combine the plesiosaurs with the pliosaurs, but there are enough differences in functional morphology to separate them, at least for this nontechnical discussion. Appearing first in the early Jurassic, the short-necked pliosaurs developed into the apex predators of the Mesozoic, gobbling up sharks, large squids, ichthyosaurs, plesiosaurs, and probably smaller pliosaurs as well. Whereas the teeth of plesiosaurs were often narrow and needle-like, as befits fish eaters, those of the short-necked pliosaurs were conical, massive, sharp, and ridged. Their heads were often disproportionately large, and their jaws were powered by huge muscles. The name *pliosaurs* means "more lizardlike" and was bestowed on them by Richard Owen in 1842, because they appeared to him to be even more lizard-like than the plesiosaurs. He wrote, "The Enaliosaurs* are immediately connected with the Crocodilian reptiles by an extinct genus, represented by species of gigantic size. The Reptile in question is essentially a modified Plesiosaurus, but its modifications appear to entitle it to be regarded as a distinct genus, which, as it is more closely allied to the true Sauria, I propose to call it Pliosaurus."

One reason to combine the plesiosaurs with the pliosaurs is the existence of some forms that seem to be intermediate between the two, such as *Macroplata* ("long blades," named for its scapulae), which was either a short-necked plesiosaur or a (relatively) long-necked pliosaur. Based on its powerful forelimbs (attached to large bony plates that braced the front paddles), it was probably a fast swimmer. It had an elongated, crocodile-like skull that was 28 inches long and a tapering, rather inflexible neck composed of 29 short, flattened cervical vertebrae. Its total length was about 16 feet. Tate and Blake (1876) originally named the first recognized species *Plesiosaurus longirostris*, but the name *Macroplata longirostris* ("long rostrum") was applied by White in 1940. The second species of similar size (15 feet total length) was *Macroplata tenuiceps* ("narrow head") from the Lower Lias (Hettangian) of Warwickshire, En-

* *Enaliosaurus* means simply "sealizard" (from the Greek *enalios*, meaning "of or from the sea") and was introduced by Owen in 1839 as a catchall term to include all the ichthyosaurs and plesiosaurs known at that time. "As we shall see later," wrote Williston (1914), "the plesiosaurs are really of remote kinship to the ichthyosaurs, and there is no such natural group as the Enaliosauria."

gland. Like *M. longirostris,* it had a neck about twice the length of its sharp-snouted, crocodile-like head; like other short-necked plesiosaurs, *M. tenuiceps* had a shoulder girdle with coracoids that were proportionately much larger than the scapulae, indicating a powerful forward stroke for fast swimming. As Darren Naish wrote in a letter to me, "Most workers now agree that there is no simple dichotomy between 'long-necked' and 'short-necked' forms, but this does not mean goodbye to the Plesiosauroidea and Pliosauroidea. Some plesiosauroids are short-necked, and likewise some pliosauroids are long-necked."

Another possibly "intermediate" form was originally named *Plesiosaurus arcuatus* by Owen in 1840, but an examination of the material, particularly the skull, convinced Arthur Cruickshank (1994b) that it should be reclassified *Eurycleidus arcuatus* (*arcuatus* means "curved" and refers to the shape of the vertebrae), as per the 1922 analysis of Andrews. The 13-foot-long specimen, which probably came from the Lyme Regis area, "seems to possess a suite of characters intermediate between those of the pliosauroids and the plesio-sauroids . . . [which is] important and interesting in itself, as further study of more complete Lower Jurassic plesiosaurs might help to elucidate the process of change from one superfamily to another." The back of the skull of *Eurycleidus* resembled that of the plesiosauroids, but the large teeth in the front were indicative of pliosaurs. Cruickshank wrote, "Because of the lack of fusion of significant skull elements [and other anatomical differences], it is confirmed that this is not only a small specimen of the species *Eurycleidus arcuatus,* but most likely an immature juvenile." In his 1996 review of the short-necked plesiosaurs of North America, Kenneth Carpenter wrote: "Traditionally, all short-necked plesiosaurs have been grouped together into the Pliosauridae. However . . . the term 'pliosaur' should not be used indiscriminately for any short-necked plesiosaur. . . . I therefore conclude that the short neck has appeared independently at least twice in the Plesiosauria, and the term 'pliosaur' to refer to any short-necked plesiosaur should be abandoned to avoid any phyletic implications."

*Archaeonectrus rostratus,* previously known as *Plesiosaurus rostratus,* was a very primitive pliosaur with a wide geographic range, with fossil remains from the Lower Lias (Sinemurian) of England and possibly the early Jurassic of Siberia. This 12-foot-long animal resembled the true pliosauroids in its large, elongated head, and for an early Jurassic form, it had an unusually short neck, only about one and a half times the length of the skull. Its teeth were pointed, conical, and curved back. In typical pliosaurid fashion, the forelimbs were somewhat smaller than the hind ones. Some of the centra of the tail vertebrae were vertically compressed, suggesting a vertical tail fin. It is not clear whether *Archaeonectrus* represents the earliest member of the Pliosauridae or if it is simply an early type that independently evolved pliosaurid-like features. In his 1999 *Plesiosauria Translation and Pronunciation Guide,* Ben Creisler summarized the plesiosaur-pliosaur debate:

> Traditionally, the small, short-necked, large-headed plesiosaurs have been considered "pliosaurs," and classified either in the family Pliosauridae itself or as a distinct family (Polycotylidae) in the superfamily Pliosauroidea. New research questions this assumption. Carpenter (1996, 1997) interprets polycotylids as a group of short-neck plesiosauroids, closely related to elasmosaurids based on common features in the skull; Bardet (1998) has

supported this reclassification. By contrast, Bakker (1993) has argued that polycotylids are true pliosauroids and that long-necked Cretaceous elasmosaurs such as *Brancasaurus,* etc., evolved not from long-necked Jurassic plesiosauroids but from small pliosauroids that were ancestral to *Leptocleidus* and polycotylids.

*Pliosaurus,* the nominal genus, is known from the Middle to Upper Jurassic, approximately 154 to 140 million years ago. The first species (described by Owen in 1842) was *Pliosaurus brachydeirus* ("short-necked," for the compressed cervical vertebrae); others include *P. rostratus, P. andrewsi, P. macromerus,* and *P. brachyspondylus.* Although most of these pliosaur specimens were unearthed in the nineteenth century, an almost complete *Pliosaurus brachyspondylus* was uncovered in the Blue Circle Cement Works in Westbury (Wiltshire) in 1994.* An amateur fossil hunter named Simon Carpenter was prospecting in a newly excavated quarry when he came across a skull that was 7 feet long with 6-inch-long teeth. The other bones were scattered around, and some had been destroyed by the excavating process, but when the fossils were excavated and brought out (often with the quarry's heavy equipment), it turned out to be "undoubtedly the best pliosaur specimen found anywhere in the world" (Storrs 1995).

In their detailed analysis of the Westbury *Pliosaurus* skull, Taylor and Cruickshank (1993) concluded that this 30-foot-long reptile had large eyes that enabled it to hunt in dark or cloudy water; the large orbits were equipped with sclerotic plates that enabled it to change its focus underwater. Its nostrils were much too small for breathing, so it probably breathed through its mouth and might have used its nostrils for smelling underwater, like *Rhomaleosaurus.* Although *P. brachyspondylus* was about twice the size of *Rhomaleosaurus,* its nostrils were the same size. Taylor and Cruickshank wrote, "We thus reconstruct *Pliosaurus brachyspondylus* as a large visual predator, perhaps capable of

---

* The Blue Circle Cement Works has proven to be a rich source of vertebrate fossils. A list reproduced in Grange et al. (1996) includes fragments of two turtles, several ichthyosaurs, some dinosaur parts, and, in addition to teeth and bones from other pliosaurs (including *Liopleurodon*), a complete skull of *P. brachyspondylus* in 1980 and another almost complete skeleton of the same species in 1994.

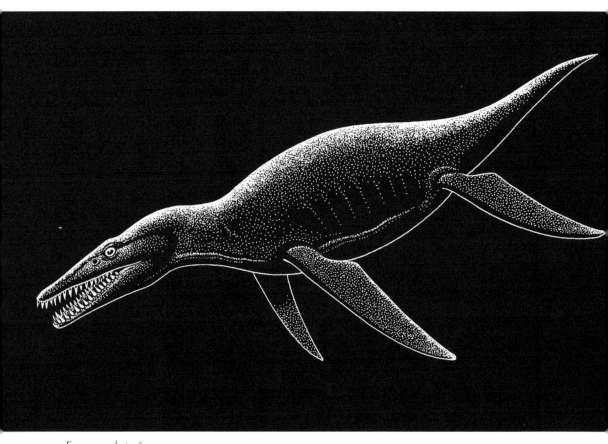

*From an analysis of the skull, investigative paleontologists have deduced that the 20-foot-long Rhomaleosaurus hunted by smell, the way most sharks do today. It is thought that other plesiosaurs relied primarily on sight.*

underwater olfaction, and probably fed opportunistically on a wide variety of food, including fishes, cephalopods, and other reptiles as available. It was apparently a dominant carnivore which despatched large prey such as fishes and reptiles with deep bites with its strong caniniform anterior dentition, and then used its broad, unobstructed palate, widened posterior gape and hooked posterior dentition to help move the prey down the gullet." In other words, *P. brachyspondylus* was a formidable predator, capable of attacking and eating anything and everything that it encountered – including dead dinosaurs. During the excavation, three armored scutes (horn-covered bony plates set in the skin) were found, obviously not from a pliosaur. Taylor, Norman, and Cruickshank (1993) identified them as belonging to an unidentified armored ornithischian dinosaur such as an ankylosaur or a stegosaur and tentatively concluded "that the pliosaur had been scavenging a dinosaur corpse shortly before its own death, and that the scutes were transported inside the pliosaur's stomach."

One of the more spectacular of the English pliosaurs was *Rhomaleosaurus* (from the Greek *rhomaleos,* meaning "strong"). The first *Rhomaleosaurus* fossil was found in an alum quarry in Yorkshire in 1848 and described by Alexander Carte and W. H. Baily in 1863. (They named it *Plesiosaurus cramptoni,* but it was renamed *Rhomaleosaurus zetlandicus* in 1874.) The magnificent specimen, 23 feet in total length and complete except for one of the flippers, which had been destroyed before the fossil was spotted, was displayed for five years in Mulgrave Castle, home of the Marquis of Normanby, owner of the alum mine. In 1853, the fossil was brought to Dublin, where it was displayed at the Zoological Society of Ireland, whose annual report included this description:

It was presented by the Marquess of Normanby to Sir Philip Crampton, who has kindly put it at the disposal of the Society for exhibition. The most interesting relic, one of "the great Sea Dragons" of the ancient world, will no doubt, prove eminently attractive, not only to the citizens of Dublin, but to the many scientific and other visitors likely to visit this city during the next few months. Its size is so great that the Council felt obliged to construct a special building of 36 feet long for its due exhibition.

After its original triumphs, *Rhomaleosaurus* was exhibited in various buildings of what is now the Natural History Museum of Ireland and finally broken up. "For those who want to see the specimen," wrote Roger Osborne in his idiosyncratic discussion of Yorkshire's geological and paleontological history, "there is bad news and good news. The bad news is that the body of the fossil is broken up and kept in crates in storage. . . . The good news is that during the last 140 years several casts of the specimen have been taken, and these can now be seen in the Natural History Museum in London, the Bath Literary and Scientific Institution, and Cornell University in New York."

What sort of animal was this "great sea dragon"? It was one of the earliest of the giant sauropterygian predators that "fed on a wide variety of active prey, and forcibly dismembered larger prey by shaking and twisting them" (Taylor 1992). For some 30 or 40 million years, the 18-foot-long, crocodile-headed rhomaleosaurs were among the top predators in the ocean. Their jaws ended in a flattened, spoon-shaped structure (sometimes known as a rosette) armed with particularly large tusks, probably useful in getting a grip on the prey before twisting off a piece. As expected in aquatic animals, *Rhomaleosaurus* had no eardrum. The tympanum is an adaptation to hearing airborne sound, and a primarily aquatic animal has less need for a tympanum because it can hear by direct conduction from the water. "The ears were not acoustically isolated from the braincase," wrote Taylor (1992), "so underwater directional hearing was poor, and sonar was not possible." The large eyes suggest that they were visual hunters, and the presence of a sclerotic ring meant that they could adjust the shape of the eyeball underwater for increased visual acuity. *Rhomaleosaurus zetlandicus* — and perhaps the short-necked Cretaceous polycotylids and the elasmosaurs — had additional modifications that made them even more efficient predators. In his detailed analysis of the head of *R. zetlandicus*, Taylor (1992) concluded that it could swim with its mouth slightly open, allowing water to pass through scoop-shaped openings in the roof of the mouth, then through a channel where smell sensors were located, and out through the external nostrils. This arrangement would have enabled this 18-foot plesiosaur to hunt its prey by smell — like a shark (Cruickshank et al. 1991). Brown and Cruickshank (1994) suggested that *Cryptoclidus* also breathed through its mouth, and like all rhomaleosaurs, it could detect scents underwater. But unlike the powerful pliosaurid *Rhomaleosaurus*, the skull and jaws of *Cryptoclidus* were lightly built, and it probably fed on soft-bodied cephalopods and small fishes. Brown and Cruickshank concluded, "The general structure is compatible with a filter feeding habit suggested for cryptoclidids by Brown (1981a) and resembles that of modern 'krill' feeders described by Massare (1987)."

One of the most unusual plesiosaur fossils — in fact, one of the most unusual fossils of *anything* — is the plesiosaur found in 1986 in an underground opal mine at Coober Pedy, South Australia. The fossil, which was in thousands of pieces, was found by a miner named Joe Vida, whose clumsy attempts to excavate it resulted in many of the smaller pieces being lost. Paul Willis painstakingly reassembled it, and it is now an almost complete skeleton of a small plesiosaur about 6 feet long, with the skull, lower jaw, teeth,

vertebral column, ribs, and most of the pelvic and pectoral girdles composed of solid opal. Willis named it "Eric," after a nonsense Monty Python song called "Eric the Half-a-Bee." (The opalized fish gastroliths and vertebrae that were found in the gut regions were named "Wanda.") Entrepreneur Sid Londish bought "Eric" and paid Willis to restore it, but he went bankrupt and put the opalized fossil up for public auction. Because the entire fossil was made of precious opal, its value was estimated at $300,000, and there was no way of guaranteeing that someone would not buy it and cut it into small pieces. (Opal is a mineral that consists of silica that has filled-in fissures and cavities of rock. It is usually colorless, but in gem opal, tiny silicate microspheres reflect light in a brilliant play of iridescence, usually in red, green, or blue.) Alex Ritchie, curator of paleontology at the Australian Museum in Sydney, came up with the idea of raising the money on national television, and $340,000 was donated by individuals and companies to purchase the precious fossil and keep it intact.

"Eric" has now been assigned to the genus *Leptocleidus* ("slender clavicle") and probably represents a new species. The opalized "Eric" was found with

*"Eric," the Australian plesiosaur with an opalized skeleton, once looked something like this.* Leptocleidus *was about 10 feet long.*

fish vertebrae inside the gut, suggesting a small-prey diet, and gastroliths that may have aided in digestion or even been used as ballast. The other *Leptocleidus* species (which all have proper names) are less dramatic in substance; all are smallish plesiosaurs with a triangular skull that has a distinct crest. The nominal species *(Leptocleidus superstes)* was found in England (Andrews 1922a), and representative fossils have also been found in South Africa *(L. capensis)*. A western Australian specimen is *L. clemai*, named for John Clema, who sponsored the expedition that excavated the fossils. *Leptocleidus clemai* was the largest species, reaching about 10 feet in length; the other species were about porpoise sized, and their size and structure suggest that they might have been inshore or even freshwater inhabitants. "Leptocleidids," wrote Cruickshank et al. in 1999, "are relatively small plesiosaurs which probably fed on fish and cephalopods in the surf zone or estuaries, and seem to be related to the 5 m long Early Jurassic genus *Rhomaleosaurus.*" This has been borne out by O'Keefe's 2002 cladistic analysis, which shows that *Leptocleidus* is indeed a member of the Rhomaleosauridae.

Another opalized plesiosaur skeleton was found in 1967 by John and Molly Addyman, opal miners from Andamooka, South Australia. In November 2000, the "Addyman plesiosaur" was bought by the Adelaide newspaper the *Advertiser* for $25,000 and donated to the South Australian Museum. It was studied by the museum's paleontologist Ben Kear (he is also examining an ichthyosaur skull to see if the animal was deaf), who assigned it to the genus *Leptocleidus,* but he did not identify the species. The skeleton, which is about 80 percent complete, is just over 2 feet long. Because it was "by far the smallest and most immature example of the genus yet discovered," Kear realized that it was a baby, or, in paleo-speak: "Small size coupled with incomplete fusion of the basicranial elements, vertebral centra, neural arches and cervical ribs, and poorly ossified articular surfaces on humerus and femur indicate that the specimen is at an early stage in its ontogeny." But even for its small size, this specimen (cataloged as SAM P15980) had very large flippers. Kear wrote:

> The most distinct growth related change evident in SAM P15980 is the disproportionately large size of the propodial elements, which equal around 17.5% of the estimated 700 mm total body length. This contrasts

with more mature specimens of *Leptocleidus* spp., in which the propodials are considerably smaller, generally representing only around 9%–11%. The relative proportions of the propodial elements also appears to vary with ontogenetic stage, juveniles showing very nearly equal humeral and femoral lengths unlike more mature individuals in which the femur is around 6% larger. The functional implications of this disparity in limb proportions might reflect the presence of differing locomotion and buoyancy regimes between adult and juvenile individuals. Indeed Wiffen *et al.* (1995) suggested that juvenile plesiosaurs might have specifically employed slower swimming speeds and a more hydrostatic (passive) regulation of body trim. In the case of taxa such as *Leptocleidus,* in which both juveniles and adults appear to have exclusively occupied freshwater to shallow near-shore marine depositional environments, alternative behavioural strategies such as migration, differing prey preference and/or feeding zones within the water column might also have been present to avoid intraspecific competition between age groups.

One of the biggest and most formidable of the pliosaurs was *Kronosaurus,* from the early Cretaceous of Australia. (The name comes from *Kronos,* the Greek mythological figure that ate his children.) In 1931–1932, an expedition from the Museum of Comparative Zoology of Harvard University, headed by W. E. Schevill, discovered an almost complete skeleton of *Kronosaurus* in the Army Downs region of Queensland. It was dynamited out by Schevill's assistant, and about four tons of rock and fossil was wrapped in bloodied sheepskins and sent back to Harvard. In the 1950s, renowned paleontologist Alfred Sherwood Romer helped mount the new Queensland material in Harvard's Museum of Comparative Zoology, but the bones were badly eroded and required much plaster and even more imagination to reconstruct the skeleton. (Cynics referred to it as "Plasterosaurus" at the time, because so much of the original fossil material was encased in plaster.) As assembled by Romer and his colleagues, *Kronosaurus* had 43 presacral (forward of the pelvis) vertebrae, which stretched it to a length of 42 feet, the size of a humpback whale. Subsequently unearthed pliosaur fossils – substantially more complete than "Plasterosaurus" – have had no more than 35 dorsal vertebrae, making

Romer's original estimate somewhat suspect, and reducing the Harvard *Kronosaurus* to a more modest 35 feet. (Despite the revisionists, however, in 1999, Cruickshank et al. wrote, "*Kronosaurus queenslandicus* is a giant form reaching nearly 14 m [45 feet] as shown by the reconstructed skeleton on display at the Harvard Museum of Comparative Zoology.") The massive, crested skull of the Harvard specimen measures 110.7 inches (more than 9 feet) long, which makes it more than twice as long as that of *Tyrannosaurus*, the largest of the terrestrial carnivores, whose skull has been measured at 52 inches. (Both wither in comparison to the skull of today's sperm whale, which can be 18 *feet* long.) Even at the reduced length of 35 feet, the early Cretaceous *Kronosaurus* was one of the largest marine reptiles and certainly one of the most terrifying predators that ever lived. Its massive jaws held an array of teeth that were 11 inches long, longer than the canines of the Pleistocene saber-toothed cats, and equaled today only by the lower jaw teeth of sperm whales.*

The type specimen for *Kronosaurus queenslandicus* is based on a jaw fragment with six teeth that was discovered by Andrew Crombie in 1899 near Hughenden in central Queensland and described by Heber Longman in 1924, 1930, and 1932. In 1929, more material was found at the same location, and under Longman's supervision (he was the director of the Queensland Museum), a restoration of the specimen was attempted (Longman 1932). The skull is broad, low, and flat—very different from the Harvard specimen, which is deeper and more robust and has had an unwarranted sagittal crest applied to it in plaster. It is likely that it is from a different species, although both are still classified as *K. queenslandicus.* In 1998, Australian paleontologist John Long wrote, "Molnar (1991) doubts that the Harvard skeleton is really the same species as the type material described as *Kronosaurus queenslandicus* by Longman (1924) since the two specimens came from different aged strata." As Tony Thulborn and Susan Turner (1993) wrote, "it is difficult to judge the extent of

---

* Of course, there are teeth longer than 11 inches today, such as the ivory tusks of walruses and elephants and the spiraling tooth of the narwhal, but none of these are used for biting. In fact, it is questionable whether the sperm whale bites anything with its massive ivory pegs; most of the squid eaten by the teuthophagous sperm whales show no sign of having been bitten, and it is now believed that the whales send out focused bursts of sound that stun or even kill the squid, which the whales then gobble up.

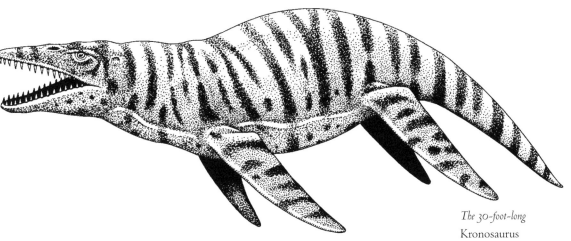

The 30-foot-long
Kronosaurus
queenslandicus,
*known from the
early Cretaceous of
Australia, was one
of the most fearsome
predators that ever
lived on Earth. Its
massive, flat-topped
skull was 9 feet
long, more than
twice as long as that
of* Tyrannosaurus
rex, *the largest of
all terrestrial
carnivores.*

any differences in skull shape, given that a considerable part of the Harvard specimen has been restored in plaster." Plaster or no plaster, it is a curious thing that "we still do not have a description of the skeleton, despite its relative completeness" (Long 1998).

Colin McHenry of Canowindra, New South Wales, has a thing about giant pliosaurs and wrote his Ph.D. dissertation on *Kronosaurus.* In a letter to me in 2002, he said:

> The main thing about *Kronosaurus,* from an overall appearance point of view, is that the body is much shorter than the Harvard mount. The head also doesn't have that crest, or huge bulbous protrusion on the top of the skull that they reconstructed. . . . Rather than looking like a killer whale with big flippers, *Kronosaurus* was more of a sea lion with the skull of a croc. The differences between it and other types of plesiosaurs are quite subtle, and are to do with the small differences in the proportions of the neck, flippers, and body.

In 1992, Oliver Hampe of the Frankfurt Museum described a very large, short-necked pliosaur from the Boyaca region of northern Colombia. He named it *Kronosaurus boyacensis,* but its thickened ribs (not known in any other pliosaur) indicate that it might be different enough from *Kronosaurus* to warrant the erection of a new genus for the South American form. It was

*With the head and teeth of a crocodile and the body of a sea lion, the 50-foot-long Liopleurodon was the terror of the late Jurassic seas of Europe.*

missing only the tail, and with nineteen dorsal vertebrae, it was estimated to have reached a total length of 30 feet. At this length, *Kronosaurus boyacensis* would have been a fearsome predator; its sharp, ribbed teeth were the size of bananas.

The gigantic pliosaur *Kronosaurus* (of whatever species) has been implicated in a direct attack on the elasmosaur *Woolungasaurus.* When Australian paleontologists Thulborn and Turner (1993) examined the skull of the elasmosaur found in Queensland in 1980, they saw that it was crushed so badly that no one had noticed the tooth marks. (Indeed, the skull was in such bad shape that it was actually broken in half, and the two pieces were sent to two different institutions, the Queensland Geological Survey and the Australian Museum in Sydney.) Thulborn and Turner described some of the damage to the reassembled skull as "not readily explicable as the results of post-mortem crushing and distortion" and concluded that it had been inflicted by a predator with exceptionally large teeth, probably *Kronosaurus.* Of the possible encounter, they wrote:

> The long and extremely flexible neck of the elasmosaurs, sometimes comprising more than 70 vertebrae, was probably an adaptation for seizing fast-moving fishes and cephalopods; the head could be swept smoothly and rapidly through a wide range, both sideways and dorsoventrally [up and down], in pursuit of such elusive prey. . . . at the same time, this long

neck was probably a major liability, since it would be an obvious point of attack for predators such as pliosaurs. A single bite to the neck might sever the spinal cord, thus immobilizing the animal. In the present case, the pliosaurian predator may have bitten rather far forwards on the neck and into the skull of *Woolungasaurus,* either by mischance or because the elasmosaur was attempting some evasive maneuver.

As large as or larger than *Kronosaurus* was *Liopleurodon,* a gigantic predatory pliosaur that one source (Haines 1999) said is "25 metres [82 feet] long and weighs almost 150 tonnes. Each flipper measures over 3 metres, and at the end of his huge mouth he carries a crown of dagger-like teeth for impaling prey." (The name *Liopleurodon* means "smooth and ribbed teeth," from the Greek *leios,* for "smooth"; *pleuron,* for "rib"; and *odon,* for "tooth." The teeth, triangular in cross section, have one smooth face and another that is strongly ridged.) Tim Haines is the author of the book *Walking with Dinosaurs* and produced the BBC television program of the same name that aired in Britain in October 1999. The book includes a limited bibliography, but there is a list of scientists who are acknowledged for their expertise, and one of these advisers is David Martill of the University of Portsmouth, who studies plesiosaurs. He has examined fragments of giant individuals of *Liopleurodon ferox* from the clays of Oxford, hinting that these pliosaurs may have been in the 50-foot range. (In the 1991 *Fossils of the Oxford Clay,* he wrote, "The skull of *Liopleurodon* may have been up to 3 m long, making it the largest known marine reptile, and possibly the largest carnivorous reptile. A specimen in excess of four metres in length . . . was discovered during preparation of this book.") It appears that Martill provided some information on the gigantic pliosaurs, but Haines (like Romer) was apparently unsatisfied with a pliosaur "only" 50 feet long and increased its size on his own. Estimates of total length for *Liopleurodon* are based on very large but fragmentary specimens that suggest a length of around 60 to 65 feet, but for the BBC to claim that it weighed 150 tons—as much as a blue whale—seems irresponsible and sensationalistic.*

* Following the airing of the television series and the publication of the accompanying book (also called *Walking with Dinosaurs*), Dave Martill and Darren Naish wrote *Walking with Dinosaurs, The Evidence: How Did They Know That?* In answer to the question "How big was

In any event, the description of *Liopleurodon's* "crown of dagger-like teeth" appears to be incorrect, since Noè (2001) has shown that this "spatulate rosette" of teeth did not exist in life and was caused by crushing of the fossil. Other large pliosaurs, such as the recently described *Maresaurus coccai* from Argentina (Gasparini 1997), were said to have had a spatulate rostrum fitted with a rosette of large, caniniform teeth, but there too, the splayed-out teeth did not exist in the living animal. *Maresaurus,* which means "sea lizard," reached a length of 20 feet. With its mouthful of sharp teeth and its powerful paddles, these pliosaurs probably resembled today's great white shark in their attack strategies; they rushed at their victims from below and took great bites out of them. Noè (2001) uses the term "bolt-shake feeding" to describe the technique of pliosaurs that took huge chunks out of their prey by violently shaking their heads while holding on with their teeth. Whether they were 30, 40, or 50 feet long, there is no question that the large pliosaurs — *Liopleurodon, Kronosaurus, Maresaurus, Brachauchenius, Megalneusaurus, Pliosaurus,* and *Peloneustes* — with their massive jaws filled with big, sharp teeth and their short, heavily muscled necks, were probably close relatives and the predominant marine predators of their time. Here's how Haines described an imaginary encounter between *Liopleurodon* and the ichthyosaur *Ophthalmosaurus:*

> He *[Liopleurodon]* raises his massive head slowly and then drives his flippers down. As he lurches forward, ammonites are sent tumbling through the water and fish are dragged off the coral in his wake. His mouth opens and snaps firmly shut round the mid-portion of the struggling Ophthalmo-saurus. The power of the attack carries both his head and his prey clean

---

*Liopleurodon,*" they wrote: "Because it is not possible to simply put whales onto weighing scales, experts disagree over the weights of these animals. Some say that the largest blue whales may reach an astonishing 200 tonnes, while others say that they probably don't even reach 100 tonnes. Regardless, weights within the range were then applied to *Liopleurodon.* However, most of a whale's bulk is carried in the thick blubber layers it carries for use on its long migrations, and to insulate it from the cold of the polar seas it often frequents. *Liopleurodon* was a denizen of warm tropical seas and would not have had such blubber. We therefore estimate that even the biggest pliosaurs would not have weighed as much as the biggest whales."

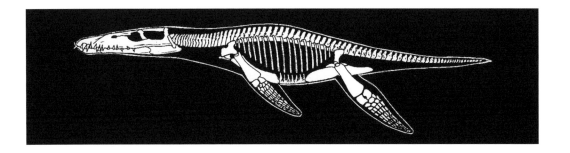

out of the water, where they hang for a moment before he brings both down with explosive force. Among all the spray and blood, his victim dies instantly, her body punctured by his long teeth and her back broken. He adjusts her limp corpse in his mouth, repeatedly biting and shaking it. Eventually it breaks into three pieces and, grasping the front portion, he rises to the surface, flicking to the back of his gaping pink throat and swallowing.

*Skeletal reconstruction of the giant pliosaur* Liopleurodon *(after Newman and Tarlo 1967). Notice the prominent belly ribs (gastralia).*

Although most of the skeleton was destroyed in the process of removing it, a Russian *Liopleurodon* was discovered on the right bank of the Volga River in 1938. The remainder, which consisted of the skull and pectrum, was saved and described in 1948 by the Soviet paleontologist Novozhilov as *Pliosaurus rossicus.* Then the ubiquitous Beverly Halstead (1971) recognized it as *Liopleurodon* and renamed it *Liopleurodon rossicus.* In 1966, Ken Carpenter described a somewhat smaller version of *Liopleurodon,* which he named *Plesiopleurodon* ("near *Liopleurodon*"), found in the Belle Fourche Shale of Wyoming. Like its larger namesake, *Plesiopleurodon* had powerful jaws and eight pairs of caniniform teeth, which were smooth and not striated like those of other, similar species. (In his thesis, Noè [2001] says that *Plesiopleurodon* is different enough from *L. ferox* to suggest that it might belong to another genus altogether.)

In 1984, a fragmentary skeleton was discovered by a student near the village of Aramberri, in Nuevo Leon, northwestern Mexico. It was originally thought to have come from some sort of dinosaur, but later examination revealed it to have belonged to a pliosaur. Eberhard ("Dino") Frey, Céline Buchy, and Wolfgang Stinnesbeck examined the material in the museum in Linares, Mexico, and discussed it in a presentation at the European Workshop on Vertebrate Paleontology, held in Florence in September 2001. When the press got hold of the story, the vertebrae (about which Frey et al. had said "a precise identification is not possible for the moment") had somehow grown into a nearly complete 65-foot-long skeleton of *Liopleurodon*, possibly the biggest marine reptile that ever lived, with "machete-sized teeth and jaws powerful enough to chew through granite" (BBC News, December 30, 2002). A granite-chewing pliosaur may be a bit over the top, but a Mexican pliosaur (even if it is not *Liopleurodon*) is indeed newsworthy, as no comparable fossils have been described from there. Much more work is required on the fossil known as the "Monster of Aramberri" (half of it is still in the ground), but it is possible that in life this giant pliosaur weighed as much as 50 tons, about the weight of a full-grown bull sperm whale.* Evidence of a massive bite mark on the skull suggests a battle between this monster and another, and if this one was the loser, imagine how big the winner must have been. It appears that the great marine reptiles are on the way to achieving a reputation previously accorded only such infamous terrestrial carnivores as *Tyrannosaurus rex* — but no *T. rex* weighed more than 7.5 tons.

Evidence of another specimen of *Liopleurodon ferox* was found in northwestern France (Bardet et al. 1993), confirming the connection between the Oxford Clay of England and the northern coast of Normandy, immediately across the English Channel. A mandible about 3¼ feet long was found in a quarry at Argences, probably representing a juvenile. In a 1999 presentation on the pliosaurs of the Oxford Clay, Noè wrote, "As predaceous marine reptiles, pliosaurs were wonderfully adapted to a marine environment. Stream-

---

* Animals supported by water and therefore spared the debilitating pull of gravity can achieve greater weight and bulk than their terrestrial counterparts. The largest and heaviest land mammal alive today is the African elephant, which can reach a weight of 8 tons, but the sauropod dinosaurs were the heaviest animals ever to walk the earth; Colbert (1962) estimated the weight of *Brachiosaurus* at 78 tons. (It was originally believed that such gigantic animals could not possibly support themselves on land and had to spend most of their lives in the water, but this idea has now been thoroughly rejected.) The weight of a full-grown fin whale is about 76 tons, and right whales and bowheads regularly go over 100 tons. The blue whale, which Lyall Watson (1981) calls "the largest animal the world has ever known," weighs in at well over 150 tons; Watson reports the "recorded maximum of 178,000 kg (196 tons)."

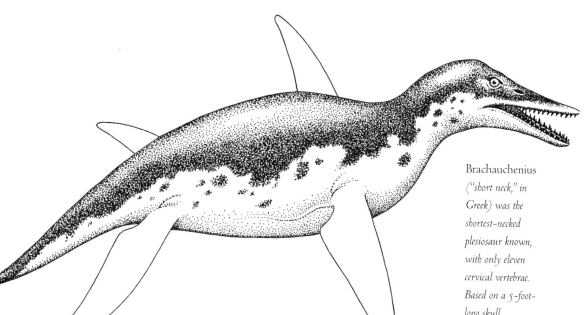

Brachauchenius ("short neck," in Greek) was the shortest-necked plesiosaur known, with only eleven cervical vertebrae. Based on a 5-foot-long skull, Brachauchenius is estimated to have reached a length of 36½ feet, making it one of the last of the great mega-predators of the late Cretaceous.

lining reduced drag, hydrofoil limbs permitted motion through a dense, yet buoyant medium, and an enlarged head mounted on a shortened neck allowed large prey to be tackled. . . . The large head, with massive jaw muscles to exert a powerful bite, sharp teeth and powerful neck made pliosaurs top predators in Mesozoic food webs." The narrow, elongated skull and widely spaced sharp teeth suggest that *Peloneustes* was a fish eater; with its wide skull and powerful (often broken) teeth, *Liopleurodon* obviously favored large, hard-boned prey.

Another of the more formidable giant pliosaurs was *Brachauchenius lucasi*, identified by Samuel Williston in 1903 from a skull and vertebrae found in the Benton Formation of Ottawa County, Kansas. He called it *Brachauchenius* ("short neck" in Greek) because it was "the shortest-necked plesiosaur known" at the time, with only eleven cervical vertebrae in a neck that was about 75 percent as long as the skull; *lucasi* was for Frederick A. Lucas of the U.S. National Museum, "who has done much valuable work in American paleontology." The short neck and relatively long skull are pliosaurian features, and the skull is distinctive for its broad, triangular, mosasaur-like shape that ends in a point, unlike that of other large pliosaurs such as *Liopleurodon* and *Pliosaurus,* whose skulls taper into a narrow, blunt snout. The large teeth have striations that branch toward the root, unlike the straight grooves on the teeth of Jurassic pliosaurs. Known from three nearly complete skulls with mandibles and two partial skeletons, and based on a 5-foot-long skull, *Brachauchenius* is estimated to reach up to 36½ feet in length and is therefore one of the last of the great mega-predators, dating from the Cenomanian-Turonian (early late Cretaceous). These gigantic forms are younger than the kronosaurs and pliosaurs and may have evolved – possibly from unknown short-necked elasmosaurids – to fill the ecological niche left vacant by the disappearance of the earlier gigantic species of the Cenomanian and early Turonian. An alternative explanation is that *Brachauchenius* is actually a short-necked pliosaurid. After the first *Brachauchenius lucasi* from Kansas, a second specimen was collected from the Eagle Ford Formation near Austin, Texas, and was described by Williston in 1907. A third specimen, more complete and somewhat better preserved, was collected from the Greenhorn Limestone in Russell County, Kansas, and is on display at the Sternberg Museum in Hays, Kansas.

Judy Massare has studied the eating habits of the plesiosaurs, but she does not attempt to resolve the bothersome question of how these gigantic reptiles could maintain enough energy in the cold ocean to swim so fast and attack so viciously. In her 1987 analysis of the "tooth morphology and prey preference of Mesozoic marine reptiles," she wrote that "the teeth of many plesiosauroids, such as *Plesiosaurus dolichodeirus, P. brachypterygius, Muraenosaurus leedsi,* and *Cryptoclidus eurymerus,* are very long, slender cones with sharply pointed apices"; they were similar to the teeth of ichthyosaurs, in that they rarely show wear and were probably used to pierce soft prey. She compares the sharp, ridged teeth of *Liopleurodon* to the teeth of killer whales, saying that they are frequently broken and worn, "suggesting a diet of fleshy prey with fairly large bones, such as very large fish and other reptiles."

In a discussion published in 1959 ("*Pliosaurus brachyspondylus* [Owen] from the Kimmeridge Clay"), Tarlo wrote:

In the centre aisle of the University Museum, Oxford, there is on exhibition a giant mandible belonging to a Pliosaur from the Kimmeridge Clay of Cumnor, Berkshire. It was first noted by Prestwich and seems to have been acquired by the Museum some time between 1880 and 1888. In 1933 Mr. H. J. Hambidge completed the long and arduous task of renovating this specimen which he had first known in 1907. Professor W. J. Sollas had intended to describe the mandible in 1936, but unfortunately he died the same year. Since that time, this remarkable mandible has remained unidentified and undescribed and no recognition has been given to the skilful work of Mr. Hambidge.

Tarlo then describes the mandible, which, if complete, would have been 9¾ feet long. "Without doubt," he wrote, "it belongs to the largest pliosaur ever recorded, somewhat exceeding the size of the Cretaceous *Kronosaurus*." (In 1959, *Kronosaurus* was believed to have been 45 feet long.) Tarlo wrote that the giant pliosaurs had previously been lumped into *Pliosaurus macromerus*, but "a detailed examination of these remains has demonstrated the existence of two different Pliosaur genera represented by the species *Pliosaurus brachydeirus* and *Stretosaurus macromerus*. (*Stretosaurus* was the genus that Tarlo erected for the newly described material, but the name would not last long.)

When Tarlo examined pliosaur fossils from the Kimmeridge Clay formation in Ely (Wiltshire), he found that the Kimmeridgian pliosaurs could be separated into two groups: one contained *Pliosaurus brachyspondylus* and *P. brachydeirus*, and the other was a new genus that he proposed to call *Stretosaurus*, after the village of Stretham, where the giant pliosaur fossil had been discovered in 1952. Further study, however, revealed that the bone he took to be a scapula was actually an ilium, which meant that his analysis was wrong, so he made *Stretosaurus* a junior synonym of *Liopleurodon*. In his 1989 study, Halstead wrote, "The basis for the erection of a new genus likewise foundered and the name *Stretosaurus* is now redundant and should be replaced by the long-established *Liopleurodon*." (In his 1959 paper on *Stretosaurus*, Tarlo suggested that this giant pliosaur might have been even larger than *Liopleurodon*, but now that the two genera have been synonymized, *Liopleurodon* retains the title of largest pliosaur known.) Again employing the peculiar approach that resulted from his midcareer name change, Halstead managed to criticize himself when he wrote: "As shall be seen Tarlo (1958, 1959b) was certainly also mistaken in trying to insist that the fore- and hindlimbs moved differently."

In McNamara and Long's 1998 book *The Evolution Revolution*, there is an almost casual mention of a presentation by Colin McHenry, Arthur Cruickshank, David Martill, and Leslie Noè (at the 1996 meeting of the Palaeontological Society in Birmingham, England) of "a giant pliosaurid from the 160-million-year old Late Jurassic Oxford Clay. This gargantuan beast of the sea had neck vertebrae 40% larger than those of *Kronosaurus*. Such a megapliosaur may have reached lengths of 18–20 metres and weighed up to 50 tonnes." Ben Creisler (1998) picks up the story:

> The excitement centered on a single vertebra found years ago in the Oxford Clay and stored at the Peterborough Museum in Cambridgeshire, England. The long-neglected piece was in rather poor condition and covered in blue paint for some unexplained reason. A number of plesiosaur experts reexamined the bone and detected similarities to a neck vertebra of a pliosaur—except that the Peterborough specimen was 245 mm across compared to 182 mm across in *Kronosaurus!* The reidentification raised a few problems—the specimen seemed to lack the characteristic plesiosaur foramina (small holes) on the underside of the centrum, while the rib articulations had thin buttresses up to the neural arch, unlike in typical plesiosaurs.

The latest salvos were fired by Darren Naish, Leslie Noè, and Dave Martill, who wrote an article for *Dino Press*, a Japanese dinosaur magazine. As translated into English, the article reintroduces the giant pliosaurs that reached stupendous sizes. A massive lower jaw was found in the Kimmeridge Clay Formation and assigned by Beverly Tarlo (1959a) to *Pliosaurus macromerus*. Extrapolating from the mandible, the skull would measure "an impressive 2.9 m [9.5 feet]. Complete pliosaur skeletons suggest that the total length of these animals is about six times longer than the total length of the skull. It appears possible, therefore, that the Berkshire mandible represents an animal of an amazing 18 m [59 feet] long!" The authors refer to this creature as "megapleurodon," but they insist that this is just a nickname and should have no scientific standing.

Another large pliosaur found in the Oxford Clay is *Simolestes* ("snub-nosed robber") *vorax* ("voracious"), which reached a length of 20 feet—maybe more. The ends of its jaws were expanded into a spatulate rosette armed with huge caniniform teeth, which suggested a powerful bite-and-twist feeding style: "The rosette of symphysial teeth was probably used for tearing large chunks of flesh from its prey, or for biting chunks out of larger ammonites" (Martill 1991). Tarlo (1960) described this arrangement as follows: "The symphysis is extremely short and so expanded that its 5 pairs of large caniniform teeth are set almost in a circle. I find it difficult to offer any functional explanation of this remarkable dentition." There is an explanation, but it is not a functional one. In his 2001 Ph.D. dissertation, Noè wrote:

> The holotype of *Simolestes vorax* NHM R3319 preserves the majority of the teeth, *in situ*, in both the upper and lower jaws. The anterior caniniforms splay out around the mandibular symphysis and this arrangement has baffled generations of paleontologists. . . . Examination of the holotype indicates that the skull has been subject to considerable dorso-ventral crushing, splaying the anterior caniniform teeth laterally. . . . In life, the teeth of *Simolestes* did not splay out as preserved in the holotype, and no functional explanation is needed for the apparently bizarre teeth.

When the teeth of *Simolestes* were believed to have been splayed out, it was assumed that the animal fed on large vertebrate prey, but with Noè's revision, "*Simolestes* is reinterpreted as primarily teuthophagous [squid eating], consuming belemnites, soft teuthids or ammonites."

From the Harrar region of Ethiopia, von Huene (1938) described a fragment of the snout of a pliosaur that he identified as *Simolestes nowackianus*, but in 1996, Nathalie Bardet and Stéphane Hua wrote that the supposed African species *Simolestes nowackianus* is based on part of a jaw belonging to the teleosaurid crocodile *Machimosaurus*. The newly described *Maresaurus coccai* from Argentina (Gasparini 1997) is also a simolestine pliosaur, with a spatulate, tooth-studded rosette on the end of its jaws. (It now appears that the spatulate, tooth-studded rosette is likely an artifact of crushing and did not exist in life in any pliosaurs.) *Maresaurus* is known only from a yard-long skull and a few cervical vertebrae, but its 20-foot-long body was probably like that of other pliosaurids. (According to Noè, *Simolestes* and *Maresaurus* might be synonymous, and both might be synonyms for an older taxon called *Eurysaurus*.)

There were gigantic pliosaurs in Jurassic North America too. In 1898, Wilbur Knight found a fossil he christened *Megalneusaurus*, or "great swimming lizard," and described it as "the largest known animals of the Sauropterygia." Its forelimbs were said to be 7 feet long (Williston 1903), but the actual remains appear to have been lost. Recently, a smaller specimen was found in southern Alaska (Weems and Blodgett 1996), but the classification of this specimen remains unresolved. According to Creisler, Robert Bakker is currently studying the material to provide a more detailed, updated description. Although the skull was not preserved, Bakker has suggested that the animal's head may have been 11 feet long — at least based on the Harvard reconstruction of *Kronosaurus*. The fossils of *Megalneusaurus* were found in the upper part of the late Jurassic Sundance Formation of Wyoming. Williston (1903) wrote, "A large portion of the type species is known; the parts so far described are the vertebrae and limbs." However, some of the original remains (ribs, vertebrae) mentioned by Knight and Williston have apparently been lost, since the surviving specimen consists only of a forepaddle, some vertebrae, and fragments of a pectoral girdle — material that many researchers (but not all) consider inadequate to diagnose a genus and species. "A full-grown *Megalneusaurus* may have been in the 35–40-foot range or larger," wrote Creisler, "but such estimates should be greeted with caution until more hard facts are known."

When workers on U.S. Highway 81, south of Concordia, Kansas, came across some fossilized bones in a road cut, they carefully dug the material out and turned it over to the University of Kansas Museum of Vertebrate Paleontology. The fossils were described in a 1944 publication by Elmer S. Riggs. He had "the skull with mandible, fifty vertebrae, many ribs, most of the pectoral girdle . . . and the ischia almost entire" — enough to recognize it as a new species of plesiosaur that he named *Trinacromerum* ("three-tipped femur") *willistoni* (after Samuel Williston). The genus *Trinacromerum* had been named in

1888 by Cragin and was applied first to *T. bentonianum,* named for the Benton Formation in Kansas where it was found. Riggs's paper consisted entirely of a description of the fossil (e.g., "The sutures joining the pedicles and the cervical ribs to the centra are plainly marked"), and there was no speculation as to what *Trinacromerum* looked like. In 1996, in response to a tendency to make *Dolichorhynchops* ("long snout face") a synonym for *Trinacromerum,* Ken Carpenter wrote that "the polycotylids *Trinacromerum* and *Dolichorhynchops* are separated by autapomorphies in the skull of *Dolichorhynchops,*" making them separate genera after all. As shown by a life-size model on display in the Sternberg Museum, *Trinacromerum* was a small, short-necked plesiosaur (a pliosaur), approximately the size of a modern sea lion. It is shown on the beach, suggesting (surprisingly) that it might have been able to come ashore.

S. P. Welles (1962) wrote, "The nomenclatorial confusion surrounding the short-necked Upper Cretaceous plesiosaurs from North America has been resolved by eliminating the names *Piratosaurus* and *Polycotylus* as nomina vana. Our concept is based on the first adequately known genus, *Dolichorhynchops.*" The Polycotylidae were the last of the short-necked pliosaurs. In some classifications they are included under the Pliosauridae. They were generally smaller than the pliosaurids proper, averaging about 10 feet long. The head was large, at least as long as the neck, and the snout was generally very elongate. They were short-necked, with uniform conical teeth and none of the massive caniniform teeth that characterized the other pliosaurs. According to Dawn Adams (1997), *Trinacromerum bonneri* was the "last and fastest pliosaur of the Western Interior Seaway." Its flippers were "the longest wing-fins known," equal in length to its dorsal spinal column, enabling the animal to achieve unprecedented speed in the water. ("Pliosaurs," she wrote, "have always been regarded as particularly high-speed swimmers . . . highly maneuverable animals, capable of changing direction skillfully in pursuit of large prey.") A "tongue and groove" articulation of the digits "further increased wingfin strength and rigidity along the longitudinal axis and minimized torsion of the wingfin as a whole, which permitted the development of longer wingfins with more wingloading and greater propulsive power."[*] Bakker

* For this paper, Adams also drew a reconstruction of *Trinacromerum bonneri* that might have

(1993b) wrote that this type of long-snouted pliosaur (called dolichorhyn-chopine because of *Dolichorhynchops*) became the most common short-necked plesiosaurs in the Western Interior Seaway after the extinction of the ich-thyosaurs at the end of the Jurassic period. Indeed, they began to resemble ichthyosaurs, with their enlarged eye sockets, longer jaws, and reduced teeth.

———

been better conceived. The proportions are commensurate with her description, but for some reason, she chose to picture the animal as if it were chrome-plated, which, if correct, would probably have cut down water resistance and increased its not inconsiderable speed even more, but it raises a whole new set of questions about the integument of pliosaurs.

This suggests that they filled the gap left by the departing ichthyosaurs, which were also fast-swimming ambush predators.

When Cruickshank, Martill, and Noè (1996) examined the ribs of a previously undescribed pliosaur fossil found in 1994 in the Oxford Clay (middle Jurassic) of Cambridgeshire, England, they named it *Pachycostasaurus* because the bones were much heavier than those of other pliosaurs — a characteristic known technically as *pachyostosis*. This condition is known today in manatees, animals that spend much of their time grazing on the bottom, so it was suggested that *Pachycostasaurus dawni* (for Alan Dawn, who found the fossil) was, like the manatees, a bottom-feeder. No gastroliths were found in conjunction with the 10-foot-long fossil, suggesting that its dense bone structure may have been sufficient ballast to allow it to sink and feed on or near the bottom. The teeth of *Pachycostasaurus* were striated, sharp, and conical, which indicated predacious feeding, but because the skull was comparatively light and delicate, the authors suggested that this large pliosaur probably did not attack big, strong prey animals. They wrote, "We speculate that *Pachycostasaurus* fed on nektobenthic arthropods, cephalopods, or possibly on the assumed nektobenthic, heavily scaled ganoid fishes. *Pachycostasaurus* might have fed on mid-dwelling, soft-bodied prey that didn't put up much of a struggle, such as burrowing shrimps."

*Pachycostasaurus* was one of the primary subjects of Noè's 2001 study (the others were *Liopleurodon and Simolestes*), and in his thesis, he modified his earlier description of the hunting strategies of this dense-boned creature. He wrote, "*Pachycostasaurus* is here interpreted as preying on hard-boned vertebrate prey, the exceptionally stout and heavily ornamented teeth indicating prey even more difficult to subdue than that tackled by *Liopleurodon*." The only *Pachycostasaurus* fossil was 10 feet long, much smaller than *Liopleurodon* (which may have been 50 feet long), and it may have been a juvenile. But thus far, it is the only specimen known, and, wrote Noè, the "definitive interpretation of preferred prey will have to await the discovery of further examples of *Pachycostasaurus*."

McHenry (personal communication 2002) has attempted to resolve the confused and confusing state of pliosaur systematics by recognizing five major groups, or "families." They are the Rhomaleosauridae, Pliosauridae,

Leptocleididae, Brachaucheniidae, and Polycotylidae. The breakdown is as follows:

*Rhomaleosauridae.* Small to large pliosauroids. The have a relatively short skull on the end of a long neck with 26 to 30 cervical vertebrae. The rostrum tends to be small in proportion to the overall size of the skull (*Macroplata* is an exception). The trunk has about 20 vertebrae, and the tail has about 37 vertebrae. The humerus and femur are of about equal size. The limbs are large relative to overall body size. Some taxa reach large body sizes (less than 20 feet?). Included genera: *Rhomaleosaurus, Archaeonectrus, Eurycleidus, Macroplata.* Lower Jurassic.

*Pliosauridae.* Medium to large pliosauroids. They have a large skull, with a long rostrum relative to overall skull size. The neck contains 18 to 22 vertebrae, the trunk approximately 22 vertebrae, and the tail approximately 28 vertebrae. The humerus is significantly smaller than the femur. Specimens reach up to 33 feet body length. Included genera: *Pliosaurus, Liopleurodon, Peloneustes, Simolestes, Maresaurus, ?Megalneusaurus, Plesiopleurodon, ?Polyptychodon.* Middle Jurassic to ?Upper Cretaceous.

*Leptocleididae.* Small pliosauroids with a small skull. The rostrum is very small compared with overall skull length. The neck is long but is shorter than that of the rhomaleosaurids — with approximately 24 vertebrae. The trunk has 20 to 24 vertebrae. Length of the tail is unknown. The humerus and femur are of equal size. Overall body size is less than 10 feet. Included genera: *Leptocleidus.* Lower Cretaceous.

*Brachaucheniidae.* Large pliosauroids with a massive skull. The rostrum is large relative to overall skull length. The neck is short, with 12 to 13 vertebrae. There are 22 trunk vertebrae and an unknown number of tail vertebrae. The humerus is significantly smaller than the femur. Overall body size is up to 33 to 36 feet. Included genera: *Kronosaurus, Brachauchenius.* Lower Cretaceous to Upper Cretaceous.

*Polycotylidae.* Small to medium pliosauroids with a large skull and a long neck. The rostrum is long relative to overall skull length. There are 19 to 26 neck vertebrae, approximately 20 trunk vertebrae, and approximately 24 tail vertebrae. The humerus and femur are almost equal in size. Included genera: *Polycotylus, Dolichorhynchops, Trinacromerum, Edgarosaurus.* Lower Cretaceous to Upper Cretaceous.

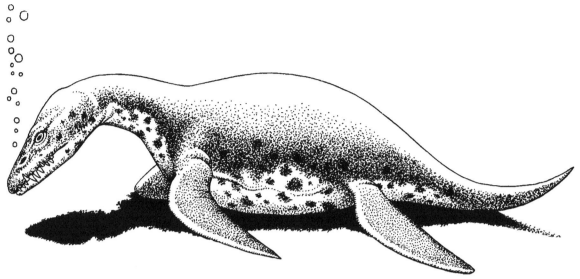

From the late Jurassic to the early late Cretaceous, giant pliosaurs were the terrors of the seas. Like all members of the Plesiosauria, they had heavily constructed bodies, short tails, and four powerful paddles used to swim and steer. In the past, paleontologists applied the term *pliosaur* to any type of plesiosaur with a short neck and a large head. The real evolutionary story may be more complex, and some researchers now think that the pliosaur design may have developed more than once. Each of the fearsome short-necked forms— *Pliosaurus, Liopleurodon, Brachauchenius, Polyptychodon, Kronosaurus*—had a huge skull with the biting power of killer whales and crocodiles. Exactly how large these great predatory sea dragons grew remains an intriguing question. There is no question, however, that these prehistoric reptiles are the quintessential sea monsters; twice as long and ten times as heavy as the largest living crocodiles, the pliosaurs were probably the most terrifying marine predators that ever lived. They dominated the seas the way the carnivorous dinosaurs dominated the land. Were it not for the fossil evidence that unquestionably demonstrates their existence, they would surely be relegated to the realm of nightmares.

*The dense bones of the pliosaur Pachycostasaurus dawni suggest that it sank to the bottom and fed on mud-dwelling, soft-bodied prey such as burrowing shrimps. Pachycostasaurus was about 10 feet long.*

# The Mosasaurs

Although there are mosasaur fossils aplenty in what was once a vast inland sea in North America, the first mosasaur fossil was found in 1780 in Maastricht, the Netherlands. Workers in a limestone mine 90 feet deep discovered a huge fossilized skeleton of a sort that had never been seen before. An army surgeon named C. K. Hoffmann directed the quarrymen to bring the whole rock containing the fossil to the surface, but while he was trying to extricate the fossil from the matrix, a clergyman named Goddin, who owned the land in which the mine was sunk, sued him and won possession of the rock-bound monster. He also got Dr. Hoffmann's money, because the unfortunate surgeon was made to pay the costs of the legal action as well. Goddin built a chapel to house the fossil, but during the 1795 siege of Maastricht by Napoleon's army, it mysteriously disappeared. When it was located (it had been "liberated" by Napoleon's grenadiers), it was sent to Paris, where various people argued about what it was. Because of its size, Pieter Camper, a renowned Dutch anatomist,

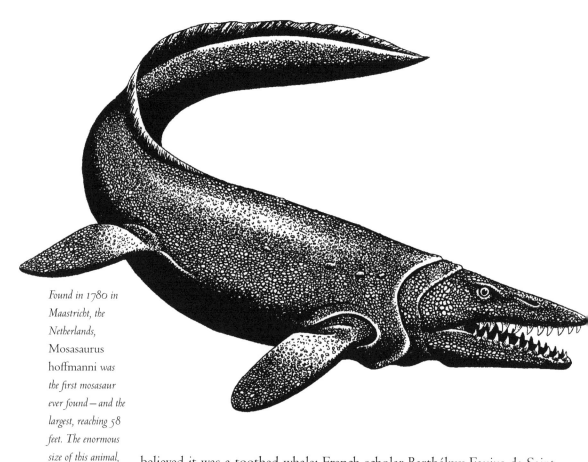

*Found in 1780 in Maastricht, the Netherlands,* Mosasaurus hoffmanni *was the first mosasaur ever found — and the largest, reaching 58 feet. The enormous size of this animal, along with its powerful jaws and teeth, meant that almost any creature was potential prey, including hard-shelled turtles and probably even other mosasaurs.*

believed it was a toothed whale; French scholar Barthélmy Faujus de Saint-Fond (known as Faujus) published an elaborate description in which he compared it with a crocodile. Unimpressed with its size, Pieter Camper's son Adriaan Gilles Camper correctly compared it with a varanid lizard, and based on his correspondence with Adriaan Camper, Baron Cuvier opined that *le grand animal fossile de Maastricht* should be placed somewhere between iguanas and varanid lizards. "The lizard status of mosasaurus," wrote Lingham-Soliar in 1995, "was first communicated by A. G. Camper in letters to Cuvier in 1790 and 1791 and followed in several later publications," but because he was so much better known, Cuvier is usually given credit for correctly identifying the mosasaur as a lizard. In 1820, Samuel Sömmering suggested the name *Lacerta gigantea* for the Maastricht mosasaur, but it turns out that he was describing a crocodilian that came from an iron mine in Bavaria, and he eventually changed the name to *Geosaurus* (Camp 1942). It was not until 1822 that the animal was awarded a Linnean binomial, when the Reverend Conybeare called it *Mosasaurus*—from *Mosa*, the Latin name of the Maas (Meuse) River near Maastricht, and *saurus*, for "lizard." Later, Dr. Hoffmann's name became a permanent part of the binomial.*

Theagarten Lingham-Soliar, now of the University of Durban-Westville in Kwazulu-Natal, South Africa, published a detailed description of *Mosasaurus hoffmanni* in 1995, when he was a Royal Society of London research fellow at the Geological Institute of the University of Tübingen in Germany. He wrote, "Although the first specimen was described over 200 years ago, it is here fully described for the first time to provide detailed insights into its anatomy, functional morphology and evolution." In accordance with Cope's rule (that, over time, there is a general trend toward greater size), *M. hoffmanni* was one of the latest and largest of the mosasaurs, reaching a length of 58 feet.† Its skull was telescoped, with the nostrils moved back from the end of the snout, but less so than in the modern cetaceans. The teeth were more complex than those of any earlier mosasaur species, with multifaceted edges that made for more effective cutting or breaking of prey items. Its eyes were large, but its binocular vision was limited, as it was in most mosasaurs except

---

* On August 8, 1998, in the St. Pietersburg quarry at Maastricht, another specimen of *Mosasaurus hoffmanni* was found. Subsequent excavations by staff members of the Natural History Museum of Maastricht and members of the Dutch Geological Society revealed that the skeleton, dispersed over an area of more than 40 square meters, included portions of both lower jaws and parts of the upper jaw, as well as vertebrae and ribs. With the exception of the missing tail bones, the skeleton is more or less complete.

† In *The Evolution of Complexity* (1988), John Tyler Bonner wrote that well-known examples of Cope's rule include the theropod dinosaurs (which culminated in *T. rex*) and also camels, elephants, and horses. Bonner points out that N. D. Newell (1949) also showed that "the same principles apply to invertebrates [including] foraminiferans, arthropods, echinoderms, brachiopods and ammonites, all widely separated groups." But then Bonner says that "a close, more finely tuned inspection of the fossil record shows that there is as much getting smaller as there is getting larger," which would indicate that Cope's rule is tautologically applicable only in those taxa where there is a demonstrable increase in size in the fossil record.

for *Plioplatecarpus houzeaui*, which had the best binocular vision of any mosasaur. The enormous size of this animal, along with its powerful jaws and teeth, meant that almost any creature was potential prey, including hard-shelled turtles and probably even other mosasaurs.

Around 1829, a mosasaur fossil was found by Major Benjamin O'Fallon near the Great Bend of the Missouri River, between Fort Lookout and Fort Pierre in what is now central South Dakota. He transported it to his garden in St. Louis, where it was seen by Prince Maximilian of Wied, who bought it from O'Fallon, brought it back to Germany, and placed it in the museum at Bonn. In 1845, German paleontologist August Goldfuss described it and named it *Mosasaurus maximiliani*, after his patron. In 1830, when Richard Harlan was given the end of the snout, he believed that it came from an ichthyosaur, so he named it *Ichthyosaurus missouriensis*. In the section on mosasaurs in *Water Reptiles of the Past and Present*, Williston (1914) mentioned Harlan's misidentification, and wrote that "some time previously, it has since been found, some fragments of the same species were described by Harlan, an American author, under the name *Ichthyosaurus missouriensis*." But in his 1967 monograph on American mosasaurs, Dale Russell lists *M. missouriensis* as one of the mosasaur species from the Pierre Shale and identifies three other specimens, one from Montana and two from South Dakota. The end of the snout that Harlan had mistaken for part of an ichthyosaur was likely a missing piece of the O'Fallon-Goldfuss mosasaur, so *M. missouriensis* can take its rightful place as a proper mosasaur after all.*

In 1899, Louis Dollo described another species of mosasaur that had been found in the vicinity of Mons in Belgium, some distance from Maastricht but from the same Upper Cretaceous formation as the original *Mosasaurus*. According to Lingham-Soliar and Nolf's 1989 description of *Prognathodon* (originally named *Dollosaurus*), it was a 14-foot-long mosasaur similar in shape to another mosasaur called *Plioplatecarpus*. The forward portion of the upper jaw (premaxilla) was armed with a clublike arrangement of four teeth, which looked like a four-fingered paw and was responsible for the name *Prognathodon*

---

* In fairness to Harlan, he later recognized that the piece had come from a mosasaur, and after showing it to Richard Owen, he tried to change its name to *Batrachiosaurus* ("frog-like lizard"), but the name was officially changed to *Mosasaurus missouriensis* in an 1839 publication.

("projecting jaw teeth"). The rest of its dental armament consisted of large, ridged jaw teeth and a particularly nasty set of palatal teeth.

Throughout the long history of vertebrate evolution, several unrelated groups have abandoned the land for an aquatic (or semiaquatic) lifestyle. Cetaceans (whales and dolphins), which are descended from terrestrial quadrupeds, began their return to the sea about 45 million years ago. With the loss of their hind legs and the transformation of forelegs into flippers and tail into flukes, they have achieved a totally aquatic existence. Sirenians (manatees and dugongs) accomplished the same thing, and they too lost their hind legs and acquired flukes (the dugong has a forked tail, and the manatee has a rounded one). Pinnipeds (seals, sea lions, walruses) appear to be in a transitional mode, not yet fully aquatic and spending a large portion of their time on land. The penguins, descended from flying birds, have traded their wings for flippers and now do all their "flying" underwater. The ichthyosaurs are descended from land reptiles of some sort, but we have no idea what the latter might have looked like—the earliest ichthyosaurs looked much like the later ichthyosaurs, only less streamlined—but in order to take the plunge, the plesiosaurs developed such adaptations as pachyostotic gastralia, ventrally located limb girdles, hydrofoil limbs, and specialized ears, eyes, and palates. Perhaps connected with the demise of the ichthyosaurs, the mosasaurs appeared rather suddenly in the fossil record in about the middle of the Cretaceous, some 90 million years ago in what is now the chalk hills of Kansas, as well as in Alabama, central Africa, and northern Europe. (The inundation of their habitat no doubt accelerated the evolution of aquatic lizards, but it provides no explanation for the disappearance of the ichthyosaurs, their predecessors as the seaway's dominant predators.)

Around 90 million years ago, a kind of marine lizard appeared in various oceanic environments around the world. Almost certainly descended from terrestrial lizards, the mosasaurs took to the water, and rather quickly—at least in geological terms—they became fully aquatic. They traded their feet for flippers, and whereas their ancestors laid eggs on land, they developed the ability to deliver their young alive in the water, a trait that appears to be a prerequisite for a seagoing lifestyle. (Among the marine reptiles that evolved during the Mesozoic are the sea turtles, which are almost completely aquatic but have to come ashore to lay their eggs.) They did not enter a realm devoid of predators, for the ichthyosaurs and plesiosaurs had colonized the oceans long before the mosasaurs did, but the ichthyosaurs were in decline by the time the mosasaurs arrived. The disappearance of the ichthyosaurs may be one of those mysteries of extinction with no answer, and it may have been nothing more than an evolutionary coincidence. Dale Russell (1967), however, believes there is a connection: "The remarkable convergence of some of the later mosasaurs with primitive Triassic ichthyosaurs shows that they were an ecological replacement of the declining ichthyosaurs." "Some mosasaurs may have been a belated ecological replacement of Triassic ichthyosaurs," wrote Lingham-Soliar in a letter to me, "but not of the Late Cretaceous thunniform ichthyosaurs. Triassic ichthyosaurs were ambush predators, and gave rise to pursuit predators at the beginning of the Jurassic, all long before mosasaurs. The vacated Triassic ichthyosaur ecological niche was partially filled by marine crocodiles and much later by aigialosaurs. Then mosasaurs came along and did the job of ambush predation better than the others put together and some may have filled a similar ecological niche to that of Triassic ichthyosaurs."

Whatever they were, the ancestors of mosasaurs have not been identified, but they probably looked a lot like aigialosaurs. In their 1992 survey of these mid-Cretaceous varanid lizards, Robert Carroll and Michael DeBraga noted, "we know almost nothing of the history of lizards between the end of the Jurassic and the Late Cretaceous, by which time most of the modern families had differentiated." The exception is the aigialosaurs, terrestrial lizards 3 feet long or more, with a tail as long as the head and body combined, not unlike today's monitor lizards (Varanidae). There are several nearly complete skeletons, representing five species: *Aigialosaurus dalmaticus, A. novaki, Opetiosaurus buccichi, Carsosaurus marchesetti,* and *Proaigialosaurus hueni,* all similar enough to suggest that they might belong to the same species. However they are classified, the aigialosaurs were probably part of the ancestry of the mosasaurs. But, as Lingham-Soliar (1994c) wrote, "Aigialosaurs demonstrate many conditions that might make them a suitable ancestor for the Mosasauridae, but there are problems: for instance, aigialosaur material is scanty and aigialosaurs and mosasaurs are both known only from Upper Cretaceous deposits. This poses problems regarding an aigialosaur ancestry unless it could be established that

*Aigialosaurs were smallish terrestrial lizards, 3 feet long or less, with a tail as long as the head and body combined, not unlike today's monitor lizards. The ancestors of mosasaurs (and varanid lizards) might have looked something like this.*

they had arisen earlier." As Carroll and DeBraga (1992) wrote, "No significant characters of the skull are known that distinguish aigialosaurs from primitive mosasaurs. In contrast, the trunk vertebrae and limbs are indistinguishable from those of terrestrial varanoids." They are considered a "sister-group" of the mosasaurs, which "suggests an earlier Cretaceous dichotomy separating advanced varanids and aigialosaurs from the more primitive genera now included in the Varanidae."

From the very limited fossil record (all aigialosaur material comes from Yugoslavia except *Proaigialosaurus*, which was found in the Solnhofen limestone of Bavaria), it appears that even if aigialosaurs cannot be identified as ancestral mosasauroids, then something very similar began the mosasaur line, which Gorden Bell (1997a) called a "27 million—year procession of vertebrate evolution so complete that it may well rival the example provided by the fossil record of horses." This may be exaggeration for emphasis. Although we do have a fairly good chronology of mosasaur development, the comparison of mosasaur ancestry to that of horses might not be entirely justified. The fossil record for horses shows replacements over time along natural lines of descent, where one can see an increase in size, increase of speed through modification of the limbs, elongation of the head and neck, and so on, but no horse species has actually been shown to be ancestral to any other.* There are still many unresolved problems with mosasaur ancestry and mosasaur phylogeny. It is more than likely that the mosasaurs were highly marine aigialosaur-like animals. One might even say that aigialosaurs were monitor lizards caught in the act of becoming mosasaurs. (Although the mosasaur skull was like that of the monitor lizards, with a joint in the middle of the lower jaw, the mosasaurs had all died out by the end of the Cretaceous, so the marine mosasaurs are not ancestral to the monitors.)

The fossil record is, as paleontologists term it, "scrappy," meaning that their research is restricted to the occasional fossil that appears in a serendipitously uncovered layer of shale or sandstone. There is deeply buried evidence of mosasaurids that no human eyes will ever see; therefore, paleontologists have to postulate a family tree with a lot of the branches missing. Still, enough fossilized mosasaur pieces have turned up to enable scientists to

* Colin McHenry (personal communication 2002) wrote, "In fact, it is almost paleontological dogma that we will never know what the ancestor of any animal looked like. For all the fossils we have found, we have probably never found a fossil that was ancestral to anything else. The odds against it are just too long for anything represented by a fossil to be an actual ancestor. But fossils do represent relatives of the ancestor, and show us what the ancestors probably looked like — thus they make good models for the elusive ancestor. So we are able to reconstruct, sometimes quite confidently, what the ancestor of a certain group must have looked like."

hypothesize a progression of mosasaur evolution, from the earliest known creature that can be categorized as a mosasaur to the last of the known mosasaurs, which became extinct about 65 million years ago. In 1977, Martin and Stewart identified what they believed to be the oldest mosasaurs, from Kansas in the Cenomanian period, 98.9 to 93.5 million years ago; however, a subsequent examination of the fossils showed them to be from various ichthyodectiform fishes (Stewart and Bell 1994). Some of the oldest known mosasaur fossils (so far) were found in the Fairport Chalk deposits (middle Turonian) of Kansas and consisted of two caudal vertebrae and a piece of a jawbone. A search of the collections at the University of Kansas Museum of Natural History turned up several more vertebrae from the Turonian, which can be dated at approximately 90 million years ago (Russell 1967). Other early mosasaur material, identified as *Clidastes,* has come from the Eagle Ford Shale of Texas, also Turonian. It is possible that the mosasaurs originated in Africa and spread to Europe and North America 100 million years ago, when shallow seaways covered most of the continents because sea level was 300 to 500 feet higher than it is today, and also because the continents have been uplifted since the Cretaceous. The presence of mosasaur fossils in Europe, Africa, and North America proves as conclusively as sedimentary deposits that these regions were once underwater or, in some cases, riverine.

Within some 3 million years of their arrival, giant mosasaurs such as *Tylosaurus* and *Platecarpus* appeared to dominate the Western Interior Seaway, as well as European and even New Zealand waters. *Tylosaurus proriger* was 46 feet long, the size of a humpback whale. But whereas the whale has baleen strainers, the mosasaur had bone-crushing jaws and gigantic teeth, the better to bite anything and everything that crossed its path. Discovered in the late Cretaceous deposits of Haumuri Bluff, South Island (New Zealand), *Tylosaurus haumuriensis* was, according to Long (1998), "the second-largest known [New Zealand] species . . . the total length of this animal can be estimated as being about 7 m [23 feet]." (As we shall see, 23 feet is relatively small in tylosaur terms.) A few million years later, the even larger and more ferocious *Mosasaurus* entered the picture at an astonishing 58 feet in length. The mosasaurs, among the largest and most powerful carnivorous animals that ever lived, dominated the world's oceans and inland seas for 25 million years, and then, with the K-T extinction event, they abruptly vanished. By then, the ichthyosaurs were long gone, and the pliosaurs were already in decline, so the passing of the mosasaurs marks the end of an era as incredible as the reign of the terrestrial dinosaurs: the time when reptiles ruled the seas.

By the mid-Cretaceous, some 90 million years ago, the continents were arranged more or less where they are now, except that Australia was still attached to Antarctica, and India, still attached to Madagascar, had not yet begun its northward journey. Worldwide sea levels had risen dramatically, and much of North America and Europe was underwater, covered by the shallow Tethys Sea. At this time, the mosasaurs began the colonization of the shallow waters that had been vacated by the ichthyosaurs. Within a geological moment, they had radiated to become the top predators of the Cretaceous seas. Their legs, originally equipped with feet designed for walking, developed paddle-shaped flippers, and their tails lengthened and became flattened like those of eels or crocodiles. In her 1994 analysis of the swimming capabilities of Mesozoic marine reptiles, Judy Massare wrote, "Not surprisingly, mosasaurs displayed many adaptations for rapid acceleration that are characteristic of ambush predators. The elongate shape resulted in a high surface-to-volume ratio for pushing against the water, and a relatively small frontal area for pushing against it. . . . [The] expanded caudal area may have been an adaptation for increasing thrust production in the distal part of the tail." The tylosaurs had evolved a blunt prow on the end of the rostrum, which they may have used as a battering ram to injure or incapacitate their prey. During the 25 million years that they prospered, the mosasaurs spread throughout the major oceans of the world, ranging almost from pole to pole. (The ichthyosaurs lived for 150 million years, and the plesiosaurs for 140 million.)

Mosasaurs are characterized by a lizard-like skull in which there are two openings behind the orbit. This condition, known as *diapsid*, occurs in lizards, snakes, and dinosaurs. The smallest mosasaurs, at a maximum length of 12 feet, are those of the genus *Clidastes* ("locker," from the interlocked vertebrae); they were the most lizard-like in form, with a thin, elongated body and a low, triangular fin on the dorsal surface of the tail. Of all the mosasaurs, *Clidastes* had the shortest tail relative to body length, but also the best-developed tail fin for marine locomotion, making them more advanced than the ancestral

*A shallow water inhabitant,* Clidastes *was one of the smaller mosasaurs, rarely reaching 15 feet.*

semiaquatic forms. The skull was short, the teeth smooth and sharp, and, as Russell (1967) wrote, "the long, slender jaws of *Clidastes* were probably adapted to rapid biting . . . and might have been effective in sawing a large object into pieces of swallowable size." As for where in the water column *Clidastes* hung out, there are differences of opinion. Williston (1914) believed that this species was a surface swimmer, and in their 1989 examination of bone necrosis in diving mosasaurs, Martin and Rothschild opined that *Clidastes* probably lived near shore and "did not regularly engage in deep diving." However, in a 1997 study of mosasaur bone microstructure, Amy Sheldon found that *Clidastes* had particularly *low* bone density (a condition she calls *osteoporosis*,* which would have provided neutral buoyancy in deeper waters,

---

* In general usage, *osteoporosis* is a disease in which bones become increasingly porous, brittle, and subject to fracture. *Pachyostosis*, which means "thickening of the bone," is the natural condition of bones that are denser or thicker than normal, a factor "largely confined to the Sirenia and some extinct reptiles" (Domning and Buffrénil 1991). The term is also used for pachycephalosaurs, ornithischian dinosaurs that had a thick bony dome on top of the skull, probably used in intraspecific head-butting, as in bighorn sheep. In personal communications, various names have been suggested to describe a normal condition in which the bone is unusually light, including *pneumatic* ("air-filled," like the bones of most birds), *tenuiosis* (from *tenuis*, meaning "thin"), and *elaphrosty* (from the Greek *elaphro*, meaning "light in weight"), but there is no generally accepted term.

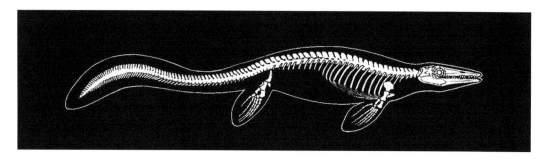

and like *Tylosaurus*, it was likely a deep diver. (No matter how deeply a mosasaur could dive, however, it had to come up for air; like all other reptiles, past and present, mosasaurs were air breathers.)

"The seas that rolled over Kansas in Cretaceous times," wrote Charles Gilmore in 1921, "contained thousands of these animals [mosasaurs] and in the chalk bluffs of that region their remains are in such a state of preservation that we are not only acquainted with their skeletal structure but with their external appearance as well." A 25-foot-long *Tylosaurus* specimen found by Charles Sternberg in Kansas in 1917 showed that "in life they were covered with small, overlapping scales." In examining the specimen, Samuel Williston detected "color markings" that consisted of "narrow, diagonally-placed parallel bars" (there was, however, no indication of the actual color). Like all mosasaurs, *Tylosaurus* had an articular joint in the middle of each of the lower jaws, which, combined with the very loose attachment at the front, allowed these animals to swallow large objects.

World sea level was at its highest during the Mesozoic, so there were vast areas for the lizards to inhabit, and the remains that sank to the bottom were preserved as fossils. The largest number of mosasaur fossils have been collected in Kansas, from the formation known as the Niobrara Chalk. About 600 feet thick, the Niobrara Chalk extends from southwestern Kansas to south-central Manitoba, but it is best exposed in northwestern Kansas, where badlands have been cut along the bluffs of the Smoky Hill River and its tributaries. It is composed of the compacted plates (coccoliths) that are remnants of the abundant, microscopic, golden brown algae (Chrysophyceae) that lived in the warm, shallow sea. The upper portion of these deposits was laid down between 87 and 82 million years ago during a period when the

Western Interior Seaway covered most of midwestern North America from the Gulf of Mexico to the Arctic Circle, incorporating all of Saskatchewan, North and South Dakota, Kansas, Nebraska, Oklahoma, and most of Texas. As of Russell's 1993 summary, the Niobrara Chalk formations of Kansas had yielded no fewer than 1,823 mosasaur specimens, the great majority of which were collected by the O. C. Marsh and E. D. Cope expeditions of the late nineteenth century. Since that time, more have been found in Kansas and elsewhere, but no other location on Earth has provided so much material for the study of these marine lizards. Here is Cope's immodest description of one of his finds, as it appeared in a report prepared for Frederick Hayden's 1871 *U.S. Geological Survey of the Territories:*

> The giants of the *Pythonomorpha* of Kansas have been called *Liodon proriger,* Cope, and *Liodon dyspelor,* Cope. The first must have been abundant, and its length could not have been far from seventy-five feet; certainly not less. . . . The *Liodon dyspelor*\* was probably the longest of known reptiles, and probably equal to the great finner whales of modern oceans. The circumstances attending the discovery of one of these will always be a pleasant recollection to the writer. A part of the face, with teeth, was observed projecting from the side of a bluff by a companion in exploration, Lieut. James H. Whitten, United States Army, and we at once proceeded to follow up the indication with knives and picks. Soon the lower jaws were uncovered, with

\* *Liodon dyspelor* Cope was probably a tylosaur, but its identification was based on fossil material that could not be identified specifically, except that it belonged to some kind of mosasaur. Russell (1967) included *Tylosaurus dyspelor* in his list of "Mosasaurs of Uncertain Taxonomic Position" and wrote, "*Tylosaurus dyspelor* cannot be referred to either of the two species of Niobrara *Tylosaurus,* and must be regarded as a *nomen vanum.*" He seemed to think that the *T. dyspelor* material might belong to *Tylosaurus proriger* because of its larger size, but he could not find any features that clinched the match with certainty. *Nomen vanum* is an old term meaning "empty name," no longer recognized by the International Code of Zoological Nomenclature. The term now used is *nomen dubium* (doubtful name), usually indicating a name that has appeared in the literature with a description but, according to other authors, cannot be applied with certainty to a recognized taxon at a species level because the original material lacks diagnostic features or, in some cases, is lost and cannot be reexamined (Creisler, personal communication).

their glistening teeth, and then the vertebrae and ribs. Our delight was at its height when the bones of the pelvis and part of the hind limb were laid bare, for they had never been seen before in this species, and scarcely in the order.

*Tylosaurus proriger* was originally named *Macrosaurus proriger* by Cope in 1869, but Cope's arch-nemesis, O. C. Marsh, renamed it *Rhinosaurus* and then *Tylosaurus* in 1872.* *Proriger* means "prow-bearing," referring to "the cylindrical prolongation of the premaxillary bone beyond the teeth and a similar flat prolongation of the extremity of the dentary" (Cope 1869c). One of the largest of the mosasaurs, *Tylosaurus proriger* lived in the Niobrara Sea during the late Cretaceous, some 85 million years ago. It was 20 to 50 feet long and had a long, slim body; huge jaws; heavy, sharp, conelike teeth; and paddle-like fore and hind limbs. It preyed on fish, shellfish, and probably smaller mosasaurs, plesiosaurs, and hesperornithiform birds. *Tylosaurus* means "knob lizard," from the Greek *tylos* for "knob" and *sauros* for "lizard." The elongated cylindrical muzzle (rostrum) projected beyond the front-most teeth in the upper jaw; the tip of the snout was probably similar in function to the "ram" or "beak" that the ancient Greeks and Romans mounted on the prows of warships to ram and sink enemy vessels. *Tylosaurus* might have used its "ram" snout to stun prey, defend against sharks or other predators, or battle rivals of its own species.

* This constant nomenclatural revision is a handicap to those trying to write about the fossils themselves. In order to chronicle the finds, one must identify the species that Cope and Marsh named, which were often renamed by later workers. In such cases, a synonymy is included in the later description, which enables the researcher to track the often convoluted taxonomic history of a particular species. Here, for example, is Russell's 1967 synonymy for the mosasaur we now know as *Tylosaurus proriger* (the year following the paleontologist's name represents the date of publication of the scientific name):

> *Macrosaurus proriger* Cope 1869
> *Macrosaurus pririger* Cope 1869
> *Liodon proriger* Cope 1869–1870
> *Rhinosaurus proriger* Marsh 1872
> *Rhinosaurus micromus* Marsh 1872
> *Tylosaurus proriger* Marsh 1872

One of the largest of the mosasaurs, Tylosaurus proriger *lived in the Niobrara Sea during the late Cretaceous, some 85 million years ago. It preyed on fish, shellfish, and probably smaller mosasaurs, ichthyosaurs, and plesiosaurs — anything and everything that swam.*

Mike Everhart (2002a) reexamined the tylosaur material in the collections of the Sternberg and other museums, particularly the fossils of *Tylosaurus nepaeolicus*. (Everhart writes that the name probably "comes from 'Nepaholla,' an earlier Indian name for the Solomon River . . . meaning 'water on a hill.'") The first specimens, probably collected by George Sternberg (the older brother of Charles), were described by Cope (1874) and named *Liodon nepaeolicus*. Cope concluded that *T. nepaeolicus* was about a third smaller than the more common *T. proriger* but was a separate species and not a juvenile. Everhart concluded:

Since its description in 1874, *Tylosaurus nepaeolicus* has been considered to be significantly smaller than *T. proriger*. The lack of complete specimens of *T. nepaeolicus* seems to have discouraged further studies of this taxon. Although it remains one of the lesser known mosasaurs from the lower Smoky Hill Chalk Member in Kansas, a sufficient number of specimens now is available to provide a more accurate assessment of its size range in comparison to *T. proriger*. New material shows that adults of this species were significantly larger than the "one third" of the size of *T. proriger* originally estimated by Cope (1874) or even the specimens measured by Russell (1967). In addition, large vertebrae from the lower one-third of the Smoky Hill Chalk Member (upper Coniacian) indicate the presence of a *Tylosaurus* that was about 8–9 m in body length. Although minor morphological features separate the two species, the fossil record indicates clearly that by the end of the Coniacian (86 mya) *T. nepaeolicus* was approaching the same adult size observed in *T. proriger* remains from the lower to middle Santonian and later.

The rivalry between Cope and Marsh involved mostly Eocene mammals and dinosaurs, but their conflicts over mosasaurs were equally acrimonious. In 1868, Cope traveled to Kansas and described several species of mosasaurs, including *Clidastes, Platecarpus, Mosasaurus,* and one that he named *Liodon,* a corruption of Owen's already existing *Leiodon.* Based on his preliminary examination of the mosasaur material, Cope developed some strange notions about these reptiles, and in 1869, he classified them into a new order, the Pythonomorpha, because he believed that they were snakelike in form. (In the same paper, he erected the order Streptosauria to include the elasmosaurs with their vertebrae reversed.) Of the mosasaurs, he wrote (1869b):

> We may now look upon the mosasaurs and their allies as a race of gigantic, marine, serpent-like reptiles, with powers of swimming and running, like the modern Ophidia. Adding a pair of short anterior paddles, they are not badly represented by old Pontoppidan's figure of a sea serpent. That terrestrial representatives, unknown to us, inhabited the forests and swamps of the Mesozoic continents, and strove for mastery with the huge dinosaurs, that also sought their shades, is probable. . . . Thus in the mosasaurids, we almost realize the fictions of snake-like dragons and sea serpents, which men have been ever prone to indulge. On account of the ophidian part of their affinities, I have called this order the Pythonomorpha.

Marsh described many mosasaurs, including one that he named—in an uncharacteristic burst of generosity—*Mosasaurus copeanus* (or perhaps Marsh's combination of the words *Cope* and *anus* was not such a generous act after all). Louis Dollo, a Belgian paleontologist, named *Plioplatecarpus marshi* after Marsh, who had drawn attention to the characters that distinguished it from *Mosasaurus hoffmanni.* Then Joseph Leidy (like Cope, from Philadelphia) reported fragmentary mosasaur fossils from New Jersey, Alabama, and Mississippi, and shortly thereafter, reports began coming in from New Zealand, Belgium, France, and Russia. Around the turn of the century, John C. Merriam described many new species from the Niobrara Chalk of Kansas, including a second species of *Halisaurus,* a new species of *Platecarpus,* and another *Clidastes.* In 1898, Samuel Williston reviewed the known mosasaurs to date and published the results, complete with detailed anatomical drawings, in the *University Geological Survey of Kansas.* In his 1914 book *Water Reptiles of the Past and Present,* Williston wrote:

> Perhaps nowhere in the world are the fossil remains of marine animals more abundantly and better preserved than in these famous chalk deposits of Kansas. The exposures are of great extent—hundreds of square miles— and the fossil treasures they contain seem inexhaustible. Long-continued explorations by collectors have brought to light thousands of specimens of these swimming lizards, some of them of extraordinary completeness and perfect preservation, so complete and so perfect that there is scarcely anything concerning the mosasaurs which one might hope to learn from their fossil remains that has not been yielded up by these many specimens.

Although the opening salvos of their lifelong battle were fired over the misplaced head of the plesiosaur *Elasmosaurus* in 1869, Cope and Marsh remained bitter enemies until death brought an end to their hostilities. (Cope died in 1897; Marsh two years later.) Their feud escalated in 1871, when Cope made an expedition to Kansas, covering ground that Marsh considered his exclusive province. Then Cope invaded Wyoming, another of Marsh's favorite hunting grounds, where he found a hitherto unknown trove of Eocene mammal fossils. It was around this time that Marsh utilized the newly raised telegraph lines to relay his discoveries to New Haven, and the battle was

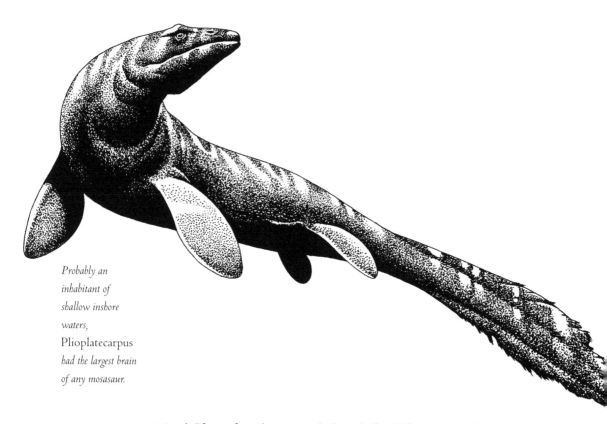

*Probably an inhabitant of shallow inshore waters,* Plioplatecarpus *had the largest brain of any mosasaur.*

joined. If one found a particularly rich fossiliferous site, the other moved in immediately, luring away the other's workers by offers of higher pay, destroying markers, and occasionally even stealing the other's specimens. The "bone hunters" of Cope and Marsh went into the field armed not only with picks and hammers but with pistols and rifles as well. Of course, the guns were used to hunt game and shoot buffaloes, and the various Indian tribes were more than a little perturbed at being driven off their lands, but each man also felt the need for protection against his rival's troops. (General George Custer and his cavalry were slaughtered by Sitting Bull and Crazy Horse at the Little Big Horn in 1876, and a mere week later, the fossil hunter Charles Sternberg, who was then working for Cope, was sent into the Black Hills of Montana to look for dinosaur fossils.) Backed by the money of his uncle George Peabody (who had founded the museum at Yale and endowed a chair in paleontology for his nephew), Marsh could better afford this pitched paleontological battle; Cope drove himself to the brink of bankruptcy trying to compete.

Along with actually finding the fossils (or having them found by someone in your employ), the question of first publication was the primary battlefield. Naming an animal (fossil or otherwise) gets your name permanently attached to it, and Cope and Marsh tried to bestow their names on as many new species as possible. This competition often resulted in too-hasty identifications (or simultaneous identifications of the same fossil, each of them giving it a different name), and as a result, an unrealistically large number of fossil animals was identified, particularly mosasaurs. In Samuel Williston's 1898 revision of the mosasaurs, he wrote that "four fifths of all the described species must be abandoned," largely because the differences identified by Cope and Marsh in their haste were artifacts of preservation and did not warrant the erection of a new species. In his extensive 1967 review of American mosasaurs, Dale Russell wrote, "Marsh and Cope led field parties into the Niobrara Chalk of western Kansas in 1870–71 and soon began describing new mosasaur material. Far too many species were named; all were inadequately diagnosed; and the resulting confusion has been a serious handicap to subsequent workers."

Charles Sternberg (1850–1943) was a professional fossil hunter who originally hoped to prospect for Marsh, but when he was turned down, he went to work for Cope, who sent Sternberg the $300 that began a long and fruitful collaboration. Working with his son Levi in 1918, Sternberg collected numerous fossil reptiles in the Niobrara Chalk of Logan County, Kansas, three of which were sold to the Paleontological Museum in Uppsala, Sweden. For the museum, Carl Wiman bought a *Pteranodon,* a *Platecarpus* mosasaur, and a nearly complete skeleton of a mosasaur identified as *Clidastes sternbergii* (Wiman 1920). ("Ward's Natural History Establishment of Rochester [New York] has negotiated the purchases and with customary generosity Swedish shipowners have granted free transport.") The mosasaur was renamed *Halisaurus* ("sea lizard") by Russell (1967) and has been subjected to taxonomic peregrinations ever since. The type specimen, *Halisaurus platyspondylus,* was originally named by Marsh in 1869 for the broadened, compressed shape of the vertebrae. Russell (1970) referred *Clidastes sternbergii* to the genus *Halisaurus,* so the current name of this species is *Halisaurus sternbergi* (Russell also respelled the specific name, dropping the extra "i"). Lingham-Soliar (1991b) didn't agree with Russell that *H. sternbergi* should be referred to *Halisaurus,* and he wanted to include *Phosphorosaurus* (named by Dollo in 1889) in the genus *Halisaurus.* Holmes and Sues (2000) argued that *Phosphorosaurus* should probably remain distinct from *Halisaurus.*

Charles Camp, who discovered the giant ichthyosaur graveyard in Nevada, also found some new mosasaurs in California. In his 1942 publication "California Mosasaurs," he wrote:

> The evolution of the mosasaurs from early Cretaceous varanoid lizards such as *Aigialosaurus* is an instructional example of the changes that occur in the passage from a land to a marine habitus in reptiles. The walking foot of the land lizard became larger, with longer and more slender fingers in the earliest known aquatic forms. Presumably these were webfooted. Some of the early mosasaurs were also slender-figured, with a loosely-knit, sea-turtle-like paddle. In advanced mosasaurs such as *Mosasaurus* and *Kolposaurus* the digits were adpressed, the number of phalanges was increased, and there was no doubt a thick, fibrous envelope around the hand, as in whales.

Camp created a new genus of California mosasaurs that he called *Kolposaurus,* which means "bay lizard" (from the Greek *kolpos,* meaning "bay" or "gulf"). He included two new species, *Kolposaurus bennisoni* (named for Allan Bennison, the high school student who found the fossil in 1937) and *K. tuckeri* (named for Professor W. M. Tucker, who found the second fossil). Both specimens were large, long-tailed mosasaurs 30 to 40 feet long. Each had a slender, pointed skull; a mouthful of sharp teeth; and very large eyes, which suggest that this species was a fast-swimming predator that probably fed on surface fishes. In 1951, having learned that the name *Kolposaurus* was "preoccupied" (by a nothosaur), Camp changed the genus name to *Plotosaurus,* which means "swimmer lizard," so his California mosasaurs are now *Plotosaurus bennisoni* and *P. tuckeri.*

At a maximum of 21 feet, the *Platecarpus* mosasaurs were exceptionally fast and flexible, but their teeth were relatively small, suggesting a diet of small fishes and cephalopods, especially belemnites.* In his 1970 review of the mosasaurs of the Selma Formation (Alabama), Russell wrote, "If belemnites normally formed a large proportion of the diet of the slender-toothed plioplatecarpines (*Platecarpus, Plioplatecarpus, Ectenosaurus*) it might be expected that these animals might be less abundant in southern waters." A couple of belemnites were preserved with a *Plioplatecarpus houzeaui* specimen housed at the Institut Royal des Sciences Naturelles de Belgique, and a few can be seen with the *Plioplatecarpus* specimen at the Teylers Museum in Haarlem, the Netherlands.

But, wrote Russell in 1967, "Because belemnites are rarely found in the Niobrara Chalk, they could not have formed an important food source for *Platecarpus* [in Kansas]." *P. tympaniticus* is the most common mosasaur fossil in the Smoky Hill Chalk of Kansas, and the members of the genus *Platecarpus* later gave rise to the more specialized form *Plioplatecarpus*, which showed some very strange modifications indeed. Those grouped with *Tylosaurus* were the largest and most formidable of all and probably the most widely distributed, having been found throughout North America as well as in Europe, New Zealand, and possibly Antarctica. (In addition to a duckbilled dinosaur [hadrosaur] and a piece of a foot bone of an ancient bird, several mosasaur fossils were found on Vega Island, on the eastern side of the Antarctic peninsula, by a joint Argentinean-American paleontological expedition in 1998.)

* Belemnites were marine cephalopods similar to modern squids and cuttlefishes, in that they were dartlike, rapid swimmers and could move tailward or tentacleward with equal facility. (The word comes from the Greek *belemnon*, meaning "dart" or "javelin.") In those rare fossils in which the soft tissue has been preserved, it can be seen that belemnites had ten tentacles of equal length, set with rows of little hooks instead of suckers, and, like the modern cephalopods, they had an ink sac. The belemnites' squidlike body enclosed a cone-shaped internal shell (the phragmocone), which terminated at the tail end in a solid, pointed element known as the rostrum or guard. The phragmocone resembled a straightened nautiloid shell, and the pro-ostracum corresponded to the calcified pen or gladius of living squids and cuttlefishes, but no living cephalopod has a solid guard at the posterior end, so the function of this bullet-shaped element can only be guessed at.

Everything we know about mosasaurs comes from the analysis of fossils, but from this material, we can tell quite a lot about the lifestyle of these large seagoing lizards. The size of *Tylosaurus*, for example, is easy enough to determine; it ranged in size from 20 to 50 feet, about half of which was tail. How much did it weigh? A 17-foot-long great white shark weighs about 3,000 pounds, but it doesn't have a particularly long tail, so a better comparison might be the saltwater crocodile *(Crocodylus porosus)*, which has a pretty long tail and, at a length of 20 feet, weighs about 2,500 pounds. At 50 feet, the "Bunker" *Tylosaurus*, found in western Kansas around 1910, was one of the largest mosasaurs ever found in the United States. Its skull was 6 feet long, and it had 72 sharp, backward-curving teeth in its jaws. It might have weighed as much as 8 tons.

The genus *Mosasaurus* includes the Maastricht species and probably the first mosasaur ever found in America. In 1804, Lewis and Clark found the remains of a huge "snake" on an island in the Missouri River in what is now South Dakota, but the fossil was sent back to Washington and lost. (It was probably *M. missouriensis*, which Williston originally named *M. horridus*.) There was great variety among the mosasaurs; some were the size of dolphins, and others were as big as small whales. The round-toothed *Globidens* is unlike any other mosasaur, and *Plioplatecarpus marshi* may have flown through the water like a gigantic penguin.

But where? Holmes, Caldwell, and Cumbaa (1999) examined a specimen of *Plioplatecarpus* found in the Scabby Butte Formation of Alberta and wrote that "the morphology of the well-preserved forelimb indicates that the animal cannot be reconstructed as a subaqueous flyer, but probably used its forelimbs for paddling. The associated matrix . . . suggests that this mosasaur was able to exploit estuarine and freshwater environments." Most mosasaurs were marine, but this specimen was found in sediments that strongly suggest "an overbank deposit representing flooding of a coal swamp occurring as a lateral equivalent to the deltaic channel system." The geological evidence ("the only robust diagnostic clues for hypothesizing paleoenvironments") indicates that this large-flippered *Plioplatecarpus* lived inland, perhaps in a freshwater estuary. When Kenneth Wright and Samuel Shannon (1988) found "an unusual mosasaur" in the uncataloged collections of the University of Alabama Museum of Natural History, they recognized it as having come from the Moore-ville Chalk Formation around Selma. It was a plioplatecarpine mosasaur that somewhat resembled the North American genus *Ectenosaurus* and the African *Goronyosaurus*, but it was different enough to warrant its own genus. They named it *Selmasaurus russelli*—the generic name for the location, and the specific name for Dale Russell, "for his extensive work on the Mosasauridae."

Until quite recently, there was no evidence one way or the other to show how mosasaurs were born. Williston (1914) wrote, "The legs were so completely adapted to an aquatic mode of living that the animals must have been practically helpless on land, able perhaps to move about in a serpentine way when accidentally stranded upon the beaches, but probably never seeking the land voluntarily. . . . If the mosasaurs were viviparous, as were the ichthyosaurs, and probably the plesiosaurs, and as are some living land lizards, the apparently entire absence of embryonic bones associated with often nearly complete skeletons of the mosasaurs is inexplicable; certainly *some* mosasaurs must have died a short time before the birth of their young." In 1989, Russell suggested that "perhaps, like some living reptiles . . . they sought the secluded beaches of isolated islets and atolls in which to lay their eggs," but this seemed unlikely to some, because these giant lizards would probably have been too large and too ungainly to move themselves about on land to lay eggs.

But then Gorden Bell, one of the world's foremost authorities on mosasaurs, found the fragmentary remains of the mosasaur *Plioplatecarpus primaevus* in South Dakota, along with the bones of two prenatal mosasaur embryos (Bell et al. 1996). The bones were disarticulated, but this was attributed to the scavenging by an opportunistic school of dogfish sharks *(Squalicorax),* whose presence was evidenced by more than 2,000 shark teeth in the immediate vicinity of the fossil embryos. It now appears that the mosasaurs, like the ichthyosaurs, gave birth to live young at sea. (The juvenile mosasaurs on Vega Island suggested another behavior previously unsuspected: they might have cared for their young as crocodilians do.) Further support for the idea of viviparous mosasaurs came in 2001, when Caldwell and Lee published a description of a fossilized aigialosaur *(Carsosaurus)* with "at least four advanced embryos distributed along the posterior two-thirds of the trunk region. This orientation suggests that they were born tail first (the nostrils emerging last) to reduce the possibility of drowning, an adaptation shared with other highly aquatic amniotes such as cetaceans, sirenians, and ichthyosaurs. . . . Viviparity in early medium-sized amphibious aigialosaurs may have freed them from the need to return to land to deposit eggs, and permitted the subsequent evolution of gigantic totally marine mosasaurs." Mike Everhart (2002b) wrote, "Despite problems related to the preservation of smaller individuals, a review of more recently collected material shows that immature mosasaurs (estimated body length = 2 m or less) are well represented throughout the [Niobrara] chalk. The recent discovery of fetal material associated with a mosasaur from South Dakota, and with a mosasaurid from Slovenia, provide compelling evidence that these marine reptiles bore live young."

Additional evidence of sharks scavenging on mosasaur skeletons was unearthed near Liège, Belgium, by Bardet et al. (1998). They found caudal vertebrae identified as belonging to *Plioplatecarpus marshi*, a mosasaur found in the Netherlands and Belgium, but very little cranial material, because this species had a particularly fragile skull. The vertebrae had "elongate and slender grooves on the neural spine, which are here interpreted to be the result of scavenging by the common dogfish (squalid) shark, *Centrophorodes appendiculatus*." (This shark, whose teeth resembled those of the living dogfish *[Squalus]*, lived during the Maastrichtian stage, as did *Plioplatecarpus*.) Tim Tokaryk (1993) of the Saskatchewan Museum of Natural History wrote that "interest is resurfacing in North American mosasaurs, as illustrated by the work performed by Rothschild and Martin (1987) on avascular necrosis, discoveries of sub-adults by Bell and Sheldon (1986) and discussion on tooth morphology and its relevance to preferred prey by Massare (1987)." The fossil Bell found was a small mosasaur, *Plioplatecarpus primaevus*, but it was the most complete specimen ever found in North America.

In September 1996, Mike and Pam Everhart removed the skull and seven cervical vertebrae of a very large mosasaur from an exposure of the Smoky Hill Chalk called Horsethief Canyon in Gove County, Kansas:

The locality was near the site of Sternberg's famous "fish-in-a-fish" *(Xiphactinus audax)* specimen, and was from about the middle of the Smoky

Hill Chalk member (Late Cretaceous) of the Niobrara formation. The remains are approximately 85 million years old. The skull was 4 feet in length and was found laying on its left side. Based on the size of the skull, the entire animal would have been about 30 feet in length. Evidence from the site indicates that at least some of the rest of the specimen is still in place. . . . Many complete or nearly complete specimens of this species from Kansas are in major museums around the world thanks to the efforts of early paleontologists such as Cope, Marsh, and Sternberg.

In the late Cretaceous, parts of Alabama — or what is now called Alabama — were evidently mosasaur heaven. As early as 1850, vertebrae and teeth collected from the "rotten limestone of Alabama" were described by Robert Gibbes, and 20 years later, Cope (1869b) described the new species *Clidastes propython,* based on an Alabama specimen. Joseph Leidy, a gentle man who would soon fade into the background as Cope and Marsh slugged it out in public, found an Alabama "*Platecarpus*" (which was later identified as *Globidens*); then C. W. Gilmore (1912) named the first of the round-toothed mosasaurs *(Globidens alabamaensis)* from Alabama material in the U.S. National Museum. In 1945, the Field Museum of Chicago sent an expedition under Rainer Zangerl to collect in the Selma Formation of Alabama, and although Zangerl listed some of the finds, the mosasaurs were not described in detail until 1970, when Dale Russell published a paper on the mosasaurs of the Selma Formation of Alabama. The species included *Halisaurus sternbergi, Clidastes propython, Globidens alabamaensis, Platecarpus* sp., *Prognathodon* sp., and *Tylosaurus zangerli,* a new species (which turned out to be synonymous with *T. proriger*). More than three-quarters of the material found by the Zangerl expedition belonged to the species first found by Cope, *Clidastes propython,* which is also known from the Niobrara fauna. In his reports, Zangerl noted that "the presence of turtles, small pterodactyls, and toothed birds . . . indicated shallowing water and an approaching shoreline" (Russell 1970), and it was on this basis that Russell considered *Clidastes* a shallow-water mosasaur.

Shallow waters tend to be warmer than deeper waters, and the presence of *Clidastes,* as well as *Platecarpus* and *Globidens,* lends "a definite Tethyan or tropical cast to the mosasaur assemblage from the Mooreville Chalk" (Russell 1970).

In 2002, Caitlin Kiernan published a study of "more than 600 mosasaur specimens from the Tombigbee Sand Member (Eutaw Formation) and Selma group of west and central Alabama." After examining most of this material, she recognized "significant stratigraphic segregation among taxa." Because the geology of various areas differed, suggesting that different conditions prevailed during the time of the mosasaurs, certain mosasaur fossils were found in some areas and not others. Kiernan identified three biostratigraphic zones: the *Tylosaurus* acme zone (where *Tylosaurus* fossils predominated), the *Clidastes* acme zone, and the *Mosasaurus* acme zone. *Tylosaurus* evidently lived in shallower, nearshore waters, while *Clidastes* lived in deeper water, farther offshore. Kiernan mentioned a "mostly unprepared" skeleton of 55-foot *Mosasaurus*—probably *hoffmanni*—"by far the most complete mosasaur (or any other fossil vertebrate) to come from the Prairie Bluff Chalk." Lingham-Soliar (1995), describing *M. hoffmanni* from the Netherlands, wrote that it "lived in fairly deep nearshore waters of 40–50 m (131–164 feet) depth, with changing temperatures and rich vertebrate and invertebrate life." He also called it "the largest marine reptile ever known,"* and it is interesting to realize that these gigantic predators plied the Cretaceous seas of Europe, North America, and, now, western Asia. In 2002, Bardet and Tonoğlu published a description of maxillary fragments (with teeth) of a mosasaur that they identified as *M. hoffmanni* found in the late Maastrichtian deposits at Kastamonu, northern Turkey.

There are well-exposed Cretaceous deposits in two main areas of Belgium—the Hesbaye-Maastricht district in the northeast (where the first mosasaur was found) and the Mons Basin in the southwest. "Both areas," wrote Lingham-Soliar (2000b), "have yielded a large number of mosasaur specimens collected and preserved in the Institut Royal des Sciences Naturelles Belgique in Brussels." Although the Maastricht mosasaur is the best known, many more specimens have come from the Ciply Phosphatic Chalk in the Mons Basin. Between 1880 and 1895, an astonishing 52 skeletons were found in various quarries around the town of Ciply, many of them complete

* It may not hold this title for long. As discussed on pp. 89–90, Betsy Nicholls of the Royal Tyrrell Museum of Alberta is currently excavating a fossil ichthyosaur whose skull was 18 feet long and whose total length has been estimated at 75 feet.

or nearly so. Dollo's original *Hainosaurus bernardi* came from Ciply, and there are examples of five other mosasaur species—*Carinodens belgicus, Plioplatecarpus houzeaui, Prognathodon giganteus, Prognathodon solvayi,* and an unnamed *Halisaurus* species—but most of the material has been referred to *Mosasaurus lemonnieri,* which Russell (1967) suggested synonymizing with the American species *Mosasaurus conodon.* But in 2000, Lingham-Soliar restored *Mosasaurus lemonnieri* to the status of full species, writing that the "previous assignment to *M. conodon* is rejected here." The original material was found at Ciply, through a collaboration between Louis Dollo of the Belgian Royal Institute and the engineers L. Bernard and A. Lemonnier of the phosphate company. (Dollo named *Hainosaurus bernardi* and *Mosasaurus lemonnieri* for these two gentlemen.) The great majority of the material from the Ciply phosphates belongs to the species *M. lemmonier,* which is differentiated from the very similar—but much larger—*M. hoffmanni* by size and certain skeletal characteristics. The durophagous genera *Globidens* and *Carinodens* were also found in Belgium and the Netherlands, demonstrating that these lowland countries represent some of the most important sites in the world for the study of mosasaurs.

In 1998, Dutch paleontologist Ruud Dortangs was fossicking in the cement quarry at the Maastricht site when he noticed a bone protruding from the limestone. It turned out to be a caudal vertebra of a large mosasaur, and with his associates from the Natural History Museum, Dortangs began to excavate the remainder of the skeleton. They found an almost complete skull, more tail vertebrae, the shoulder girdle, some teeth, and the rib cage. When they had removed and examined the bones, they "more or less routinely" identified them as belonging to the giant Maastricht mosasaur *M. hoffmanni,* but "subsequent preparation revealed features and skull inconsistent with such an assignment" (Dortangs et al. 2001). They realized that this 45-foot mosasaur was a new species of *Prognathodon.* An animal this size would have had few natural enemies, but the bones were scratched as if from sharks' teeth. It cannot be known whether the sharks killed the mosasaur and then fed on it or came upon its carcass after it had died, but the scratches on the bones and the sharks' teeth found alongside the fossil indicate that sharks had fed on the mosasaur, which was named *Prognathodon saturator. Saturator* means "one who gives satisfaction" in Latin, and the name was chosen because the mosasaur

*Found in a quarry in Maastricht, the Netherlands,* Prognathodon saturator *is the most recently discovered mosasaur. At a length of 45 feet, it was also one of the largest.*

had given satisfaction to the hungry sharks (Dortangs et al. 2002). On exhibit at the Natural History Museum in Maastricht, *P. saturator* has been named "Bèr," which is a common nickname for Albert or Hubert in Dutch.

Outside of Kansas and the Netherlands, some of the best mosasaur material comes from Africa. In 1912, Robert Broom (who would go on to discover *Australopithecus robustus,* now known as *Paranthropus robustus*) wrote about a fragmentary specimen of *Tylosaurus* from the Upper Cretaceous of Pondoland, South Africa, that he felt was "manifestly not *Tylosaurus proriger* Cope" but was quite similar to *T. dyspelor,* so he named it *Tylosaurus capensis.* When W. E. Swinton (1930b) of the British Museum found the first mosasaur in Nigeria, he named it *Mosasaurus nigeriensis* (according to Lingham-Soliar [1991b], Swinton's material actually consists of a number of mosasaur taxa lumped together as *Mosasaurus nigeriensis*). Otto Zdansky of the Egyptian University published a paper in 1935 on the mosasaurs of Egypt and other parts of Africa, identifying ten different species, eight of which were found in Egypt. In 1969–1970, an expedition from the University of Florence headed for Nigeria in search of fossils, and in the Goronyo district of Sokoto State, they hit pay dirt (Azzaroli et al. 1975). The Dukamaje Formation was so rich in vertebrate fossils that they called it the "Mosasaur Shales," and they found, described,

* Evidently, Azzaroli et al. erected the genus *Goronyosaurus* on the basis of "some highly aberrant features" of the skull, but when Soliar (1988) examined the material, he found their description incorrect in some respects, "but other characters described by them, plus the

and named the 25-foot-long *Goronyosaurus nigeriensis*,* a new species that resembled no other mosasaur, and another specimen that resembled *Halisaurus*.

Theagarten Lingham-Soliar has been working with the African mosasaurs since 1988, when he published a paper (under the name T. Soliar; Lingham was added later) on *Goronyosaurus* from the Upper Cretaceous of Sokoto State, Nigeria, which had been named for the Goronyo district by Azzaroli et al. in 1972. In a later discussion, Lingham-Soliar (1999b) called *Goronyosaurus* "one of the most enigmatic extinct marine reptiles, manifesting the largest number of derived characters in the Mosasauridae." The skull of *Goronyosaurus* differs from that of any other mosasaurs in that it is not tapered toward the front; rather, it can be described as an elongated cylinder. It resembled a crocodile in the way its teeth, including the first caniniforms in mosasaurs (only mammals have true canines), fit into deep sockets in the opposing jaws. The estimated length of an adult *Goronyosaurus* was 21 feet, making it one of the larger known mosasaurs. (For comparison, *M. hoffmanni*, the largest of the mosasaurs, was more than twice as long.) The large teeth and powerful jaws suggest that it fed on large fish and other reptiles. Its eyes were relatively small, but its sense of smell was keen, and it probably fed much the way the marine crocodiles do: by ambushing their prey and then tearing it apart with their powerful jaws and teeth. Lingham-Soliar (1999b) wrote:

> In addition the long body form of mosasaurs, suited to ambush predation, was a distinct advantage in the changing environment of the Late Cretaceous. The fast, highly evasive teleost fishes were experiencing a major radiation at this time and the pursuit form of predatory tactics in marine reptiles would have become energetically very expensive. It therefore seems no coincidence that pursuit predators such as the ichthyosaurs became extinct at this point and the plesiosaurs were reduced from six families to two.

Lingham-Soliar was so impressed with the teeth of *Goronyosaurus* that he devoted two papers to them and their implications. In the paper quoted above

---

new information added here, vindicates the erection of a new genus, which can be tentatively assigned to the Tylosaurinae." A new subfamily might be warranted here, but so far, only the single species has been found.

Found in the Upper
Cretaceous of the
Goronyo district,
Sokoto State,
Nigeria, the 21-
foot-long
Goronyosaurus
was one of the larger
mosasaurs. With
teeth that fit into
opposing sockets like
those of a crocodile,
this reptile was a
formidable predator.

(1999b), he showed the restored skull with the teeth in place, pointing out that the size and structure of the caniniform teeth "suggest that they were not designed for impact against bone but rather shearing into flesh." He devoted a later paper (2002b) only to the caniniform teeth and how *Goronyosaurus* might have used them: "Taken together with skull strengthening features discussed in a functional study of the skull of *Goronyosaurus*, the enlarged teeth . . . seem to be a novel mosasaurian development of the dentition and a food trap. Such features are more characteristic of some crocodiles and much earlier terrestrial carnivores. . . . *Goronyosaurus* represents an exemplar of a giant, marine reptilian predator at the end of the Late Cretaceous."

"The Iullemmeden Basin [southwest Niger] provided one of the richest environments in the world for mosasaur evolution and diversification," wrote Lingham-Soliar (1998a).* Here he discovered *Pluridens walkeri*, which had twice as many teeth as any other mosasaur (*Pluridens* means "many teeth"), and their structure suggested that it fed on small fishes and thin-shelled invertebrates, rather like some of the ichthyosaurs. Somewhere around 65 million years ago, in the period we call the Upper Cretaceous, this many-toothed mosasaur

* Niger and Nigeria are two different countries, although the great Niger River runs through both. Niger (pronounced Ni-zher), directly north of Nigeria, is largely composed of semiarid lands or Saharan desert. Nigeria has a long coastline on the Gulf of Guinea; it consists of mangrove swamps near the coast and, farther inland, savannas, rain forests, and high plains.

swam in the Trans-Saharan Seaway, a part of the Tethys Sea extending from the Gulf of Guinea in the west to the Mediterranean in the northeast, essentially bisecting the African continent. Lingham-Soliar envisions *Pluridens* "as an ambush predator, as are most mosasaurs, accelerating rapidly by means of the long tail when prey was sighted."

"Recent studies," wrote Lingham-Soliar (1994a), "show that mosasaurs were also prevalent in Zaire and Angola. The picture therefore is that of an almost continuous band of mosasaur localities stretching from Egypt, across to Morocco and Algeria, then southwards to Niger, Nigeria, Zaire, Angola, and South Africa. Hence, African mosasaurs must today rival the historical and present-day discoveries of two of the greatest mosasaur bearing regions of the world, North America and Belgium/The Netherlands." Lingham-Soliar found mosasaur fossils from A to Z – Angola to Zaire – in Africa. He identified fragmentary mosasaur material – mostly teeth – referable to four species in Zaire: *Plioplatecarpus, Prognathodon, Halisaurus,* and *Mosasaurus.* He examined a new species that had been found in Angola and named *Angolasaurus bocagei,* but "reassessment of the material indicates that it clearly belongs to a new species of *Platecarpus,*" geographically the most widespread member of the Mosasauridae and inhabiting the waters of (what is now) North America, Europe, Africa, and New Zealand. Of *Plioplatecarpus marshi,* he wrote, "With needle-sharp, strongly backwardly recurved teeth, it drew in prey by what is known as ratchet feeding similar to that of snakes – 'walking' the jaws over the prey. . . . It is interesting that the animal also shows early signs in its morphology of adopting a penguin-like mode of locomotion, underwater flight, that would have been highly useful in the complex, crowded habitats it is believed to have inhabited."

Like sub-Saharan Africa – or Kansas, for that matter – the Negev Desert of Israel is one of the last places one would expect to find the remains of extinct aquatic reptiles. But in Cretaceous times, these areas were all underwater, and the waters were occupied by mosasaurs. In 1993, workers at the Oron phosphate field 30 miles south of Be'er Sheva unearthed a fossil mosasaur, and it was shipped to Copenhagen, where preparator Sten Jakobsen worked on it for two years. Paleontologists Niels Bonde and Per Christiansen then began the scientific analysis of the 5½-foot-long skull that was encased in silicified sandstone as hard as concrete. The wide, heavy skull, with its massive jaw teeth and especially large, curved palatal teeth, suggested that *Oronosaurus*—nicknamed for the place it was found—was a mega-predator, well designed to prey on large vertebrates. From the length of the skull, Bonde and Christiansen estimated the total length of the animal at about 40 feet, making Israel's first mosasaur one of the largest known. The skull, which is the largest fossil of anything ever unearthed in Israel, now resides at the Geological Institute of the University of Copenhagen, but because it belongs to Ben Gurion University in Be'er Sheva, it will be returned there when a museum is built in which to display it.*

In September 2002, the description was finally published in the *Journal of Vertebrate Paleontology*. Christiansen and Bonde named the new species *Prognathodon currii* (after Phil Curry, a famed Canadian dinosaur paleontologist) and wrote that it "represents one of the largest mosasaurid skulls ever discovered, rivaled only by the giant tylosaurine *Hainosaurus bernardi*, and the plotosaurine *Mosasaurus hoffmanni*, which appears to have been subequal in size to *P. currii*." They estimated its total length at about 36 feet and wrote that its powerful skull and teeth suggest that it was "a top predator, which had become adapted for predominantly hunting large, vertebrate prey, a suggestion further corroborated by the unusually large size of the palatal teeth.

---

* The rules of scientific nomenclature are varied and complex. When Bonde and Christiansen discussed *Oronosaurus* at a symposium in Copenhagen in 1999, they were fairly certain that this gigantic mosasaur specimen represented a new genus and felt comfortable giving it a new name. For the most part, however, a scientific name is officially accepted only when it is published in a journal, and *Oronosaurus* did not qualify. In fact, it now turns out that it isn't a new genus after all. In a letter to me in December 2001, Christiansen wrote: "The giant is no longer called *Oronosaurus*. When I did phylogenetic analyses using only the American prognathodons (and, of course a larger number of other taxa) the specimen consistently (under various optimizations) came out as the sister taxon to all of the other mosasaurines. As the sister taxon to all other mosasaurines it had to be a new genus. However, the American prognathodons are different from the European type species *P. solvayi*, and when this animal was included in the analysis, results changed. Now our monster consistently emerged as the sister taxon to *P. solvayi*, with the American prognathodons forming successive out-groups to the pair. Thus, our animal *is* a *Prognathodon*, albeit an enormous, and highly derived species—and it very evidently is a new species."

Evidently, *P. currii* is a superior candidate to the title of marine tyrannosaur than any of the other large mosasaurids."

Although the first New Zealand plesiosaur fossils were uncovered in 1859, recent discoveries have put this isolated island group right in the middle of marine reptile research. Ichthyosaur fossils were found in 1954, at Mangahouanga on North Island. Amateur collector Joan Wiffen (affectionately known as the "Dragon Lady") has found the remains of plesiosaurs, sharks, and turtles and several large fragments and skulls of various mosasaurs, including *Tylosaurus haumuriensis*, *Mosasaurus mokoroa*, and a new species she discovered and named—*Moanasaurus mangahouangae*. Much of this material is now being studied; the most recent description (Bell et al. 1999) can be found in the abstracts from the Society of Vertebrate Paleontology's annual meeting:

Recent fieldwork in the Upper Cretaceous marine sandstones of New Zealand has clarified several longstanding problems regarding the paleo-ecology and systematics of Late Cretaceous mosasaurs in the southern hemisphere. Collecting near Kaikoura (South Island), at Haumuri Bluff, produced the skull of the enigmatic tylosaurine mosasaur *Taniwhasaurus oweni* Hector, 1874. This specimen, and study of previously collected specimens, indicates that *Tylosaurus haumuriensis* is the junior synonym of *Taniwhasaurus*. *Taniwhasaurus* shows important similarities to the North American and West European tylosaurine *Hainosaurus bernardi* Dollo, 1885. The presumably enigmatic and endemic mosasaur *Moanasaurus* Wiffen, 1980, is a valid and very important taxon that is morphologically unique, and is represented by at least two species ranging through the Campanian. Specimens assigned to *Rikkisaurus* Wiffen, 1990, *Prognathodon* cf. *overtoni*, and *Mosasaurus flemingi* are reassigned to *Moanasaurus*. Phylogenetic analysis indicates that the moanasaurines are sister-group to the Plotosaurini (*Mosasaurus* and *Globidens*); clidastines are the sister-group to moanasaurines and Plotosaurini. Mosasaur fossils occur in giant concretions formed within near-shore marine clastics, the beds of which are marked by intense bioturbation. New Zealand mosasaurs were occupying nearshore environments and may have used coastlines to radiate and migrate between continents.

Some mosasaurs had a special adaptation that enabled them to eat the slippery fishes and squid that probably made up most of their diet. In addition to the regular teeth in the upper and lower jaws, the pterygoid bones that made up the hard palate on the roof of the animal's mouth were also equipped with teeth that kept the prey items from wriggling free after they had been grabbed by the jaw teeth. But there are some mosasaur fossils that indicate that these huge reptiles were not all fish eaters. In 1987, James Martin and Phillip Bjork described the stomach contents (which they referred to as "gastric residues") of a South Dakota fossil of *Tylosaurus proriger* that included the remnants of the diving bird *Hesperornis*, a bony fish, a lamnid shark, and the smaller mosasaur *Clidastes*.

Working in the American South in the early decades of the twentieth century, Charles W. Gilmore of the U.S. National Museum found evidence of some remarkable mosasaurs that ate only shellfish, rather than chasing down fast-moving prey items and snagging them with their big, sharp teeth. The genus known as *Globidens* ("round teeth"), first discovered by Gilmore in Alabama in 1912 and subsequently unearthed in Kansas and South Dakota, had rounded teeth instead of the more typical conical spikes. From the partial jawbones that have been excavated, it has been estimated that *Globidens* reached a length of 20 feet, and perhaps even more. Although a reptile of this size

*The 20-foot-long Globidens was a mosasaur that crushed shells with its round teeth, hence its name. Specimens have been found in Alabama, Belgium, and the Netherlands.*

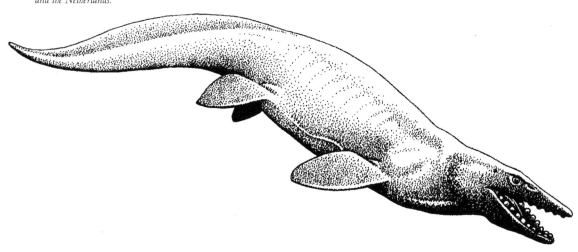

would have been a formidable predator, its rounded teeth were designed to crush shellfish—probably ammonites. Because we know that mosasaurs occasionally fed on ammonites, it is not that much of a leap to imagine a mosasaur species that evolved to eat *only* these cephalopods. (A modern analogue is the horn shark, *Heterodontus* sp., with pavement-like teeth in the back of its jaws that are used specifically for crushing the hard shells of oysters and clams.) Two tooth types are identified in *Globidens:* a spherical type, fairly smooth and with a small nubbin or point, and a subspherical form, with a highly striated surface and a large apical nubbin.

Smaller than *Globidens* but with similarly rounded teeth were the mosasaurs *Carinodens belgicus* and *C. fraasi,* which were only 10 to 12 feet long and probably searched the sea floor for brittle mollusks and sea urchins to crack open. (*Carinodens* was originally named *Compressidens* by Dollo in 1924.) *Globidens* and *Carinodens* from the Upper Cretaceous of Belgium and the Netherlands were the first marine reptiles since the placodonts of the Triassic and the ichthyosaur *Grippia* from the Triassic of Spitsbergen that were specialized for feeding on shelled animals. Based on just a few teeth on a slender jaw, Lingham-Soliar (1999a) reconstructed the entire dental row of *Carinodens* to show, in lateral view, pointed teeth anteriorly, triangular teeth toward the middle, and rectangular teeth posteriorly. Both the tooth shape and the wrinkled surface played an important part in the stresses the teeth were subjected to. *Carinodens* probably fed on thin-shelled invertebrates and *Globidens* on thicker-shelled invertebrates and vertebrates. The round-toothed mosasaurs were the only ones that did not have teeth on the pterygoid bones of the palate; crushed shellfish did not have to be "walked" to the throat like struggling vertebrates. Feeding on hard-shelled animals (durophagy) also occurred in other mosasaurs such as *Mosasaurus hoffmanni, Prognathodon,* and the tylosaurs, although in these forms it was probably opportunistic and part of a wider feeding strategy.

Louis Dollo (1904) was among the first to record the feeding potential of mosasaurs when he showed the fossilized remains of a large turtle in the gut cavity of the 50-foot-long mosasaur *Hainosaurus* found in Belgium. Even with its hinged lower jaw, it remains a mystery how *Hainosaurus* could have swallowed the turtle's carapace (Lingham-Soliar 1992b). Said by some to have been the largest of all mosasaurs, *Hainosaurus* has also been found in the Kristianstad Basin in Skåne, southern Sweden, and (maybe) in the Pierre Shale of Manitoba. The Manitoba specimen, found in the pits of the Pembina Mining Company, was named *Hainosaurus pembinensis* and was described in 1988 by Betsy Nicholls, now of the Royal Tyrrell Museum. It was the first record of *Hainosaurus* from North America.* This species is the longest of the mosasaurs because it had more precaudal vertebrae than any other species; it had 53, compared with the 35 of *Tylosaurus.* The teeth are minutely serrated, and the narrow skull is shaped like an arrowhead. Although unspecialized feeders, these giant mosasaurs were highly specialized in their killing mechanism, involving not only a huge and somehow expandable mouth but also a large, solid rostrum at the tip of the snout that could be used as a battering ram to stun or kill prey by smashing into it, not unlike the way a bottlenose dolphin uses its "beak" to fight off sharks.

An animal with a built-in battering ram is likely to use it, and there is evidence that one large mosasaur killed another by a powerful blow to the head. The victim was a subadult *Mosasaurus hoffmanni,* and the suspected perpetrator was *Hainosaurus bernardi.* Examining a cast of the braincase of *M. hoffmanni* in the collection of the Institut Royal des Sciences Naturelles de Belgique, Lingham-Soliar (1998c) found "some unusual damage," consisting of a severed and displaced cerebellum, that could only have come from "a powerful concentrated blow to the prootic region of the braincase. The prootic would have sprung inwards, facilitated by ligamentous sutures, bro-

---

* Lingham-Soliar wrote to me that he is not convinced that this is *Hainosaurus:* "Nicholls based her analysis on Dollo's distinction between *Hainosaurus* and *Tylosaurus* which is purely on allometric variations of the skull in the two species. However, to this date, despite the enormous numbers of tylosaur species in North America no studies have been made to investigate intraspecific variations of this nature. Having looked at mosasaurs such as *Mosasaurus lemonnieri* (Lingham-Soliar 2000b), of which there are a number of specimens in the Institute Royal in Belgium, in both cranial and postcranial measurements there are considerable intraspecific variations. I personally would not have created this new North American species, with all its ramifications, without a thorough investigation of the bountiful *Tylosaurus* specimens in the USA. In Dollo's day I think it was understandable, particularly with his penchant for telegraphic descriptions."

The 50-foot-long mosasaur Hainosaurus, shown crushing an ammonite whose ink sac has burst. The head of the mosasaur was modeled after a drawing by Lingham-Soliar that appeared on the cover of the European magazine Science Spectra in 1999.

ken internally thereby causing the brain to be severed and sprung out again." What sort of animal could (or would) ram a gigantic mosasaur? Probably an animal that was designed to do just that. The tylosaur *Hainosaurus* had a large, bony rostrum; was capable of bursts of speed; and had a mouthful of strong, sharp teeth and an enormous appetite. Of course, we will never know what caused the death of *M. hoffmanni,* but the clues, as read by "Sherlock" Lingham-Soliar, point strongly in the direction of *Hainosaurus.* It had the weapon, the opportunity, and the motive.

In 1991, Lingham-Soliar wrote a paper called "Locomotion in Mosasaurs" in which he rieewed the early speculations on mosasaur swimming, many of which had the reptiles undulating their entire bodies like snakes or eels. After a careful analysis of the structure of the vertebrae, he concluded that they were "potentially capable of the axial subundulatory mode of swimming," which means that the forward part ("the anterior third to half of the body") is stiffened, while the rear portion undulates. The examples he gave were the cod *(Gadus morhua)*, the American alligator *(Alligator mississippiensis)*, and the Galápagos marine iguana *(Amblyrhynchus cristatus)*. As shown by Massare (1988), mosasaurs were probably slow swimmers and therefore were not likely to have been pursuit predators. They were, however, capable of short bursts of speed, which suited them to the role of ambush predator.

But only a year later, Lingham-Soliar proposed that the large mosasaur *Plioplatecarpus marshi* actually *flew* underwater. In his previous study (1991a), he had written that, as with crocodilians, undulatory swimming was ubiquitous in mosasaurs (the "axial subundulatory mode"). However, prompted by new material he had unearthed in the Natural History Museum of London, he wrote (1992a): "the enormous pectoral girdle and highly unusual bones of the forelimb . . . viewed in the context of the morphology of the animal as a whole, led to the conclusion that one mosasaur, *P. marshi,* uniquely swam using subaqueous flight—a previously undescribed mode of swimming in mosasaurs." Subaqueous flight differs from "rowing," where the foreflippers are used to pull the animal through the water, like the oars of a rowboat or the arms and hands of a swimming human, or, as Lingham-Soliar described it, "the propulsive force in rowing involves a powerful anteroposterior stroke driving the animal forward; the recovery stroke involves 'feathering' the 'oar' in order to return it to the beginning of the power stroke." "Flying" involves an up-and-down movement of the flippers, with the downstroke providing the propulsive power; as the animal moves forward, the stroke cycle can be diagrammed as an oval or a circle. We are obviously unable to see *P. marshi* in action, but the California sea lion *(Zalophus)* has a similarly exaggerated shoulder blade, and there are any number of observations of these popular pinnipeds "flying" through the water. In short, the large surface area and tapered shape of the "wing," combined with powerful musculature attached to a brace (the pectoral girdle) that can withstand strong pressures, lead to the conclusion that this animal "flew" through the water. As to why this species would have flown while other mosasaurs propelled themselves with caudal undulations, Lingham-Soliar opines that its shallow-water lifestyle required greater maneuverability than the deeper-water types, "and it seems that the unusual structure of *Plioplatecarpus marshi* led to adaptations for pursuit of fast and/or elusive prey in a structurally complex environment."

The idea of underwater flight in mosasaurs has led to a spirited controversy within the paleontological community. For instance, Nicholls and Godfrey (1994) accepted Lingham-Soliar's original interpretation, but not the revised version. They recognized that the spine of *Plioplatecarpus marshi* was stiffened by especially heavy vertebrae, but they said that in all other subaqueous "fliers" (such as penguins) the tail is greatly reduced, and "mosasaurs traditionally have long, laterally compressed tails, and there is no reason to believe that *Plioplatecarpus* was any different in this respect." They contended that the huge flippers of this mosasaur would not have been particularly effective as wings, and that the powerful pectoral girdle "may be associated with a number of other functions, such as an increase in maneuverability in a structurally complex environment." Furthermore, "sharks which shake their prey have well-developed pectoral girdles. Sharp movements of the pectoral fins are transmitted to the head to achieve the vigorous shaking needed to dismember the prey. The massive deltopectoral crest and pectoral girdle seen in *Plioplatecarpus* might have allowed them to feed in this fashion." In his discussion of "Carrier's Constraint," Cowen (1996) wrote that the body was indeed stiffened, but not for underwater flying. Why was it stiffened? "I suggest," wrote Cowen, "that *Plioplatecarpus* was beginning to solve Carrier's Constraint, by decoupling flexure of the thorax from swimming propulsion, which increasingly involved only the posterior of the animal. Such an adaptation would only be important for an animal swimming at sustained speed in surface waters. Therefore, I suggest, this animal was the best sustained surface swimmer among mosasaurs, even if it did not fly underwater."

If the locomotion of *Plioplatecarpus marshi* "increasingly involved only the posterior of the animal," one would expect a tail fin at least as prominent as those of *Clidastes*, *Plotosaurus*, and the various *Mosasaurus* species, but the neural spins of the caudal vertebrae of *Plioplatecarpus marshi* are the shortest known in mosasaurs, indicating the unlikelihood of a reasonably developed tail fin. Surface swimming in a large mosasaur such as *P. marshi* would be very expensive energetically because of increased drag resulting from wave action and water movement for several feet below the surface. In the 1999 paper in which they described a plioplatecarpine mosasaur from an estuarine environment, Holmes, Caldwell, and Cumbaa rejected Lingham-Soliar's reconstruction and biomechanical analysis of *P. marshi*. They wrote that "his analysis required extensive reconstruction of limb elements, most of which were not present in the specimen available to him." Lingham-Soliar hypothesized that the paddle of *P. marshi* was used in subaqueous flying, but Holmes et al. believe that *Plioplatecarpus* did not "fly" at all but paddled for initial acceleration with its foreflippers, then tucked them in (presumably to reduce drag) and used its tail for sustained swimming. The foreflippers would also be used to effect sudden changes in direction, both laterally and vertically.

In the past, paleontologists often examined and analyzed fossils, believing that their responsibility began and ended with osteological descriptions (e.g., "the tubular bassioccipitalia are partially concealed by the underlap of the pterygoids"), but nowadays, most paleontologists believe that they can—and should—postulate a lifestyle from the fossil evidence. Lingham-Soliar is a charter member of the modern group. In a 1993 article entitled "The Mosasaur *Leiodon* Bares Its Teeth," he indulged in the usual descriptions of the bones (which are, in this case, mostly the teeth of the title), as in, "anteriorly there is a small rounded edentulous process," but his analysis was directed toward an understanding of how the mosasaur might have used those teeth. After differentiating *Leiodon* ("smooth teeth") from other mosasaur species (the name was first employed by Richard Owen in a series of papers in 1840–1845) and laying the requisite osteological and taxonomic groundwork, he gets to the core of his discussion:

The powerful, highly specialized teeth of *Leiodon* were probably the most efficient in the Mosasauridae for tearing off chunks of soft bodied prey such as fishes or other marine reptiles. *L. mosasauroides* was the most advanced member of the genus in this respect, with razor sharp anterior and posterior carinae. Clearly, *Leiodon* was a formidable predator, the nearest mosasaur analogue to sharks such as *Cretolamna* and *Carcharodon*. Like sharks also, *Leiodon* (as in all mosasaurs) had a system of continual tooth replacement that ensured an ever-sharp battery of teeth. . . . A possible further method of predation in the large *L. mosasauroides* would involve lunging at full speed at the underbelly of bigger prey, and at the last moment, tilting the head away to allow the teeth to rip open the gut. In this way, even very large prey can be immobilised, as is often seen on land when carnivores e.g., hyaenas, subdue large prey.

John Colagrande devotes a chapter of *In the Presence of Dinosaurs* to coastal wildlife in the Niobrara Sea, which includes the feeding plesiosaurs discussed earlier and a vivid description of the hunting technique of the mosasaur *Tylosaurus:*

> If a hunting tylosaur makes contact with a school of ammonites, it will generally circle it at least once, widely, then dive. When it is directly under the mollusks, it will swim up into them, gnashing its great jaws and teeth this way, trying to injure as many of the cephalopods as it can. The attack scatters the school in all directions, leaving only the injured swimming erratically through flecks of broken shell slowly fluttering to the bottom. These crippled mollusks now have the tylosaur's undivided attention. It grasps each one by its tentacled head and shakes it violently, sending much of the damaged shell flying, so that the animal inside can be swallowed – a messy but effective technique.

In 1960, Erle Kauffman and Robert Kesling published "An Upper Cretaceous Ammonite Bitten by a Mosasaur," in which they went into incredible detail to show that "the shell was bitten repeatedly, and bears dramatic evidence of the fatal encounter." They plotted the tooth patterns of the mosasaur against the holes and published 9 pages of photographs to accompany the 45-page paper. They suggested that the mosasaur that did the biting was "most likely a deep diver of the Platecarpinae, a close relative of *Platecarpus brachycephalus* and *Ancylocentrum overtoni.*" As they described the event:

> The initial attack was directed at the upper side of the conch, providing the ammonite was swimming in the normal position used by its living relative, *Nautilus.* The mosasaur must have dived at it from above to seize it. The attack was pertinaceous, resulting in at least sixteen bites. As shown by the marks of the pterygoid teeth in the sequence of bites, the mosasaur

evidently tried to swallow the entire ammonite, pulling it as far back into the throat as possible.

This is what happened to the ammonite:

> The shell walls bear numerous subround perforations, crushed areas, and dents of several sizes which were made by the teeth of a mosasaur. These marks are present on both sides of the shell, but are best developed on the left side, which shows an almost complete set of maxillary impressions. A dorsal sector of the conch has been fractured and slightly displaced, and the living chamber, which makes up about half of the outer whorl of *Placenticeras,* has been severely crushed and slightly torn at its apertural margin.

There are those, however, who believe that the dramatic event, presented in such graphic detail by Kauffman and Kesling, did not happen at all. In his 1998 book *Time Machine,* cephalopod specialist Peter Ward devotes an entire chapter to "The Bite of a Mosasaur," in which he recounts his observations of a sea turtle attack on a nautilus in captivity in New Caledonia, during which the nautilus's shell was fragmented like a porcelain plate hit with a hammer. Then he tells of his examination of a collection of *Placenticeras* shells in which the holes "seemed to conform to the sizes and shapes produced by limpets." He includes a discussion of graduate student Erica Roux's attempt to make round holes in nautilus shells, a close approximation of unfossilized ammonite shells:

> Erica constructed an artificial mosasaur jaw. It did not look much like the real thing, being fabricated of metal with series of teeth made out of nails and screws, but nevertheless it approximated the real thing in many ways. The "teeth" descended onto the shell surface just as a mosasaur jaw would have, and a gauge attached to the jaw showed the amount of pressure needed to produce a break. A nautilus shell was put between the jaws and the type of damage inflicted on the shell was observed. For several days [the lab] reverberated with cracks and snaps, as shell after shell fell victim to those jaws of death. An army of mosasaurs could not have had so much fun. And in all the carnage that ensued, not once was a round circular hole approximating the size of a mosasaur's tooth ever produced.

Like many others, Ward believes that mosasaurs did indeed eat ammonites; they just crushed the shells to get at the soft, edible bits.

In 1998, Kase et al. published their findings in "Alleged Mosasaur Bites on Late Cretaceous Ammonites Are Limpet (Patellogastropod) Home Scars." Using a robot mosasaur jaw, they demonstrated that the pressure exerted by a mosasaur's teeth would utterly fracture a cephalopod's shell (there being no fresh ammonites available, they used nautiluses). More significantly, they examined the holes supposedly made by the teeth of mosasaurs on ammonite shells and found clear evidence of limpets "grazing" on the shells with their radular teeth. They concluded:

> We do not deny that mosasaurs may have preyed on ammonites by crushing. Any that escaped swallowing had the potential to be preserved as fossils. However, it is difficult to determine whether any resulting fragments are attributable to mosasaur bites or to other geologic processes. We cannot accept that both limpet home scars and tooth punctures are present on the ammonite shells. It is improbable that two unrelated kinds of punctures should always occur at the same localities and only in a narrow stratigraphic interval. We conclude that all the holes in ammonites attributed to mosasaur bites are limpet hole scars that were altered by diagenesis [the chemical, physical, and biological changes undergone by a sediment after its initial deposition, and during and after its lithification, exclusive of surface alteration]. Our findings are important in revising Late Cretaceous marine food webs and the alleged role of mosasaurs as ammonite predators.

Also in 1998, Seilacher wrote "Mosasaur, Limpets or Diagenesis," in which he said, "The claimed 'mosasaur bites' are probably all caused by limpets rasping on necroplanktonic *Placenticeras* shells, compactual puncturing of the pits and diagnostic beveling of the rims." In other words, Seilacher believed that the ammonites were already dead when they were colonized by the limpets.

But Tsujita and Westermann (2001) believe that even if limpets made some of the holes, it is highly unlikely that they made all of them, and they support Kauffman and Kesling's parsimonious suggestion that hungry mosasaurs punched holes in the ammonite shells with their powerful jaws and teeth. Tsujita and Westermann examined more than 150 specimens of *Placenticeras* from the Upper Cretaceous Bearpaw Formation of southern Alberta and found, as had Kauffman and Kesling, that many of the shells exhibited holes in straight rows or even in a V-shaped pattern, which conformed to the jaw shape of mosasaurs but was highly unlikely to result from random assemblages of limpets. Furthermore, they said, "fossil limpet shells are much too rare in the Bearpaw Formation to account for all the perforations." The designers of the robot jaws employed on nautilus shells assumed "that mosasaurs always closed their jaws in a violent snapping motion" that shattered the shells, but that assumption is unwarranted; indeed, the "unusually loose jaw structure of mosasaurs probably allowed for a great deal of controlled variation in biting habit," and they would therefore not crush the shells as the robots did. "Many aspects of the perforations and associated features preserved in *Placenticeras* shells that can easily be accounted for by the mosasaur-bite hypothesis, are impossible to explain by the limpet hypothesis. . . . We confidently conclude that the vast majority of perforated specimens of *Placenticeras*, at least those from Alberta, record evidence of predation and that the mosasaur-bite mark hypothesis has been unjustly dismissed by proponents of the limpet home scar hypothesis."

I lean toward the mosasaur-bite hypothesis, and I believe that Kauffman and Kesling are correct. Tsujita and Westermann are convincing, in that limpets were unlikely to have arranged themselves in patterns that so closely resembled the tooth rows of mosasaurs, and their detailed analysis of the jaws of mosasaurs explains why ammonite shells would not be shattered. It is unlikely that Kase, Seilacher, Ward, and the rest of the proponents of the limpet scar hypothesis are going to concede — after all, Tsujita and Westermann reexamined the same evidence they did, not something new and definitive — and the argument is certainly not settled. To understand the mosasaurs' feeding habits, we really need Peter Ward's time machine.

Like the other marine reptiles, the mosasaurs were probably partially endothermic, but the question of where the energy came from for sustained locomotion is not often addressed (Lingham-Soliar does not mention it). Massare (1994) wrote, "The physiology of the animal is the most important factor in estimating sustained swimming speeds. Mosasaurs, related to monitor lizards, were almost certainly ectotherms." (Monitor lizards, believed by some to be closely related to mosasaurs, are surely ectotherms.) Although he did not know if they dived deeply, Russell (1967) indicated that *Tylosaurus* and *Platecarpus* frequented the deeper parts of the water column on a regular basis. Although the surface waters of the interior seaway might have been warmer than the ocean, the depths were certainly cool, and we are pretty sure that some mosasaurs were capable of deep dives (estimates of the greatest depth of the interior seaway rarely exceed 600 feet).

When they examined the fossilized vertebrae of some North American mosasaurs, Rothschild and Martin (1987) found evidence of avascular necrosis in two of the most common genera, *Tylosaurus* and *Platecarpus.* This bone disease, which was present in nearly every skeleton they examined, occurs when the blood supply to the bones is cut off, and it indicates an episode of decompression sickness ("the bends"), which results from nitrogen bubbles entering the bloodstream under pressure as an animal ascends after a deep dive. No such diseased vertebrae were found in specimens of *Clidastes,* which was not a particularly deep diver, as far as we know. Necrotic bone in *Tylosaurus* and *Platecarpus* suggests that these were deep-water species that may have dived too deeply and too often.

Williston (1898), the earliest authority on mosasaurs, believed that *Clidastes* was a swift surface hunter, but given what we know about living ocean predators, such as dolphins, sprinting in pursuit of prey at the surface is a very uncommon technique. Dolphins play or bow-ride at or near the surface but do most of their hunting while submerged. The same is true of sharks, which may take their prey at the surface but stalk it from below. (The great white shark, which feeds on seals and sea lions, approaches them from below and consummates the attack at or near the surface.) The fish variously known as the dorado, mahi-mahi, or *Coryphaena hippurus* is probably the closest thing to a "swift surface hunter." Considered one of the fastest of all fishes, *Coryphaena* chases flying fishes at the surface and occasionally even catches them in the air. Like dolphins—and unlike dorados and sharks—mosasaurs had to surface to breathe, so the opportunity to take prey at the surface was always there. Williston believed that *Tylosaurus* was a predator of other marine reptiles and that *Platecarpus* was a deep diver. Martin and Rothschild (1989) also wrote that in the Pierre Shale of South Dakota they "have collected skeletons of these giant forms [of mosasaurs] in the same area as the remains of giant extinct squids that may have been 6.2 to 9.2 meters [20 to 30 feet] long. It is possible that *Tylosaurus* may have dived to great depths to capture squid, as the modern sperm whale does now."

On the deep-diving ability of *Platecarpus*, Amy Sheldon (1997) disagrees with Martin and Rothschild. She wrote, "*Platecarpus* shows pachyostosis [an increase in bone density] which requires an increase in lung volume. This suggests a shallower and narrower range of neutral buoyancy." Sheldon believes that "bone microstructure seems to correlate with ecology"; that is, those animals with increased bone density are negatively buoyant even in shallow water, and the heavy bones, like a diver's weight belt, keep the animals submerged. (Sirenians, with some of the densest bones of any animals, inhabit *only* shallow waters, and Steller's sea cow *[Hydrodamalis]* probably could not submerge at all.) Sheldon wrote, "Many cetaceans, such as dolphins and some whales, ichthyosaurs, and some turtles, have very porous, light bone, and many swim swiftly."*

An inclination to get the bends is what evolutionary biologists call "mal-

---

* In one living whale species, the bones are the densest known for any animal. Blainville's beaked whale, also known as the dense-beaked whale *(Mesoplodon densirostris)*, is a species known from stranded specimens and occasional sightings at sea. Examining the rostrum (the forward, pointed portion of the upper jaw) of a specimen in the Museum National d'Histoire Naturelle de Paris, Buffrénil et al. (2000) found that the bone was 22 percent denser than any other known mammalian bone. Since no one has ever seen a dense-beaked whale diving or hunting, the authors could only speculate as to the function of this incredibly heavy bone. They discounted the idea that it might be used for intraspecific fighting because its density renders it brittle, and "bones adapted for shock loading, such as deer antlers, have the opposite structural characteristics." It might, they thought, be used as an ultrasound transmitter, but not enough information is known on sound production in beaked whales. Does it help in deep diving? Probably not. The authors concluded: "In the absence of experimental investigation, the true functional role of this feature is largely a matter of conjecture." If we can't figure out why a living whale needs such a dense rostrum, imagine how difficult it is to understand the physiological requirements of creatures that have been extinct for 100 million years.

adaptive" — a development that should produce a population that will eventually be doomed by its own habits. (Humans who get this disease are operating far outside the regular parameters of their biology.) Did such a situation contribute to the downfall of the mosasaurs — or at least those that, like *Tylosaurus,* were believed to be the deepest divers? Martin and Rothschild (1989) do not think so:

> It seems unreasonable to assume that every deep dive would result in decompression syndrome. If this were the case, how could deep diving behavior have evolved? It seems likely that decompression events were the direct result of crises such as the need to escape from predators or injudicious pursuit of prey. . . . Did decompression syndrome have any role in the final extinction of the mosasaurs? We do not think so. The fact that they lasted for at least 25 million years — a long time by most standards — suggests they were relatively successful organisms. . . . That the final disappearance of the mosasaurs occurred simultaneously with the extinction of such dissimilar organisms as dinosaurs and various types of phytoplankton strongly suggests that the cause was something other than a special maladaptation.

For the past 30 years, Mike Everhart has been uncovering fossil reptiles from the Kansas shales and has found numerous mosasaur bones that show distinct evidence of shark attack. From teeth embedded in the mosasaur's bones, the species of shark can be identified: it was *Cretoxyrhina mantelli,* a lamnid that is known to have reached a length of 20 feet. After excavating most of a fossilized mosasaur, Everhart realized that the ribs on the reptile's right side had been bitten completely through. We will never know whether the shark attacked a living mosasaur or scavenged a floating carcass. (Since the extinct shark had no common name, Everhart christened it *ginsu shark,* "because it fed by slicing up its victim into bite-sized pieces." It is now popularly known as the ginsu mako.) *Cretoxyrhina* is known from the fossil faunas of Africa, Europe, and North America, and *C. mantelli,* described by Agassiz in 1843, is common in the Upper Cretaceous sediments of the Western Interior Seaway, the warm, shallow sea that inundated central North America during the Cretaceous. From the shape of the teeth, it is clear that *Cretoxyrhina* was similar in shape (and probably in habits) to today's great white and mako sharks.

Everhart (1999) identified the shark-bitten mosasaurs of the seaway as *Tylosaurus, Platecarpus,* and *Clidastes.* A large *Plioplatecarpus* mosasaur from the Cretaceous Pierre Shale in Griggs County, North Dakota, was found in 1995 by two local fossil collectors, Mike Hanson and Dennis Halvorson. They contacted John Hoganson, the paleontologist for the North Dakota Geological Survey, and spent almost two years excavating the fossil. The specimen is around 70 percent complete, missing only the flippers, pelvis, a few ribs, and parts of the tail. It is the largest *Plioplatecarpus* ever found, 25 percent larger than the next largest, and a new species. The skeleton is 23 feet long; the near-complete skull alone is 3 feet long. Like the Kansas mosasaurs, this fossil showed numerous shark teeth embedded in the bone, leading to the speculation that this mosasaur had either been killed by sharks or scavenged as it floated.

The relationship of mosasaurs to other reptiles was long a subject of controversy, but Dale Russell's 1967 study, "Systematics and Morphology of the American Mosasaurs," alleviated much of the confusion. Still, according to Gorden Bell (whose 1997 summary I have abridged here), "although many authors have favored varanid-mosasaurid relationships, such a hypothesis has not been rigorously tested using modern phylogenetic methods." But, writes Bell, "as for the relationships among mosasaurids, the picture is much clearer. Many of the relationships proposed by Russell (1967) have been supported by two fairly vigorous phylogenetic analyses using many characters." Carroll (1988) included aigialosaurs and mosasaurs in his discussion of "aquatic varanoid lizards" and said that *Opetiosaurus* (an aigialosaur) was about 3¼ feet long, with a laterally compressed tail with the tip pointed downward and a skull that was nearly identical to that of the mosasaurs. Both had a prominent intramandibular joint, which opened the lower jaw unusually wide to help in the bolting of large food items, suggesting an affinity of the aigialosaurs and mosasaurs with snakes.

The sudden disappearance of these powerful, effective predators is, according to Lingham-Soliar (1999a), "an enigma of the K-T extinction." He wrote, "Their feeding potential, aided by an arsenal of tools—crushers, gougers,

The mosasaur Tylosaurus attacking a smaller mosasaur. Ranging in size from 20 to 50 feet, the tylosaurs were the major predators of the Niobrara Sea during the Cretaceous period.

slicers, snappers, piercers, graspers, rammers and crunchers—was unequaled by other marine reptiles. They were among the most adaptable of animals, and clearly flourished during this period of changing temperatures and receding sea-levels. So what went wrong?" According to Dale Russell (personal communication 1999):

> The mosasaurs were undergoing a great radiation toward the end of the Cretaceous, and were becoming much more sealion-like and whale-like (the marine mammals later mimicked them through parallel selection/ evolution). But the mosasaurs were exterminated before they reached anything like their evolutionary potential. There are about 10 times as many mosasaur specimens preserved as there are specimens of dinosaurs, but the sample size is still too small to serve as a statistical basis for demonstrating rapidity of extinction. But as far as I am concerned, the crash in marine phytoplankton was amply sufficient to fatally interrupt the food chain toward mosasaurs, and I have little doubt that the mosasaurs were exterminated in the general productivity crisis at the end of Cretaceous. Sixty-five million years ago, they seemed to be expanding in speciation, and there was certainly no predator alive at the time that could threaten a 50-foot-long carnivorous lizard with a mouthful of powerful teeth and bone-crushing jaws.

In 1995, Lingham-Soliar wrote, "the indications are that the demise of the mosasaurs was sudden and unexpected," and four years later, he was prepared to accept the notion that they had been wiped out by some sort of extraterrestrial event. He wrote (1999d), "Thus mosasaurs, uniquely among the major reptile groups, provide a biological argument in favor of sudden extinction." But the latest known mosasaur (Prognathodon waiparensis) was collected from a site on New Zealand's Waipara River and was found approximately 6½ feet below the section that marks the K-T boundary. "There is," wrote Michael Caldwell (personal communication 2002), "a lot of time and a lot of sediment separating the critter from the event. Unless the fauna was watching the night sky for 50,000 years prior to the impact, and then dying en masse from fear, the empirical observation linking mosasaur extinctions to bolide impacts is missing at this point."

But if, as Michael Lee (1997) has written, snakes and mosasaurs are sister groups (both arising from a single common ancestor), the mosasaurs are not officially extinct at all. Lee combined mosasaurs and snakes in a group he named Pythonomorpha, a name originally coined by Cope in 1869 to include the mosasaurs and snakes and based on the mythological serpent Python, which was produced from the mud left after Deucalion's flood. McNamara and Long (1998) summed up Lee's unanticipated analysis by writing:

> True terrestrial snakes appear by the Late Cretaceous, at the same time that the radiation of mosasaurs was peaking. For many years the origin of snakes was clouded in mystery due to lack of adequate fossil evidence. But now Lee and Caldwell have blown away the cobwebs, by taking a fresh, rigorous, and very detailed look at the known material. . . . So when you are next out snorkeling and are startled by a sea snake [McNamara and Long are Australians] it may not only be some highly derived snake that you are frantically paddling away from, but all that remains of a great radiation of a great tradition of aquatic reptiles that once dominated the seas.

In 1966, in response to the confused and inconclusive state of the study of snake evolution at that time, Alfred Sherwood Romer wrote, "in contrast to the extinction or seeming evolutionary stagnation of other reptile types, the snakes are today a group of reptiles still 'on the make.'" Minton and Heatwole (1978) wrote, "The snakes appeared late in the Mesozoic, and there is some evidence that, quite early in their history, they produced some huge marine species. Apparently these giant sea snakes were not very successful, for they endured but a short time and left a very scanty fossil record." According to Heatwole (1999), "Other snakes from the Cretaceous are known only from incomplete fossils and as no good skull material exists the most that can be said of them is that they were snakes with some characteristics intermediate between those of lizards and modern snakes."

The earliest snakes are known from isolated and rather uninformative vertebrae. The best preserved early snakes had an elongate body, reduced limbs, and adaptations for chemosensory hunting. They are descended from lizards and manifest many lizard-like characters. In 1997, Caldwell and Lee published a description of *Pachyrhachis problematicus,* a fossil snake that was found in the limestone quarries of Ein Yabrud, some 12 miles north of Jerusalem. (The name comes from *pachys*, which means "thick," and *rhachis*, which means "spine"; *problematicus* is self-explanatory.) Although it was certainly a snake, it had tiny hind legs consisting of femur, tibia, fibula, and tarsals, as well as other characters that provided "additional support for the hypothesis that snakes are most closely related to Cretaceous marine lizards (mosasauroids)." It was later determined that a fossil snake known as *Ophiomorphus*, also from the quarries at Ein Yabrud, was actually another specimen of *Pachyrhachis problematicus*, and although neither skeleton was complete, there was enough material for paleontologists to postulate its morphology and relationships. Its heavy bones indicated that its overall density was very close to that of seawater, and it was probably a very slow swimmer. Although its head was tiny, it had powerful jaws and was believed to strike swiftly at its prey.

Since Minton and Heatwole bemoaned the lack of primitive snake fossils, their "giant marine snakes" have begun appearing, but, as with many things paleontological, newly unearthed fossils often confuse rather than clarify things. Consider *Haasiophis terrasanctus*, a particularly well-preserved fossil that was found in the same limestone quarry in the Judean Hills as *Pachyrhachis*. (*Haasiophis* was named for Professor Haas, who found the fossil in 1976; *terrasanctus* means "Holy Land" in Latin.) The *Pachyrhachis* and *Haasiophis* fossils are from the mid-Cretaceous, 95 million years ago, but the analysis of the *Haasiophis* fossil by Tchernov et al. (2000) produced conflicting conclusions from those of Caldwell and Lee (1997). The fossil *Haasiophis*, which was about 3 feet long, also had legs, but its jaw structure suggested to Tchernov et al. that it was more closely related to the larger, living snakes of today and that both *Pachyrhachis* and *Haasiophis* were not primitive at all but advanced snakes that had reevolved legs. (Many living pythons retain rudimentary hind limbs, so reevolving limbs is a possibility.) The limbs of *Pachyrhachis* and *Haasiophis* are too small in relation to body size to have had any locomotor function, so they may have been used as an aid in mating, as are the hind limb buds of pythons today.

Then Lee, Caldwell, and Scanlon (1999) reexamined *Pachyophis woodwardi*, which had originally been described as a snake by Nopsca in 1923, but "the evidence was not compelling, and later workers have been reluctant to accept this view." In their reevaluation, Lee and his colleagues believed that they showed that *Pachyophis* was indeed a very primitive snake. The fossil was found in East Herzegovina, in the same locality as another snake known as *Mesophis nopscai*, which is now lost. The fossil of *Pachyophis* is smaller than that of *Pachyrhachis*, but its ribs are much heavier, indicating that it was not a juvenile of the latter form. The thickened bone—a condition known as *pachyostosis*—is characteristic of marine animals because it increases their density, which strongly suggests that this species (and also *Pachyrhachis*) were marine. "However," wrote the authors, "at the moment, whether or not all snakes went through a marine phase in their evolution remains equivocal."

In 2001, Caldwell and Albino published a discussion of the paleoenvironment and paleoecology of the marine snakes *Pachyophis* and *Pachyrhachis* and the terrestrial snake *Dinilysia*. As mentioned earlier (Scanlon et al. 1999), *Pachyrhachis* was shown to have inhabited interreef systems of the Tethyan seaway, and with its small head and muscle attachments that correspond to those of modern striking snakes, it was probably competent at plucking its prey from within cracks and crevices. Because the type specimen of *Pachyrhachis* contains a partial tooth plate from a pycnodont fish, it might have eaten fairly large prey and been able to spread its jaws widely, as do many modern snakes. At a length of 4 feet, *Pachyrhachis* was nearly twice as large as *Pachyophis*, but because they shared many physical characteristics, their hunting methods were probably the same.

The descent of snakes is one of the most contentious areas in vertebrate biology. Tchernov et al. (2000) were more than a little critical of the conclusions of Lee et al. (1999) and wrote, "*Haasiophis* and *Pachyrhachis* have no particular bearing on snake-mosasaurid relationships or snake origins. . . . Basal snakes, including basal macrostomatans, retain rudimentary hind limbs, which, however, remain much more incomplete than those of *Haasiophis*." But as Caldwell (personal communication 2002) notes, he and Lee "never said that they did [have such a bearing]. It is also very important to realize that Tchernov et al. did not repeat the study of Caldwell and Lee (1997) which included all squamates and a number of fossil lizards, but rather restricted their analysis to only snakes. They rearranged the ingroup relationships of snakes and concluded that all snakes were unrelated to mosasaurs. This is a spurious claim as no other lizards of any kind were included in their analysis. . . . Tchernov and his collaborators have no replacement hypothesis for the sister group relationship of snakes—only that Caldwell and Lee are wrong. That sort of statement is not science."

In the essay that introduced the Tchernov paper in *Science,* Greene and Cundall criticized the approach (and conclusions) of Caldwell and Lee (1997), who "showed their drawings and reconstructions of *Pachyrhachis* to a number of nonscientists who use 'snake' in the vernacular sense, and all identified *Pachyrhachis* as a snake rather than a lizard." Even though it had legs, the dense, heavy bones of *Pachyrhachis* suggest that it was a water dweller, and the location of the fossil in marine deposits seems to confirm this suggestion. Because of similarities in the jaw structure, Lee et al. (1999) concluded that it (and all other snakes) had evolved from mosasaurs. In remarks published in *New Scientist* (Hecht 2000), Mike Caldwell said, "Rieppel's analysis fails to compare the legged snakes with mosasaurs, their closest relatives." In 1998, Hussam Zaher published a revision of the phylogenetic position of *Pachyrhachis,* and two years later, Caldwell (2002b) responded by writing:

> The origins and relationships of snakes continue to be fascinating and intriguing problems. The complex and conflicting characters present in a number of well-preserved Cretaceous snakes have now been added to the pool of data used to examine snake phylogeny. As a result of ingroup and outgroup analysis of snake interrelationships, a marine origin for snakes is now a reasonable alternative to the received position that snakes originated from a burrowing or fossorial ancestor. Such "assaults" on conventional hypotheses are always resisted forcibly, and justifiably so. However, Zaher's (1998) hypothesis is not a well-supported criticism of Caldwell and Lee (1997) despite its appeal to more conventional phylogenetic hypotheses, and its underlying support for the fossorial origins of snakes.

Michael Lee believes that the mosasaurs are the nearest relatives of snakes. Like snakes, mosasaurs had pterygoid (palatal) teeth and hinged lower jaws. Snakes have developed a rigid skull structure from which the highly flexible jaws are suspended, which facilitates the engulfment of large prey items—in some cases, larger than the snake's head. In 1999, with Gorden Bell and Michael Caldwell, he wrote, "Here we present evidence that mosasaurs—large, extinct marine lizards related to snakes—represent a crucial intermediate stage. Mosasaurs, uniquely among lizards, possessed long, snakelike palatal teeth for holding prey. Also, although they retained the rigid upper jaws typical of lizards, they possessed highly flexible lower jaws that were not only morphologically similar to those of snakes, but also functionally similar. . . . In terms of skull structure, the large, limbed marine mosasaurs were functionally, as well as phylogenetically, intermediate between the lizards and snakes."

In a 2000 article delightfully entitled "Nice Snake, Shame about the Legs," Michael Coates and Marcello Ruta reviewed the hypotheses about the evolutionary origins of snakes. They wrote:

> *Pachyrhachis problematicus* from Israel rapidly assumed a central position in the debates about snake phylogeny. It has miniature hindlimbs articulated with a rudimentary pelvic girdle, but sadly, its feet are missing. Currently described from only two specimens, it was originally interpreted as an aquatic relative of terrestrial varanoids and was therefore thought to be morphologically convergent with snakes. However, it has recently been interpreted as a true snake, based on its loosely articulated upper jaws, intramandibular joint, the condition of several skull bones, the absence of forelimb and pectoral girdle, body elongation and vertebral structure.

They said that according to Caldwell and Lee, *Pachyrhachis* is the most primitive known snake and "has gained classic 'transitional' status, bridging the gulf between two highly specialized squamate clades," the mosasauroid-snake shared ancestry and modern snakes. Rieppel and Zaher take an opposite view, maintaining that the scolecophidians (extant blind snakes) are the most primitive snakes. The questions of snake developmental evolution are not resolved. Coates and Ruta concluded: "it is worth remembering that phylogeny is an ongoing research program and that large parts of the evolutionary tree remain unwritten, unexplored, and deeply uncertain.

As if to show that the derivation of snakes from lizards isn't so strange after all, Wiens and Slingluff (2001) published "How Lizards Turn into Snakes: A Phylogenetic Analysis of Body-Form Evolution in Anguid Lizards." For the most part, anguid lizards already look like snakes: they are the "glass snakes" (*Ophisaurus*, confusingly translated as "snake lizard") and "slowworms" (*Anguis fragilis*) of Africa, Europe, and Asia, which have no legs at all; and the alligator lizards (*Gerrhonotus*) of western North America, which have extremely short legs and long, sinuous bodies. To the layperson, it is obvious that they are not snakes because they have closable eyelids and a notched (as opposed to a forked) tongue. They can shed their tails to escape predators, something no snake can do. (The glass snake is so named because besides being able to shed its tail, it can shatter it into several pieces to distract predators even more.) Any study labeled "A Phylogenetic Analysis" is going to be heavy going for the layperson, and this one is no exception. It is replete with sentences like this, selected at random: "The best-fitting model was then used in a heuristic search to find the overall best likelihood topology using tree-bisection-reconnection branch swapping and 10 random addition sequence replicates." If you're not a phylogeneticist, such a sentence probably won't help you understand how lizards turn into snakes, but the authors summarized their findings by writing, "Our results support the hypothesis that limb reduction is correlated with body elongation and that digit loss is correlated with limb reduction."

In the chapter "Wonder of the Kansas Plains" in his 1887 book *Sea and Land: An Illustrated History of the Wonderful and Curious Things of Nature Existing before and since the Deluge*, J. W. Buel expressed the public's amazement at the discovery of gigantic sea lizards in the badlands of the American West:

> The fabulous monsters that were believed in in the olden times, the dragons, serpents, etc., are thrown in the shade by these truly ancient monsters that once swam in the ocean that finally became land-locked, and the bottom of which is now raised high above the water level. The shore line of the ancient ocean is distinctly marked. Imagine the water between New York and London a dry plain, its whales and fishes stranded in the mud, on the sides of the great hills, and on the plateaus that we know exist, an idea can be formed of the *mauvaise terres*. Professor Marsh says that in one place he counted from his horse the remains of five huge monsters

spread upon the plain. One of the largest of these, a reptile called the *Liodon,* exceeded in size the largest whale.

From the moment that the *grand animale de Maastricht* was hauled up from the limestone mine in 1780, mosasaurs have been among the most intriguing of prehistoric animals. Named for the Meuse River, that specimen gave its name to all the mosasaurs that followed it into the limelight of paleontology. The mosasaurs arose, diversified, and flowered 25 million years before the end-Cretaceous event and departed with the last of the terrestrial, nonavian dinosaurs. Mosasaur fossils have been found in Canada, the Netherlands, Sweden, Africa, Australia, New Zealand, Antarctica, and, in the United States, in Kansas, Nebraska, New Mexico, Colorado, Texas, Georgia, Alabama, North and South Dakota, Montana, Arkansas, and New Jersey. The rocks have revealed something of the lives of the mosasaurs, but much of their existence remains hidden. They may have descended from terrestrial lizards; they may have given rise to snakes; but during their brief reign, they rose to a position of marine dominance that would not be equaled until the whales and dolphins arrived on the scene 50 million years later. Some reached enormous sizes, and with their flexible jaws and powerful teeth, they became the apex predators of the open seas. Others lurked in the shallows, ready to ambush anything that happened by. Still others developed heavy, rounded teeth that enabled them to crush the thick shells of bivalves. They may or may not have punched through ammonite shells with their teeth. They were big, fast, powerful, and dangerous to other Mesozoic marine life-forms. Entombed in the rocks, they left us tantalizing glimpses of an ancient way of life in the water.

# The "Reason" for Extinction

At one time, the reason for the extinction of the (nonavian) dinosaurs was regarded as unknown and probably unknowable. Dinosaurs roamed the earth, and then they didn't. George Gaylord Simpson, writing in 1953, said, "No one knows exactly why the dinosaurs and a host of other ancient forms became extinct. This is not because there is anything mysterious or metaphysical about extinction or because the possible causes are unknown. It is just because there are many reasonable possibilities, and the record does not enable us to say in the particular case which of them were actually involved. All we can say is that something changed and the dinosaurs did not." In 1968, in *The Evidence of Evolution,* Smithsonian Institution paleontologist Nicholas Hotton wrote, "It is sometimes assumed that a sudden major change in climate at the end of the Mesozoic era was the chief cause of the dinosaurs' demise. However, other episodes of climactic change during the Mesozoic do not appear to have bothered the dinosaurs excessively, and the suddenness of dinosaur extinction may be more apparent than real."

In 1980, a group of scientists at the University of California at Berkeley—Nobel Prize–winning physicist Luis Alvarez, his geophysicist son Walter, and geochemists Frank Asaro and Helen Michel—recognized the trace element iridium in a thin layer of clay at the boundary layer between Cretaceous formations and Tertiary formations in Gubbio, Italy, and, later, at other locations around the world. Because iridium is rare in the earth's crustal rocks but common in asteroids and stony meteorites, its presence in this layer suggested that it was a result of fallout from some sort of an explosion, and the amount of iridium in this layer around the world (calculated from the known iridium content of meteorites) indicated that a gigantic body, roughly approximating the mass of Mount Everest, had crashed into the earth at approximately 100,000 miles per hour.

The discovery of a huge crater off the Yucatán peninsula in 1991 lent credence to the impact theory, because up to that time, the only evidence to support it had been the enigmatic iridium particles and the disappearance of so many species. The Chicxulub Crater (named for an ancient Mayan village near the site and pronounced CHEEK-zhu-loob), which is buried under about 600 feet of sedimentary rock that has accumulated since the impact, is 125 to 185 miles across and was known to Mexican petroleum engineers long before anyone connected it with the impact. Supporters of the Alvarez et al. (1980) theory of dinosaur destruction—and there are many—believe that the impact induced a global environmental collapse of such magnitude that it culminated in biological devastation. They believe that the uppermost layers of rock where the asteroid hit were heated to such temperatures that carbon dioxide and sulfate aerosols were released into the atmosphere, creating a worldwide climate of acid rain and smog, not to mention the darkening effect of dust clouds circling the earth, which would lower temperatures drastically—the so-called impact winter. Fiery debris ignited continent-sized fires that burned for years. A cataclysm of this magnitude brings out the hyperbole in writers, even if they are scientists. In *Night Comes to the Cretaceous*, James Powell wrote: "A few minutes later, the mixture of vaporized meteorite and rock, still traveling at ballistic velocities of 5 km/sec to 10 km/sec, began to reenter the atmosphere. The individual globules were traveling so fast that they ignited, producing a literal rain of fire. Over the entire globe, successively later the greater the distance from the target, the lower atmosphere burst into a wall of flame, igniting everything below. . . . Everything that could burn did."

It is hard to resist such persuasively purple prose, but there are those who have managed to do so. They say that meteorites approach the earth all the time, and although some have actually landed with a significant impact, they have had little effect on the earth's atmosphere. And although the 1815 eruption of the Indonesian volcano Tambora may have darkened the skies and killed off the year's corn crop in North America, it otherwise did no permanent damage. Besides, they say, the fossil record does not show that the land dinosaurs died within a couple of years; rather, they died over a much longer period, perhaps tens or even hundreds of thousands of years. There is little doubt that a meteorite struck the earth about 65 million years ago, because shocked quartz (an indicator of high-temperature impact) and iridium-laden layers have now been found around the world at the corresponding stratigraphic levels. There was certainly an impact at Chicxulub, and because it coincided with the mass extinction of the dinosaurs and many other kinds of animals, it is difficult to deny a relationship between the two events, but the nature of that connection remains unresolved.

Whether something killed them or they died of unknown causes, the great terrestrial dinosaurs were all gone after the dust cleared from whatever it was that happened 65 million years ago. Contrary to popular conceptions, all the dinosaurs were not marching around as the Cretaceous came to its abrupt halt. By that time, most of them were extinct already, and many had been extinct for tens or even hundreds of millions of years. For example, the carnivore *Allosaurus* was gone 135 million years ago, as was *Apatosaurus,* the great sauropod that used to be known as *Brontosaurus.* The feathered reptile *Archaeopteryx,* originally found in shales from 150 million years ago, was gone 30 million years later, and *Iguanodon,* the first known dinosaur, vanished 110 million years ago. *Deinonychus,* the dinosaur described as warm-blooded by John Ostrom in 1969, disappeared from the fossil record 100 million years ago, and *Protoceratops,* the predominant dinosaur of the Gobi Desert, was last recorded from strata dated at 75 million years old. In fact, as far as we can tell from the scanty fossil record, almost all the dinosaurs had died out except for those in western North America. *Saltosaurus, Ankylosaurus, Pachycephalosaurus, Gallomimus, Triceratops,* and the great *Tyrannosaurus* were the last remnants of the line of giant reptiles that had dominated the land for 150 million years. When the asteroid hit, it was these dinosaurs that were somehow eliminated. After the impact, no terrestrial dinosaurs have been recorded. For the most part, their fossils have been found in the Hell Creek region of Montana. Although this does not mean that Montana was the last refuge of the last of the dinosaurs, it does mean that we have not found many fossils elsewhere. It was also at this time that the last of the mosasaurs died out. By the time the asteroid struck, the ichthyosaurs and the plesiosaurs had been extinct for 20 million years.

The demise of the terrestrial dinosaurs is probably paleontology's greatest mystery. For every detective who believes he has found the culprit, there is another who has identified a different suspect or group of suspects. But despite the efforts of the best minds, the earth has kept the answer—if there is an answer—hidden in the rocks. A concise summary can be found in Michael Novacek's 1996 book *Dinosaurs of the Flaming Cliffs,* in which the author, one of the American Museum's "dinosaur hunters" of the Gobi Desert in the 1990s, wrote:

Does that mean the long-standing mystery—what killed the dinosaurs?—has been solved? Well, not entirely. Even if such an impact did occur at sixty-five million years before present (give or take a half million), we cannot be sure it had the global impact ascribed to it. There is some evidence that a drastic decline in non-avian dinosaurs may have occurred well before the end of the Cretaceous. Moreover, this devastation was neither so overwhelming nor so rampant as the extermination at the end of the Permian. True, many families of mammals, birds, fishes, ammonites, belemnites, and bivalves (clams, oysters, and other dual-shelled species) went extinct. Over fifty percent of various marine planktonic groups were also erased. But numerous important lineages—many of the frogs, salamanders, turtles, lizards, mammals, crocodiles, birds, fishes, angiosperms, conifers, arthropods (insects, spiders, crabs, and sundry), gastropods (snails and kin), echinoderms, and nearly half the plankton species—went right on through the Cretaceous boundary. One of the real mysteries of Cretaceous extinction is therefore its taxonomic selectivity.

Why were the non-avian dinosaurs so persecuted? And if such an event was caused, as currently argued by many scientists, by a cataclysmic impact of a giant asteroid, why was this pattern of extinction so discriminating? Why did some dinosaurs, feathery, flying creatures of high metabolism that surely would not do well in clouds of metallic vapors, survive the event? Why did many other vertebrates, animals, plants, and marine organisms make it? The fact that this extinction event, like the Permo-Triassic extinction and other events before it, was selective really complicates the theory. It forces us to consider the subtleties of cause and effect relating to the survival of biological systems. Namely, we need to know how exactly such an event *selectively* snuffed out Cretaceous species. These are subtle connections for which we have few insights.

Unlike the cataclysmic demise of the dinosaurs, there was no single event to mark the departure date of the great marine reptiles. Also, when the Niobrara and the Tethys Seas were closed by tectonic forces and dried up, their water-dependent inhabitants dried up too. It wasn't like pulling the plug from a bathtub, of course; the drying up and reduction of the inland seas took millions of years, and during that time, many marine reptiles became extinct without succumbing to evaporation. Moreover, not all the reptiles lived in bodies of water that disappeared; many lived in oceans and seas that were more or less where they are today. The marine reptiles passed into extinction over a 20 million–year stretch, the ichthyosaurs departing slowly, and the plesiosaurs and the mosasaurs making their final curtain call around the K-T boundary. The Chicxulub impact certainly wreaked ecological havoc on the oceans, raining deadly chemicals on the waters, disrupting food chains, generating massive tsunamis, and affecting virtually every form of marine life.

The latest known plesiosaur fossil has been dated as late Cretaceous (middle Campanian to Maastrichtian), about 65 million years ago: on Seymour Island, Antarctic peninsula, fragmentary remains of an unidentified plesiosaur were found (Chatterjee and Zinsmeister 1982), along with the partial skull of a very large mosasaur, provisionally identified as either *Hainosaurus* or *Tylosaurus*. Many elasmosaur fossils are known from the late Maastrichtian rocks of the Maastricht region of Belgium. More recently, remains of elasmosaurid plesiosaurs have been collected from the lower part of the late Cretaceous López de Bertodano Formation on Seymour Island, Antarctica, by the Polish Antarctic Expeditions (Fostowicz-Frelik and Gazdzicki 2001):

The bone material includes pectoral, dorsal, and caudal vertebral centra, femur, tibia, and fragments of the humerus, scapula, and ischia, that most probably belonged to the one specimen. The microstructure of the bone tissue shows rather dense structure with Haversian remodeling well underway and the areas of intensive growth, suggesting subadult stage of ontogeny. The dense pachyostotic character of the rib and girdle tissue, together with a relative small size of the bones (approximated length of the animal about two meters) may indicate that described material belongs to the not fully grown elasmosaur, which may have lived in shallow water environment. The studied remains share some similarities with those of *Mauisaurus* from the Maastrichtian of New Zealand.

Extinction, the mysterious and powerful converse (or complement) of evolution, can sometimes be explained in Darwinian terms. If there is no adaptation to compensate for an environmental change, the creature will be unable to function effectively in its modified environment and, in time, will die out. In these cases, it does not require global warming or cooling, over-specialization, a deadly infectious disease, or an extraterrestrial impact to eliminate a species (although these can certainly speed up the process), but only the inability of the creature to adapt to its changing world. There is, so far, no equation that can predict with any certainty when a particular species will become extinct, but the near universality of extinction strongly suggests that whatever the time sequence or the cause, everything will eventually die out. To exemplify the title of his provocative book *Extinction: Bad Genes or Bad Luck?* David Raup introduces the trilobites, which lived for more than 300 million years and died about 245 million years ago. He asks: "Why? Did the trilobites do something wrong? Were they fundamentally inferior organisms? Were they stupid? Or did they just have the bad luck to be in the wrong place at the wrong time?" Raup's idea (developed with Jack Sepkoski) was that meteors and comets have been crashing into Earth since the planet was formed and that they are somehow related to the principal extinction events, which have occurred approximately every 26 million years. The connection between mass extinctions and extraplanetary collisions is not evident, but Raup and Sepkoski believe that there might be one. "My own view," wrote Raup, "is that periodicity is alive and well as a description of extinction history during the past 250 million years—despite the lack of a viable mechanism."

Raup argues that normal environmental stresses (temperature changes, raising and lowering of sea level, wandering continents, and so forth) usually produce adaptations or migrations, not extinctions. He wrote, "most plants and animals have evolved defenses against the normal vicissitudes of their environment." But a stress that has never been experienced previously and for which the species has no defense—such as epidemic disease—can certainly devastate a species and perhaps even lead to its extinction. Because the earth has been bombarded by a steady stream of icy comets, stony asteroids, and meteorites, it is conceivable that all extinctions are connected to these visits of space debris. In conclusion, Raup answers the question posed by the title of his book:

> Extinction is evidently a combination of bad genes and bad luck. Some species die out because they cannot cope in their normal habitat or because superior competitors or predators push them out. But as is surely clear from this book, I feel that most species die out because they are unlucky. They die because they are subjected to biological stresses not anticipated in their prior evolution and because time is not available for Darwinian natural selection to help them adapt.

Still, it is hard to imagine why the ruling reptiles of the sea did not endure. From the fossil evidence, we can see that they were numerous, efficient, and highly diversified. Cetaceans had not yet arrived on the scene, so there was no competition from them, and the only other large predators were sharks. Animals can become extinct without a catastrophe, and the vast majority of the millions of extinctions that have occurred in the geological past have been caused by a combination of factors whose synergistic influences we simply do not understand. Groups of animals rise and fall in cycles that are largely unknown and unpredictable, but many extinctions were probably related to global change as the continents slid around, mountains were pushed up, and oceans cooled, warmed, dried up, or were formed anew. Tectonic changes are certainly responsible for massive climatic modifications, but we can only wonder what, if any, effect these earth movements may have had on the lives of animals.

During their time, the marine reptiles dominated their environment; they were the apex predators of the oceans, rather like killer whales or great white sharks today. An interesting parallel might be drawn between the extinct giant marine reptiles and *Carcharodon megalodon,* a gigantic, predatory shark that resembled the great white but was three times longer. The largest known great white measured 21 feet; *Megalodon* has been estimated at 60 feet. And whereas the largest white shark teeth are a little more than 2 inches long, fossil *Megalodon* teeth can be 6 inches. *Megalodon* (which means "great tooth") is extinct, gone from the oceans for at least 100,000 years, but it is difficult to say why. It was obviously a powerful predator, and it is known that it preyed on whales, but the whales are still here and the predator is long gone. The watery climate may have changed in such a way that warm-blooded mammals could survive but cold-blooded reptiles and fishes could not; or perhaps the prey species of the great marine reptiles gradually disappeared, which would have sent the predators drifting hungrily toward extinction. But because we really don't know what the primary prey of the large marine reptiles was — some theorists hold that it was smaller marine reptiles — the question remains unanswered, and maybe unanswerable.

The only extinctions we truly understand are those that we ourselves engineered: the great auk, dodo, passenger pigeon, Carolina parakeet, quagga, Tasmanian wolf, Caribbean monk seal, Steller's sea cow, and hundreds of others, all eliminated in the brief moment that we have had to strut and fret our apocalyptic hour upon the evolutionary stage. As for why so many other species disappeared long before Mr. Sapiens arrived on the scene with his clever weapons and his special kind of havoc, let us give the final word on the subject to Charles Darwin:

> We need not marvel at extinction; if we must marvel, let it be at our own presumption in imagining for a moment that we understand the many complex contingencies on which the existence of each species depends. If we forget for an instant that each species tends to increase inordinately, and that some check is always in action, yet seldom perceived by us, the whole economy of nature will be utterly obscured. Whenever we can precisely say why this species is more abundant in individuals than that; why this species and not another can be naturalised in a given country; then, and not until then, may we justly feel surprise why we cannot account for the extinction of any species or group of species.

# References

Adams, D. A. 1997. *Trinacromerum bonneri,* new species, last and fastest pliosaur of the Western Interior Seaway. *Texas Jour. Sci.* 49(3):179–98.

Ahlberg, P. E., and R. A. Milner, 1994. The origin and early diversification of tetrapods. *Nature* 338:507–14.

Alexander, R. M. 1989. *Dynamics of Dinosaurs and Other Extinct Giants.* Columbia University Press.

——. 1990. Size, speed and buoyancy adaptations in aquatic mammals. *American Zoologist* 30:189–96.

Alvarez, L. W. 1983. Experimental evidence that an asteroid impact led to the extinction of many species 65 million years ago. *Proc. Natl. Acad. Sci.* 80:627–42.

Alvarez, L., W. Alvarez, F. Asaro, and H. V. Michel. 1980. Extraterrestrial cause for the Cretaceous-Tertiary extinction. *Science* 208:1095–108.

Andrews, C. W. 1909. On some new Plesiosauria from the Oxford Clay of Peterborough. *Ann. Mag. Nat. Hist.* 4:418–29.

——. 1910. *A Descriptive Catalogue of the Marine Reptiles of the Oxford Clay, Based on the Leeds Collection in the British Museum (Natural History), London, Part I.* British Museum.

——. 1912. Description of a new plesiosaur (*Plesiosaurus capensis,* sp. nov.) from the Uitenhage Beds of Cape Colony. *Ann. S. Afr. Mus.* 7:309–22.

——. 1922a. Description of a new plesiosaur from the Weald Clay of Berwick (Sussex). *Q. Jour. Geol. Soc. London* 78:285–98.

——. 1922b. Note on the skeleton of a new plesiosaur (*Rhomaleosaurus thorntoni,* sp. n.) from the Upper Lias of Northamptonshire. *Ann. Mag. Nat. Hist.* 9(10):407–15.

Appleby, R. M. 1956. The osteology and taxonomy of the fossil reptile *Ophthalmosaurus. Proc. Zool. Soc. London* 126:403–47.

——. 1959. The origins of ichthyosaurs. *New Scientist* 6:758–60.

——. 1961. On the cranial morphology of ichthyosaurs. *Proc. Zool. Soc. London* 137:333–70.

Archibald, J. D. 1996. *Dinosaur Extinction and the End of an Era: What the Fossils Say.* Columbia University Press.

——. 1997. Extinction, Cretaceous. In P. J. Currie and K. Padian, eds., *Encyclopedia of Dinosaurs,* pp. 221–30. Academic Press.

Archibald, J. D., and W. A. Clemens. 1982. Late Cretaceous extinctions. *American Scientist* 70:377–85.

Aronson, R. 1990. Rise and fall of life at sea. *New Scientist* 128(1741):34–37.

Augusta, J., and Z. Burian. 1964. *Saurier der Urmeere.* Artia.

Azzaroli, A., C. de Giuli, G. Ficcarelli, and D. Torre. 1972. An aberrant mosasaur from the Upper Cretaceous of north-western Nigeria. *Memorie Accademia nazionale dei Lincei. Classe di scienze fisiche matematiche e naturali* 52(3):53–56.

——. 1975. Late Cretaceous mosasaurs from the Sokoto district, Nigeria. *Memorie Accademia nazionale dei Lincei. Classe di scienze fisiche matematiche e naturali* 13(2):21–34.

Bains, S., R. D. Norris, R. M. Corfield, and K. L. Faul. 2000. Termination of global warmth at the Paleocene/Eocene boundary through productivity feedback. *Nature* 407:171–74.

Bakker, R. T. 1968. The superiority of dinosaurs. *Discovery* 3(2):11–22.

——. 1971. Dinosaur physiology and the origin of mammals. *Evolution* 25:636–58.

——. 1972. Anatomical and ecological evidence for endothermy in dinosaurs. *Nature* 238:81–85.

——. 1975. Dinosaur renaissance. *Scientific American* 232(4):58–78.

——. 1986. *The Dinosaur Heresies.* Morrow.

——. 1993a. Jurassic sea monsters. *Discover* 14(9):78–85.

——. 1993b. Plesiosaur extinction cycles—events that mark the beginning, middle and end of the Cretaceous. In W. G. E. Caldwell and E. G. Kaufmann, eds., *Evolution of the Western Interior Basin,* pp. 641–63. Geological Association of Canada.

Barber, L. 1980. *The Heyday of Natural History.* Doubleday.

Bardet, N. 1992. Stratigraphic evidence for the extinction of the ichthyosaurs. *Terra Nova* 4:649–56.

——. 1994. Extinction events among Mesozoic marine reptiles. *Historical Biology* 7:313–24.

Bardet, N., and M. Fernández. 2000. A new ichthyosaur from the Upper Jurassic lithographic limestones of Bavaria. *Jour. Paleo.* 74(3):503–11.

Bardet, N., and S. Hua. 1996. *Simolestes nowackianus* Huene, 1938 from the Upper Jurassic of Ethiopia is a teleosaurid crocodile, not a pliosaur. *N. Jb. Geol. Paläeont. Mh.* 1996(2):65–71.

Bardet, N., and X. P. Suberbiola. 2001. The basal mosasaurid *Halisaurus sternbergii* from the late Cretaceous of Kansas (North America): A review of the Uppsala type specimen. *Comptes Rendus de*
l'Académie des Sciences, ser. IIA, Earth and Planetary Science 332:395–402.

Bardet, N., and C. Tonoğlu. 2002. The first mosasaur (Squamata) from the late Cretaceous of Turkey. *Jour. Vert. Paleo.* 22(3):712–15.

Bardet, N., P. Godefroit, and J. Sciau. 1999. A new elasmosaurid plesiosaur from the Lower Jurassic of southern France. *Palaeontology* 42(5):927–52.

Bardet, N., J. W. M. Jagt, M. M. M. Kuypers, and R. W. Dortangs. 1998. Shark tooth marks on a vertebra of the mosasaur *Plioplatecarpus marshi* from the late Maastrichtian of Belgium. *Publicaties van het Natuurhistorisch Genootschap in Limburg* 41(1):52–55.

Bardet, N., G. Pennetier, E. Pennetier, and J. Queromain. 1993. Presence du pliosaure *Liopleurodon ferox* Sauvage dans le Jurassique Moyen (Callovien) de Villiers-sur-Mer, Normandie. *Bull. Trim. Soc. Géol. Normandie et Amis Muséum du Havre* 80:11–14.

Bardet, N., P. Wellnhofer, and D. Herm. 1994. Discovery of ichthyosaur remains (Reptilia) in the Upper Cenomanian of Bavaria. *Mitt. Bayer. Staatsslg. Paläont. Hist. Geol.* 34:213–20.

Bartholomai, A. 1966. The discovery of plesiosaurian remains in freshwater sediments in Queensland. *Aust. Jour. Sci.* 28:437–38.

Baur, G. H. C. L. 1887. On the morphology of the Ichthyopterygia. *Amer. Nat.* 21:837–40.

——. 1890. On the characters and systematic position of the large sea-lizards, Mosasauridae. *Science* 16(405):262.

Beaumont, C., G. M. Quinlan, and G. S. Stockmal. 1993. The evolution of the Western Interior Basin: Causes, consequences and unsolved problems. In W. G. E. Caldwell and E. G. Kaufmann, eds., *Evolution of the Western Interior Basin,* pp. 97–117. Geological Association of Canada.

Bell, B. A., A. Murray, and L. W. Osten. 1982.

*Coniasaurus* Owen, 1850 from North America. *Jour. Paleo.* 56:520–24.

Bell, G. L. 1995. Middle Turonian (Cretaceous) mosasauroids from Big Bend National Park, Texas. In V. L. Santucci and L. McClelland, eds., *National Park Service Paleontological Research,* vol. 2. Technical Report NPS/NRPO/NRTR-95/16, pp. 34–39.

——. 1997a. Introduction. In J. M. Callaway and E. L. Nicholls, eds., *Ancient Marine Reptiles,* pp. 281–92. Academic Press.

——. 1997b. A phylogenetic revision of the North American and Adriatic Mosasauroidea. In J. M. Callaway and E. L. Nicholls, eds., *Ancient Marine Reptiles,* pp. 293–332. Academic Press.

Bell, G. L., M. W. Caldwell, R. Holmes, J. Wiffen, and J. McKee. 1999. Sea monsters of the South Pacific: On the Late Cretaceous mosasaurs of New Zealand. *Jour. Vert. Paleo.* 19(suppl. to 3):32A.

Bell, G. L., M. A. Sheldon, J. P. Lamb, and J. E. Martin. 1996. The first direct evidence of live birth in Mosasauridae (Squamata): Exceptional preservation in Cretaceous Pierre Shale of South Dakota. *Jour. Vert. Paleo.* 16(suppl. to 3):21A.

Bennett, S. C. 2000. Inferring stratigraphic position of fossil vertebrates from the Niobrara Chalk of western Kansas. *Kansas Geological Survey, Current Research in Earth Sciences, Bulletin* 244(1):1–26.

Benton, M. J. 1985. Classification and phylogeny of the diapsid reptiles. *Zool. Jour. Linn. Soc. London* 84:97–164.

——. 1989. Mass extinctions among tetrapods and the quality of the fossil record. *Phil. Trans. Roy. Soc. London* B325:369–86.

——. 1990a. *The Reign of the Reptiles.* Crescent.

——. 1990b. Scientific methodologies in collision: The history of the study of the extinction of the dinosaurs. In M. K. Hecht, B. Wallace, and R. J. McIntyre, eds., *Evolutionary Biology,* pp. 371–400. Plenum.

——. 1991. The myth of the Mesozoic cannibals. *New Scientist* 132(1790):40–44.

——. 1993. Late Triassic extinctions and the origin of the dinosaurs. *Science* 260:769–70.

——. 1997a. Reptiles. In P. J. Currie and K. Padian, eds., *Encyclopedia of Dinosaurs,* pp. 637–43. Academic Press.

——. 1997b. *Vertebrate Paleontology.* Chapman and Hall.

Benton, M. J., and P. S. Spencer. 1995. *Fossil Reptiles of Great Britain.* Chapman and Hall.

Benton, M. J., and M. A. Taylor. 1984. Marine reptiles from the Upper Lias (Lower Toarcian, Lower Jurassic) of the Yorkshire coast. *Proc. Yorkshire Geol. Soc.* 44:399–429.

Benton, M. J., M. A. Wills, and R. Hitchin. 2000. Quality of the fossil record through time. *Nature* 403:534–36.

Blake, R. W. 1983. Energetics of leaping dolphins and other aquatic animals. *Jour. Mar. Biol. Assoc. U.K.* 63:61–70.

Bonner, J. T. 1988. *The Evolution of Complexity by Means of Natural Selection.* Princeton University Press.

Brinkman, D. B., Z. Xijin, and E. L. Nicholls. 1992. A primitive ichthyosaur from the Lower Triassic of British Columbia, Canada. *Palaeontology* 35(2):465–74.

Broom, R. 1912. On a species of *Tylosaurus* from the Upper Cretaceous beds of Pondoland. *Ann. S. Afr. Mus.* 7:332–33.

Brown, B. 1904. Stomach stones of plesiosaurs. *Science* 19:184–85.

——. 1907. Gastroliths. *Science* 25(636):392.

——. 1913. A new plesiosaur, *Leurospondylus,* from the Edmonton Cretaceous of Alberta. *Bull. Amer. Mus. Nat. Hist.* 32:605–15.

Brown, D. S. 1981. The English Upper Jurassic

Plesiosauroidea (Reptilia) and a review of the phylogeny and classification of the Plesiosauria. *Bull. Br. Mus. Nat. Hist. (Geol.)* 35(4):253–347.

Brown, D. S., and A. R. I. Cruickshank. 1994. The skull of the Callovian plesiosaur *Cryptoclidus eurymerus*, and the sauropterygian cheek. *Palaeontology* 37(4):941–53.

Brown, D. S., A. C. Milner, and M. A. Taylor. 1986. New material of the plesiosaur *Kimmerosaurus langhami* Brown from the Kimmeridge Clay of Dorset. *Bull. Br. Mus. Nat. Hist. (Geol.)* 40(5):225–34.

Brown, N. N.d. The Western Interior Seaway: An introduction to the general history, paleogeography, and ammonite record. *http://gs.ucsd.edu.paleontology/seaway.html.*

Buchholtz, E. A. 2001. Swimming styles in Jurassic ichthyosaurs. *Jour. Vert. Paleo.* 21(1):61–73.

Buel, J. W. 1887. *Sea and Land: An Illustrated History of the Wonderful and Curious Things of Nature Existing before and since the Deluge. A Natural History of the Sea, Land Creatures, the Cannibals and Wild Races of the World.* Historical Publishing Co.

Buffetaut, E. 1989. Evolution. In C. A. Ross, ed., *Crocodiles and Alligators*, pp. 14–25. Facts on File.

Buffrénil, V. de, L. Zylberberg, W. Traub, and A. Casinos. 2000. Structural and mechanical characteristics of the hyperdense bone of the rostrum of *Mesoplodon densirostris* (Cetacea, Ziphiidae): Summary of recent observations. *Historical Biology* 14:57–65.

Cadbury, D. 2000. *The Dinosaur Hunters: A True Story of Scientific Rivalry and the Discovery of the Prehistoric World.* Fourth Estate.

Caldwell, M. W. 1994. Developmental constraints and limb evolution in Permian and extant lepidosauromorph diapsids. *Jour. Vert. Paleo.* 14(4):459–71.

———. 1995. The pectoral girdle and forelimb of *Carsosaurus marchesetti* (Aigialosauridae), with a preliminary phylogenetic analysis of mosasauroids and varanoids. *Jour. Vert. Paleo.* 15(3):516–31.

———. 1996. Ontogeny and phylogeny of the mesopodial skeleton in mosasauroid reptiles. *Zool. Jour. Linn. Soc.* 116:407–36.

———. 1997a. Limb ossification patterns of the ichthyosaur *Stenopterygius*, and a discussion of the proximal tarsal row of ichthyosaurs and other neodiapsid reptiles. *Zool. Jour. Linn. Soc.* 120:1–25.

———. 1997b. Limb osteology and ossification patterns in *Cryptoclidus* (Reptilia: Plesiosauroidea) with a review of sauropterygian limbs. *Jour. Vert. Paleo.* 17:295–307.

———. 1997c. Modified perichondral ossification and the evolution of paddlelike limbs in ichthyosaurs and plesiosaurs. *Jour. Vert. Paleo.* 17(32):534–47.

———. 1999a. Description and phylogenetic relationships of a new species of *Coniasaurus* Owen, 1850 (Squamata). *Jour. Vert. Paleo.* 19:438–55.

———. 1999b. Squamate phylogeny and the relationships of snakes and mosasaurids. *Zool. Jour. Linn. Soc.* 125:115–47.

———. 2000a. On the aquatic squamate *Dolichosaurus longicollis* Owen, 1850 (Cenomanian, Upper Cretaceous), and the evolution of elongate necks in squamates. *Jour. Vert. Paleo.* 20(4):720–35.

———. 2000b. On the phylogenetic relationships of *Pachyrhachis* within snakes: A response to Zaher. *Jour. Vert. Paleo.* 20(1):187–90.

———. 2002. From fins to limbs to fins: Limb evolution in fossil marine reptiles. *Amer. Jour. Med. Genet.* 9999:1–15.

Caldwell, M. W., and A. M. Albino. 2001. Palaeoenvironment and palaeoecology of three Cretaceous snakes: *Pachyophis*, *Pachyrachis*, and *Dinilysia*. *Acta Palaeontol. Polon.* 46(2):203–18.

——. 2002. Exceptionally preserved skeletons of the Cretaceous snake *Dinilysia patagonica* Woodward, 1901. *Jour. Vert. Paleo.* 22(4):861–66.

Caldwell, M. W., and G. Bell. 1995. *Halisaurus* sp. (Mosasauridae) from the Upper Cretaceous (?Santonian) of east-central Peru, and the taxonomic utility of mosasaur cervical vertebrae. *Jour. Vert. Paleo.* 15(3):532–44.

Caldwell, M. W., and J. Cooper. 1999. Redescription, paleobiogeography, and paleoecology of *Coniasaurus crassidens* Owen 1850 (Squamata) from the English Chalk (Cretaceous, Cenomanian). *Zool. Jour. Linn. Soc.* 127:423–52.

Caldwell, M. W., and M. S. Y. Lee. 1997. A snake with legs from the marine Cretaceous of the Middle East. *Nature* 386:705–9.

——. 2001. Live birth in Cretaceous marine lizards (mosasauroids). *Proc. Roy. Soc. London, Biol. Sci.* 268(1484):2397–401.

Caldwell, M. W., R. L. Carroll, and H. Kaiser. 1995. The pectoral girdle and forelimb of *Carsosaurus marchesetti* (Aigialosauridae), with a preliminary phylogenetic analysis of mosasauroids and varanoids. *Jour. Vert. Paleo.* 15(3):516–31.

Caldwell, W. G. E., and E. G. Kaufmann, eds. 1993. *Evolution of the Western Interior Basin.* Geological Association of Canada.

Callaway, J. M. 1997a. Ichthyosauria. In J. M. Callaway and E. L. Nicholls, eds., *Ancient Marine Reptiles,* pp. 3–16. Academic Press.

——. 1997b. A new look at *Mixosaurus.* In J. M. Callaway and E. L. Nicholls, eds., *Ancient Marine Reptiles,* pp. 45–59. Academic Press.

Callaway, J. M., and D. R. Brinkman. 1989. Ichthyosaurs (Reptilia, Ichthyosauria) from the Lower and Middle Triassic Sulphur Mountain Formation, Wapiti Lake area, British Columbia. *Can. Jour. Earth Sci.* 26:1491–500.

Callaway, J. M., and J. A. Massare. 1989a. Geographic and stratigraphic distribution of the Triassic Ichthyosauria (Reptilia; Diapsida). *N. Jb. Geol. Paläeont.* 178:37–58.

——. 1989b. *Shastasaurus altispinus* (Ichthyosauria, Shastasauridae) from the Upper Triassic of the El Antimonio district, northwestern Sonora, Mexico. *Jour. Paleo.* 63(6):930–39.

Camp, C. L. 1942. California mosasaurs. *Mem. Univ. Calif.* 13(1):1–68.

——. 1951. *Plotosaurus,* a new generic name for *Kolposaurus* Camp, preoccupied. *Jour. Paleo.* 35(6):822.

——. 1980. Large ichthyosaurs from the Upper Triassic of Nevada. *Palaeontographica, Abteilung A.* 170:139–70.

Carey, F. G. 1973. Fish with warm bodies. *Scientific American* 228(2):36–44.

Carlton, J. T., J. B. Geller, M. L. Reaka-Kudla, and E. A. Norse. 1999. Historical extinctions in the sea. *Annu. Rev. Ecol. Syst.* 30:515–38.

Carpenter, K. 1989. *Dolichorhynchops* ≠ *Trinacromerum.* *Jour. Vert. Paleo.* 9(suppl. to 3):15A.

——. 1992. Monsters of the sea and air. In B. Preiss and R. Silverberg, eds., *The Ultimate Dinosaur,* pp. 232–43. Byron Preiss Visual.

——. 1996. A review of short-necked plesiosaurs from the Cretaceous of the Western Interior, North America. *N. Jb. Geol. Paläeont. Abh.* 201(2):259–87.

——. 1997. Comparative cranial anatomy of two North American Cretaceous plesiosaurs. In J. M. Callaway and E. L. Nicholls, eds., *Ancient Marine Reptiles,* pp. 191–216. Academic Press.

——. 1999. Revision of North American elasmosaurs from the Cretaceous of the Western Interior. *Paludicola* 2(2):148–73.

Carrier, D. R. 1987. The evolution of locomotor

stamina in tetrapods: Circumventing a mechanical constraint. *Paleobiology* 13:326–41.

———. 1991. Conflict in the hypaxial musculo-skeletal system: Documenting an evolutionary constraint. *American Zoologist* 31:644–54.

Carroll, R. L. 1981. Plesiosaur ancestors from the Upper Permian of Madagascar. *Phil. Trans. Roy. Soc. London* 297:315–83.

———. 1988. *Vertebrate Paleontology and Evolution.* Freeman.

———. 1997. Mesozoic marine reptiles as models of long-term large-scale evolutionary phenomena. In J. M. Callaway and E. L. Nicholls, eds., *Ancient Marine Reptiles,* pp. 3–16. Academic Press.

Carroll, R. L., and M. DeBraga. 1992. Aigialosaurs: Mid-Cretaceous varanid lizards. *Jour. Vert. Paleo.* 12(1):66–86.

Carroll, R. L., and P. Gaskill. 1985. The nothosaur *Pachypleurosaurus* and the origin of plesiosaurs. *Phil. Trans. Roy. Soc. London,* ser. B, 309:343–93.

Carte, A., and W. H. Baily. 1863. Description of a new species of *Plesiosaurus,* from the Lias, near Whitby, Yorkshire. *Jour. Roy. Dublin Soc.* 4:160–70.

Chaloner, W. G., and A. Hallam, eds. 1989. *Evolution and Extinction.* Cambridge University Press.

Charig, A. 1989. The Cretaceous-Tertiary boundary and the last of the dinosaurs. *Phil. Trans. Roy. Soc. London* B 325:387–400.

———. 1993. Disaster theories of dinosaur extinction. *Modern Geology* 18:299–318.

Chatterjee, S., and B. S. Creisler. 1994. *Alwalkeria* (Thyeropoda) and *Mortuneria* (Plesiosauria), new names for preoccupied *Walkeria* Chatterjee, 1897 and *Turneria* Chatterjee and Small, 1989. *Jour. Vert. Paleo.* 14(1):142.

Chatterjee, S., and B. J. Small. 1989. New plesiosaurs from the Upper Cretaceous of Antarctica. *Geol. Soc. London Spec. Pub.* 47:197–215.

Chatterjee, S., and W. J. Zinsmeister. 1982. Late Cretaceous marine vertebrates from Seymour Island, Antarctic Peninsula. *Antarctic Journal* 17(5):66.

Christiansen, P., and N. Bonde. 1999. Anatomy and phylogenetic affinities of a gigantic mosasaur from Israel. In E. Hoch and A. K. Brantsen, eds., *Secondary Adaptation to Life in Water,* p. 11. University of Copenhagen Geologisk Museum.

———. 2002. A new species of gigantic mosasaur from the late Cretaceous of Israel. *Jour. Vert. Paleo.* 22(3):629–44.

Cicimurri, D. J., and M. J. Everhart. 2001. An elasmosaur with stomach contents and gastroliths from the Pierre Shale (late Cretaceous) of Kansas. *Trans. Kansas Acad. Sci.* 104(3–4):129–43.

Clarke, J., and S. Etches. 1991. Predation amongst Jurassic marine reptiles. *Proc. Dorset Nat. Hist. Archaeol. Soc.* 113:202–5.

Coates, M. I., and J. A. Clack. 1990. Polydactyly in the earliest known tetrapod limbs. *Nature* 347:66–69.

Coates, M. I., and M. Ruta. 2000. Nice snake, shame about the legs. *Trends in Ecology and Evolution* 15(12):503–7.

Colagrande, J. 2000. *In the Presence of Dinosaurs.* Time-Life Books.

Colbert, E. H. 1949. A new Cretaceous plesiosaur from Venezuela. *Amer. Mus. Novitates* 1420:1–22.

———. 1955. *Evolution of the Vertebrates.* John Wiley.

———. 1962. The weights of dinosaurs. *Amer. Mus. Novitates* 2076:1–16.

———. 1963. *Dinosaurs: Their Discovery and Their World.* Hutchinson.

———. 1965. *The Age of Reptiles.* W. W. Norton.

———. 1973. *Wandering Lands and Animals.* Dutton.

Colbert, E. H., R. B. Cowles, and C. M. Bogert. 1946. Temperature tolerances in the American alligator and their bearing on the habits, evolution, and extinction of the dinosaurs. *Bull. Amer. Mus. Nat. Hist.* 86:331–73.

Coles, H. 1853. On the skin of the *Ichthyosaurus. Proc. Geol. Soc. London* 9(1):79–81.

Collin, R., and C. M. Janis. 1997. Morphological constraints on tetrapod feeding mechanisms: Why there were no suspension-feeding marine reptiles. In J. M. Callaway and E. L. Nicholls, eds., *Ancient Marine Reptiles,* pp. 451–66. Academic Press.

Conway Morris, S. 2002. We were meant to be. . . . *New Scientist* 176(2369):26–29.

Conybeare, W. D. 1822. Additional notes on the fossil genera *Ichthyosaurus* and *Plesiosaurus. Trans. Geol. Soc. London* 1(2):103–23.

——. 1824. On the discovery of an almost perfect skeleton of the Plesiosaurus. *Trans. Geol. Soc. London* 2:381–90.

Cope, E. D. 1867. The fossil reptiles of New Jersey. *Amer. Nat.* 1:23–67.

——. 1868a. A large new enaliosaur. *Proc. Acad. Nat. Sci. Phila.* 20:92–93.

——. 1868b. On a new large enaliosaur. *Amer. Jour. Sci.* 46(137):263–64.

——. 1868c. On some Cretaceous reptilia. *Proc. Acad. Nat. Sci. Phila.* 20:233–242.

——. 1869a. The fossil reptiles of New Jersey. *Amer. Nat.* 3:84–91.

——. 1869b. On the reptilian orders Pythonomorpha and Streptosauria. *Proc. Boston Soc. Nat. Hist.* 12:250–66.

——. 1869c. Remarks on *Thoracosaurus brevispinus, Ornithotarsus immanis,* and *Macrosaurus proriger. Proc. Acad. Nat. Sci. Phila.* 11(81):123.

——. 1869d. Specimens of extinct reptiles. *Nature* 1:121–22.

——. 1870a. Additional note on *Elasmosaurus. Amer. Jour. Sci.* 50(149):268–69.

——. 1870b. On *Elasmosaurus platyurus* Cope. *Amer. Jour. Sci.* 50(148):140–41.

——. 1870c. On some reptilia of the Cretaceous formation of the United States. *Proc. Amer. Phil. Soc.* 11:271–74.

——. 1871a. Note of some Cretaceous vertebrates in the State Agricultural College of Kansas, U.S.A. *Proc. Amer. Phil. Soc.* 12:168–76.

——. 1871b. On the geology and paleontology of the Cretaceous strata of Kansas. *Hayden's Fifth Annual Report (1871) of the U.S. Geological Survey of the Territories,* pp. 318–49.

——. 1871c. On some species of Pythonomorpha from the Cretaceous beds of Kansas and New Mexico. *Proc. Amer. Phil. Soc.* 11:574–84.

——. 1871d. Supplement to the "Synopsis of Extinct Batrachia and Reptilia of North America." *Proc. Amer. Phil. Soc.* 12:41–52.

——. 1872a. On Kansas vertebrate fossils. *Amer. Jour. Sci.* 3(13):65.

——. 1872b. [On the structure of the Pythonomorpha]. *Proc. Acad. Nat. Sci. Phila.* 24:140–41.

——. 1873. Catalogue of the Pythonomorpha found in the Cretaceous strata of Kansas. *Proc. Amer. Phil. Soc.* 12:264–87.

——. 1874. Review of the vertebrata of the Cretaceous period found west of the Mississippi River. *U.S. Geol. Surv. Terr. Bull.* 1(2):3–48.

Cowen, R. 1996. Locomotion and respiration in aquatic air-breathing vertebrates. In D. Jablonski, D. H. Erwin, and J. H. Lipps, eds., *Evolutionary Paleobiology,* pp. 337–53. University of Chicago Press.

——. 2000. *History of Life.* Blackwell Science.

Cragin, F. 1888. Preliminary description of a new or little known saurian from the Benton of Kansas. *Amer. Geol.* 2:404–7.

Creisler, B. 1998. Giant pliosaurs – real and imaginary.

*Dino-Dispatches No. 1.* http://www.dinosauria .com/dispatches/19981108001.html.

——. 1999. Plesiosaur Translation and Pronunciation Guide. http://www.dinosauria.com/dml/ names/ples.html.

——. 2000. Mosasauridae Translation and Pronunciation Guide. http://www.dinosauria .com/dml/names/mosa.html.

Cruickshank, A. R. I. 1994a. Cranial anatomy of the Lower Jurassic pliosaur *Rhomaleosaurus megacephalus,* Stuchbury (Reptilia: Plesiosauria). *Phil. Trans. Roy. Soc. London* B 343:247–60.

——. 1994b. A juvenile plesiosaur (Plesiosauria: Reptilia) from the Lower Lias (Hettangian: Lower Jurassic) of Lyme Regis, England: A Pliosaurid-plesiosaurid intermediate? *Zool. Jour. Linn. Soc.* 112:151–78.

——. 1997. An early Cretaceous pliosauroid from South Africa. *Ann. S. Afr. Mus.* 105:207–26.

Cruickshank, A. R. I., and R. E. Fordyce. 2002. A new marine reptile (Sauropterygia) from New Zealand: Further evidence for a late Cretaceous Austral radiation of cryptoclidid plesiosaurs. *Palaeontology* 45(3):557–75.

Cruickshank, A. R. I., and J. A. Long. 1997. A new species of pliosaurid reptile from the early Cretaceous Birdsong Sandstone of Western Australia. *Rec. W. Aust. Mus.* 18:263–76.

Cruickshank, A. R. I., R. E. Fordyce, and J. A. Long. 1999. Recent developments in Australasian sauropterygian palaeontology (Reptilia: Sauropterygia). *Rec. W. Aust. Mus. Suppl.* 57:201–5.

Cruickshank, A. R. I., D. M. Martill, and L. F. Noè. 1996. A pliosaur (Reptilia, Sauropterygia) exhibiting pachyostosis from the middle Jurassic of England. *Jour. Geol. Soc. London* 153:873–79.

Cruickshank, A. R. I., P. G. Small, and M. A. Taylor. 1991. Dorsal nostrils and hydrodynamically driven underwater olfaction in plesiosaurs. *Nature* 352:62–64.

Cuppy, W. 1941. *How to Become Extinct.* University of Chicago Press.

Cuvier, G. 1800–1805. *Leçons d'anatomie comparée.* Paris.

Czerkas, S. J., and S. A. Czerkas. 1990. *Dinosaurs: A Global View.* Barnes and Noble.

Czerkas, S. M., and D. F. Glut. 1982. *Dinosaurs, Mammoths and Cavemen: The Art of Charles R. Knight.* Dutton.

Darby, D. G., and R. W. Ojakangas. 1980. Gastroliths from an Upper Cretaceous plesiosaur. *Jour. Paleo.* 54:548–56.

Darwin, C. 1859. *On the Origin of Species.* John Murray.

Dawson, J. W. 1903. *The Story of Earth and Man.* Harper and Brothers.

DeBraga, M., and R. L. Carroll. 1993. The origin of mosasaurs as a model of macro-evolutionary patterns and processes. *Evol. Biol.* 27:245–322.

Deeming, D. C., L. B. Halstead, M. Manabe, and D. M. Unwin. 1993. An ichthyosaur embryo from the Lower Lias (Jurassic: Hettangian) of Somerset, England, with comments on the reproductive biology of ichthyosaurs. *Modern Geology* 18:423–42.

De la Beche, H. T., and W. D. Conybeare. 1821. Notice of the discovery of a new fossil animal, forming a link between the *Ichthyosaurus* and the crocodile, together with general remarks on the osteology of the *Ichthyosaurus. Trans. Geol. Soc. London* 5:559–94.

Delair, J. B., and W. A. S. Sarjeant. 1975. Joseph Pentland—a forgotten pioneer in the osteology of marine reptiles. *Proc. Dorset Nat. Hist. Archaeol. Soc.* 1975:12–16.

Desmond, A. J. 1976. *The Hot-Blooded Dinosaurs.* Dial Press.

——. 1982. *Archetypes and Ancestors: Palaeontology in*

*Victorian London 1850–1875.* University of Chicago Press.

Dietz, L. F., and W. A. S. Sarjeant. 1993. L. B. Halstead: A bibliography of his published writings. *Modern Geology* 18:61–81.

Dingus, L., and T. Rowe. 1997. *The Mistaken Extinction: Dinosaur Evolution and the Origin of Birds.* Freeman.

Dingus, L., E. S. Gaffney, M. A. Norell, and S. D. Sampson. 1995. *The Halls of Dinosaurs: A Guide to Saurischians and Ornithischians.* American Museum of Natural History.

Dollo, L. 1887. Le hainosaure et les nouveaux vertébrés fossiles du Musée de Bruxelles. *Rev. Quest. Sci.* 21:504–39; 22:70–112.

———. 1889. Première note sur les mosasauriens de Mesvin. *Bull. Soc. Belg. Geol. Paleont. Hydrol.* 3:271–304.

———. 1904. Les mosasauriens de la Belgique. *Bull. Soc. Belg. Geol. Paleont. Hydrol.* 18:207–16.

———. 1909. The fossil vertebrates of Belgium. *Ann. N.Y. Acad. Sci.* 4:99–119.

Domning, D. P., and V. de Buffrénil. 1991. Hydrostasis in the Sirenia: Quantitative data and functional interpretation. *Mar. Mam. Sci.* 7(4):331–68.

Dortangs, R. W., J. W. M. Jagt, H. H. G. Peeters, and A. S. Schulp. 2001. New records of late Cretaceous mosasaurs (Reptilia, Squamata) from the Maastrichtian type area. *Jour. Vert. Paleo.* 21(suppl. to 3):45A–46A.

Dortangs, R. W., A. S. Schulp, E. W. A. Mulder, J. W. M. Jagt, H. H. G. Peeters, and D. Th. de Graaf. 2002. A large new mosasaur from the Upper Cretaceous of the Netherlands. *Neth. Jour. Geosci.* 81(1):1–8.

Douglas, K. 1999. Dinodolphin. *New Scientist* 161(2176):14.

Doyle, P., and D. I. M. MacDonald. 1993. Belemnite battlefields. *Lethaia* 26:65–80.

Druckenmiller, P. S. 2002. Osteology of a new plesiosaur from the Lower Cretaceous (Albian) Thermopolis Shale of Montana. *Jour. Vert. Paleo.* 22(1):29–42.

Dupras, D. L. 1988. Ichthyosaurs of California, Nevada and Oregon. *California Geology* 5:99–107.

Du Toit, A. I. 1927. A geological comparison of South America with South Africa. *Carnegie Inst. Wash. Publ.* 381:1–157.

———. 1937. *Our Wandering Continents: An Hypothesis of Continental Drifting.* Oliver and Boyd.

Eastman, C. R. 1904. A recent paleontological induction. *Science* 20:465–66.

———. 1906. Sermons in stomach stones. *Science* 23:983.

Edinger, T. 1935. *Pistosaurus. N. Jb. Geol. Paläeont.* (74):321–59.

Eldredge, N. 1991a. *Fossils: The Evolution and Extinction of Species.* Princeton University Press.

———. 1991b. *The Miner's Canary: Unraveling the Mysteries of Evolution.* Prentice-Hall.

———. 1998. *The Pattern of Evolution.* Freeman.

———. 2000. *The Triumph of Evolution and the Failure of Creationism.* Freeman.

Ellis, R. 1999. *The Search for the Giant Squid.* Penguin.

Erickson, G. M., K. C. Rogers, and S. A. Yerby. 2001. Dinosaurian growth patterns and rapid avian growth rates. *Nature* 412:429–33.

Etheridge, R. 1888. On additional evidence of the occurrence of *Plesiosaurus* in the Mesozoic rocks of Queensland. *Proc. Linn. Soc. N.S.W.* 2:410–13.

———. 1897. An Australian sauropterygian (*Cimoliasaurus*), converted into precious opal. *Rec. Aust. Mus.* 3:21–29.

———. 1904. A second sauropterygian converted into opal from the Upper Cretaceous of White Cliffs, New South Wales. With indications of ichthyopterygians at the same locality. *Rec. Aust. Mus.* 5:306–16.

Evans, M. 1999. A new reconstruction of the skull of the Callovian elasmosaurid plesiosaur *Muraenosaurus leedsii* Seeley. *Mercian Geologist* 14(4):191–96.

Everhart, M. J. 1999. Evidence of feeding on mosasaurs by the late Cretaceous lamniform shark, *Cretoxyrhina mantelli. Jour. Vert. Paleo.* 17(suppl. to 3):43A–44A.

———. 2000a. Gastroliths associated with plesiosaur remains in the Sharon Springs Member of the Pierre Shale (Late Cretaceous), western Kansas. *Trans. Kansas Acad. Sci.* 103(1–2):64–75.

———. 2000b. Mosasaurs: Last of the great marine reptiles. *Prehistoric Times* 44:29–31.

———. 2001. Revisions to the biostratigraphy of the Mosasauridae (Squamata) in the Smoky Hill Chalk Member of the Niobrara Chalk (late Cretaceous) of Kansas. *Trans. Kansas Acad. Sci.* 104(1–2):56–75.

———. 2002a. New data on cranial measurements and body length of the mosasaur, *Tylosaurus nepaeolicus* (Squamata; Mosasauridae), from the Niobrara Formation of western Kansas. *Trans. Kansas Acad. Sci.* 105(1–2):33–43.

———. 2002b. Remains of immature mosasaurs (Squamata, Mosasauridae) from the Niobrara Formation (late Cretaceous) argue against nearshore nurseries. *Jour. Vert. Paleo.* 22(suppl. to 4):52A.

———. 2002c. Where the elasmosaurs roam. *Prehistoric Times* 53:24–27.

Everhart, M. J., and J. Bussen. 2001. First report of the mosasaur, *Plioplatecarpus* cf. *primaevus,* from the Pierre Shale (Campanian) of western Kansas. *Kansas Acad. Sci. Trans.* 20(abstracts):28–29.

Everhart, M. J., and P. A. Everhart. 1996. First report of the shell crushing mosasaur, *Globidens* sp., from the Sharon Springs Member of the Pierre Shale (Upper Cretaceous) of western Kansas. *Kansas Acad. Sci. Trans.* 15(abstracts):17.

———. 1997. Earliest occurrence of the mosasaur, *Tylosaurus proriger* (Mosasauridae: Squamata) in the Smoky Hill Chalk (Niobrara Formation, Upper Cretaceous) of western Kansas. *Jour. Vert. Paleo.* 17(suppl. to 3):44A.

Everhart, M. J., P. A. Everhart, and K. Shimada. 1995. New specimen of shark-bitten mosasaur vertebrae from the Smoky Hill Chalk (Upper Cretaceous) in western Kansas. *Kansas Acad. Sci. Trans.* 14(abstracts):19.

Fastovsky, D. E., and D. B. Weishampel. 1996. *The Evolution and Extinction of the Dinosaurs.* Cambridge University Press.

Fernández, M. S. 1994. A new long-snouted ichthyosaur from the early Bajocian of the Neuquén Basin (Argentina). *Ameghiniana* 31:291–97.

———. 1997. A new ichthyosaur from the Tithonian (late Jurassic) of the Neuquén Basin, northwestern Patagonia, Argentina. *Jour. Paleo.* 7:497–84.

———. 1999. A new ichthyosaur from the Los Molles Formation (early Bajocian), Neuquén Basin, Argentina. *Jour. Paleo.* 73(4):677–81.

———. 2000. Late Jurassic ichthyosaurs from the Neuquén Basin, Argentina. *Historical Biology* 14:133–36.

———. 2001. Dorsal or ventral? Homologies of the forefin of *Caypullisaurus* (Ichthyosauria: Ophthalmosauria). *Jour. Vert. Paleo.* 21(3):515–20.

Fernández, M. S., and M. Iturralde-Vinent. 2000. An Oxfordian Ichthyosauria (Reptilia) from Viñales, western Cuba: Paleobiogeographic significance. *Jour. Vert. Paleo.* 20(1):191–93.

Fish, F. E., and J. M. Battle. 1995. Hydrodynamic design of the humpback whale flipper. *Jour. Morphol.* 225:51–60.

Flannery, T. 2001. *The Eternal Frontier: An Ecological History of North America and Its People.* Heinemann.

Fleming, C. A., D. R. Gregg, and S. P. Welles. 1971. New Zealand ichthyosaurs—a summary including new records from the Cretaceous. *N.Z. Jour. Geol. Geophys.* 14(4):734–41.

Fortey, R. S. 1998. *Life: A Natural History of the First Four Billion Years of Life on Earth.* Knopf.

Fostowicz-Frelik, L., and A. Gazdzicki. 2001. Anatomy and histology of plesiosaur bones from the late Cretaceous of Seymour Island, Antarctic Peninsula. In A. Gazdzicki, ed., *Palaeontological Results of the Polish Antarctic Expeditions. Part III. Palaeontol. Polon.* 60:7–32.

Frey, E., and J. Riess. 1982. Considerations concerning plesiosaur locomotion. *N. Jb. Geol. Paläeont.* 164:193–94.

Frey, E., M.-C. Buchy, and W. Stinnesbeck. 2001. The monster of Aramberri and friends: New finds of marine reptiles in the Mesozoic of northeastern Mexico (abstract). *Eur. Workshop Vert. Paleo., Florence, Sept. 19–22,* p. 30.

Gasparini, Z. 1985. Los reptiles marinos Jurásicos de América del Sur. *Ameghiniana* 22:23–34.

———. 1988. *Ophthalmosaurus monocharactus* Appelby (Reptilia, Ichthyopterygia) en las calizas litográficas del Area Los Catutos, Neuquén, Argentina. *Ameghiniana* 25:3–16.

———. 1997. A new pliosaur from the Bajocian of the Neuquén Basin, Argentina. *Palaeontology* 40:135–37.

Gasparini, Z., and L. Spalletti. 1993. First Callovian plesiosaurs from the Neuquen Basin, Argentina. *Ameghiniana* 30(3):245–54.

Gasparini, Z., N. Bardet, and M. Iturralde-Vinent. 2002. A new cryptoclidid plesiosaur from the Oxfordian (late Jurassic) of Cuba. *Geobios* 35:201–11.

Gibson, C. D. 1981. A history of the swordfishery in the northwestern Atlantic. *American Neptune* 41(1):36–65.

———. 1998. *The Broadbill Swordfishery in the North Atlantic.* Ensign.

Gilmore, C. W. 1912. A new mosasauroid reptile from the Cretaceous of Alabama. *Proc. U.S. Natl. Mus.* 41(1870):479–84.

———. 1921. An extinct sea-lizard from western Kansas. *Scientific American* 74(14):273, 280.

———. 1927. Note on a second occurrence of the mosasaurian reptile *Globidens. Science* 66:452.

Gish, D. T. 2001. *Dinosaurs by Design.* Master Books.

Gore, R. 1989. Extinctions: What caused the earth's great dyings? *National Geographic* 175(6):662–69.

Gould, S. G., and N. Eldredge. 1977. Punctuated equilibria: The tempo and mode of evolution reconsidered. *Paleobiology* 3:115–51.

Gould, S. J. 1990. Bent out of shape. *Natural History* 5(90):12–25.

Grange, D. R., G. W. Storrs, S. Carpenter, and S. Etches. 1996. An important marine vertebrate-bearing locality from the Lower Kimmeridge Clay (Upper Jurassic) of Westbury, Wiltshire, *Proc. Geol. Assoc.* 107:107–16.

Haines, T. 1999. *Walking with Dinosaurs: A Natural History.* BBC Worldwide.

Hallam, A. 1972. Continental drift and the fossil record. *Scientific American* 227(11):56–66.

———. 1986. End-Cretaceous mass extinction event: Argument for terrestrial causation. *Science* 238:1237–42.

———. 1989. The case for sea-level change as a dominant causal factor in mass extinction of marine invertebrates. *Phil. Trans. Roy. Soc. London* B325:437–55.

Halstead, L. B. 1968. *The Pattern of Vertebrate Evolution.* Freeman.

———. 1971. *Liopleurodon rossicus* (Novozhilov)—a

pliosaur from the Lower Volgian of the Moscow Basin. *Palaeontology* 14:566–70.

——. 1982. *The Search for the Past.* Doubleday.

——. 1989. Plesiosaur locomotion. *Jour. Geol. Soc. London* 146:37–40.

Halstead, L. B., and J. Halstead. 1987. *Dinosaurs.* Sterling.

Harlan, R. 1834a. Notice of the discovery of the remains of the *Ichthyosaurus* in Missouri, N.A. *Trans. Amer. Phil. Soc.* 4:405–8.

——. 1834b. Notice of fossil bones found in the Tertiary formation of the state of Louisiana. *Trans. Amer. Phil. Soc.* 4:397–403.

——. 1842. On the discovery of the *Basilosaurus* and the *Batrachiosaurus. Proc. Geol. Soc. London* 3:23–24.

Hawkins, T. 1834. *Memoirs of Ichthyosauri and Plesiosauri, Extinct Monsters of the Ancient Earth.* Relfe and Fletcher.

Heatwole, H. 1999. *Sea Snakes.* Krieger.

Hecht, J. 2000. Prehistoric pins. *New Scientist* 165:15.

Herald, E. S. 1961. *Living Fishes of the World.* Doubleday.

Heyning, J. E., and J. G. Mead. 1996. Suction feeding in beaked whales: Morphological and observational evidence. *Contrib. Sci. L.A. County Mus. Nat. Hist.* 464:1–12.

Hildebrand, A. R., G. T. Penfield, D. A. Kring, M. Pilkington, Z. Camargo, D. S. Jacobsen, and W. V. Boynton. 1991. Chicxulub crater: A possible Cretaceous-Tertiary boundary impact crater on the Yucatán peninsula. *Geology* 19:867–71.

Hodge, R. P., and B. W. Wing. 2000. Occurrences of marine turtles in Alaska waters, 1960–1998. *Herp. Rev.* 31(3): 148–51.

Hoffman, A. 1989. What, if anything, are mass extinctions? *Phil. Trans. Roy. Soc. London* B 325:13–21.

Hogler, J. A. 1992. Taphonomy and paleoecology of *Shonisaurus popularus* (Reptilia: Ichthyosauria). *Palaios* 7:108–17.

——. 1993. Tail-bends of Triassic ichthyosaurs: A reappraisal. *Jour. Vert. Paleo.* 13(3):41A.

——. 1994. Speculations on the role of marine reptile deadfalls in Mesozoic deep-sea paleoecology. *Palaios* 9(1):42–47.

Holmes, R. 1996. *Plioplatecarpus primaevus* (Mosasauridae) from the Bearpaw Formation (Campanian, Upper Cretaceous) of the North American Western Interior Seaway. *Jour. Vert. Paleo.* 16(4):673–87.

Holmes, R., and H.-D. Sues. 2000. A partial skeleton of the basal mosasaur *Halisaurus platyspondylus* from the Severn Formation (Upper Cretaceous: Maastrichtian) of Maryland. *Jour. Paleo.* 74(2):309–16.

Holmes, R., M. W. Caldwell, and S. L. Cumbaa. 1999. A new specimen of *Plioplatecarpus* (Mosasauridae) from the Lower Maastrichtian of Alberta: Comments on allometry, functional morphology, and paleoecology. *Can. Jour. Earth Sci.* 36:363–69.

Home, E. 1814. Some account of the fossil remains more nearly allied to fishes than any other classes of animals. *Phil. Trans. Roy. Soc. London* 104:571–77.

——. 1816. Some further account of the fossil remains of an animal, of which a description was given to the society in 1814. *Phil. Trans. Roy. Soc. London* 106:318–21.

——. 1818. Additional facts respecting the fossil remains of an animal, on the subject of which two papers have been printed in the *Philosophical Transactions,* showing that the bones of the sternum resemble those of *Ornithorhynchus paradoxus. Phil. Trans. Roy. Soc. London* 108:24–32.

——. 1819a. An account of the fossil skeleton of the Proteosaurus. *Phil. Trans. Roy. Soc. London* 109:209–11.

——. 1819b. Reasons for giving the name *Proteosaurus*

to the fossil skeleton which has been described. *Phil. Trans. Roy. Soc. London* 109:212–16.

Hotton, N. 1968. *The Evidence of Evolution*. Van Nostrand.

Howe, S. R., T. Sharpe, and H. S. Torrens. 1981. *Ichthyosaurs: A History of Fossil Sea-Dragons*. National Museum of Wales.

Humphries, S., and G. D. Ruxton. 2002. Why did some ichthyosaurs have such large eyes? *Jour. Exp. Biol.* 205:439–41.

Hungerbühler, A. 1994. Recently identified type material of the Lower Jurassic ichthyosaur *Stenopterygius* in the Geological-Paleontological Institute, Tübingen. *Paläontol. Z.* 68(1–2):245–58.

Iturralde-Vinent, M., and M. A. Norell. 1996. Synopsis of late Jurassic marine reptiles from Cuba. *Amer. Mus. Novitates* 3164:1–17.

Jagt, J. W., E. W. A. Mulder, W. B. Gallagher, and A. S. Schulp. 1999. A new specimen of *Mosasaurus hoffmanni* from the type locality at Maastricht, the Netherlands. *Jour. Vert. Paleo.* 19(suppl. to 3):55.

Kase, T., P. Johnston, A. Seilacher, and J. B. Boyce. 1998. Alleged mosasaur bite marks on late Cretaceous ammonites are limpet (patellogastropod) home scars. *Geology* 26(10):947–50.

Kass, M., and D. Smith. 2001. Preliminary report on new material for *Prognathodon stadtmani*. *Jour. Vert. Paleo.* 21(suppl. to 3):67A.

Kauffman, E. G. 1984. Paleobiogeography and evolutionary response dynamic in the Cretaceous Western Interior Seaway of North America. In G. E. G. Westermann, ed., *Jurassic-Cretaceous Biochronology of North America*, pp. 273–306. Geol. Soc. Canada Spec. Paper 27.

Kauffman, E. G., and W. G. E. Caldwell. 1993. The Western Interior Basin in space and time. In W. G. E. Caldwell and E. G. Kaufmann, eds., *Evolution of the Western Interior Basin*, pp. 1–30. Geological Association of Canada.

Kauffman, E. G., and R. V. Kesling. 1960. An Upper Cretaceous ammonite bitten by a mosasaur. *Univ. Mich. Mus. Paleont. Contrib.* 15:193–248.

Kear, B. P. In press. A juvenile pliosaur from the early Cretaceous of South Australia. *Lethaia*.

Kiernan, C. R. 2002. Stratigraphic distribution and habitat segregation of mosasaurs in the Upper Cretaceous of western and central Alabama, with an historical review of the Alabama mosasaur discoveries. *Jour. Vert. Paleo.* 22(1):91–103.

Kirton, A. M. 1983. A review of British Upper Jurassic ichthyosaurs. Ph.D. diss., University of Newcastle.

Knight, C. R. 1935. *Before the Dawn of History*. McGraw-Hill.

Kosch, B. F. 1990. A revision of the skeletal reconstruction of *Shonisaurus populatis* (Reptilia: Ichthyosauria). *Jour. Vert. Paleo.* 10(4):512–14.

Langton, J. 1994. "Revealed: The Loch Ness picture hoax. Monster was a toy submarine." *Sunday Telegraph*, March 13, pp. 1, 3.

Lee, M. S. Y. 1997. The phylogeny of varanoid lizards and the affinities of snakes. *Phil. Trans. Roy. Soc. London* B 352:56–91.

——. 1998a. Anatomy and relationships of *Pachyrhachis problematicus*, a primitive snake with hind limbs. *Phil. Trans. Roy. Soc. London* 353(1575):1521–22.

——. 1998b. Convergent evolution and character correlation in burrowing reptiles: Towards a resolution of squamate relationships. *Biol. Jour. Linn. Soc.* 65:369–453.

——. 2000. Snake origins and the need for scientific agreement on vernacular names. *Paleobiology* 27(1):1–6.

Lee, M. S. Y., and M. W. Caldwell. 1998. Anatomy and relationships of *Pachyrhachis problematicus*, a primitive snake with hindlimbs. *Phil. Trans. Roy. Soc. London* B 353:1521–52.

——. 2000. *Adriosaurus* and the affinities of mosasauroids, dolichosaurs, and snakes. *Jour. Paleo.* 74(1):915–37.

Lee, M. S. Y., G. L. Bell, and M. W. Caldwell. 1999. The origin of snake feeding. *Nature* 400:655–59.

Lee, M. S. Y., M. W. Caldwell, and J. D. Scanlon. 1999. A second primitive marine snake: *Pachyophis woodwardi* from the Cretaceous of Bosnia-Herzegovina. *Jour. Zool. London* 248:509–20.

Leidy, J. 1870a. On the *Elasmosaurus platyurus* of Cope. *Amer. Jour. Sci.* 49(147):392.

——. 1870b. [Remarks on *Poicilopleuron valens, Clidastes intermedius, Leiodon proriger, Baptemys wyomingensis,* and *Emys stevenosonianus*]. *Proc. Acad. Nat. Sci. Phila.* 22:3–5.

Ley, W. 1951. *Dragons in Amber.* Viking.

Li, C. 1999. Ichthyosaur from Guizhou, China. *Chinese Sci. Bull.* 44:1318–21.

Li, C., and H.-L. You. 2002. *Cymbospondylus* from the Upper Triassic of Guizhou, China. *Vertebrata PalAsiatica* 40(1):9–16.

Li, J.-L., J. Liu, and O. Rieppel. 2002. A new species of *Lariosaurus* (Sauropterygia: Nothosauridae) from Triassic of Guizhou, southwest China. *Vertebrata PalAsiatica* 40(2):114–26.

Lingham-Soliar, T. 1991a. Locomotion in mosasaurs. *Modern Geology* 16:229–48.

——. 1991b. Mosasaurs from the Upper Cretaceous of Niger. *Palaeontology* 34(3):653–70.

——. 1992a. A new mode of locomotion in mosasaurs: Subaqueous flying in *Platecarpus marshi. Jour. Vert. Paleo.* 12:405–21.

——. 1992b. The tylosaurine mosasaurs (Reptilia, Mosasauridae) from the Upper Cretaceous of Europe and Africa. *Bull. Inst. Roy. Sci. Nat. Belg.* 62:171–94.

——. 1993. The mosasaur *Leiodon* bares its teeth. *Modern Geology* 18:443–58.

——. 1994a. First record of mosasaurs from the Maastrichtian (Upper Cretaceous) of Zaire. *Paläontol. Z.* 68(1–2):259–65.

——. 1994b. Going out with a bang: The Cretaceous-Tertiary extinction. *Biologist* 41(5):215–18.

——. 1994c. The mosasaur "*Angolasaurus*" *bocagei* (Reptilia: Mosasauridae) from the Turonian of Angola re-interpreted as the earliest member of the genus *Platecarpus. Paläontol. Z.* 68(1–2):267–82.

——. 1995. Anatomy and functional morphology of the largest marine reptile known, *Mosasaurus hoffmanni* (Mosasauridae, Reptilia) from the Upper Cretaceous Upper Maastrichtian of the Netherlands. *Phil. Trans. Roy. Soc. London* 347:155–80.

——. 1998a. A new mosasaur *Pluridens walkeri* from the Upper Cretaceous, Maastrichtian of the Iullemmeden Basin, southwest Niger. *Jour. Vert. Paleo.* 18(4):709–17.

——. 1998b. Taphonomic evidence for fast tuna-like swimming in Jurassic and Cretaceous ichthyosaurs. *N. Jb. Geol. Paläont. Abh.* 207(2):171–83.

——. 1998c. Unusual death of a Cretaceous giant. *Lethaia* 31:308–10.

——. 1999a. The durophagous mosasaurs (Lepidosauromorpha, Squamata) *Globidens* and *Carinodens* from the Upper Cretaceous of Belgium and the Netherlands. *Paleo. Jour.* 33(6):638–46.

——. 1999b. A functional analysis of the skull of *Goronyosaurus nigeriensis* (Squamata: Mosasauridae) and its bearing on the predatory behavior and evolution of this enigmatic taxon. *N. Jb. Geol. Paläeont. Abh.* 213(3):355–74.

——. 1999c. Rare soft tissue preservation showing fibrous structures in an ichthyosaur from the Lower Lias (Jurassic) of England. *Proc. Roy. Soc. London* B 266:2367–73.

———. 1999d. What happened 65 million years ago? *Science Spectra* 17:20–29.

———. 2000a. Doing the locomotion: The plesiosaur flew through the Mesozoic seas – but probably on two wings rather than four. *Guardian,* November 16.

———. 2000b. The mosasaur *Mosasaurus lemonnieri* (Lepidosauromorpha, Squamata) from the Upper Cretaceous of Belgium and the Netherlands. *Paleo. Jour.* 34(2):S225–37.

———. 2000c. Plesiosaur locomotion: Is the four-wing problem real or merely an atheoretical exercise? *N. Jb. Geol. Paläeont. Abh.* 217(1):45–87.

———. 2001. The ichthyosaur integument: Skin fibers, a means for a strong, flexible and smooth skin. *Lethaia* 34:287–302.

———. 2002a. Extinction of ichthyosaurs: A catastrophic or evolutionary paradigm? *N. Jb. Geol. Paläeont. Abh.* (in press).

———. 2002b. First occurrence of premaxillary caniniform teeth in the Varanoidea: Presence in the extinct mosasaur *Goronyosaurus* (Squamata: Mosasauridae) and its functional and paleoecological implications. *Lethaia* 35:1–44.

Lingham-Soliar, T., and D. Nolf. 1989. The mosasaur *Prognathodon* (Reptilia, Mosasaurida) from the Upper Cretaceous of Belgium. *Bull. Inst. Roy. Sci. Nat. Belg.* 59:137–90.

Long, J. A. 1995. *The Rise of Fishes: 500 Million Years of Evolution.* Johns Hopkins University Press.

———. 1998. *Dinosaurs of Australia and New Zealand, and Other Animals of the Mesozoic Era.* Harvard University Press.

Long, J. A., and A. R. I. Cruickshank. 1998. Further records of plesiosarian reptiles of Jurassic and Cretaceous age from western Australia. *Rec. W. Aust. Mus.* 19:47–55.

Longman, H. A. 1924. A new gigantic marine reptile from the Queensland Cretaceous, *Kronosaurus queenslandicus* new genus and species. *Mem. Qld. Mus.* 8:26–28.

———. 1930. *Kronosaurus queenslandicus,* a gigantic Queensland pliosaur. *Mem. Qld. Mus.* 10:1–7.

———. 1932. Restoration of *Kronosaurus queenslandicus. Mem. Qld. Mus.* 10:98.

———. 1935. Palaeontological notes. *Mem. Qld. Mus.* 10:236–39.

Lydekker, R. 1889. On an ichthyosaurian paddle showing the contour of the integuments. *Geol. Mag.* 3(6):388–90.

Maisch, M. W. 1998a. A new ichthyosaur genus from the Posidonia Shale (Lower Toarcian, Jurassic) of Holzmaden, SW Germany with comments on the phylogeny of post-Triassic ichthyosaurs. *N. Jb. Geol. Paläeont. Abh.* 209(1):47–78.

———. 1998b. The temporal region of the middle Jurassic ichthyosaur *Ophthalmosaurus* – further evidence for the non-diapsid cranial architecture of the Ichthyosauria. *N. Jb. Geol. Paläeont. Mh.* 1998(7):401–14.

———. 2000. Observations on Triassic ichthyosaurs. Part VI. On the cranial osteology of *Hastasaurus alexandrae* Merriam 1902 from the Hosselkus Limestone (Carnian, late Triassic) of northern California with a revision of the genus. *N. Jb. Geol. Paläeont. Abh.* 217(1):1–25.

———. 2001. Observations on Triassic ichthyosaurs. Part VII. New data on the osteology of *Chaohusaurus geishanensis* Young & Dong, 1972 from the Lower Triassic of Anhui, China. *N. Jb. Geol. Paläeont. Abh.* 219(3):305–27.

Maisch, M. W., and A. T. Matzke. 1997. Observations on Triassic ichthyosaurs. Part I. Structure of the palate and mode of tooth implantation in *Mixosaurus cornalianus* (Bassani, 1886). *N. Jb. Geol. Paläeont. Mh.* 1997(12):717–32.

———. 1998a. Observations on Triassic ichthyosaurs.

Part II. A new ichthyosaur with palatal teeth from Monte San Giorgio. *N. Jb. Geol. Paläeont. Mh.* 1998(1):26–41.

——. 1998b. Observations on Triassic ichthyosaurs. Part III. A crested, predatory mixosaur from the middle Triassic of the Germanic Basin. *N. Jb. Geol. Paläeont. Abh.* 209:105–34.

——. 1998c. Observations on Triassic ichthyosaurs. Part IV. On the forelimb of *Mixosaurus* Baur, 1887. *N. Jb. Geol. Paläeont. Abh.* 209(2):247–72.

——. 2000. The mixosaurid ichthyosaur *Conectopalatus* from the middle Triassic of the German Basin. *Lethaia* 33:71–74.

——. 2001a. The cranial osteology of the middle Triassic ichthyosaur *Contectopalatus* from Germany. *Palaeontology* 44(6):1127–56.

——. 2001b. Observations on Triassic ichthyosaurs. Part VIII. A redescription of *Phalarodon major* (von Huene, 1916) and the composition and phylogeny of the Mixosauridae. *N. Jb. Geol. Paläeont. Abh.* 220(3):431–47.

Maisch, M. W., and M. Rücklin. 2000. Cranial osteology of the sauropterygian *Plesiosaurus brachypterygius* from the Lower Toarcian of Germany. *Palaeontology* 43(1):29–40.

Mantell, G. A. 1837. On the structure of the fossil saurians. *London's Mag. Nat. Hist.* 10:281, 341.

Márquez, M. R. 1990. *FAO Species Catalogue.* Vol. 11. *Sea Turtles of the World.* FAO Fisheries Synopsis 11 (125):1–81.

Marsh, O. C. 1869. Notice of some new mosasauroid reptiles from the Greensand of New Jersey. *Amer. Jour. Sci. Arts* 48(144):392–97.

——. 1872a. Discovery of the dermal scutes of mosasaurid reptiles. *Amer. Jour. Sci.* 3(16):290–92.

——. 1872b. Notice of a new reptile from the Cretaceous. *Amer. Jour. Sci.* 4(23):406.

——. 1872c. On the structure of the skull and limbs in mosasaurid reptiles, with descriptions of new genera and species. *Amer. Jour. Sci.* 3(18):448–64.

——. 1879. A new order of extinct reptiles (Sauronodonta) from the Jurassic formation of the Rocky Mountains. *Amer. Jour. Sci.* 3:85–86.

——. 1880. New characters of mosasauroid reptiles. *Amer. Jour. Sci.* 3:83–87.

Martill, D. M. 1991. Marine reptiles. In D. M. Martill and J. D. Hudson, eds., *Fossils of the Oxford Clay,* pp. 226–43. Palaeontological Association.

——. 1993. Soupy substrates: A medium for the exceptional preservation of ichthyosaurs of the Posidonia Shale (Lower Jurassic) of Germany. *Kaupia* 2:77–97.

——. 1995. An ichthyosaur with well preserved soft tissue from the Sinemurian of southern England. *Palaeontology* 38:897–903.

Martill, D. M., and J. D. Hudson, eds. 1991. *Fossils of the Oxford Clay.* Palaeontological Association.

Martill, D. M., and D. Naish. 2000. *Walking with Dinosaurs, the Evidence: How Did They Know That?* BBC.

Martin, J. E. 1994. A baby plesiosaur from the late Cretaceous Pierre Shale, Fall River County, South Dakota. *Jour. Vert. Paleo.* 14(suppl. to 3):35–36A.

Martin, J. E., and P. R. Bjork. 1987. Gastric residues associated with a mosasaur from the late Cretaceous (Campanian) Pierre Shale in South Dakota. *Dakoterra* 3:68–72.

Martin, L. D. 1984. A new Hesperornithid and the relationships of Mesozoic birds. *Trans. Kansas Acad. Sci.* 87(3–4):141–50.

——. 1994. S. W. Williston and the exploration of the Niobrara Chalk. *Earth Sci. Hist.* 13(2):138–42.

Martin, L. D., and B. M. Rothschild. 1989. Paleopathology and diving mosasaurs. *American Scientist* 77:46–67.

Martin, L. D., and J. D. Stewart. 1977. The oldest

(Turonian) mosasaurs from Kansas. *Jour. Paleo.* 51(5):973–75.

——. 1982. An ichthyornithiform bird from the Campanian of Canada. *Can. Jour. Earth Sci.* 19:324–27.

Massare, J. A. 1987. Tooth morphology and prey preference of Mesozoic marine reptiles. *Jour. Vert. Paleo.* 7(2):121–37.

——. 1988. Swimming capabilities of Mesozoic marine reptiles: Implications for methods of predation. *Paleobiology* 14:187–205.

——. 1992. Ancient mariners. *Natural History* 101(9):48–53.

——. 1994. Swimming capabilities of Mesozoic marine reptiles: A review. In L. Maddock, Q. Bone, and J. M. V. Rayner, eds., *Mechanics and Physiology of Animal Swimming*, pp. 133–52. Cambridge University Press.

Massare, J. A., and J. M. Callaway. 1988. Live birth in ichthyosaurs: Evidence and implications. *Jour. Vert. Paleo.* 8(3):21A.

——. 1990. The affinities and ecology of Triassic ichthyosaurs. *Geol. Soc. Amer. Bull.* 102:409–16.

——. 1994. *Cymbospondylus* (Ichthyosauria: Shastasuridae) from the Lower Triassic Thaynes Formation of southeastern Idaho. *Jour. Vert. Paleo.* 14(1):139–41.

Massare, J. A., and J.-A. Faulkner. 1997. Sharks as morphological analogs for ichthyosaurs. *Paudicola* 1(3):117–25.

Mather, C. O. 1976. *Billfish*. Saltaire.

Mazin, J.-M., V. Suteethorn, E. Buffetaut, J.-J. Jaeger, and R. Helmke-Ingavat. 1991. Preliminary description of *Thaisaurus chonglakmanii* n.g., n. sp. a new ichthyosaurian (Reptilia) from the early Triassic of Thailand. *Comptes Rendus de l'Académie des Sciences*, ser. 2, 313:1207–12.

Mazzotti, F. J. 1986. Structure and function. In C. A.

Ross, ed., *Crocodiles and Alligators*, pp. 42–57. Facts on File.

McClintock, J. 2000. Romancing the bone. *Discover* 21(6):81–90.

McCoy, F. 1867. On the occurrence of *Ichthyosaurus* and *Plesiosaurus* in Australia. *Ann. Mag. Nat. Hist.* 19:355–56.

McGowan, C. 1972a. The distinction between longipinnate and latipinnate ichthyosaurs. *Life Sciences Occasional Papers, Royal Ontario Museum* 20:1–12.

——. 1972b. The systematics of Cretaceous ichthyosaurs with particular reference to material from North America. *Contributions to Geology* 11(1):9–29.

——. 1973a. The cranial morphology of the Lower Liassic latipinnate ichthyosaurs of England. *Bull. Br. Mus. (Nat. Hist.) Geol.* 24(1):3–109.

——. 1973b. Differential growth in three ichthyosaurs: *Ichthyosaurus communis, I. breviceps,* and *Stenopterygius quadriscissus* (Reptilia, Ichthyosauridae). *Life Sci. Contrib. Roy. Ontario Mus.* 93:1–21.

——. 1973c. A note on the most recent ichthyosaur known: An isolated coracoid from the Upper Campanian of Saskatchewan (Reptilia, Ichthyosauria). *Can. Jour. Earth Sci.* 10:1346–49.

——. 1974a. A revision of the latipinnate ichthyosaurs of the Lower Jurassic of England (Reptilia: Ichthyosauria). *Life Sci. Contrib. Roy. Ontario Mus.* 100:1–30.

——. 1974b. A revision of the longipinnate ichthyosaurs of the Lower Jurassic of England, with descriptions of two new species (Reptilia: Ichthyosauria). *Life Sci. Contrib. Roy. Ontario Mus.* 97:1–37.

——. 1976. The description and phenetic relationships of a new ichthyosaur genus from the Upper Triassic of England. *Can. Jour. Earth Sci.* 13(5):668–83.

——. 1978a. Further evidence for the wide geographical distribution of ichthyosaur taxa. *Jour. Paleo.* 52:1155–62.

——. 1978b. An isolated ichthyosaur coracoid from the Maastrichtian of New Jersey. *Can. Jour. Earth Sci.* 15(1):169–71.

——. 1979a. A revision of the Lower Jurassic ichthyosaurs from Germany with a description of two new species. *Paleontographica* 166:93–135.

——. 1979b. Selection pressure for high body temperatures: Implications for dinosaurs. *Paleobiology* 5(3):285–95.

——. 1983. *The Successful Dragons.* Samuel Stevens.

——. 1986. A putative ancestor for the swordfish-like ichthyosaur *Eurhinosaurus*. *Nature* 322(6078):454–56.

——. 1988. Differential development of the rostrum and mandible of the swordfish (*Xiphias gladius*) during ontogeny and its possible functional significance. *Can. Jour. Zool.* 66:496–503.

——. 1989a. Computed tomography reveals further details of *Excalibosaurus*, a putative ancestor for the swordfish ichthyosaur *Eurhinosaurus*. *Jour. Vert. Paleo.* 9(3):269–81.

——. 1989b. The ichthyosaurian tailbend: A verification problem facilitated by computer tomography. *Paleobiology* 15(4):429–36.

——. 1989c. *Leptopterygius tenuirostris* and other long-snouted ichthyosaurs from the English Lower Lias. *Palaeontology* 32(3):409–27.

——. 1990a. Computed tomography confirms that *Eurhinosaurus* (Reptilia Ichthyosauria) does have a tailbend. *Can. Jour. Earth Sci.* 27(11):1541–45.

——. 1990b. Problematic ichthyosaurs from southwest England: A question of authenticity. *Jour. Vert. Paleo.* 10(1):72–79.

——. 1991a. *Dinosaurs, Spitfires, and Sea Dragons.* Harvard University Press.

——. 1991b. An ichthyosaur forefin from the Triassic of British Columbia exemplifying Jurassic features. *Can. Jour. Earth Sci.* 28:1553–60.

——. 1992a. The ichthyosaurian tail: Sharks do not provide an appropriate analogue. *Palaeontology* 35:555–70.

——. 1992b. Unusual extensions of the neural spines in two ichthyosaurs from the Lower Jurassic of Holzmaden. *Can. Jour. Earth Sci.* 29(2):380–83.

——. 1993. A new species of large, long-snouted ichthyosaur from the English Lower Lias. *Can. Jour. Earth Sci.* 30(6):1197–1204.

——. 1994a. *Diatoms to Dinosaurs: The Size and Scale of Living Things.* Penguin.

——. 1994b. A new species of *Shastasaurus* (Reptilia: Ichthyosauria) from the Triassic of British Columbia: The most complete exemplar of the genus. *Jour. Vert. Paleo.* 14:168–179.

——. 1994c. The taxonomic status of the Upper Liassic ichthyosaur *Eurhinosaurus longirostris*. *Palaeontology* 37(4):747–53.

——. 1994d. *Temnodontosaurus risor* is a juvenile form of *T. platydon*. *Jour. Vert. Paleo.* 14:472–79.

——. 1995a. A new and typically Jurassic ichthyosaur from the Upper Triassic of British Columbia. *Can. Jour. Earth Sci.* 33:24–32.

——. 1995b. A remarkable small ichthyosaur from the Upper Triassic of British Columbia, representing a new genus and species. *Can. Jour. Earth Sci.* 32:292–303.

——. 1995c. The taxonomic status of *Leptopterygius* Huene, 1922 (Reptilia: Ichthyosauria). *Can. Jour. Earth Sci.* 33:439–43.

——. 1996. Giant ichthyosaurs of the early Jurassic. *Can. Jour. Earth Sci.* 33(7):1011–21.

——. 1997a. The taxonomic status of the late Jurassic ichthyosaur *Grendelius mordax*: A preliminary report. *Jour. Vert. Paleo.* 17(2):428–30.

——. 1997b. A transitional ichthyosaur fauna. In

J. M. Callaway and E. L. Nicholls, eds., *Ancient Marine Reptiles*, pp. 61–80. Academic Press.

——. 2001. *The Dragon Seekers.* Perseus.

McGowan, C., and A. C. Milner. 1999. A new Pleinsbachian ichthyosaur from Dorset, England. *Palaeontology* 42(5):927–52.

McGowan, C., and R. Motani. 1999. A reinterpretation of the Upper Triassic ichthyosaur *Shonisaurus. Jour. Vert. Paleo.* 19(1):42–49.

McNab, B. K. 1983. Energetics, body size, and the limits to endothermy. *Jour. Zool. London* 199:1–29.

McNamara, K., and J. Long. 1998. *The Evolution Revolution.* Wiley.

Merriam, J. C. 1910. The skull and dentition of a primitive ichthyosaurian from the middle Triassic. *Bull. Dept. Geol. Univ. Calif.* 5:381–90.

Minton, S. A., and H. Heatwole. 1978. Snakes and the sea. *Oceans* 11(2):53–56.

Moodie, R. L. 1912. The "stomach stones" of reptiles. *Science* 35(897):377–78.

Motani, R. 1996. Redescription of the dental features of an early Triassic ichthyosaur *Utatsusaurus hataii. Jour. Vert. Paleo.* 16(3):396–402.

——. 1997a. New information on the forefin of *Utatsusaurus hataii* (Ichthyosauria) *Jour. Paleo.* 71(3):475–79.

——. 1997b. New technique for retrodeforming tectonically deformed fossils, with an example for ichthyosaurian specimens. *Lethaia* 30:221–28.

——. 1997c. Redescription of the dentition of *Grippia longirostris* (Ichthyosauria) with a comparison with *Utatsusaurus hataii. Jour. Vert. Paleo.* 17(1):39–44.

——. 1997d. Temporal and spatial distribution of tooth implantations in ichthyosaurs. In J. M. Callaway and E. L. Nicholls, eds., *Ancient Marine Reptiles*, pp. 81–103. Academic Press.

——. 1998. First complete forefin of the ichthyosaur *Grippia longirostris* from the Triassic of Spitsbergen. *Palaeontology* 41(4):591–99.

——. 1999a. On the evolution and homologies of ichthyopterygian forefins. *Jour. Vert. Paleo.* 19(1):28–41.

——. 1999b. Phylogeny of the Ichthyopterygia. *Jour. Vert. Paleo.* 19(3):472–95.

——. 2000a. Is *Omphalosaurus* ichthyopterygian? A phylogenetic perspective. *Jour. Vert. Paleo.* 20(2):295–301.

——. 2000b. Rulers of the Jurassic seas: The reign of ichthyosaurs. *Scientific American* 283(6):52–59.

——. 2000c. Skull of *Grippia longirostris:* No contradiction with a diapsid affinity for the ichthyopterygia. *Palaeontology* 43(1):1–14.

——. 2002. Scaling effects in caudal fin propulsion and the speed of ichthyosaurs. *Nature* 415:309–12.

Motani, R., and H. You. 1998a. The forefin of *Chenosaurus chaoxianensis* (Ichthyosauria) shows delayed mesopodial ossification. *Jour. Paleo.* 72(1):133–36.

——. 1998b. Taxonomy and limb ontogeny of *Chaohusaurus geishanensis* (Ichthyosauria), with a note on the allometric equation. *Jour. Vert. Paleo.* 18(3):533–40.

Motani, R., M. Manabe, and Z.-M. Dong. 1997. The status of *Himalayasaurus tibetensis* (Ichthyopterygia). *Paludicola* 2(2):174–81.

Motani, R., N. Minoura, and T. Ando. 1998. Ichthyosaurian relationships illuminated by new primitive skeletons from Japan. *Nature* 393:255–57.

Motani, R., B. M. Rothschild, and W. Wahl. 1999. Large eyeballs in diving ichthyosaurs. *Nature* 402:747.

Motani, R., H. You, and C. McGowan. 1996. Eel-like swimming in the earliest ichthyosaurs. *Nature* 382:347–48.

Mulder, E. W. A. 2001. Co-ossified vertebrae of

mosaurs and cetaceans: Implications for the mode of locomotion of extinct marine reptiles. *Paleobiology* 27(4):724–34.

Mulder, E. W. A., N. Bardet, P. Godefroit, and J. W. M. Jagt. 2000. Elasmosaur remains from the Maastrichtian type area, and a review of latest Cretaceous elasmosaurs (Reptilia, Plesiosauroidea). *Bull. Inst. Roy. Sci. Nat. Belg.* 70:161–78.

Naish, D. 1998. Did ichthyosaurs fly? *Dinosaur World* 4:27–29.

Naish, D., L. F. Noè, and D. M. Martill. 2001. Giant pliosaurs and the mysterious "Megapleurodon." *Dino Press* 4:98–103.

Newell, N. D. 1949. Phyletic size increase, an important trend illustrated by fossil invertebrates. *Evolution* 3:103–24.

Newman, B., and B. Tarlo. 1967. A giant marine reptile from Bedfordshire. *Animals* 10(2):61–63.

Nicholls, E. L. 1976. The oldest known North American occurrence of the Plesiosauria (Reptilia: Sauropterygia) from the Liassic (Lower Jurassic) Fernie Group Alberta, Canada. *Can. Jour. Earth Sci.* 13:185–88.

———. 1988. The first record of the mosasaur *Hainosaurus* (Reptilia: Lacertilia) from North America. *Can. Jour. Earth Sci.* 25:1564–70.

Nicholls, E. L., and D. B. Brinkman. 1993. A new specimen of *Utatsusaurus* (Reptilia: Ichthyosauridae) from the Lower Triassic Sulphur Mountain Formation of British Columbia. *Can. Jour. Earth Sci.* 30:486–90.

Nicholls, E. L., and S. J. Godfrey. 1994. Subaqueous flight in mosasaurs – a discussion. *Jour. Vert. Paleo.* 14:450–52.

Nicholls, E. L., and M. Manabe. 2001. A new genus of ichthyosaur from the late Triassic Pardonet Formation of British Columbia: Bridging the Triassic-Jurassic gap. *Can. Jour. Earth Sci.* 38:983–1002.

Nicholls, E. L., and A. P. Russell. 1990. Paleobiogeography in the Western Interior Seaway of North America: The vertebrate evidence. *Palaeogeography, Palaeoclimatology, Palaeoecology* 79:149–69.

Nicholls, E. L., D. B. Brinkman, and J. M. Callaway. 1999. New material of *Phalarodon* (Reptilia: Ichthyosauria) from the Triassic of British Columbia and its bearing on the interrelationships of mixosaurs. *Palaeontographica* 252:1–22.

Nicholls, E. L., C. Wei, and M. Manabe. 2003. New material of *Qianichthyosaurus* Li, 1999 (Reptilia, Ichthyosauria) from the late Triassic of southern China, and implications for the distribution of Triassic ichthyosaurs. *Jour. Vert. Paleo.* 22(4):759–65.

Noè, L. 1999. The Callovian pliosaurs of the Oxford Clay – evidence and implications for the consumption of marine invertebrates. In E. Hoch and A. K. Brantsen, eds., *Secondary Adaptation to Life in Water*, pp. 38–40. University of Copenhagen Geologisk Museum.

———. 2001. A taxonomic and functional study of the Callovian (middle Jurassic) Pliosauroidea (Reptilia, Sauropterygia). Ph.D. diss., University of Derby.

Norman, D. 1994. *Prehistoric Life.* Macmillan.

Novacek, M. J. 1996. *Dinosaurs of the Flaming Cliffs.* Anchor Doubleday.

Obradovich, J. D. 1993. A Cretaceous time scale. In W. G. E. Caldwell and E. G. Kauffman, eds., *Evolution of the Western Interior Basin*, pp. 379–96. Geologic Association of Canada.

O'Keefe, F. R. 2001. Ecomorphology of plesiosaur flipper geometry. *Jour. Evol. Biol.* 14(6):987–91.

———. 2002a. A cladistic analysis and taxonomic

revision of the Plesiosauria. *Acta Zool. Fennica* 213:1–63.

———. 2002b. The evolution of plesiosaur and pliosaur morphotypes in the Plesiosauria (Reptilia: Sauropterygia). *Paleobiology* 28(1):101–12.

———. 2002c. Inference of plesiosaur hunting styles from flipper geometry: Parallels among birds, bats, and airplanes. *Jour. Vert. Paleo.* 22 (suppl. to 3):93A.

Orndorff, R. L., R. W. Wieder, and H. F. Filkorn. 2001. How the west was swum. *Natural History* 110(5):22–24.

Osborn, H. F. 1898. Models of extinct vertebrates. *Science* 7(182):841–45.

———. 1899. A complete mosasaur skeleton, osseous and cartilaginous. *Amer. Mus. Nat. Hist. Mem.* 1(4):167–88.

———. 1900. Intercentra and hypapophyses in the cervical region of mosasaurs, lizards and Sphenodon. *Amer. Nat.* 34(397):1–7.

Osborne, R. 1998. *The Floating Egg: Episodes in the Making of Geology.* Cape.

Ostrom, J. H. 1969. Osteology of *Deinonychus antirrhopus,* an unusual theropod from the Lower Cretaceous of Montana. *Bull. Peabody Mus. Nat. Hist.* 30:1–165.

Owen, R. 1838. A description of the Viscount Cole's specimen of *Plesiosaurus macrocephalus* (Conybeare). *Proc. Geol. Soc. London* 2:663–66.

———. 1840. Note on the dislocation of the tail at a certain point observable in many ichthyosauri. *Trans. Geol. Soc. London* 5:511–14.

———. 1840–1845. *Odontography.* Hippolyte Bailliere.

———. 1842. Observations on the teeth of the Zeuglodon, Basilosaurus of Dr. Harlan. *Proc. Geol. Soc. London* 3:24–28.

———. 1860. *Report of the Twenty-ninth Meeting of the British Association for the Advancement of Science.* John Murray.

———. 1862. Monograph on the fossil reptilia from the Kimmeridge Clay, *Pliosaurus grandis. Monog. Palaeont. Soc. London,* pp. 27–28.

———. 1869. Monographs on the British fossil reptilia from the Kimmeridge Clay, containing *Pliosaurus grandis, P. trochanterius* and *P. portlandicus. Monog. Palaeont. Soc. London* 111:1–12.

———. 1877. On the rank and the affinities in the reptilian class of the Mosasauridae, Gervais. *Quart. Jour. Geol. Soc. London* 33:682–715.

———. 1883. On generic characters in the order Sauropterygia. *Quart. Jour. Geol. Soc. London* 33:133–38.

Palmer, D. 1999. *Atlas of the Prehistoric World.* Discovery Books.

Páramo-Fonseca, M. E. 2000. *Yaguarasaurus columbianus* (Reptilia, Mosasauridae), a primitive mosasaur from the Turonian (Upper Cretaceous) of Colombia. *Historical Biology* 14:121–31.

Parrish, J. T., and D. L. Gautier. 1993. Sharon Springs Member of the Pierre Shale: Upwelling in the Western Interior Seaway? In W. G. E. Caldwell and E. G. Kaufmann, eds., *Evolution of the Western Interior Basin,* pp. 319–32. Geological Association of Canada.

Paton, R. L., T. R. Smithson, and J. A. Clack. 1999. An amniote-like skeleton from the early Carboniferous of Scotland. *Nature* 398:508–13.

Pearce, F. 2002. Oldest fossilized vomit pile uncovered. *New Scientist* 173(2330):9.

Pearce, J. C. 1846. Notice of what appears to be an embryo of an *Ichthyosaurus* in the pelvic cavity of *Ichthyosaurus (communis?). Ann. Mag. Nat. Hist.* 17:44–46.

Perkins, S. 2002. Sea dragons. *Science News* 162(8):122–24.

Persson, P. O. 1982. Elasmosaurid skull from the

Lower Cretaceous of Queensland (Reptilia: Sauropterygia). *Mem. Qld. Mus.* 20:647–55.

Pitman, R. L., D. M. Palacios, P. L. R. Brennan, B. J. Brennan, K. C. Balcomb, and T. Miyashita. 1999. Sightings and possible identity of a bottlenose whale in the tropical Indopacific: *Indopacetus pacificus? Mar. Mam. Sci.* 15(2):531–49.

Polcyn, M., and G. L. Bell. 1994. *Coniasaurus crassidens* and its bearing on varanoid-mosasauroid relationships. *Jour. Vert. Paleo.* 14(suppl. to 3):42A.

Pollard, J. E. 1968. The gastric contents of an ichthyosaur from the Lower Lias of Lyme Regis, Dorset. *Palaeontology* 11:376–88.

Powell, J. L. 1998. *Night Comes to the Cretaceous.* Freeman.

Randerson, J. 2002. Reptiles at four o'clock. *New Scientist* 173:17.

Raup, D. M. 1984. Death of species. In M. H. Nitecki, ed., *Extinctions*, pp. 1–19. University of Chicago Press.

———. 1989. The case for extraterrestrial cases of extinction. *Phil. Trans. Roy. Soc. London* B 325:421–35.

———. 1991a. Extinction: Bad genes or bad luck? *New Scientist* 131(1786):46–49.

———. 1991b. *Extinction: Bad Genes or Bad Luck?* Norton.

———. 1994. The role of extinction in evolution. *Proc. Natl. Acad. Sci.* 91:6758–63.

Raup, D. M., and J. J. Sepkoski. 1982. Mass extinctions in the marine fossil record. *Science* 215:1501–3.

———. 1986. Periodic extinction of families and genera. *Science* 231:833–36.

Raup, D. M., and S. M. Stanley. 1971. *Principles of Paleontology.* Freeman.

Raup, D. M., J. J. Sepkoski, and S. M. Stigler. 1982. Mass extinctions in the fossil record. *Science* 219:1240–41.

Rees, J., and N. Bonde. 1999. Plesiosaur remains from the early Jurassic Hale Formation, Bornholm,

Denmark. In E. Hoch and A. K. Brantsen, eds., *Secondary Adaptation to Life in Water*, p. 70. University of Copenhagen Geologisk Museum.

Reeves, R. R., B. S. Stewart, P. J. Clapham, and J. A. Powell. 2002. *National Audubon Society Guide to Marine Mammals of the World.* Knopf.

Rich, T. H., R. A. Gangloff, and W. R. Hammer. 1997. Polar dinosaurs. In P. J. Currie and K. Padian, eds., *Encyclopedia of Dinosaurs*, pp. 562–73. Academic Press.

Rieppel, O. 1988. A review of the origin of snakes. *Evol. Biol.* 22:37–130.

———. 1994. Osteology of *Simosaurus gaillardoti* and the relationships of stem-group Sauropterygia. *Fieldiana Geol.* 28:1–85.

———. 1997. Sauropterygians. In J. M. Callaway and E. L. Nicholls, eds., *Ancient Marine Reptiles*, pp. 107–19. Academic Press.

———. 1998. Ichthyosaur remains (Reptilia, Ichthyosauria) from the middle Triassic of Makhtesh Ramon, Negev, Israel. *N. Jb. Geol. Paläeont. Mh.* 1998:537–44.

———. 2001a. The cranial anatomy of *Placochelys placodonta* Jaekel, 1902 and a review of the Cyamodontoidea (Reptilia, Placodonta). *Fieldiana Geol.* 45:1–104.

———. 2001b. A new species of *Nothosaurus* (Reptilia: Sauropterygia) from the Upper Muschelkalk (Lower Lindian) of southwestern Germany. *Palaeontographica* 263:137–61.

Rieppel, O., and H. Hagedorn. 1997. Paleogeography of middle Triassic sauropterygia in central and western Europe. In J. M. Callaway and E. L. Nicholls, eds., *Ancient Marine Reptiles*, pp. 121–44. Academic Press.

Rieppel, O., and R. R. Reisz. 1999. The aquatic origin of turtles. In E. Hoch and A. K. Brantsen, eds., *Secondary Adaptation to Life in Water*, p. 59. University of Copenhagen Geologisk Museum.

Riess, J. 1986. Fortbewegunsweise, Schwimmbiophysik und phylogenie der ichthyosaurer. *Paleontographica* A 192:93–155.

Riess, J., and E. Frey. 1982. Considerations concerning plesiosaur locomotion. *N. Jb. Geol. Paläeont.* 164:193–94.

Riggs, E. S. 1944. A new polycotylid plesiosaur. *Univ. Kansas Bull.* 30:77–87.

Ritchie, A. 1979. Sea monster in opal – or the one that got away? *Aust. Nat. Hist.* 19:408–13.

———. 1988. Who should pay for Australia's past? *Aust. Nat. Hist.* 22(8):368–70.

———. 1990. Return of the great sea monsters. *Aust. Nat. Hist.* 23(7):538–45.

Robinson, J. A. 1975. The locomotion of plesiosaurs. *N. Jb. Geol. Paläeont.* 149(3):286–332.

———. 1977. Intracorporal force transmission in plesiosaurs. *N. Jb. Geol. Paläeont.* 153:86–128.

Romer, A. S. 1948. Ichthyosaur ancestors. *Amer. Jour. Sci.* 246(2):109–21.

———. 1956. *Osteology of the Reptiles.* University of Chicago Press.

———. 1966. *Vertebrate Paleontology.* University of Chicago Press.

———. 1968. *The Procession of Life.* World.

———. 1974. Aquatic adaptation in reptiles – primary or secondary? *Ann. S. Afr. Mus.* 64:221–30.

Romer, A. S., and A. D. Lewis. 1959. A mounted skeleton of the giant plesiosaur *Kronosaurus*. *Breviora* 112:1–15.

Roper, C. F. E., and K. J. Boss. 1982. The giant squid. *Scientific American* 246(4):96–105.

Ross, C. A., ed. 1989. *Crocodiles and Alligators.* Facts on File.

Rothschild, B. M., and L. D. Martin. 1987. Avascular necrosis: Occurrence in diving Cretaceous mosasaurs. *Science* 236:75–77.

Rothschild, B. M., and D. Tanke. 1992. Paleopathology of vertebrates: Insights to lifestyle and health in the geological record. *Geoscience Canada* 19(2):73–82.

Rowe, M. P. 2000. Inferring the retinal anatomy and visual capacities of extinct vertebrates. *Palaeontologia Electronica* 3(1). http://palaeo-electronica.org/2000_1/retinal/other.htm.

Rudwick, M. J. S. 1972. *The Meaning of Fossils.* University of Chicago Press.

———. 1992. *Scenes from Deep Time.* University of Chicago Press.

———. 1997. *Georges Cuvier, Fossil Bones, and Geological Catastrophes.* University of Chicago Press.

Russell, D. A. 1964. Intercranial mobility in mosasaurs. *Postilla* 86:1–19.

———. 1967. Systematics and morphology of the American mosasaurs. *Bull. Peabody Mus. Nat. Hist. Yale Univ.* 23:1–237.

———. 1970. The vertebrate fauna of the Selma Formation of Alabama. Part VII. The mosasaurs. *Fieldiana Geol. Mem.* 3(7):369–80.

———. 1975a. A new species of *Globidens* from South Dakota, and a review of globidentine mosasaurs. *Fieldiana Geol.* 33(13):235–56.

———. 1975b. Reptilian diversity and the Cretaceous-Tertiary transition in North America. In W. G. E. Caldwell, ed., *The Cretaceous System in the Western Interior of North America*, pp. 119–36. Geological Association of Canada.

———. 1989. *An Odyssey in Time: The Dinosaurs of North America.* University of Toronto Press, National Museum of Natural Sciences.

———. 1993. Vertebrates in the Cretaceous Western Interior Sea. In W. G. E. Caldwell and E. G.

Kaufmann, eds., *Evolution of the Western Interior Basin*, pp. 665–80. Geological Association of Canada.

Sander, P. M. 1988. A fossil reptile embryo from the middle Triassic of the Alps. *Science* 239:780–83.

——. 1989a. The large ichthyosaur *Cymbospondylus buscheri*, sp. nov. from the middle Triassic of the Monte San Giorgio (Switzerland) with a survey of the genus in Europe. *Jour. Vert. Paleo.* 9(2):163–73.

——. 1989b. The pachypleurosaurids (Reptilia: Nothosauria) from the middle Triassic of Monte San Giorgio (Switzerland), with the description of a new species. *Phil. Trans. Roy. Soc. London B* 325:561–670.

——. 1992. *Cymbospondylus* (Shastasauridae: Ichthyosauria) from the middle Triassic of Spitsbergen: Filling a paleobiogeographic gap. *Jour. Paleo.* 66(2):332–37.

——. 1997. The paleobiogeography of *Shastasaurus*. In J. M. Callaway and E. L. Nicholls, eds., *Ancient Marine Reptiles*, pp. 17–43. Academic Press.

——. 2000. Ichthyosauria: Their diversity, distribution, and phylogeny. *Paläontol. Z.* 74(1–2):1–35.

Sander, P. M., and H. Bucher. 1990. On the presence of *Mixosaurus* (Ichthyopterygia: Reptilia) in the middle Triassic of Nevada. *Jour. Paleo.* 64(1):161–64.

——. 1993. An ichthyosaur from the uppermost Toarcian of southern France. *N. Jb. Geol. Paläeont. Mh.* 10:631–40.

Sander, P. M., O. C. Rieppel, and H. Bucher. 1997. A new pistosaurid (Reptilia: Sauropterygia) from the middle Triassic of Nevada and its implications for the origin of the plesiosaurs. *Jour. Vert. Paleo.* 17(3):526–33.

Sarjeant, W. A. S. 1993. Lambert Beverly Halstead (1933–1991): His life, his discoveries and his controversies. *Modern Geology* 18:5–59.

Sato, T., and G. W. Storrs. 2000. An early polycotylid plesiosaur (Reptilia: Sauropterygia) from the Cretaceous of Hokkaido, Japan. *Jour. Paleo.* 74(5):907–14.

Sato, T., and K. Tanabe. 1998. Cretaceous plesiosaurs ate ammonites. *Nature* 394:629–30.

Scanlon, J. D., and M. S. Y. Lee. 2000. The Pleistocene serpent *Wonambi* and the early evolution of snakes. *Nature* 403:416–20.

Scanlon, J. D., M. S. Y. Lee, M. W. Caldwell, and R. Shine. 1999. The paleoecology of the primitive snake *Pachyrachis*. *Historical Biology* 13:127–52.

Schwimmer, D. R., J. D. Stewart, and G. D. Williams. 1997. Scavenging by sharks of the genus *Squalicorax* in the late Cretaceous of North America. *Palaios* 12:71–83.

Scott, W. B., and S. N. Tibbo. 1968. Food and feeding habits of the swordfish, *Xiphias gladias*, in the western North Atlantic. *Jour. Fish. Res. Bd. Can.* 25(5):903–19.

Seeley, H. G. 1874. On *Muraenosaurus leedsi*, a plesiosaurian from the Oxford Clay. *Q. Jour. Geol. Soc. London* 30:197–208.

——. 1877a. On *Mauisaurus gardneri*, Seeley, an elasmosaurian from the base of the Gault of Folkestone. *Q. Jour. Geol. Soc. London* 33:541–46.

——. 1877b. On the vertebral column and pelvic bones of *Pliosaurus evansi* (Seeley), from the Oxford Clay of St. Neots. *Q. Jour. Geol. Soc. London* 30:716–23.

——. 1880. Report on the mode of reproduction of certain species of *Ichthyosaurus* from the Lias of England and Wurtemburg. *Rep. Br. Assoc. Adv. Sci.* 50:68–76.

——. 1888. On the mode of development of the young in *Plesiosaurus*. *Rep. Br. Assoc. Adv. Sci.* 1887:697–98.

———. 1908a. On the extremity of the tail in Ichthyosauria. *Ann. Mag. Nat. Hist.* 8(1):436–41.

———. 1908b. On the interlocking of the neural arches in ichthyosauria. *Ann. Mag. Nat. Hist.* 8(1):436–41.

Seilacher, A. 1998. Mosasaurs, limpets or diagenesis: How *Placenticeras* shells got punctured. *Geowissenschaftliche Reihe* 1:93–102.

Sheldon, M. A. 1987. Juvenile mosasaurs from the Mooreville Chalk of Alabama. *Jour. Vert. Paleo.* 7(suppl. to 3):25A.

———. 1989. Implications of juvenile mosasaur recognition on taxonomy. *Jour. Vert. Paleo.* 9(suppl. to 3):38A.

———. 1990. Immature mosasaurs from the Niobrara: A sampling problem? *Jour. Vert. Paleo.* 10(suppl. to 3):42A.

———. 1992. Ontogenetic changes in mosasaur bone microstructure. *Jour. Vert. Paleo.* 12(suppl. to 3):51A.

———. 1997. Ecological implications of mosasaur bone microstructure. In J. M. Callaway and E. L. Nicholls, eds., *Ancient Marine Reptiles*, pp. 333–54. Academic Press.

Sheldon, M. A., and G. L. Bell. 1999. Paedomorphosis in Mosasauridae (Squamata): Evidence from fossil bone microstructure. *Paludicola* 2(2):190–205.

Sheldon, M. A., G. L. Bell, and J. P. Lamb. 1996. Histological characters in prenatal specimens of the mosasaur, *Plioplatecarpus primaevus. Jour. Vert. Paleo.* 16(suppl. to 3):64A.

Shuler, E. W. 1950. A new elasmosaur from the Eagle Ford Shale of Texas. Part II. *Fondren Sci. Ser., S. Methodist Univ.* 2:1–33.

Shuler, E. W., and S. P. Welles. 1947. New elasmosaur from the Upper Cretaceous of Texas. *Bull. Geol. Soc. Amer.* 58:1263.

Simpson, G. G. 1953. *Life of the Past.* Yale University Press.

Smellie, W. R. 1915. On a new plesiosaur from the Oxford Clay. *Geol. Mag.* 2:341–43.

Snow, F. H. 1878. On the dermal covering of a mosasauroid reptile. *Trans. Kansas Acad. Sci.* 6:54–58.

———. 1879. The scales of *Liodon. Amer. Nat.* 13(2):132.

Soliar, T. 1988. The mosasaur *Goronyosaurus* from the Upper Cretaceous of Sokoto State, Nigeria. *Palaeontology* 31:747–62.

Sollas, W. J. 1881. On a new species of plesiosaur (*P. conybeari*) from the Lower Lias of Charmouth; with observations on *P. megalocephalus*, Stutchbery, and *P. brachycephalus*, Owen. *Jour. Geol. Soc. London* 37:472–81.

Spotila, J. R. 1995. Metabolism, physiology, and thermoregulation. In K. A. Bjorndal, ed., *Biology and Conservation of Sea Turtles*, pp. 591–92. Smithsonian Institution Press.

Spotila, J. R., M. P. O'Connor, and F. P. Paladino. 1997. Thermal biology. In P. L. Lutz and J. L. Musick, eds., *The Biology of Sea Turtles*, pp. 297–314. CRC Press.

Stanley, S. M. 1984a. Marine mass extinctions: A dominant role for temperature. In M. H. Nitecki, ed., *Extinctions*, pp. 69–117. University of Chicago Press.

———. 1984b. Mass extinctions in the ocean. *Scientific American* 250(6):64–72.

———. 1987. *Extinction.* Scientific American Library.

Sternberg, C. H. 1907. Some animals discovered in the fossil beds of Kansas. *Trans. Kansas Acad. Sci.* 20:122–24.

———. 1908. My expedition to the Kansas chalk for 1907. *Trans. Kansas Acad. Sci.* 21:111–14.

———. 1909. *The Life of a Fossil Hunter.* Henry Holt.

———. 1917. *Hunting Dinosaurs in the Bad Lands of the Red Deer River, Alberta, Canada.* Lawrence, Kans.: n.p. 1985 reprint, NeWest Press.

——. 1922. Explorations of the Permian of Texas and the chalk of Kansas, 1918. *Trans. Kansas Acad. Sci.* 30(1):119–20.

Stewart, J. D., and G. L. Bell. 1989. The earliest reputed North American mosasaur records are not mosasaurs. *Jour. Vert. Paleo.* 9:39A (abstract).

——. 1994. North America's oldest mosasaurs are teleosts. *Contrib. Sci. Nat. Hist. Mus. L.A. County* 441:1–9.

Storrs, G. W. 1984. *Elasmosaurus platyurus* and a page from the Cope-Marsh war. *Discovery* 17(2):25–27.

——. 1991. Anatomy and relationships of *Corosaurus alcovensis* (Diapsida: Sauropterygia) and the Triassic Alcova Limestone of Wyoming. *Bull. Peabody Mus. Nat. Hist.* 44:1–151.

——. 1993a. Function and phylogeny in sauropterygian (Diapsida) evolution. *Amer. Jour. Sci.* 293-A:63–90.

——. 1993b. The quality of the Triassic sauropterygian fossil record. *Rev. Paleobiol.* 7:217–28.

——. 1993c. The systematic position of *Silvestrosaurus* and a classification of Triassic sauropterygians. *Paläontol. Z.* 67(1–2):177–91.

——. 1994. A juvenile specimen of *?Plesiosaurus* sp. from the Lias (Lower Jurassic, Pleinsbachian) near Charmouth, Dorset, England. *Proc. Dorset Nat. Hist. Archaeol. Soc.* 116:72–76.

——. 1995. Jurassic jaws surface in Wiltshire. *Dinosaur Soc. U.K. Quarterly* 1(2):6–7.

——. 1997. Morphological and taxonomic clarification of the genus *Plesiosaurus*. In J. M. Callaway and E. L. Nicholls, eds., *Ancient Marine Reptiles*, pp. 145–90. Academic Press.

——. 1999. An examination of plesiosauria (Diapsida: Sauropterygia) from the Niobrara Chalk (Upper Cretaceous) of central North America. *Univ. Kansas Paleo. Contrib.* 11:1–15.

Storrs, G. W., and M. A. Taylor. 1996. Cranial anatomy of a new plesiosaur genus from the lowermost Lias (Rhaetian/Hettangian) of Street, Somerset, England. *Jour. Vert. Paleo.* 16:403–20.

Storrs, G. W., M. S. Arkhangel'skii, and V. M. Efimov. 2000. Mesozoic marine reptiles of Russia and other former Soviet republics. In M. J. Benton, M. A. Shiskin, D. M. Unwin, and E. N. Kurichkin, eds., *The Age of Dinosaurs in Russia and Mongolia*, pp. 187–210. Cambridge University Press.

Stukely, W. 1719. An account of the impression of an almost entire skeleton of a large animal in a very hard stone from Nottinghamshire. *Phil. Trans. Roy. Soc. London* 30:693–68.

Sues, H.-D. 1987a. On the skull of *Placodus gigas* and the relationships of Placodontia. *Jour. Vert. Paleo.* 7:138–44.

——. 1987b. Postcranial skeleton of *Pistosaurus* and interrelationships of the Sauropterygia (Diapsida). *Zool. Jour. Linn. Soc. London* 90:109–31.

——. 1989. The place of crocodiles in the living world. In C. A. Ross, ed., *Crocodiles and Alligators*, pp. 14–25. Facts on File.

——. 1990. Two dietary developments. *Nature* 346:14–15.

——. 2001. Ruffling feathers. *Nature* 410:1036–37.

Swinton, W. E. 1929. Ichthyosaur embryos. *Natural History* 2:8–12.

——. 1930a. A new plesiosaur from Warwickshire. *Nat. Hist. Mag.* 2:271–75.

——. 1930b. On fossil reptilia from Sokoto province. *Biol. Geol. Surv. Nigeria Bull.* 1:42–48.

——. 1930c. Preliminary account of a new genus and species of plesiosaur. *Ann. Mag. Nat. Hist.* 10(6):206–9.

——. 1931. The plesiosaurs in the Bristol Museum. *Rep. Br. Assoc. Adv. Sci.* 1930:340–41.

——. 1948. Plesiosaurs in the City Museum, Bristol. *Proc. Bristol Nat. Soc.* 27:343–60.

——. 1973. *Fossil Reptiles and Amphibians.* British Museum.

Tarlo, L. B. 1958. The scapula of *Pliosaurus macromerus,* Phillips. *Palaeontology* 1:193–99.

——. 1959a. *Pliosaurus brachyspondylus* (Owen) from the Kimmeridge Clay. *Palaeontology* 1(4):283–91.

——. 1959b. *Stretosaurus* gen. nov., a giant pliosaur from the Kimmeridge Clay. *Palaeontology* 2(1):39–55.

——. 1960. A review of the Upper Jurassic pliosaurs. *Bull. Br. Mus. (Nat. Hist). Geol.* 4(5):147–89.

Tarsitano, S., and J. Riess. 1982a. Considerations concerning plesiosaur locomotion. *N. Jb. Geol. Paläeont. Abh.* 164:193–94.

——. 1982b. Plesiosaur locomotion – underwater flight versus rowing. *N. Jb. Geol. Paläeont. Abh.* 164:188–92.

Tate, R., and J. F. Blake. 1876. *The Yorkshire Lias.* Van Voorst.

Taylor, M. A. 1981. Plesiosaurs – rigging and ballasting. *Nature* 290:628–29.

——. 1986. Lifestyle of plesiosaurs. *Nature* 319:179.

——. 1987a. How tetrapods feed in water: A functional analysis by paradigm. *Zool. Jour. Linn. Soc.* 91:171–95.

——. 1987b. A reinterpretation of ichthyosaur swimming and buoyancy. *Palaeontology* 30(3):531–35.

——. 1987c. Reptiles that took on the sea. *New Scientist* 116(1588):46–50.

——. 1989a. The other dinosaurs. *New Scientist* 121(1655):65.

——. 1989b. Sea-dragons all aswim. *Nature* 338:381.

——. 1989c. Sea-saurians for skeptics. *Nature* 338:635–36.

——. 1992. Functional anatomy of the head of the large aquatic predator *Rhomaleosaurus zetlandicus* (Plesiosauria, Reptilia) from the Toarcian (Lower Jurassic) of Yorkshire, England. *Phil. Trans. Roy. Soc. London* 335:247–80.

——. 1993. Stomach bones for feeding or buoyancy? The occurrence and function of gastroliths in marine tetrapods. *Phil. Trans. Roy. Soc. London* B 341:163–75.

——. 1994. The plesiosaur's birthplace: The Bristol Institution and its contribution to vertebrate paleontology. *Zool. Jour. Linn. Soc. London* 112:179–96.

——. 1995. The sea monster of Dorset. *Natural History* 104(10):69.

——. 1997. Before the dinosaur: The historical significance of the fossil marine reptiles. In J. M. Callaway and E. L. Nicholls, eds., *Ancient Marine Reptiles,* pp. xix–xlvi. Academic Press.

——. 2000. Functional significance of bone ballasting in the evolution of buoyancy control strategies by aquatic tetrapods. *Historical Biology* 14:15–31.

Taylor, M. A., and A. R. I. Cruickshank. 1993. Cranial anatomy and functional morphology of *Pliosaurus brachyspondylus* (Reptilia: Plesiosauria) from the Upper Jurassic of Westbury, Wiltshire. *Phil. Trans. Roy. Soc. London* 341:399–418.

Taylor, M. A., and H. S. Torrens. 1995. Fossils by the sea. *Natural History* 104(10):66–71.

Taylor, M. A., D. B. Norman, and A. R. I. Cruickshank. 1993. Remains of an ornithischian dinosaur in a pliosaur from the Kimmeridgian of England. *Palaeontology* 36(2):357–60.

Tchernov, E., O. Rieppel, H. Zaher, M. J. Polcyn, and L. J. Jacobs. 2000. A fossil snake with limbs. *Science* 287(5460):2010–12.

Thompson, K. S. 1976. On the heterocercal tail in sharks. *Paleobiology* 2:19–38.

Thompson, K. S., and D. E. Simanek. 1977. Body form and locomotion in sharks. *American Zoologist* 17:343–54.

Thulborn, R. A. 1982. Liassic plesiosaur embryos reinterpreted as shrimp burrows. *Palaeontology* 25:351–59.

Thulborn, T., and S. Turner. 1993. An elasmosaur bitten by a pliosaur. *Modern Geology* 18:489–501.

Thurmond, J. T. 1968. A new polycotylid plesiosaur from the Lake Waco Formation (Cenomanian) of Texas. *Jour. Paleo.* 42:1289–96.

——. 1969. Notes on mosasaurs from Texas. *Texas Jour. Sci.* 21(1):69–79.

Thurmond, J. T., and D. E. Jones. 1981. *Fossil Vertebrates of Alabama.* University of Alabama Press.

Tibbo, S. N., L. R. Day, and W. F. Doucet. 1961. The swordfish (*Xiphias gladius* L.): Its life history and economic importance in the Northwest Atlantic. *Bull. Fish. Res. Bd. Can.* 130:1–47.

Tichy, G. 1995. Ein früher, durophager Ichthyosaurier (Omphalosauridae) aus der Mitteltrias der Alpen. *Geologisch-Paläontologische Mitteilungen Innsbruck* 20:349–69.

Tierchert, C., and R. S. Matheson. 1944. Upper Cretaceous ichthyosaurian and plesiosaurian remains from western Australia. *Aust. Jour. Sci.* 6:167–78.

Tokaryk, T. T. 1993. A plioplatecarpine mosasaur from the Bearpaw Shale (Upper Cretaceous) of Saskatchewan, Canada. *Modern Geology* 18:503–9.

Torrens, H. S. 1995. Mary Anning (1799–1847) of Lyme: "The greatest fossilist the world ever knew." *Br. Jour. Hist. Sci.* 28:257–84.

Tsujita, C. J., and G. E. G. Westermann. 2001. Were limpets responsible for the perforations in the ammonite *Placenterias? Palaeogeography, Palaeoclimatology, Palaeoecology* 169:245–70.

Vaughn, P. P., and M. R. Dawson. 1956. On the occurrence of tympanic membranes in the mosasaur *Platecarpus. Trans. Kansas Acad. Sci.* 59(3):382–84.

Verne, J. 1864. *A Journey to the Center of the Earth.* 1986 Signet Classic edition.

Von Huene, F. 1938. Ein pliosauride aus Abessinien. *Zbl. Miner. Geol. Paläont.* 10:370–76.

Wade, M. 1984. *Platypterygius australis,* an Australian Cretaceous ichthyosaur. *Lethaia* 17:99–113.

——. 1990. A review of the Australian Cretaceous longipinnate ichthyosaur *Platypterygius* (Ichthyosauria, Ichthyopterygia). *Mem. Qld. Mus.* 28:115–37.

Wagner, A. 1853. Die characteristic eine neuen art von *Ichthyosaurus* aus den lithographischen schiefern und eines zahnes von *Polyptychodon* aus dem gründsandsteine von Kellheim. *Bull. der königlische Akademie der Wissenschaft, Gelehrte Anzeigen* 6:661–70.

Ward, P. D. 1992. *On Methuselah's Trail.* Freeman.

——. 1997. *The Call of Distant Mammoths.* Copernicus.

——. 1998. *Time Machine: Scientific Explorations in Deep Time.* Copernicus.

Ward, P. D., and D. Brownlee. 2000. *Rare Earth.* Copernicus.

Watson, D. M. S. 1924. The elasmosaurid shoulder-girdle and fore-limb. *Proc. Zool. Soc. London* 2:885–917.

Watson, L. 1981. *Sea Guide to Whales of the World.* Hutchinson.

Weems, R. E., and R. B. Blodgett. 1996. The pliosaurid *Megalneusaurus:* A newly recognized occurrence in the Upper Jurassic Neknek Formation of the Alaska peninsula. *Bull. U.S. Geol. Surv.* 2152:169–75.

Welles, S. P. 1939. Plesiosaur from the Upper Cretaceous of the San Joaquin Valley. *Bull. Geol. Soc. Amer.* 50:1974.

——. 1943. Elasmosaurid plesiosaurs with a description of the new material from California and Colorado. *Univ. Calif. Mem.* 13:125–254.

——. 1949. A new elasmosaur from the Eagle Ford

Shale of Texas. *Fondren Sci. Ser., S. Methodist Univ.* 1:1–28.

———. 1952. A review of the North American Cretaceous elasmosaurs. *Univ. Calif. Pub. Geol. Sci.* 29:46–144.

———. 1962. A new species of elasmosaur from the Aptian of Colombia, and a review of the Cretaceous pliosaurs. *Univ. Calif. Pub. Geol. Sci.* 46:1–96.

———. 1970. The longest neck in the ocean. *Univ. Nebraska Mus. Notes* 43:1–2.

Welles, S. P., and J. D. Bump. 1949. *Alzadasaurus pembertoni*, a new elasmosaur from the Upper Cretaceous of South Dakota. *Jour. Paleo.* 23:521–35.

Welles, S. P., and D. R. Gregg. 1971. Late Cretaceous reptiles of New Zealand. *Rec. Canterbury Mus.* 9:1–111.

Welles, S. P., and B. H. Slaughter. 1963. The first record of the plesiosauria genus *Polyptychodon* (Pliosauridae) from the New World. *Jour. Paleo.* 37:131–33.

Wendt, H. 1959. *Out of Noah's Ark.* Houghton Mifflin.

———. 1968. *Before the Deluge.* Doubleday.

Werth, A. 2000. A kinematic study of suction feeding and associated behavior in the long-finned pilot whale (*Globicephala melas* Traill). *Mar. Mam. Sci.* 16(2):299–325.

Whetstone, K. N. 1976. A new plesiosaur from the Coon Creek Formation of Tennessee. *Jour. Paleo.* 51(2):424–25.

White, T. E. 1935. On the skull of *Kronosaurus queenslandicus* Longman. *Occasional Papers Boston Soc. Nat. Hist.* 8:219–28.

———. 1940. Holotype of *Plesiosaurus longirostris* Blake and the classification of the plesiosaurs. *Jour. Paleo.* 14:451–67.

Whitear, M. 1956. On the colour of an ichthyosaur. *Ann. Mag. Nat. Hist.* 9:742–44.

Whittle, C. H., and M. J. Everhart. 2000. Apparent and implied evolutionary trends in lithophagic vertebrates from New Mexico and elsewhere. In S. G. Lucas and A. B. Heckert, eds., *Dinosaurs of New Mexico*, pp. 75–82. New Mexico Museum of Natural History.

Wiens, J. J., and J. J. Slingluff. 2001. How lizards turn into snakes: A phylogenetic analysis of body-form evolution in anguid lizards. *Evolution* 55(11):2303–18.

Wiffen, J., 1980. *Moanasaurus*, a new genus of marine reptile (family Mosasauridae) from the Upper Cretaceous of North Island, New Zealand. *N.Z. Jour. Geol. Geophys.* 23:507–28.

———. 1990. New mosasaurs (Reptilia; family Mosasauridae) from the Upper Cretaceous of North Island, New Zealand. *N.Z. Jour. Geol. Geophys.* 33:67–85.

———. 1991. *Valley of the Dragons: The Story of New Zealand's Dinosaur Woman.* Random Century.

Wiffen, J., and W. Moisley. 1986. Late Cretaceous reptiles (families Elasmosauridae and Pliosauridae) from the Mangahouanga Stream, North Island, New Zealand. *N.Z. Jour. Geol. Geophys.* 29:205–52.

Wiffen, J., V. de Buffrénil, A. de Ricqlés, and J.-M. Mazin. 1995. Ontogenetic evolution of bone structure in late Cretaceous Plesiosauria from New Zealand. *Geobios* 28:625–40.

Wilford, J. N. 1986. *The Riddle of the Dinosaurs.* Knopf.

Williams, G. D., and R. L. Stelck. 1975. Speculations on the Cretaceous paleogeography of North America. In W. G. E. Caldwell, ed., *The Cretaceous System in the Western Interior of North America*, pp. 1–20. Geological Society of Canada.

Williston, S. W. 1893. An interesting food habit of the plesiosaurs. *Trans. Kansas Acad. Sci.* 13:121–22.

———. 1889. A new plesiosaur from the Niobrara

Cretaceous of Kansas. *Trans. Kansas Acad. Sci.* 12:174–78.

———. 1890. Structure of the plesiosaurian skull. *Science* 16(405):262.

———. 1891. Kansas mosasaurs. *Science* 18(463):345.

———. 1893. Mosasaurs. Part II. Restoration of *Clidastes. Kansas Univ. Quart.* 2(2):83–84.

———. 1894. A food habit of the plesiosaurs. *Amer. Nat.* 28(325):50.

———. 1897. Range and distribution of the mosasaurs with remarks on synonymy. *Kansas Univ. Quart.* 4(4):177–85.

———. 1898. Mosasaurs. *Univ. Geol. Surv. Kansas, Paleontology* 4(5):81–347.

———. 1902. Restoration of *Dolichorhynchops osborni,* a new Cretaceous plesiosaur. *Kansas Univ. Sci. Bull.* 1(9):241–44.

———. 1903. North American plesiosaurs. Part I. *Field Columbian Mus. Pub.* 2:1–77.

———. 1904a. The relationships and habits of the mosasaurs. *Jour. Geol.* 12:43–51.

———. 1904b. The stomach stones of the plesiosaurs. *Science* 22:565.

———. 1906. North American plesiosaurs: *Elasmosaurus, Cimoliasaurus,* and *Polycotylus. Amer. Jour. Sci.* 21:221–36.

———. 1907. The skull of *Brachauchenius,* with special observations on the relationships of the plesiosaurs. *Proc. U.S. Nat. Mus.* 32:477–89.

———. 1908a. The evolution and distribution of the plesiosaurs. *Science* 27:726–27.

———. 1908b. North American plesiosaurs: *Trinacromerum. Jour. Geol.* 16:715–35.

———. 1914. *Water Reptiles of the Past and Present.* University of Chicago Press.

Wilson, E. O. 1992. *The Diversity of Life.* Harvard University Press.

Wiman, C. J. 1920. Some reptiles from the Niobrara group in Kansas. *Bull. Geol. Instn. Uppsala* 18:9–18.

Winchester, S. 2001. *The Map that Changed the World: William Smith and the Birth of Modern Geology.* HarperCollins.

Wood, R. C. 1976. *Stupendemys geographicus,* the world's largest turtle. *Breviora* 436:1–31.

Wright, K. R. 1985. A new specimen of *Globidens alabamaensis* from Alabama. *Jour. Alabama Acad. Sci.* 56(3):102 (abstract).

———. 1988. The first record of *Clidastes liodontus* (Squamata, Osasauridae) from the eastern United States. *Jour. Vert. Paleo.* 8(3):343–45.

Wright, K. R., and S. W. Shannon. 1988. *Selmasaurus russelli,* a new plioplatecarpine mosasaur (Squamata, Mosasauridae) from Alabama. *Jour. Vert. Paleo.* 8:102–7.

Yoda, K., K. Sato, Y. Niizuma, M. Kurita, C. Bost, Y. Le Maho, and Y. Naito. 1999. Precise monitoring of porpoising behaviour of Adélie penguins determined using acceleration data loggers. *Jour. Exp. Biol.* 202(22):3121–26.

Young, G. 1821. Account of a singular fossil skeleton, discovered at Whitby in February 1819. *Wernerian Nat. Hist. Soc. Mem.* 3:450–57.

Zaher, H. 1998. The phylogenetic position of *Pachyrhachis* within snakes (Squamata, Serpentes). *Jour. Vert. Paleo.* 18:1–13.

Zaher, H., and O. Rieppel. 1999. The phylogenetic relationships of *Pachyhachis problematicus,* and the evolution of limblessness in snakes. *Comptes Rendus Acad. Sci. Paris* 329:831–37.

Zawisha, P. H., and L. Lee. 1995. The preparation, design, fabrication, engineering and installation of a mount for *Thalassomedon haningtoni* (long-necked plesiosaur). *Jour. Vert. Paleo.* 15(suppl. to 3):61A.

Zdansky, O. 1935. The occurrence of mosasaurs in Egypt and in Africa in general. *Bull. Inst. Égypte* 17:83–94.

# Index

Gastroliths. *See* Stones

*Geosaurus*, 197

Germany

   *Henodus* fossils, 40

   Holzmaden, 9, 74–75, 81, 86

   ichthyosaur fossils, 74–75, 81, 86, 96–97, 114

   pistosaur skeleton, 119–120

   Solnhofen, 9, 96–97, 202

*Gerrhonotus* (alligator lizard), 250

Giant squid, 109–110n

Gibbes, Robert, 219

Gilmore, Charles W., 206, 219, 228

Ginsu sharks, 241–242

Gish, Duane T., 63–64

Gizzards, 156, 157

Glass snakes (*Ophisaurus*), 250

*Globidens*, 216, 219, 221, 227, 228(illus.), 228–229

   *alabamaensis*, 219

Godefroit, P., 161

Godfrey, S. J., 233

Goldfuss, August, 198

*Goronyosaurus*, 217, 223–224, 224(illus.)

   *nigeriensis*, 222–223

Gould, Stephen J., 13–14, 71n

Great Flood, 18, 23

Great white sharks (*Carcharodon carcharias*), 59, 79, 216, 239

Green, Matthew, 126–127

Green turtle (*Chelonia mydas*), 33

Gregory, Joseph, 92

*Grendelius mordax*, 109

*Grippia*, 80

Gulf of Mexico. *See* Chicxulub Crater

*Haasiophis terrasanctus*, 246, 247

Haines, Tim, 179, 180–181

*Hainosaurus*, 229–230, 231(illus.), 257

   *bernardi*, 221, 226, 227, 230–231

*pembinensis*, 230

*Halisaurus*, 211, 213, 221, 225

   *platyspondylus*, 213–214

   *sternbergi*, 214, 219

Halstead, Lambert Beverly, 73–74, 101, 143, 148, 154, 155, 181, 185–186. *See also* Tarlo, Lambert Beverly

Halvorson, Dennis, 242

Hampe, Oliver, 177

Hanson, Mike, 242

Harlan, Richard, 42, 124–125, 198

Harp seals (*Phoca groenlandica*), 111

Harvard University, Museum of Comparative Zoology, 175–176

Hawkins, Thomas W., 21, 70–71, 160

Hawkins, Waterhouse, 25–26

Hawksbill turtle (*Eretmochelys imbricata*), 33, 33(illus.)

Hayden, Frederick, 207

Heatwole, H., 245, 246

*Henodus*, 38–40, 40(illus.)

   *chelyops*, 40

*Heterodontus* (horn shark), 229

Hoffmann, C. K., 195, 197

Hoganson, John, 242

Hogler, Jennifer A., 93

Holmes, R., 214, 216, 234

Holzmaden, Germany, 9, 74–75, 81, 86

Home, Sir Everard, 67–68

Horn sharks (*Heterodontus*), 229

Horses, evolution of, 202

Hotton, Nicholas, 253

*Hovasaurus*, 35, 36(illus.)

Hua, Stéphane, 187

Humphries, Stuart, 110–111

Hungerbühler, Axel, 75

Hunting behaviors

   ambush predation, 80, 120

   of dolphins, 239

   of elasmosaurs, 154

*Polyptychodon*, 192, 193

Porbeagle sharks *(Lamna nasus)*, 62(illus.), 79

Powell, James L., 254

*Proaigialosaurus hueni*, 200, 202

*Proganochelys quenstedi*, 31, 32

*Prognathodon*, 198–199, 219, 225, 229

    *currii*, 226–227

    *giganteus*, 221

    *overtoni*, 227

    *saturator*, 221–222, 222(illus.)

    *solvayi*, 221, 226n

    *waiparensis*, 244

*Proteosaurus*, 67–68

*Protoceratops*, 255

*Pteranodon*, 213

*Pterodactyle*, 24, 69

Pythonomorpha, 210, 245

*Qianichthyosaurus*, 96

Quenstedt, Friedrich, 75

Raup, David M., 9, 258

Reproduction

    of aigialosaurs, 217–218

    of cetaceans, 30, 73

    of elasmosaurs, 147–148

    of ichthyosaurs, 43, 48–49, 72–74, 76, 97–98, 99

    of mammals, 30, 49

    of marine reptiles, 14, 29–30, 48–49, 58

    of mosasaurs, 199, 217, 218

    of plesiosaurs, 147–148, 149–151, 152

    of pliosaurs, 150–151

    viviparous, 29–30, 43, 48–49, 58, 72–74, 97–98, 99, 217–218

Reptiles

    anapsids and diapsids, 28–29, 85n

    characteristics, 27–28

    definition, 27

    ectothermic nature, 27–28, 29, 45, 52

    eggs, 27

    energy needs, 54–55

    evolution of, 29, 30

    lack of stamina, 47

    return to aquatic life, 30

    ribs, 63n

    ruling, 44

    Sphenodontidae, 84–85

    terrestrial, 29

    *See also* Lizards; Marine reptiles; Snakes; Turtles

*Rhinosaurus*, 208, 208n

Rhomaleosauridae, 172, 174, 191–192

*Rhomaleosaurus*, 169, 170(illus.), 174, 192

    *zetlandicus*, 171–172

Ridley turtles, 34

Rieppel, O., 34, 35, 249

Riess, J., 139, 144, 146

Riggs, Elmer S., 188

*Rikkisaurus*, 227

Riou, Edward, 22

Ritchie, Alex, 173

Robinson, Jane Ann, 138–140, 141, 142, 144, 146, 148

Rolex, 90

Romer, Alfred Sherwood, 63, 175, 245

Roosevelt, Theodore, 1

Rothschild, B. M., 109, 111, 205, 239, 240

Roux, Erica, 236

Rudwick, Martin J. S., 21, 22, 24, 70

Ruling reptiles, 44

Russell, A. P., 55

Russell, Dale A., 198, 200, 205, 207, 210, 213, 214, 215, 217, 219, 221, 239, 242, 244

Russia, fossils found in, 181

Ruta, Marcello, 249

Ruxton, Graeme D., 110–111

Saint-Hilaire, Geoffroy, 19

*Saltosaurus,* 255

Saltwater crocodiles (*Crocodylus porosus*), 58, 216

Sander, Martin, 76, 82, 87, 92–93, 114

Sarjeant, William A. S., 67

Sauropterygians, 34–36

Scanlon, J. D., 246–247

Schevill, W. E., 175

Schopf, Thomas J. M., 260

Sciau, J., 161

Scientific names, 3–5, 17–18

Sclerotic rings, 5, 78n
: of ichthyosaurs, 77, 96, 109
: of plesiosaurs, 160
: of pliosaurs, 169, 172

Scotland
: fossils found in, 28
: Loch Ness monster, 2, 121

Sea lions, locomotion, 137, 139, 232

Seals
: elephant, 111
: harp, 111
: *See also* Pinnipeds

Sea snakes, 47, 52, 55, 136

Sea turtles
: comparison to plesiosaurs, 3
: current species, 32–34
: egg laying, 47, 148
: endangered, 34
: extinct species, 31
: flatback, 34
: green, 33
: hawksbill, 33, 33(illus.)
: leatherback, 32, 33, 53(illus.), 53–54, 58
: locomotion, 137, 138, 139, 140
: loggerhead, 33, 34(illus.)
: metabolism, 54
: ridley, 34

similarities to marine reptiles, 40
: *See also* Turtles

Sedgwick Museum of Geology, Cambridge, 127

Seeley, Harry Gower, 72–73, 132–133, 135, 149–150, 157

Seilacher, A., 237, 238

*Selmasaurus russelli,* 217

Sepkoski, Jack, 262–263

Shannon, Samuel W., 216–217

Sharks
: ancient, 217, 221–222, 241–242, 259
: attacks on mosasaurs, 217, 221–222, 241–242
: cat-, 78–79
: circulatory systems, 47–48
: dogfish, 217, 218
: ginsu, 241–242
: great white, 59, 79, 216, 239
: horn, 229
: hunting behavior, 239
: lamnid, 47–48, 103, 241–242
: locomotion, 102, 103, 136
: mackerel, 79
: mako, 79
: porbeagle, 62(illus.), 79
: similarities to ichthyosaurs, 11
: tails, 8, 79, 102

*Shastasaurus,* 88(illus.), 93–95
: *alexandrae,* 88, 89
: *altispinus,* 89
: *careyi,* 89
: *carinthiacus,* 89
: *neoscapularis,* 88–89
: *neubigi,* 92–93
: *osmonti,* 89
: *pacificus,* 89

Sheldon, Amy, 205, 240

*Shonisaurus,* 91(illus.)
: fossils, 89–92

Williston, Samuel, 30, 119, 130, 153, 156–157, 183–184, 188, 198, 205, 206, 211, 213, 216, 217, 239–240

Wiman, Carl, 86, 87, 213

*Wimanius*, 86

Winchester, Simon, 68–69

Wood, Roger, 32

*Woolungasaurus*, 178–179
  *glendowerensis*, 132

Wright, Kenneth R., 216–217

Wyoming, fossils found in, 181, 188, 211

*Xiphias gladius* (broadbill swordfish), 107, 107(illus.)

Yale University, 127, 212–213

Yoda, K., 101

You, H., 104

Young, George, 68–69

Yugoslavia, fossils found in, 202, 247

Zaher, Hussam, 248, 249

Zaire, fossils found in, 225

*Zalophus* (California sea lion), 232

Zangerl, Rainer, 219

Zdansky, Otto, 222

*Zeuglodon*, 125

Zoological Society of Ireland, 171